Cambridge Studies in the History and Theory of Politics

EDITORS

Maurice Cowling   G. R. Elton
J. R. Pole

A PROTESTANT VISION

A PROTESTANT VISION

WILLIAM HARRISON AND THE REFORMATION OF ELIZABETHAN ENGLAND

G. J. R. PARRY

UNIVERSITY RESEARCH FELLOW, UNIVERSITY OF
QUEENSLAND, ST LUCIA

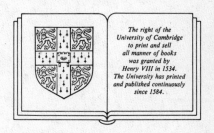

The right of the
University of Cambridge
to print and sell
all manner of books
was granted by
Henry VIII in 1534.
The University has printed
and published continuously
since 1584.

CAMBRIDGE UNIVERSITY PRESS

CAMBRIDGE

LONDON   NEW YORK   NEW ROCHELLE

MELBOURNE   SYDNEY

Published by the Press Syndicate of the University of Cambridge
The Pitt Building, Trumpington Street, Cambridge CB2 1RP
32 East 57th Street, New York, NY 10022, USA
10 Stamford Road, Oakleigh, Melbourne 3166, Australia

First published 1987

Printed in Great Britain by the University Press, Cambridge

British Library cataloguing in publication data
Parry, G. J. R.
A Protestant vision: William Harrison and
the reformation of Elizabethan England. –
(Cambridge studies in the history and theory
of politics)
1. Harrison, William. *1534–1593*
I. Title
942′.0072024   DA3.H3/

Library of Congress cataloguing in publication data
Parry, G. J. R.
A Protestant vision.
(Cambridge studies in the history and theory
of politics)
Includes index.
1. Protestantism – History – 16th century.
2. Reformation – England. 3. England – Church history –
16th century. 4. Harrison, William, 1534–1593. I. Title.
II. Series.
BX5071.P37   1987   280′.4′0942   86-17091
ISBN 0 521 32997 3

Contents

v

Preface

Every individual who reflects upon his environment does so in the light of certain historical assumptions about that environment. The unreflecting individual commonly lacks any sense of historical perspective. This study explores the connection between William Harrison's particular historical vision and his individual interpretation of his contemporary world. Harrison is now chiefly known for his *Description of Britain*, published in Holinshed's *Chronicles* in 1577 and 1587, but the discovery of a manuscript of his 'Great English Chronology', the work to which he attributed far greater importance, enables us for the first time properly to examine his thought. Far from being a narrow historical calendar, the 'Chronology' is a voluminous and fascinating history of the world, important not only as a hitherto unknown example of Elizabethan historiography, but also as a work of Protestant historical interpretation, in which Harrison continually stressed the contemporary relevance of providential historical patterns. Indeed, this study shows that when Harrison's historical vision is placed in the context of contemporary Protestant thought what historians have described as Elizabethan Puritanism appears as the thorough-going application of a common Protestant historical outlook, to which Harrison's 'Chronology' gave individual expression.

European and English Protestants thought, wrote and acted in accordance with their personal understanding of this shared historical vision, and the circumstances of temperament and situation led some English Protestants to believe that providential history cast a sinister light upon the polity and institutions of the Elizabethan Church as established in 1559. When these Puritans viewed that Church against the background of the history of the True Church, they felt themselves under an obligation to restore its polity and institutions to the ideal forms depicted in that history. The myriad individual variations within the monolithic classifications of 'Protestant' and 'Puritan' therefore reflect the respective abilities of each believer to reconcile the imperfect present with the ideal past. Fired by their historical vision, the least restrained Protestants could ignore all objective difficulties in the way of achieving their ideal, while others insisted that only the prince could safely

vii

restore the Church to its proper condition, and still more moderate thinkers discerned little difference between the ideal status and the status quo. Even more difficult for those seeking hard and fast categories, all these ways of perceiving the Elizabethan Church can be found at various times and in differing contexts in an individual such as William Harrison.

Approaching Elizabethan Puritanism through William Harrison's thought, then, can be more informative than treating Puritanism as a monolith. For such a study underlines the varieties of emphasis, mood, expression and interpretation which have to be accepted within the fundamental unity of Protestant thought. An examination of Harrison's thought also reveals that differences over Church polity were only a minor part of a wider and less acrimonious discussion amongst Protestants about the obligations which were imposed upon the members of the True Church. Harrison's thought shows that for devout Protestants those obligations extended over the whole range of political, social and economic behaviour, and also impinged upon the study and interpretation of Nature. The degree of unanimity within this wider discussion makes it more important to examine the historical assumptions upon which it was predicated, and Harrison's writings are particularly suited to this task. For his 'Chronology' and *Description* are rich in material which shows how a Protestant world-view depended upon a Protestant historical interpretation. Therefore the reader may be assured that this study of Harrison's views on important ecclesiastical, political, social and intellectual issues devotes its first three chapters to studying his historical beliefs, because that provides the best means of elucidating the prevailing assumptions within his thought. For he believed that even the minutiae of chronological and historical scholarship could not be pursued independently of his prior obligations to obey God's commandments as a member of the True Church. Essentially his Protestant interpretation of world history and his Protestant vision of Elizabethan England were two aspects of the same way of thinking.

No proper examination of Harrison's thought can ignore his social and intellectual environment, which conditioned his thinking and which in turn became subject to his searching criticism. Yet in delineating the major problems faced by William Harrison, much familiar detail has had to be sacrificed. Another book might be written about the genial Harrison of the *Description of Britain*, the garrulous commentator on contemporary dress, diet, and domestic alterations, the devoted husband and family man, the country parson throughout the high years of Elizabethan's reign. Such a study might reveal a figure more accessible to the twentieth century, but it would not, I think, reveal his true importance for students of Elizabethan history and the history of Protestant thought. As a sounding-board who gave his own particular resonances to the ideas rippling through the Elizabethan intellectual ether, Harrison is a particularly instructive lesson in the implications of the Protestant, Bible-dominated way of thinking.

Although I am entirely responsible for any errors and deficiencies in this work, its completion enables me to acknowledge my indebtedness to many individuals and institutions. Sir Geoffrey Elton's wise and careful supervision of the Cambridge Ph.D. dissertation from which this book derives was only exceeded by the persistent encouragement which he gave towards the completion of the latter. Parts of this book have benefited in many ways from the constructive criticism of Marie Axton, William Lamont, David Loades, Roy Porter and Johann Sommerville, and it is a very inadequate recompense merely to excuse them from any blame for its contents. Mr William O'Sullivan, formerly keeper of Manuscripts at Trinity College, Dublin, deserves special thanks for his help in using a remarkable collection of manuscripts unjustly ignored by English historians. I would also like to thank Mr David Preston of the Western Education and Library Board, Derry, Northern Ireland. The staffs at the Cambridge University Library, the Essex County Record Office at Chelmsford, the British Library, Guildhall Library and Public Record Office in London, and at the Bodleian Library, Oxford, have always proved extremely helpful. Mrs Melber and her staff in the Data Preparation Department of the Computer Centre at Teesside Polytechnic deserve thanks for their heroic efforts in processing the typescript on a Prime 2250 computer. Various parts of this work were written while a Research Fellow at the University of Melbourne, while a Fellow of Henry Giles House, Cambridge, and while a Lecturer at Teesside Polytechnic. I am grateful to all my colleagues at those institutions for their support. I am particularly grateful to the Humanities Department at Teesside Polytechnic which gave generous financial support towards the final preparation of this work.

Part of Chapter 5 has previously been published in *The Journal of Ecclesiastical History*, July 1984, as 'William Harrison and the Two Churches in Elizabethan Puritan Thinking', and part of Chapter 7 has previously been published in *History of Science*, September 1984, as 'Puritanism, Science and Capitalism: William Harrison and the Rejection of Hermes Trismegistus.'

PART I

A Protestant Vision of History

1

The Two Churches

William Harrison's 'Great English Chronology' shows how attitudes derived from European mainstream Protestantism when deployed in the English context could become transformed by their new environment into something identifiable as 'Puritanism'. Harrison's detailed examination of salvation history since Adam in his 'Chronology', written in the 1570s, developed a received historical model through which he also interpreted his contemporary experience of the Reformation in England. That historical viewpoint therefore helped to define the content of Harrison's radical Protestantism within the particular conditions of the Elizabethan Church, for he believed that interpreting both world history and contemporary events according to the criteria laid down by the Scriptures unanimously confirmed that the English Reformation represented yet another episode in the eternal struggle between the True Church and the satanic Church of Cain.

Drawing heavily upon the European formulators of the Protestant world-view, Harrison's 'Chronology' traced this conflict in the Scriptural account of history from the Creation, and in post-Scriptural history. Together with his well-known *Description of Britain*, the 'Chronology' applied the criteria of a True Church which he found implicit in this Scriptural interpretation to all aspects of Church and society in Elizabethan England. For the 'Chronology' also reflects the fact that Harrison had grown to maturity through the disquieting religious fluctuations of the previous four decades which in hindsight seemed to fit the universal pattern of conflict. Perhaps most importantly, the method and viewpoint of the 'Chronology' developed more fully elements of Harrison's historical thought which had originated in a period of personal evangelical crisis in the 1560s. This transformation in his thought paralleled his increasing unease about the precise status of the Elizabethan Church within his scheme of universal conflict. Harrison's thought prominently displays a close connection between his historical interpretation and his critical, Puritan view of the Elizabethan Church, for only within his scheme of salvation history could Harrison find assurance about his own role in furthering the purposes of the True Church in the world. In turn the strong historical foundations of this world-view enabled him to seek the complete reformation not only of the Elizabethan Church but also of the whole of contemporary society by reference to the criteria laid down by the True Church in its unceasing conflict with the Church of Cain.

Born in London to a small merchant family in 1535, his years as a schoolboy at St Paul's exposed Harrison both to the conservative humanism of Colet's foundation and to the new learning of Cranmer's English liturgy.[1] Probably in the reign of Edward VI he became what he self-deprecatingly called 'an unprofitable grammarian' at Westminster School under the enlightened Protestant educator, Alexander Nowell. This grounding in good letters laid the basis for his later rejection of the barbarities of scholastic Latin, especially its distortions of the Scriptures. It also introduced him to the techniques of textual criticism which when applied in the 'Chronology' helped to establish the boundaries of legitimate knowledge by diminishing the authority both of popish forgeries and Hermetic occult speculations. The reinforcement of those boundaries by reference to Scriptural revelation preoccupied Harrison when he wrote his 'Chronology'.[2] Looking back from an increasingly zealous, evangelical perspective in 1565, Harrison concluded that before the Marian reaction he had known Christ 'as well as his age permitted'.[3]

This did not prevent him from taking Roman Catholic orders as an undergraduate at Oxford. In 1556 while a member of Christ Church, he became what he later described in 1565 as 'a shaven worshipper of Baal', although he claimed to have been recalled from this 'insanity' by the powerful preaching of the Oxford Martyrs sometime before July 1558. Those words carefully described experiences which shaped two ideas dominant in his later thought, and especially evident in the 'Chronology'. The reference to the idolatrous Gentile cults of the Old Testament fore-shadows his later obsessive identification of popery with Gentilism, while the alleged means of his conversion to Protestantism encouraged the fixation

---

[1] *Harrison's description of England in Shakespeare's youth*, ed. F. J. Furnivall (4 parts. London, 1877), appendix I, p. li.

[2] *The Description of England by William Harrison*, ed. Georges Edelen (Ithaca: New York, 1968), p. 76. 'The Great English Chronology', Trinity College Dublin MS 165 (hereafter referred to as TCD MS 165), fos. 124^{a}r, 221r, 350v, praises the great classical grammarians and condemns the schoolmen. See G. J. R. Parry, 'William Harrison (1535–93) and "The Great English Chronology": puritanism and history in the reign of Elizabeth' (unpublished Cambridge Ph.D. Dissertation, 1981), chapter I for more biographical information.

[3] Harrison's autobiography, written on an end leaf of John Bale's *Scriptorum illustrium maioris Brytannie...catalogus* (Basileae, apud Ioannem Oporinum, Feb. 1559), now Derry Diocesan Library shelf-mark D.ii.d.7., translated and printed in G. Edelen, 'William Harrison', in *Studies in the Renaissance*, ix (1962), pp. 256–72, at pp. 258–9.

that preaching could produce a psychological awakening, creating a regenerate understanding of the world. The vehemence with which Harrison described his apostasy reflects the deep psychological scars left by his Oxford years, and he took pains to emphasise that he became a Protestant before Elizabeth's accession, at some risk of persecution from 'that Jezebel', Mary Tudor. This need to identify with the persecuted True Church throughout time formed an important part of the dichotomous view of world history later presented in Harrison's 'Chronology'.[4]

In 1559 Harrison became Rector of Radwinter, Essex, where he attacked ingrained popery, which he saw as the remnant of antichristian religion, through that same medium of preaching which had brought him to a regenerate understanding of the world.[5] He sharpened that vision on the whetstone of theological studies during the 1560s, taking his B.D. from Cambridge in 1571, possibly as a member of the proto-seminary at Christ's. There he breathed the supercharged atmosphere of committed evangelical Protestantism which saturated Cambridge in the 1560s, and which provided the context for his increasingly rigorous reassessment of all human knowledge according to what he perceived were the Scriptural criteria of legitimate knowledge. One casualty of this weeding-out process was the Hermetic philosophy, whose mystical interpretation of the cosmos Harrison seems to have accepted during his popish years at Oxford. In the 'Chronology' he specifically rejected several important aspects of this philosophy.[6] On the other hand the historical and chronological works which Harrison acknowledged in 1565, and which were later transformed into the 'Chronology', gained added importance by falling within what Harrison perceived to be, in this evangelical context, the legitimate bounds of human enquiry.

Indeed Harrison's account of the works which he had written by 1565 reads almost like an analysis of the separate elements of his world-view at that period, elements later combined in the 'Chronology'. None of these works survive, and although their titles reveal his already deep interest in history and chronology, not until Harrison united these two pursuits did he fully discover the mysteries inherent in the fulfilment of the divine promises, a discovery which enabled him to draw correspondingly radical conclusions in his 'Chronology'. One of these works described in 1565, a life of St Paul, made a more subtle contribution to the development of Harrison's thought. Like many another Protestant who had experienced the psychological trauma of a sudden conversion, Harrison must have been struck by the great personal relevance of Paul's life, as well as finding it an intriguing historical

---

[4] Parry, 'Puritanism and history', pp. 11–22, has more details about Harrison's Oxford experiences. Edelen, 'William Harrison', pp. 258–9.

[5] See below, pp. 154–7.   [6] See below, pp. 107–9 and 309–16.

and chronological problem. More importantly, in tracing Paul's life in the
Acts and Epistles, Harrison came to share the Pauline view of the Scriptures,
to be convinced of the direct relevance of the entire history of the Church
for the present struggle to build it up with 'lively stones'.[7]

Harrison had also written a history of Britain by 1565. British history later
formed a substantial part of the 'Chronology', but although England
consequently seemed to play a considerable role in the unfolding drama of
the Two Churches, this was merely because, as Harrison admitted, 'I regard
not gretly to dele in thantiquities of forren nations'. His historical
interpretation focussed on the universal Elect Church, not any particular
Elect Nation. Two other works from this period of intense evangelical
activity, 'Chronological computations from the beginning of the world to
his own time' and 'Reflections on the same', introduce the subject of
chronology, and underline the fact that for earnest reformers the whole course
of time only existed to give fulfilment to God's prophetic promises for His
Church.[8]

Whatever may have been the tone of Harrison's lost 'Reflections' on time,
eventually he became fascinated by its mysteries, tantalisingly revealed both
in its large-scale structure and its most intricate and obscure patterns, parallels
and symmetries. The 'Chronology' exemplifies Harrison's willingness to
discern divine meaning in chronology, and shows that this readiness to
participate in divine mysteries formed an essential part of his radicalism. The
admitted intricacies and obscurities of chronological studies should not
mislead us into dismissing as unimportant an area of knowledge which
Harrison and many of his contemporaries took so seriously. Accepting this
mystical element in Harrison's thought helps us to answer the important
question why he chose to write a chronology rather than a chronicle, for
he clearly found levels of meaning in the process of time which could not
be satisfactorily explained by a conventional narrative history.

Perhaps for this reason Harrison eventually abandoned the large history
which occupied most of his attention in 1565. He then claimed to be 'daily
writing...on an uncommon compendium of history in imitation of Aelian,
Gellius, Macrobius, Petrarch and Politian'. All these writers had practised
the late classical, Christian and humanist tradition of historical biography,
using historical examples to illustrate normative moral and political conduct.
Very probably this compendium consisted of some sort of narrative history
written with a high moral tone, but as Harrison became increasingly
preoccupied with finding providential meaning in the past such a constricting
framework must have become correspondingly less suited to displaying that

[7] Edelen, 'William Harrison', pp. 258-9. See also J. S. Coolidge, *The Pauline Renaissance in England* (Oxford, 1970)
[8] TCD MS 165 fo. 23v and Edelen, 'William Harrison', pp. 258-9, which omits cancelled references to the history of Britain and another, briefer, chronology in Harrison's list in Bale's *Scriptorum.*

meaning, and so he began his 'Chronology' about 1570.[9] Thus he came to espouse the more distinctively Protestant, and particularly German, interest in the detailed study of universal chronology and history as a means of discerning God's will, a change which paralleled his growing disquiet about the state of the Elizabethan Church. These related concerns increasingly dominated Harrison's thought as apocalyptic tensions rose throughout the 1570s.[10]

Like other sixteenth-century historians, however, Harrison also recognised the more mundane usefulness of chronology as a way of imposing some sort of order on the chaos of historical facts. Jean Bodin elevated the commonplace into a ground rule for historical research when he insisted that 'Those who think they can understand histories without chronology are as much in error as those who wish to escape the windings of a labyrinth without a guide.' The best writers were the most meticulous in dating events said Bodin, for 'without a system of time hardly any advantage is culled from history'.[11] Yet the determination of an exact chronology proved such a daunting task that the means often became an end in itself. Abraham Fleming, editor of the second edition of Holinshed's *Chronicles* to which Harrison contributed, observed that 'it is not a work for everie common capacitie, naie it is a toile without head or taile, even for extraordinarie wits, to correct the accounts of former ages so many hundred yeares received, out of uncertainties to raise certainties, and to reconcile writers dissenting in opinion and report'.[12] The fact that 'so diverse is the observation of true yeres' often troubled Harrison, for 'a man shall hardly gesse how to leane unto the likeliest'; as for errors in transcription, 'I accompt them almost infinite'. Widely differing chronological systems caused almost insoluble problems of synchronicity, and when the Septuagint differed from the Vulgate Old Testament by as much as thousands of years, only relative accuracy was possible. Polybius, whose magisterial strictures against erring chronologers Harrison acknowledged 'leaveth no place for me', set the standard, allowing that 'the matter is not great to erre in a year or two'. Harrison's efforts over two decades to achieve even finer precision went unappreciated, however, and Fleming's observation just quoted was an attempt to defend Harrison's accuracy from attacks by other members of the Holinshed group.[13]

---

[9] He used these authors merely for factual information in TCD MS 165, e.g. fos. 41r, 60r, 119v, 162v. Parry, 'Puritanism and history', pp. 412–13 on the MS's period of composition.

[10] See below pp. 125–31.

[11] J. Bodin, *Method for the Easy Comprehension of History*, trans. B. Reynolds (New York, 1945), p. 303.

[12] R. Holinshed, *The first and second volume of chronicles* (at the expenses of John Harrison et al.: London, Jan. 1587), sig. Y6r.

[13] TCD MS 165, fos. 209v, 65v–66r, 46v, and see G. J. R. Parry, 'William Harrison and Holinshed's Chronicles', in *The Historical Journal*, 27 (1984), pp. 789–810, esp. 809–10. Parry, 'Puritanism and history', p. 415, on Harrison's very precise chronological arrangement of his notes.

Harrison's declared intentions in writing his 'Chronology' not only maintain this ideal of a precise and complete record of the past but also bring us closer to the centre of his world-view, to his response to the Scriptures. Not all the trivial details of history had an obvious place in the unfolding continuum of salvation history. Yet much that we would dismiss as irrelevant lumber demanded Harrison's attention because it exemplified the truths that could be found in the Word, simply because it formed part of the unbroken chain of history which gave fulfilment to God's promises. Therefore more than frustrated pedantry caused Harrison to bemoan his failure to clarify the succession of High Priests from Herod to the Fall of Jerusalem, for he sought 'the certaintie of the historie...to the uttermost of my power next unto the preaching of the worde which is my cheefe vocation'. Harrison held the study of time and history second in importance only to the perpetual preaching function of the True Church. It absorbed his energies to such an extent that he lost all sense of proportion, and in struggling 'to be exact even in the smallest things...now and then I am constraigned to over passe some that are of more value'.[14] Such dedication found encouragement from authorities such as Philip Melanchthon, whose work Harrison admired and who argued that the precise historical fulfilment of Scriptural prophecies proved 'that our word is come of god, and that none other faith save ours is true'; a faith confirmed by chronology, for prophecy showed 'whan Christe muste come, and whan the end of the worlde is to be loked for'. In Harrison's thought we find this same nexus between true doctrine and accurate chronology, as in his comment that 'Eusebius is gretly overshoted oftentimes so well in soundness of doctrine as supputation of his times'.[15]

In Harrison's view then an important part of the meaning of the Scriptures lay in the exact knowledge of the historical experiences of the True Church which they recounted. To help to elucidate this meaning he wrote a detailed chronological treatise described on the title page of his 'Chronology', but not extant, which he claimed was the first attempt to make it 'easie for the reader of the scriptures to discerne the true time of each incident whose daie and yere is noted' in the Bible. Therefore the Scriptures not only prophesied the chronological framework of history since the Creation, but also provided much of its content and dictated its interpretation, so that a proper, faithful understanding of history and chronology complemented Scriptural learning. The mixture of tasks which Harrison set himself in his 'Chronology' makes

---

[14] Thus this succession helped him to establish that Christ had died in the extremely portentous year 4000 AM (TCD MS 165, fo. 138v) and see below, pp. 96–8 on the prophetic importance of that date.

[15] P. Melanchthon, *The thre bokes of Cronicles whyche John Carion...gathered* (trans. and pr. Walter Lynne: London, 1550), 'The use of readying hystoryes' fo. *6r., TCD MS 165, fo. 41r–v.

this connection more evident. The 'three cheifest pointes' were 'the exact correction of the time, confirmation of doctrine, or disclosing of necessary antiquitie'.[16] The reference to doctrine might seem anomalous in a work ostensibly devoted to chronology and history, but it reminds us that the Scriptures provided Harrison with a distinctive interpretation of history, an interpretation which itself formed a vital part of true doctrine and which reveals just what he meant by 'necessary antiquitie'. Taken together, the three tests of true doctrine, exact chronology and correct historical inter-pretation provided the criteria by which Harrison could judge all historical phenomena, and by which he could perceive that the Elizabethan Church, as part of the prophetic continuum of history, came under the same judgement.

Harrison believed that the Scriptural view of time and history had as much relevance to his contemporary situation as had Scriptural doctrinal teachings. In fact he found it unnecessary to distinguish between them. Within this particular historical framework the Puritan willingness to regard the Scriptural experience as directly applicable to contemporary circumstances ceases to be paradoxical. For despite the fact that history presented a prophetic continuum of discrete events, Harrison steadfastly believed in the contemporaneity of the Scriptures for all times, since all events were united by the same encounter with God. Even at the chronological level this assumption emerges in his quotation of the Hebrew proverb that 'there is neither first nor last in the scriptures, as if it should mean the Scriptures do not alwaies observe the order of time'.[17] This immediately raises the question, to put it in Harrison's terms, of whether his response to the Word depended entirely on the immediate working of the Holy Spirit, or whether it derived from human authority. In other words, how much did this idea owe to the Hebraic patterns of thought which shaped the Scriptures?

The uniformity and uniqueness of Hebrew thought can be easily overstated, a temptation particularly irresistible to the school of 'biblical theology' which flourished from the 1930s. In reaction to historical biblical criticism these theologians attempted to stress the unity, coherence and relevance of the Scriptures, mainly by contrasting Hebrew with non-biblical thought. They found the distinctive character of the Scriptures to be so obvious that they attempted to account for it by suggesting that the Hebrews had a different psychological perception of time from that of western man, that they displayed a deep sense of contemporaneity with the Scriptural

---

[16] TCD MS 165, fo. 170v.
[17] Ibid., fo. 48v, and compare H. Butterfield, *Christianity and History* (London, 1949), p. 72: the example of Israel would live for us 'if only we could rid ourselves of an obsession and genuinely convince ourselves that the history of the ancient Hebrews [in exile] was fundamentally of the same texture as our own'.

experience which made it perpetually relevant to their present circumstances. This now venerable tradition of Scriptural interpretation is often summarised in a contrast between the senses of Χρονος (linear, chronological time) and καιρος (time comprising religiously decisive moments). This interpretation distinguishes Western man's presumed chronological outlook from an alleged Hebrew perception of 'realistic' or καιρος time made up of segments distinguished by their historical contents. Such analyses frequently assert that the Hebrews held times with similar contents to be identical, that the intervention of God in history freed the Hebrews from chronological time by bringing them into simultaneous relationship with those who at all times remembered the covenant with God as part of the cult. It is therefore argued that this sense of cultic simultaneity reflected a particular type of psyche. From the modern evangelical viewpoint this Scriptural emphasis on contemporaneity makes the Bible's religious message universally relevant.[18] Some recent historians of Puritan thought have adopted similar views.[19]

However, the arguments of 'biblical theology' assume that Hebrew thought remained unchanged over many centuries, and they also depend upon a selective use of the scanty biblical evidence about Hebrew thinking on time. Hebrew words for time, chosen without regard to their various contextual meanings and historical changes in their use, have been cited in support of what are essentially theologians' philosophical generalisations about time. These lexical weaknesses need detain us no longer than the obvious point that many characteristics designated as peculiar to Hebrew thought are universally present in human nature. For the Hebrew perception of time was the same as ours. As we shall see, the undoubted sense of contemporaneity which permeates the Scriptures and to which Harrison displayed particular sensitivity has another source. Furthermore it is important to notice the Old Testament's preoccupation with chronology, which is perhaps mistakenly overlooked by apologists for the distinctiveness of Hebrew thought. For the biblical text, as Harrison found, cannot be understood without giving due attention to the detailed chronological data which impressively underpinned the Scriptures' authoritative account of history from the Creation. Chronology not only integrated the historical Scriptural books but provided the sole justification for some parts of the Bible.[20] The next chapter will examine this element in Harrison's thought

---

[18] J. Marsh, *The Fulness of Time* (London, 1952), pp. 20–52, conveniently summarises this approach, but J. R. Wilch, *Time and Event, An Exegetical Study of the Use of Eth in the Old Testament in Comparison to other Temporal Expressions in Clarification of the Concept of Time* (Leiden, 1969), pp. 1–17, succinctly analyses and criticises this whole school of interpretation. See also J. Barr, *Biblical Words for Time* (2nd edn. rev. London, 1969), pp. 11, 21–7, 33–56, 94–8.

[19] Especially Coolidge, *Pauline Renaissance*, which sometimes overstresses the contrast between 'Jewish' and 'Greek' thought.

[20] Wilch, *Time and Event*, pp. 20, 32–4, and Barr, *Biblical Words for Time*, pp. 28–31 and 158, which traces 'Biblical theology' back to Bergson's philosophy.

more fully, but here we should note this uniquely Hebraic influence on his thinking. For he clearly believed that in laboriously detailing the working out of God's will from the very beginning, he shared with the Old Testament Hebrews a compelling understanding of God's nature. From that perspective no part of linear time and history escaped God's control, for everything contributed to the fulfilment of God's promises to his Elect, and thus to the elucidation of the divine character.

Such an outlook found support in Scriptural teachings on the unity of Creation and the inextricable connections between all occurrences in it. As Bodin concluded, all events were 'by almightie God bound in such fit order and consequence, as that those things which are first have coherence with the last; and those which are in the middest with them both, and all with all combined and bound together' indissolubly. Harrison similarly read outwards from Scriptual intimations of God's purposes, to profane history. He saw in Pompey's installation of Antipater over Palestine 'how the providens of god beginneth to work, for the removing of the Scepter from Juda to thend the prophecie of Jacob may ones be fulfilled and Christ our savior sent into the worlde, which could not ere this time be worthily fulfilled'.[21] The Incarnation had been accomplished as part of the measured order of history, and so would be the end of all time. From Harrison's foreshortening perspective near what he believed would be the end of time, the purpose of chronology was to show the relationship between events juxtaposed in time only by God's will.[22] On every page of the 'Chronology' that mysterious will could be seen working itself out to its awesome doom.

The Hebrew grasp of chronological succession was not unique, despite frequent attempts to stress its independence by somewhat loose comparisons with alleged Greek cyclic views of history. Neither Hebrew nor Greek thought remained uniform, and there are fundamental methodological problems about contrasting unformulated Hebrew thought with the formulations of Greek philosophy, but in any case not all Greek philosophers taught that history moved in cycles. Nor were Greek historians influenced by these philosophical theories, and surely it is their work that must be compared with the Old Testament view of history. There would only be a complete contrast if the Greek historians posited cycles of exact, eternal recurrence of all the events they related, and clearly they did not.[23] Greeks

---

[21] *Jean Bodin: The Six Bookes of a Commonwealth*, ed. K. D. McRae (Cambridge, Mass., 1962), p. 436. TCD MS 165, fo. 130v, *cf*. Gen. 49. 10. Bodin eventually abandoned Christianity for a personal type of Judaism (D. P. Walker, *Spiritual and Demonic Magic from Ficino to Campanella* (London, 1958; 1975), p. 171, and P. L. Rose, *Bodin and the Great God of Nature* (Geneva, 1980), pp. 134–48). See below, pp. 61, 72.

[22] *Description*, ed. Edelen, p. 390, on Harrison's expectations of the End.

[23] Barr, *Biblical Words for Time*, pp. 144–7; Wilch, *Time and Event*, pp. 13–14; and esp. A. Momigliano, 'Time in ancient historiography', in *History and the Concept of Time (History and Theory)*, Beiheft 6 (1966), pp. 4–13.

would have understood the Bible's concrete account of time, while Greek historians had a strong sense of unique chronological succession in history – indeed their raw materials only achieved the status of historical evidence when they could be dated.[24]

At this point, however, an important difference between Greek and Hebrew approaches to history emerges. Greek historians applied rules of evidence, demanding eyewitness reports or at least corroboration of oral evidence; this effectively limited their history to the recent past. In contrast Hebrew historians subordinated themselves to the prophets, accepting the values of those who claimed to interpret all events because they had been shown the predestined course of time. Therefore Biblical history achieved uniqueness by its continuity from the Creation, by its presentation of a significant line of events which demonstrated the continuous intervention of God in His world. Immune from the Greek scruples about evidence, Biblical history was not distinguishable as myth, because the evidence in its favour formed part of the cult, either written down or kept in the collective memory of Israel. The Hebrews felt themselves under a religious obligation to remember all of their past, but when the earliest Christians appropriated this history it proved incomprehensible to learned pagans because it offended all their notions of historical evidence.[25]

Again only a relative distinction can be drawn between the Hebrew emphasis on historical events as divine manifestations and the beliefs of other Near Eastern cults. Contrary to what is often assumed, the so-called nature gods did not merely reveal themselves through natural cycles but also acted in history – in fact history and Nature were not clearly distinguished in the ancient Near East. The Old Testament shared many of the common traditions and motifs of other Near Eastern religions, in which ethical patterns became laid down as the word of the god found fulfilment in the moral retribution visited upon nations and individuals. The Israelite cult was really distinguished not by its understanding of history but by its different conception of the deity. Monotheism enhanced the tendency towards a unitary historical perspective, where one divine aim increasingly emerged as unchallenged.[26] The Scriptures actually referred to several divine plans which

---

[24] Until the 5th century BC chronological lists constituted most of this evidence (ibid., pp. 15–16).

[25] Ibid., pp. 16–21. This theoretical requirement persistently revived the antipathy between faith and reason. Calvin rebuked the ungodly who questioned the authority of Genesis because Moses had not seen all he recounted (*A Commentarie of John Calvine, upon the first booke of Moses called Genesis. Translated out of Latin into English by Thomas Tymme* (Henry Myddleton for John Harrison and George Bishop: London, 1578), sigs. B1r and P7v).

[26] B. Albrektson, *History and the Gods. An Essay on the Idea of Historical Events as Divine Manifestations in the Ancient Near East and in Israel* (Lund, 1967), pp. 16–23, 41, 55–67, 100–6. Albrektson concludes that by attributing relatively more importance to God's activity in history, Israel gave it more influence over the cult, e.g. in 'historicising' original agrarian feasts into the Passover (ibid., pp. 115–16).

were rarely spelled out, but for sixteenth-century readers like William Harrison the most striking fact about the assumed unitary divine plan was the recorded continuity of belief in its existence throughout both the Testaments. The stream of prophetic witnesses to the fulfilment of God's promises gave history its special character for Harrison, and persuaded him that those promises would be kept in the present. Only one medium transmitted this insight, and in the Bible's brilliant account of the Elect's successive encounters with God we find the real reason for the centrality of the Scriptures in Harrison's thought.[27]

Modern theologians have suggested that this recognition of a corporate personality, the perception of a special relationship with the people of the covenant throughout the ages, was an important feature of Hebrew thought. Therefore this suggests another way in which Harrison's thought processes echoed theirs. This way of thinking did not involve a subjective 'present actualisation' of past events, as 'biblical theologians' have claimed, but more significantly the recognition that salvation history comprised a distinctive line of events which clearly demonstrated God's continual intervention in His creation, and that there had existed a number of individuals along that line whose intimate experience of God's power gave their lives unique importance and relevance to the present. This represented not anti-historical cultic simultaneity, but a firm belief in the certainty of God's character and the continuity of His covenant, which confirmed the comparability of distinct historical circumstances. The principles derived from each encounter between God and the Elect could thus be 'actualised' in the present.[28]

William Harrison interpreted the Scriptures in this way. He perceived the biblical text as a simple, linear rendering of a complex and multi-faceted reality, a single phenomenon that comprised the whole experience of the Elect under the care of God. That experience offered edifying instruction in how to obey God's will in contemporary circumstances when the Elect still lived under God's care. The very arrangement of the Scriptural history confirmed its contemporary relevance, for the Holy Ghost, said Harrison, 'doth often by later examples set furth such things as passed before time in men of like condition and are omitted in their histories'. This way of thinking allowed Harrison to find in the Scriptures the lineaments of a complete reformation for Church and society, just as the isolated criticisms uttered by members of the Hidden Church under the medieval papacy 'gathered together and brought into one perfit treatize...wold set downe the order of a perfite reformation'. Not for the last time can we see Harrison

---

[27] The basic insight was unoriginal; its chief importance for us was its transmission to the sixteenth century by the Scriptures (ibid. p. 110).

[28] See Wilch, *Time and Event*, pp. 74–5, 51, 170; Momigliano, 'Ancient historiography', pp. 18–20; Barr, *Biblical Words for Time*, p. 150. The problem of exactly how these principles were derived is discussed below, pp. 22–6.

applying what he conceived to be a Scriptural historical pattern to non-Scriptural history. Indeed not only the internal coherence of the Scriptural account of the Elect but the coherence of that interpretation with the rest of creation, in Harrison's eyes, showed that 'the confirmation of the Scriptures is not to be had from man'.[29] Once one achieved this correct understanding of the Scriptures, confirmation of their teachings could be discovered not only within the sacred text but also in all past and present phenomena, properly interpreted according to Scriptural criteria.

Seen in the context of Reformation thought, Harrison's acceptance of the Holy Spirit revealed in the Scriptures clearly owed more to human authority than he would have liked to admit. The precise contemporary source of his Scriptural interpretation is ultimately unknowable, but he carefully enlisted the great authority of Philip Melanchthon in support of his argument that essentially the Scriptures described the perpetual combat of two churches, the True Church and the satanic Church of Cain, for to some this Protestant argument seemed distressingly novel.[30] Harrison fundamentally agreed with the outstanding German scholar, but there were equally important differences between them which show how particular English conditions reinforced Harrison's fervent interpretation of the Scriptures, while Melanchthon's experiences encouraged him to take a more sanguine view of the past and its meaning for the present.

Harrison's belief in the continuous Elect covenant line, which in its relationship with God filled past and present, echoed the argument in Melanchthon's edition of *Carion's Chronicle*, where 'he hath excellently set furth the state of the church of christ from [time] to time touching the prosperity and decaie therof and therunto infinite examples of the iustice and mercy of god right worthy to be redd and perused of all men'. The significance of this approbation lies in the nature of Melanchthon's interpretation of church history, which explains world history. Harrison did not simply admire Melanchthon's scholarship, but accepted his depiction of a fundamental pattern in history through which both men sought to explain the present, by reference to the first moments of the Church's existence. Essentially the contemporary conflict did not differ from the struggle at the foundation of the True Church and its satanic parody, the False Church of Cain. Satan's ceaseless attempts to undermine what God had set up ensured that there would always be complete and utter antipathy between what Harrison called 'the line of the right wise', founded by Adam, and the teachers of false doctrine, the sect founded by Cain when he separated from

---

29 TCD MS 165, fos. 6r, 304v and 168r. See Coolidge, *Pauline Renaissance*, pp. 33–5, on the Pauline roots of this Scriptural interpretation.

30 Heinrich Bullinger when pressing a similar case conceded that 'All thys I suppose wyll be new and straunge in many hertes', for the unlearned believed that Christianity had begun under Tiberius (*The Olde fayth*, tr. Myles Coverdale (1547), sigs. E5r–v, B11r).

his father's church. This battle filled all of time, for although, said Harrison, 'the race of the wicked following the example of their cursed father declined daily from evell to worse', the godly patriarchs established a line of personal discipleship, so that Seth, for example, 'taught his children to increase in knowledge and the fere of god'. From the very first crisis there also existed a written corpus of prophetic doctrine, revealing to the Elect the future development of Antichrist's power, for 'when Cain builded his Citie Henoch and erected his kingdome, God set up the prophet Henoch who published a boke of the celestial decrees, wherin he foresheweth evidently a discourse of the kingdom of christe and the regiment of Antichrist'.[31] Even after the Flood, Ham 'renewed the most of all those wickednesses (wherebi god was so displeased that he drowned all the world) teaching them to be lawfull and tolerable'. The success of Ham's cursed posterity only emphasised the need to obey exactly God's commands to protect the True Church, 'For as the Israelites slew not all, for Josua spared the Gibeonites (and other many mo), so gret nombers of them grew to be dispersed over most quarters of the earth. From them also proceded the first ignorauns of god and therto bondage and servitude of mankinde', warned Harrison.[32]

Ever since Augustine, Cain and Abel had traditionally symbolised the opposition between the corrupt earthly city and the heavenly city, but the sixteenth-century Reformers were the first to make this opposition an explanation of the whole of world history. Luther had found it instructive and comforting 'to trace each of the two churches from these men as the originators and to note by what a marvellous plan God has always directed their affairs'. For like Harrison in the next generation, Luther found this model a convincing explanation and remedy for contemporary troubles: 'Even then the divine promise began to work itself out…just as we experience it today', so that a correct historical interpretation became 'a source of comfort for us to learn from experience that we are being dealt with by our adversaries in the way bloodthirsty Cain dealt with the righteous Abel'.[33] Heinrich Bullinger, the Protestant theologian who held enormous influence over English evangelicals in the 1560s, when Harrison pursued his theological studies, reinforced this dualistic historical model. He popularised the notion that with Cain and Abel 'begyneth the first difference of true and false belevers', that 'these two generacions shall in no wyse agree, but be at

---

[31] TCD MS 165, fo. 219r, and see P. Fraenkel, *Testimonia Patrum: The Function of the Patristic Argument in the Theology of Philip Melanchthon* (Geneva, 1961), p. 59. TCD MS 165, fos. 1v, 4r; cf. Fraenkel, *Testimonia Patrum*, pp. 63–7. Harrison's source on Enoch was Theodore Bibliander, on whom see below, pp. 43–6.

[32] TCD MS 165, fos. 18r and 10r, where the Canaanites received only 'percell of their woefull burden which Noah laid…upon the posterity of Chanaan'.

[33] Luther, *Works*, (St Louis, 1958), i; *Lectures on Genesis Chapters 1–5*, ed. by Jaroslav Pelikan, p. 252.

variaunce in fayth and religion' throughout history. The True Church feared, honoured and served God, but the False, tempted by Satan, neither trusted nor honoured God, but loved the world and followed its lusts and temptations. Bullinger also claimed that from Ham after the Flood 'sprange ydolatrye, offryng to ymages' and false religion, which was 'brought in among other nacions by the helpe of the olde serpent', polluting the Greeks, Romans, 'and other people'.[34]

Within a similar historical framework Harrison, like other Puritans, could insist that the Elizabethan Church had exactly to obey Scriptural commands for a complete reformation, since contemporary conditions did not represent historical development away from the Scriptural conflict so much as that same perpetual struggle carried on under another guise. The True Church had to concentrate all its energies on achieving a pure reformation, for Old Testament Israel, in her encounters with the Canaanites and their successors, showed the nemesis that awaited those who faltered in the conflict with the unregenerate. Israel exemplified the fluctuating fortunes of the True Church, which waxed and waned according to the zeal with which it obeyed God, and either suppressed the False Church or foolishly allowed it to flourish. The Old Testament established through the example of Israel the perpetual and characteristic pattern of faith and apostasy, for even Israel succumbed to the seductions of degenerate Gentile religion. Harrison accepted Melanchthon's argument that in Israel only a faithful minority had opposed corruption, and he also stressed that the repeated decline in Israel's fortunes had only been arrested by the rediscovery of normative Scriptural truth and the rejection of Gentile errors, through the preaching of this faithful minority in the covenant line, in periodic reformations of varying purity. In Harrison's view the fact that this historical interpretation had been revealed to the Patriarchs of the earliest times, confirmed its relevance for the Church under Elizabeth. For Adam's disciple, Cainan, taught the motions of the moon, whose 'increase, diminution, variable condition in motion and light is a noble and evident image not only of our owne... but also of the state of the whole churche', which sometimes flourishes but often 'appereth but in a weake estate'. The present Reformation in England therefore had to be interpreted in the light of the whole history of the True Church, which had witnessed a long series of such partial reformations. These demonstrated that corruption would always follow true teaching, which would only be generally reestablished by divinely appointed teachers of truth, who themselves formed both the permanent minority of believers in each generation and the Elect covenant line stretching throughout time.[35]

For Harrison the continuity of this covenant line also proved that the

---

[34] Bullinger, *The Olde Fayth*, sigs. C4v–C5r, D1r.
[35] Fraenkel, *Testimonia Patrum*, pp. 64–5 and TCD MS 165, fo. 18r.

sixteenth-century Reformation shared the same substance with all other reformations. For God, said Harrison, 'will never leave his church voide of soch elect and chosen Vesselles as may call his people from their errors into the light of his truth and surely if you note it well their hath bene a noble succession of soch teachers even sith the very creation', a succession mainly of personal disciples.[36] With this continuous oral tradition there stood from the beginning the written corpus of faith, enshrined at first in the two pillars inscribed by Adam so that the knowledge of God's power, the time and manner of the Creation, and his 'wholesome admonitions' should not be forgotten.[37] Here again history and doctrinal teachings were indistinguishable. This narrowly defined corpus of doctrine provided both a means of detecting false doctrine and of interpreting the Old Testament, for those listed first in the Scriptural genealogies were not the eldest 'but soche onely as succeeded in the right line from Seth unto Abraham' and remained loyal to true doctrine, for only 'the title of goddes providens in his appointed vessell is to be considered in the genealogy of christ'.[38] Members of this covenant line merited justification solely by their faith in the promised Messiah, and stood out from their own times by their continuation of this revelation. In their priority in the genealogies 'we see the order of the divine election which geveth the prerogative to Sem amonge the Children of Noah, and to Abram among the children of Thare, from whom the families proceded that onely stocke unto godes promises and covenaunt.'[39]

Relying upon Paul's Epistle to the Hebrews, this christological interpretation of the Old Testament assumed that the patriarchs and prophets advanced their reformations by preaching a spiritual rather than literal interpretation of the ceremonies, as a type of Christ, or as Bullinger put it, 'to dryve awaye the mysunderstandynge whyche was rysen up among and in the people...poynte they every where from the letter unto the sprete, from the outward sacrifice unto christ Jesus'.[40] The Elect were particularly distinguished by their creative application of this prophetic insight to all aspects of their existential experience. For when Israel repeatedly trespassed beyond her already worldly interpretation of the ceremonies, to worshipping

---

[36] Ibid., fo. 6r. Harrison listed the covenant line: Adam, Methuselah, Noah, Sem, Abraham, Isaac, Jacob, the Patriarchs, Moses, Joshua, Caleb, the Judges, Samuel, David, Nathan, Ahija, the rest of the prophets to Elijah and Elisha, Isaiah, Eliseus, Jeremiah, Daniel, Aggeus, Zachary, 'and after these other mo came still on and continued to John Baptist who saw Christ' (ibid., fo. 71r). The line continued after Christ, and so did the Church of Cain, particularly in the supporters of transubstantiation (ibid., fo. 213v).

[37] God ensured that these survived the Flood. Both Harrison and Melanchthon borrowed this notion from Josephus (Fraenkel, *Testimonia Patrum*, p. 64; TCD MS 165, fo. 1v).

[38] 'Wherfore soche as hold that the line of christ is continued in order of succession according to the eldest are manifestly deceaved for by that means Ismaell should be preferred before Isaac' (ibid. fo. 8r).

[39] Ibid., fo. 20r.   [40] *The Olde Fayth*, sig. F7r.

Nature and attributing her prosperity to the Canaanite nature gods, the prophets sought to proclaim the fact that history provided the surest instruction in faithful knowledge. History was not 'dead', because the Lord of history who had given the miracles of Exodus and Settlement remained at work in the present, which shared His wider purposes. Israel's cycles of faith and apostasy therefore reflected the contest between this prophetic insight and the willingness of fallen man to be misled by Satan, to turn to Nature and misinterpret history as a record of 'dead' events, a mistake characteristic of Gentilism.[41]

Among the Gentile nations, lack of this faithful understanding and satanic influence not only distorted the true faith received from the Elect but also corrupted its corollary of true knowledge of every art and science. The priority, completeness and unity of Elect knowledge, meant that the doctrinal tradition transmitted by the covenant line established the boundaries of legitimate knowledge, which had to be faithfully observed. For amongst the Gentiles the faithless distortion of this knowledge led only to religious, social and political decline. Ever willing to embrace this corrupt knowledge and its false gods, the Israelites frequently suffered a similar fate, and reformation came only with the revival of the prophetic historical interpretation of the present by members of the covenant line. Here the lineaments of Harrison's approach to contemporary problems begin to emerge, for he saw the direct relevance of this pattern to Elizabethan England, since the human weaknesses behind Israel's desire for idolatry were 'even the same which move us to follow the papist religion and idolatry brought from Rome'.[42] Therefore the heirs of the Elect covenant line had to exercise constant vigilance against popery, or wily Satan would use it to subvert the feeble True Church beginning to re-emerge in England.

It must be stressed that Harrison acknowledged that mankind was inherently incapable of achieving a complete reformation. Because of their human frailties, individual members of the covenant line had taught only relatively pure doctrine. Therefore although Melchisedek fulfilled the office of high priest, 'in that he represented the preesthode of christ', Christ alone 'made the finall and perfite sacrifice whereof all other were but shadowes', a distinction of the Apostolic age that Melanchthon had insisted upon in *Carion's Chronicle*. He believed that only the Apostles taught pure doctrine against clear error, whereas the True Church normally fought against relative error with relative truth. Therefore while he based his christological

[41] S. G. F. Brandon, *Time and Mankind* (London, 1951), p.97; A. Richardson, *History, Sacred and Profane* (London, 1964); J. K. S. Reid, *The Authority of Scripture* (London, 1957).

[42] TCD MS 165, fo. 253v; thus the Israelite belief that idolatry brought wealth, power and 'carnall liberty', explained 'the aptnesse of the people in my time...to come hedlong into error' (ibid., fo. 59r).

interpretation of the Old Testament on the idea that the Christian faith remained at all times identical with the faith given to Adam, for 'There is but one faith in Christ's salvation, revealed in both Testaments', he believed that the Apostles taught a *novum doctrine genus*.[43] Harrison likewise discerned a qualitative difference between the Law and the Gospel, which enabled him to make Christocentric distinctions within the genealogy of the Elect. For example, he found in Joshua intellectual gifts equal to Moses, but 'he is to be preferred in that he and not Moses did bring the people into the land of promise, and therefore is a signe of Christ which the law or Moses was not able to perform'.[44]

Like Melanchthon, Harrison emphasised the continuity of the covenant line and its doctrines in the Church after Christ, for 'Even as this order was kept before Christ so sins his assention he hath left us his worde and manifold preachers of the same in like sort who from time to time have not ceased to call the people to repentauns'. In keeping with the relative impurity of their faith, however, members of the covenant line 'have swarved and clogged the lordes people' with false doctrine.[45] As in the Old Testament, these periodic reformations displayed the perpetual characteristics of apostasy and recovery, showing that Harrison did not conceive the history of the Church since Christ as a straight sliding scale of increasing corruption, but a series of troughs and peaks generally moving downwards. Not the standards of the Apostolic age but the perpetual Scriptural doctrines reintegrated by the Apostles provided the basis for assessing the status of each reformation.

This fact underlined the contemporary relevance of the conflict of the Two Churches, for as we have seen Harrison believed that the Old and New Testaments and the history of the later Church showed a sinister congruence. Satan had preyed upon human weaknesses to seduce Israel into idolatry, and those motives were 'even the same which move us to follow the papist religion'. The Elect had therefore to exercise constant vigilance in their obedience to Scriptural teachings, or wily Satan would again subvert the True Church through popery. The correct interpretation of the history of the Church since Christ reinforced this lesson, for in the context of the Two Churches Harrison could see that the idolatrous errors of Gentilism were revived in popery and summed up in the figure of Antichrist. The satanic parody of the True Church taught pernicious errors which had repeatedly infected Israel, although God had sought 'by all means to plucke his people

---

43 Ibid., fo. 24r. As soon as the Apostles preached, however, their teachings were perverted and the Church thus misled (Fraenkel, *Testimonia Patrum*, p. 76). Christ's faith was 'the same which was showed to the olde fathers' according to Bullinger, *The Olde Fayth*, sig. G5v.

44 TCD MS 165, fo. 47r; *cf.* Bullinger, *The Olde Fayth*, sig. E6r.

45 This replaced a severer assessment, that most of these teachers had 'lost the sound knowledg of the rocke christ' and through their errors 'become subiect unto the curse which is pronounced upon all soche as leade the blinde out of their waie' (TCD MS 165, fo. 71r).

from the rites and ceremonies of the gentiles' and punished disobedience.[46] The papists disobeyed this significant revelation, and 'learned of the gentiles' many of their errors. Not only did their ceremonies have sinister parallels with satanic Gentilism, but they bound 'the consciences of the true and zealous Christians' in enforcing these abominations. The process had begun with good intentions, but corruption inevitably went with divergence from the Scriptural doctrinal tradition. In their misguided zeal to suppress Jewish superstitions, early bishops of Rome had 'returned again in many things to plaine gentilisme which god had condemned and abolished amonge his chosen people'. Popery continued the threat of Gentilism not just in its ceremonies but in its intrinsic nature, epitomised in its gaudy ceremonies. For by appealing to natural man's weaknesses 'Sathan practized to reduce a christian gentilisme into the churche of christ' through Roman innovations.[47]

In contrast to this reminder of human failings, both Melanchthon and Harrison recognised that the imperfections of the series of minor reformations throughout time did not sever their connection with the original pure stream of doctrine. Indeed we have already noted Harrison's belief that this pure doctrine could be resurrected by interpreting all inherited knowledge according to perpetual Scriptural criteria, so that in this instance 'in some things (though not generally)' medieval critics of the papacy 'do espie to me and detect part of the wickedness of their times albeit that god hath not opened eche of their eyes to see the botome of all that is amisse in that Synagoge of Antichrist'.[48] Piecing together their insights according to the Scriptural doctrinal pattern would create 'a perfite reformation'. Because he felt that he shared this unchanging godly insight, Harrison believed that he could resurrect the full experience of the earliest moments of time, that in his experiences God 'set furth such things as passed before time in men of like condition'.[49] For he stood at the end of the prophetic covenant line, linked to its beginning by his inheritance of true doctrine. The secret preaching of Ridley, Latimer, and Cranmer in the time of persecution had recalled him from his temporary place as 'a shaven worshipper of Baal' in

---

[46] Ibid., fo. 69v. The New Testament gave a different external form to that spiritual truth within the ceremonial law which the Jews had misinterpreted. Harrison neither condemned nor praised 'ethnike authors'. Because Christ had not condemned them, they could be read, but extremist opponents of Gentilism 'will scasely allow the reading of any histories' but the Scriptures (ibid., fo. 167v; *cf.* Ded. to *Description of Scotland* in Holinshed's *Chronicles* (1577), sig. ✶ b.ii. ✶).

[47] Including praying to the East, images (TCD MS 165, fo. 69v). traditional customs (ibid., fo. 119r), purgatory (fos. 245r, 269r), the date of Christmas (fo. 132r), offending candles (fo. 200r), perambulations (fo. 43v), praying for each other (fo. 137r), blessing with the empty chalice (fo. 48r). The 'bestly doctrine' of transubstantiation outdid the Gentiles, however (fo. 48v). Some of these persisted in the Elizabethan Church, and Harrison abolished them at Radwinter – see below, pp. 147–54.

[48] TCD MS 165, fo. 304v.   [49] Ibid., fo. 6r.

the Church of Cain, a decisive experience which converted him to a truth which he believed had been steadfastly guarded since Adam.[50]

This inheritance had an important impact on Harrison's historical understanding. Most obviously, in his eyes it gave history a teleological dynamic, for history only existed to give realisation to prophecy. Time also acquired for him a dynamic quality which it does not have for us, because being coterminous with history it shared its purposes. Therefore Harrison felt justified in perceiving the divine will manifested in chronology, and especially its mysterious parallels, patterns and rhythms, as we shall see below. Here we should notice, however, how much he owed to the Hebrew approach to history which the early Fathers had appropriated in order to vindicate intellectually a Gospel compromised by the failure of the expected Second Advent to materialise.

At the end of the second century AD Tertullian claimed to be able to penetrate to the true nature of time and the historical continuum by relying on Moses, the first prophet. Moses not only gave 'In his book the sequence of events set in order from the beginning', a prophetically necessary order down to his own day and thereafter, but showed the meaning of such events, because 'in his own story he gave pictures of things yet to be'.[51] Here Tertullian responded to the demand for backward thinking inherent in the Hebrew teleological approach to history. Our psychological insight into the forward movement of history requires a rational examination of historical causation, but the practice of seeking events in teleological relation to their final End, which the early Christians acquired from the Hebrew prophets, meant that events occurring in disparate periods could be seen as fulfilling a given purpose in a similar way. The Hebrew prophets particularly relied upon this sort of historical interpretation. In their exhortations they utilised God's accepted pre-eminence in history, demonstrated in the supernatural successes of Exodus and Settlement. They fervently preached their historical interpretation of all kinds of phenomena to awaken a populace which had slipped into an easy acceptance of history as a *fait accompli*, content with the present enjoyment of its consequences and uninterested in its wider purposes.[52]

Drawing upon his own experience of preaching, William Harrison recognised that the prophets had faced the same problem of making their audience aware of the immanent presence of God in every daily thought and

---

[50] Harrison's autobiography in Edelen, 'William Harrison', p. 258.
[51] Tertullian, *Apology*, ed. and trans. T. R. Glover (London, 1931). p. 93.
[52] T. Boman, *Hebrew Thought Compared with Greek*, trans. J. L. Moreau (London, 1960), p. 170, argues that our insight into the movement of history owes more to the Greeks than the Hebrews, but over-emphasises the contrast between the two historiographies. Hebrew history could be non-teleological, the prophets interpreted this raw material teleologically. Brandon, *Time and mankind*, p. 97.

action. The failure to maintain this historical insight contributed to Satan's seduction of the people into idolatry. Discussing the apostasy in the Promised Land, therefore, Harrison noted the prophets' need to recall Israel from the Canaanite worship of Nature as the evidence of supernatural power, to bring her back to a recognition of the prophetic historical continuum. Harrison suggested that Israel went awhoring after false gods only when those who 'had seene the workes of the Lorde in the delivery died, after whose deathes, the people, thinking themselves at liberty as shepe without a shepherde, forgate their promise made to Joshua not long before his death'. Then Israel had promised to serve the Lord and put away strange gods, a covenant extracted after Joshua had rehearsed the history of the mighty works of God on behalf of Israel.[53] So Harrison clearly perceived that Israel's prosperity depended upon a clear understanding of the historical evidence of God's immanence and supreme power, and the utilisation of that insight in obeying God's will and adhering to true doctrine. God's historical actions thus provided the foundation for that covenant by which the True Church distinguished itself from the Church of Cain, and a correct historical interpretation was an essential part of true faith.

This contrast between history and Nature as sources of revelation requires further refinement, especially about the way in which those who heard Joshua, or the sixteenth-century audience, were shown the meaning of history. Those influenced by 'biblical theology' have stressed that God's being is not learned through propositions but revealed in actions, that revelation is an event, not a statement of eternal verities. This analysis argues that the Hebrew felt himself to be the fixed point towards which all actions were oriented, an allegedly subjective view of history often contrasted with the modern impersonal view of historical actions.[54] Yet this overlooks the fact that events are intrinsically silent on many vital questions, for example whether the Exodus rewarded Hebrew piety and righteousness, or expressed God's inscrutable love for an unworthy people. The immense contrast between election through human merits and through undeserved grace meant that Joshua had to resolve the question, as one of the divine messengers through whom God repeatedly revealed the doctrinal meaning and inner purpose of historical events. Like Joshua, the covenant line of prophets received the power to interpret contemporary events in the light of God's actions in Israel's past, and on that basis chastised contemporary sins by the threat of future punishment. Their prophecies constituted the divine revelation about history, which merely fulfilled in action the Word that had already been proclaimed.[55]

[53] TCD MS 165, fo. 47r, and Joshua 24.
[54] Boman, *Hebrew Thought*, p. 171; Reid, *Authority of Scripture*, p. 180.
[55] Albrektson, *History and the Gods*, pp. 118, 121.

This prior revelation by the covenant line thus delimited the complex of meanings which could be drawn from their own actions or indeed any Scriptural event, and eventually, in Harrison's thought, this conditioned the interpretation of the whole of history. Important as an inhibition on the rational interpretation of the Bible, this idea is probably more familiar as the Protestant argument that the Scriptures interpreted themselves. The fact that time constituted the order in which God granted realisation to prophecy in order to produce a final outcome may have been a partial key to the whole process, but without knowledge of the divine promises meditation on historical events alone could not reveal God's aims. For that reason Harrison strove to hold fast to the doctrinal revelation of the covenant line. The modern argument that the Bible details a sequence of 'ideographic' events, each with a complex of meanings exceeding the sum of its details, overlooks the fact that Protestants believed that those details expressed a prior revelation. Allegedly this 'ideographic' thinking found significance in singular events through their relationship with others in a unique continuum, not in any general principles which could be deduced from them. More importantly, John Coolidge has described this as the distinctive characteristic of sixteenth-century Puritan thinking.[56] However, this needs considerable qualification, for the prophets clearly established the general principles which could be extracted from historical events. The inspiration of divine grace behind those principles made merely rational investigation of Scriptural events fruitless, without constant reference to the divine revelation of God's purposes in His relationship with His chosen people.

Harrison's views on such problems of Scriptural interpretation not only identify the limits of human reason and free will to obey God's commands, but also show that the kind of general principles which could be drawn by human reasoning from Scriptural events were strictly limited by doctrinal criteria previously laid down by the covenant line. To the regenerate understanding, the Scriptures confirmed themselves, because their story expressed the unchanging doctrinal inheritance of the covenant line in a multitude of different ways. This central point once grasped, these criteria could be universally applied in the present, where Harrison stood at the end of the covenant line. In this context, free will was limited to the obedience of this revelation, reason stood under the tutelage of the Scriptures. Such restraints reproduced the circumstances in which the revelation had been made, for Harrison believed that the covenant line guarded an unaltered doctrine because that doctrine had been given by illumination rather than derived through the processes of imperfect human reason. While the

---

[56] Ibid., pp. 119–20; Reid, *Authority of Scripture*, p. 187, and see Coolidge, *Pauline Renaissance*, pp. 16–17, which makes much of a presumed contrast between Jewish 'ideographic' and Greek 'nomothetic' thinking.

prophets applied this doctrine to changing circumstances, they always pointed the way towards Christ. Citing the example of Isaiah, who 'excelled the rest', Harrison showed that the prophet 'had all in charge not only to foreshow of things to come whereof thei had special revelation, but also to interprete and declare the lawe and applie the doctrine therof in soche wise as might best tend to the utility and benefite of the people'. In Harrison's christological view of the covenant line, the prophets propounded a spiritual understanding of the Law which went hand in hand with their promises of punishment and mercy. The three 'principle grounds' of their interpretation were first 'the doctrine contained in the two tables, the second the promises and threatenings of the law, and the third the covenant of grace and reconciliation founded upon Christ who is the end of the law'. As the perpetual teaching of the Elect since Adam, this still applied in the present.[57]

Harrison consistently demonstrated his belief that revelation, not natural reason, determined the content and limits of this doctrine throughout history. The 'profound writer' and 'divine poete' Orpheus, for example, had not only seen 'the Hebrewe theology either in Egypt or in Palestine and redde the 5 Bookes of Moses', but just as importantly, 'sondri prophecies of Christ and such other treatizes as his predecessors had written before touching the knowledge of God and creation of the World'. To this extent Orpheus was as well-equipped as the prophets to discover the lineaments of true doctrine by submitting his reason to revelation, by creatively using this inherited knowledge to go beyond what he had learned and interpret all phenomena by Scriptural criteria, rejecting error and embracing truth. However, his reliance on rational criteria limited Orpheus to repeating what he knew of God's character from his acquaintance with true doctrine. Although he assented intellectually to the Hebrew notion of history as the fulfilment of prophecy which confirmed Elect doctrines, Orpheus' dependence on reason prevented him from rejecting his previous illusions, and he 'very often stumbled upon the errors of the gentiles, and such corrupted doctrine as he was trained up in'. In an analogous situation Harrison had sifted the knowledge he had acquired when a papist, and amongst the rejected dross was the Hermetic philosophy to which Orpheus had been deemed an important witness. Orpheus' attempt to explain parts of human experience by something other than the doctrine transmitted by the covenant line, revealed his failure to subordinate his reason to the revelations of divine grace. This crucial failing found active expression in the contrast between Orpheus' repetition of error and Isaiah's 'most vehement admonitions, reprehensions and consolations evermore applying the doctrine as he saw cause and the estate of the people and children of Israel required'. In Harrison's view Isaiah enjoyed an understanding perfected by grace, which

[57] TCD MS 165, fo. 81v.

revealed to him the whole course of history and therefore the significance of Israel's apostasy in forsaking the True Church, and its faith in the God of history, for the satanically-inspired nature religions of the Church of Cain. This insight explained both the vehemence and the perfection of his interpretation. In that Isaiah not only understood the dualistic pattern of history but also in his life and actions formed part of that pattern, he represented an ideal of immense contemporary relevance to Harrison.[58]

The importance which Harrison attached to revelation as the necessary transforming influence on human reason is brought into sharper focus if we contrast his interpretation of Isaiah's teaching with Richard Hooker's views. Hooker argued that Isaiah attacked ignorant idolatry by 'the manifest law of reason', a reflective argument which always directed Isaiah's thinking, independently of divine illumination and the interpretation of history as the conflict of the Two Churches. It thus forms part of the universal rational argument available at all times: 'That which we say in this case of idolatry, serveth all other things, wherin the like kind of general blindness hath prevailed against the manifest laws of reason'. To Harrison, however, this idolatry itself reflected the weakness of unaided human reason in the face of Satan's subversion, for the Israelites attributed Canaanite prosperity to their nature gods, and turned away from the evidence of providential history, which Isaiah reasserted (Is. 44.24–8), and to which he demanded Israel should contribute by returning to true obedience.[59] Isaiah's unaided ability to perceive the truth was no greater than that of those members of the covenant line under the medieval papacy who participated in contemporary errors and only saw the wickedness of their times so far as God 'opened eche of ther eyes'.[60]

Harrison thus recognised the special contemporary importance of the covenant line, for the prophets had been taken beyond the limits of human reasoning by immanent and inexplicable grace as much when they criticised present iniquities as when they prophesied the future. He vividly described his realisation of this fact when reading I Kings 18 and 19. 1–5, a description important for several reasons. Most obviously it describes his Puritan response to the Scriptures, his immediate involvement with the experiences of God's chosen vessels, to which the continuity of the covenant line had given such contemporary relevance. It also shows how the doctrines which he believed that covenant line had transmitted, delimited his interpretations of Scriptural events. What appears to be simply a rational deduction of a

---

[58] Ibid., fos. 56r–v, 81v.
[59] Ibid., fo. 81v; Hooker, *Lawes* (London, 1594), I.8.11, facsimile (Amsterdam, 1971), i, p. 68. Calvin believed that Isaiah asserted that Nature revealed God but fallen man was too blind to read this evidence. *The Institution of Christian Religion* (Reinold Wolfe and Richard Harrison: London, 1561), I.xiv.1, fo. 43v.
[60] TCD MS 165, fo. 304v.

general principle from disparate events appeared to Harrison as an example of human reason obeying revelation. For of many possible alternatives, true doctrine had already provided the conclusion that God required men to be taught, and the fact that the historical actions of the Elect expressed that truth made it especially impressive to human understanding. At first 'whenne I redde this history of the dealing of Helias [Elijah] with the false prophets', said Harrison, 'I could not but stand to consider how the Thesbite was so bold with Ahab and yet fered to abide the fury of his wife [Jezebel]. But this is more to be merviled that as he fled from her wrathe for fere of deth so ere long he desired of god that he might end his life for he was no better than his father.'

The spectacle of a powerful and vigorous prophet reduced to fear and self-disgust troubled Harrison, but in a moment of insight conditioned by his previous understanding of true doctrine he saw that this action revealed a vitally important fact about God's relationship with his Elect covenant line. For in common with Elijah 'Even so Peter fered not in presens of the whole rout of them which came to take Christ to draw his sword and laie manfully at Malchus and yet in presens of one pore wenche he wretchedly yelded to forsware and denie his master. Certes these examples declare that even the very best men although as sometime thei do thorow the power of god worke wonders, yet at an other thei are left unto themselves that thei maie remember and know themselves to be but men'. Once more Harrison's thinking follows his belief that the Holy Ghost expressed the same doctrines in the distinct historical actions of 'men of like condition'.[62] This participation in the Holy Spirit directed a regenerate understanding in creatively applying the knowledge gained from one part of the Scriptures to another, and by extension to 'men of like condition' in contemporary circumstances. Harrison felt confident that for the individual reasoning obedient to revelation, the totality of Scriptural teachings limited the whole perception of the world.

Harrison's 'Chronology' therefore shows that he was primarily interested in history as a source of positive information about the building up of the True Church in the present. This purpose informed his preaching and teaching, as it did that of other Protestants who found in the Scriptural account of the True Church a complete blueprint for the contemporary Reformation. Naturally, given Harrison's uninhibited eclecticism, not all the material in the 'Chronology' suited this purpose, and he could of course draw general principles from historical examples – he could even use an example from the history of Israel to support a general observation on human behaviour.[62] Yet, most importantly, these conclusions did not

---

[61] Ibid., fo. 75r; similarly Amos was 'stirred up by God, and hath both knowledge constancie and the spirit of the prophecie geven him' (ibid., fos. 80r–v).

[62] Ibid., fo. 68v; cf. 2 Sam. 10. 1–5.

contribute towards the end of building up the True Church. That could never be subordinated to the demands of unaided reason, but remained autonomous from reason and gave special meaning both to Scriptural actions and those later events which apparently fulfilled Scriptural prophecy.

The cosmic struggle between the Elect and the Gentiles gave those actions contemporary relevance, so that 'I would wish the loving reader', said Harrison, 'to consider the doings of the world as concerning the dealings of the gentiles with the old man and the discourse of the Jewish history here set furth with the proceding and conflicts of soch as be regenerate in Christ and made members of his visible or church militant'. The doctrinal inheritance of the covenant line revealed the fluctuating fortunes of the True Church to have been a reflection of Israel's apostasy and disobedience, and made of her return to obedience through God's mercy a lesson which could be directly applied to sixteenth-century believers. For 'if thou canst applie ther errors and corrections with ther recoveries and returnes unto thy self and therwithall consider the secrete and manifest working of God in the preservation of the one and favourable ponishment of the other', that is, accept the covenant line's own interpretation of these events, then in the actions of the Elect 'thou shalt see a merveilous sight for thy comforte and find a ready path as St.Peter saith to make thine election certeine'.[63]

Harrison's conviction, shared with the Hebrew prophets, that the past revealed the unchanging nature of God's relations with his Elect, had led him to 'historicise' Peter's argument. For where 2 Pet. 1. 4–10 rehearsed a list of positive but abstract Christian qualities, resembling the philosophical virtues, Harrison stressed that the Elect's finite historical actions gave external expression to revealed doctrine. The history of Israel remained a living example because it revealed the most fundamental information about the unchanging nature and will of God, and what He commanded His people to do. Above all, it revealed the need for complete obedience to God's will in all things, and the prior necessity for divine grace to bestow on mankind the abilities necessary for such obedience and righteous behaviour. For without God's help man could not completely bend his will to do what the Scriptures showed God always commanded. Therefore from an early example of religious and political decline Harrison learned 'to crave of the Lorde that he wold put ones not only into the hertes of princes but of all men without differens that thei should attempt nothing in whatsoever dealing before thei first did consult how it might safely stand with the will and pleasure of god'. Indeed this constant necessity to test all thoughts and actions by reference to God's revealed will Harrison considered 'the chief point of all religion'. The criteria for this assessment could therefore be found only

---

[63] TCD MS 165, fo. 47v. Significantly, this is Harrison's comment on God's institution of the Judgeship over Israel, which had great importance for his views on contemporary magistracy. See below, pp. 215–34.

in the Scriptures, and not only Harrison's religious views but his ideas of social and political reform developed from this fundamental premise.[64]

This doctrinal context distinguishes the Protestant use of Scriptural models from the humanist emphasis on historical examples, seen in *Carion's Chronicle*, where Harrison found so much to admire. In Melanchthon's thought at this point, humanist and Protestant approaches to the past came closest together. An outstanding humanist scholar, Melanchthon did not completely abandon the habits of mind inculcated by his earlier training; indeed, he often used historical examples for commonplace moralising purposes. Yet although Melanchthon paraphrased a traditional humanist view of history when he argued for the superiority of example over precept 'because that examples being set before us as images do not only teache openly, but do also admonish, sturre, and inflame the myndes that are honestly brought up, that they maye be kindled toward vertues and honesty with a certain pleasur and love', he made a distinctive contribution to Protestant historiography when he applied this formula to the Scriptures, where 'these thinges are moost clerely expressed'. For the Bible revealed a kind of knowledge which 'the hystoryes of the Gentyles do not teache us', an account of God's kingdom, his promises and mercy towards Christ's kingdom 'under the crosse sence the beginninge of the worlde', where are 'declared the witnesses of God's workes'. Scriptural history taught more than mere civic virtue, it showed true believers that they had to follow the godly examples of those who had rested on God's promises rather than earthly powers, for although Satan with all the power of the world assaulted the Word, 'God hath wonderfully alway kept his promise, above the understandynge and thought of men's wit or wisdome'. Like Harrison, Melanchthon found that such a history taught the fear of God to the present heirs of the True Church, a lesson inaccessible to human reason and upon which the Gentile histories were therefore silent. That silence itself underlined the historical importance of the limits of natural reason.[65]

Clearly Harrison's historical outlook could be explained away simply as one lacking any concept of anachronism, and therefore able to make everything over in its own image. Fundamentally, Harrison's relative ignorance of our sense of anachronism did allow him to discern patterns in history and chronology, because he believed that all time was homoge-

---

[64] Ibid., fo. 28r. Raleigh believed that 'there is no better guide' than God's written will – even the blind 'wisdome of man' could see that the Chronicles of Judah and Israel 'being written by men inspired with the spirit of God, instruct us chiefly, in that which is most requisite for us to know...propounding examples which illustrate this infallible rule, "The feare of the Lord is the beginning of Wisdome"' (*The History of the World* (for Walter Burre: London, 1614), II.xxi.6).

[65] Melanchthon, *Carion's Chronicle* sigs. *4v, *5v, and his preface 'Of the Use and Profyte of Histories', also reprinted in *Cooper's Chronicle* (1565), sigs. f1v – f2v.

neous. Yet two reasons save this from being a flat and uninteresting view of history. The dynamic teleological movement of history towards its goal bound past and present together, so that the full meaning of the past could be found not by reference to the present alone, but also by interpretation of the prophecies. This further suggests that it would be more accurate to think of synchronistic thinking. For there is a great difference between making many different pasts agree with the present and projecting one continuous, complete and generally recognisable prophetic historical process on to the present. The prophetic continuum of events highlighted the fact that the past and present had the same meaning. The concept of anachronism operated only within this general assumption, ensuring that circumstances only produced individual variations within a common framework. Harrison's circumstances, for example, forced him to use this framework in more radical ways than its European formulators had done. Therefore much can be learned about Harrison's outlook by examining his individual application of the concept of the Two Churches.

Harrison believed that spiritually he had been reborn early in 1558 as a member of the True Church, and that that rebirth made him contemporaneous with all the Elect in their unceasing conflict with Satan. Therefore it is more illuminating to examine what Harrison found most relevant to his own experiences in the history of the Elect than to trace the roots of his belief in their conflict with the Church of Cain. For behind Melanchthon stood Luther, whose emphasis upon the polarity of Jerusalem and Babylon merely elaborated the antipathy between the City of God and the City of Man depicted in Augustine's *De civitate Dei*.[66] It is more important to see in Harrison's own assessment of Augustine how the European ideas which Harrison received became transformed by his experience of the Reformation in England, how subjective was his identification with the Elect. For Harrison and Melanchthon had different perspectives on the past and consequently chose to emphasise their contemporaneity with different phases and figures in the history of the True Church. At this point we can see the effects of anachronistic thinking, but only operating within the general context of the Two Churches, which neither man constructed anachronistically from his own circumstances. In fact those circumstances only served to differentiate their ideas. Their different viewpoints reflect their individual perceptions of the status of their respective churches.

Melanchthon, while aware of the variable success of the repeated reformations throughout history, reserved a special place for Augustine. He believed that agreement with Augustine was 'an abbreviation for holding

---

[66] Luther's argument cited above, p. 15, that Cain's treatment of Abel foreshadowed contemporary papist attacks, referred back to *De civitate Dei*, XV.vii and Matt. 23.35 (*Works* St Louis, 1958, I, p. 252).

the Catholic faith', because the Lutheran Reformation had inherited the nature of the Augustinian Reformation.[67] Augustine, claimed Melanchthon, had combatted the excesses of the 'aetas Origenica', when truth became polluted by error, by a return 'ad fontes', re-establishing the primal teaching of the Church. This enabled Melanchthon to make an almost unqualified identification between Augustine and the Apostles. Just as those reformations agreed with the Catholic faith for all time, so Melanchthon believed in the congruence between the Wittenberg and Augustinian Reformations, whose identical characters sprang from their return to original faith, reflected in their teachings and practices and transcending our equivalence between time and change. This did not mean that at Wittenberg truth had finally triumphed over error, but that the means of that triumph had been created by a clear separation of truth and error. On this basis Melanchthon argued for an ecumenical reformation based on fundamental doctrinal, not ceremonial, grounds.[68]

This 'Magisterial' interpretation probably appeared increasingly inappropriate to Harrison in the England of the 1570s, as evangelical hopes for further gradual reform in the Church steadily dwindled. Consequently Harrison took a more radical view of Augustine, 'by whome, as by a noble light, the churche of god hath profited so moche'. He felt greater reluctance to accept Augustine's identity with the Apostles, mainly because 'among our papists this bishop is estemed for his skill in divinitie', in the same way that the pagans defended Aristotle as the ultimate authority on philosophy, 'so that among them it is heynous blasphemy either to refuse or controll the Authority of S.Augustine or not where he erreth'. To Harrison he was 'but a man, and...whatsoever man doeth maie againe by man be examined and tried' by comparison with the truth.[69] Since the papists had appropriated Augustine, Harrison felt compelled to approach his teachings with greater caution than had Melanchthon. This merely reflected the fact that Harrison felt no need to identify with a successful reformation in the past while he regarded the Elizabethan Church as only 'semi-reformed'. His position of impotent frustration gave him a greater appreciation of, and a closer commitment to, the pattern of persecution that distinguished the True Church.[70]

The clearest illustration of these contrasting positions is the fact that Harrison believed that the failures of the Elizabethan Church boded ill for

---

[67] Fraenkel, *Testimonia Patrum*, p. 94.   [68] Ibid., pp. 82–3, 94–6.

[69] TCD MS 165, fos. 175r, 28v. These remarks should not be taken out of context – where necessary Harrison used Augustine as a witness to the perpetual teachings of the covenant line, especially against the Hermetic philosophy. See below, pp. 310–11.

[70] Ibid., fo. 201v. Note that Harrison felt it necessary in 1565 to emphasise his fears about persecution from 'that Jezebel' Mary Tudor, at a time when Elizabeth's credentials as a godly prince were coming under closer scrutiny.

the future, while Melanchthon perceived greater cause for optimism about the state of the Church before the Second Advent. Like other Elizabethan radicals Harrison expressed his despair in a familiar type, which seemed to prefigure the end of the visible Church by the time immediately before the Incarnation. Then 'so small was the true church of god...that those godly which lived supposed that it had utterly bene extinguished. The scripture commendeth onely a few persons...and so shall it be also in the end of the world wherof the Jewish estate before Christ is an Image, wherein the number of true christiens shalbe very small wherfore the continuauns of the time shalbe cut of lest the wickednesse of the world shold altogether suppresse the church and no spouse of christ be found upon the erth'. Harrison's pessimistic sense of isolation explains the parallels within this vision, whereas by contrast Melanchthon looked for, and found, a symmetry between the Testaments which explained the End in terms applicable to the Wittenberg Reformation. He found in Josiah's restoration of true religion 'the figure of the last times in the church, to the which the true and sincere knowledge of the word shalbe opened, even before the end of the worlde'. Harrison considered Josiah a worthy but relatively minor reformer, whose attempt to purify the Church proved temporary.[71]

Distinctions between the 'oppressed' tradition and the 'Magisterial' interpretation of providential history can be over-emphasised. For Melanchthon believed that the sixteenth-century Reformation shared the experience of the past history of the Church because at all times the true believers suffered persecution. The Church enjoyed pure doctrine and godly members when led by God through difficulties, for 'in deserto maior fuit gloria huius populi, quam unquam florente regno in terrae Canaan'. Yet despite Melanchthon's agreement with the many Reformers who had embraced an eccclesiology of persecution, his own experience had taught him that when the Church appeared abandoned and at its last gasp, it had enjoyed divine liberation, and the freedom, in the Wittenberg Reformation, clearly to distinguish truth from error.[72] Harrison's analysis revealed a different meaning in history, and one which he found specially relevant to the unsatisfactory state of the Elizabethan Church. In David's contrasting actions while 'exercised with affliction and peniurie' and later enjoying 'rest and welth', Harrison found 'a good rule for all men', that idleness represented the greatest threat 'to the steadfast persisting of the godly', 'sithe ther is nothing that bringeth forgetfulnesse of god soner then welth and liberty to do what we list neither any meane to bring us soner to the remembrauns of our selves than affliction

---

[71] Ibid., fos. 130r, 89v; *cf.* Melanchthon, *Carion's Chronicle*, fo. 17v.
[72] P. Christianson, *Reformers and Babylon* (Toronto, 1978), p. 11, points out that for English interpreters the 'oppressed' and 'Imperial' themes were not mutually exclusive; see Fraenkel, *Testimonia Patrum*, pp. 66, 95–6.

and troble'.[73] This 'good rule' was more than a nod to convention, for it arose from the history of the True Church, pregnant with implications for the Elizabethan Church which had been momentarily reprieved from persecution. Harrison felt absolutely convinced that where Satan failed to pollute true doctrine by persecution he would, as he had in the early Christian Church, 'assaie by other practizes as rest ease, wealth, [desire of] honor, induction of new rites, ceremonies and adoration of reliques to corrupt their Integrity of Judgement, and lead them more surely into ther greater damnation'. Thus Harrison discerned the same lesson repeating itself at different times in the True Church, informing him that the false sense of security which had robbed the Elizabethan Church of its vigour and zeal for complete reformation threatened to allow the resurgence of that popery which Satan's blandishments had originally introduced. For 'how this divise prospered in his handes, I think ther are but few that can excuse themselves of ignorauns'; Satan's success could be measured by the contrasts between the primitive and the popish churches, and the same threat still clouded the horizon for the Elizabethan Church.[74]

The true depth of Harrison's dislike for the 'Magisterial' or 'Imperial' interpretation of salvation history is apparent in his discussion of Constantine, to the vast majority of Harrison's contemporaries the model of a Christian prince. This is examined in more detail below, but here we should note that Harrison clearly attributed the beginning of debilitating prosperity in the Church to the creation of an established Church under Constantine. Indeed he went even further in making Constantine personally responsible for distorting the Church from its true nature as a mystical body of the Elect in all ages, into an expression of the civil polity at one specific period.[75] Constantine made the True Church subject to worldly 'policy', and this same feature disfigured the Elizabethan Church. Therefore Harrison could not make peace with that Church, but only live with it under an uneasy truce, for the history of the True Church proved that it could remain constant only under the Cross.[76] The distinguishing features of this Puritan outlook begin to emerge in the lessons, drawn from the history of the True Church, which Harrison found directly applicable to the contemporary struggle. Their relative familiarity should not obscure Harrison's complete confidence that there existed no difference between the present confrontation with popery and, for example, the attacks of Amazias, 'the idolatrous priest of Bethel', upon the prophet Amos, for 'Thus we see how the godly have

[73] TCD MS 165, fo. 68v, and fo. 70v for similar comments on Solomon.
[74] Ibid., fo. 145r.
[75] Fraenkel, *Testimonia Patrum*, pp. 79–82, distinguishes Melanchthon from Continental Radicals in his views on Constantine. For Harrison's attitude, see below, pp. 235–43.
[76] See Chapter 4, pp. 145–87.

bene persecuted by the wicked from time to time and what platformes are oft divised to bring them to their endes'. Similarly, because the experiences of any one of the Elect remained immediately and personally relevant to every other member of the covenant line, to 'men of like condition' in Harrison's phrase, the sufferings under Ahab of the 'excellent prophete' Micah, and his conflict with the many false prophets, confirmed that 'truth is not alwaies to be found among the greatest nombers nor continually with soch as be of most authority'.[77] The last phrase especially underlines the disruptive potential of such a view, given the right circumstances in Harrison's England.

Harrison's response to the Scriptures exposes the psychological roots of his Puritanism. For one can argue that his willingness to interpret the present according to the dualistic pattern of salvation history reflects an attempt to recreate within himself that condition of dislocation which he believed distinguished the Elect throughout time, and which made it self-evident that the Church could only remain constant under the Cross. His constant internal struggle against the seductions of worldly prosperity incorporated the central feature of Puritan belief – the need to give unqualified obedience to God's commands, to rely totally upon the divine promises in God's covenant. To think and act with this sense of utter dependence, to apply Scriptural criteria in assessing all one's knowledge and actions, required the stimulus of adversity. Therefore in God's seven-fold renewal of His promises to Abraham 'we maie see how god confirmeth his promises unto his elect that rest upon his providens notwithstanding that in the meane time of there peregrinations here in erth many trobles happen unto them and those often very great', said Harrison.[78] Adverse circumstances always forced men to rely on God's power, and brought them to realise how that power had been revealed in historical events, as it would be in the present and future. Worldly prosperity destroyed human understanding of the continuity between past and present, and enticed individuals into fulfilling their own desires rather than the will of God.

Distaste for the enjoyment of the present opportunities of this world therefore accompanied a sense of contemporaneity which judged the present not in its own terms but in relation to what had gone before and what was promised to come. From Harrison's viewpoint persecution not only identified the True Church, but also repeatedly emphasised the true meaning of history and the similar experiences of other Elect individuals throughout time. The divinely-given ability to recognise and proclaim this fact distinguished the covenant line from the succession of false prophets, and in both their words and experiences the continuous minority of true prophets proclaimed man's

[77] TCD MS 165, fos. 8or, 74v.
[78] Ibid., fo. 27r.

total reliance on God's power.[79] Therefore Harrison found it essential to believe that the Church of Cain, through which Satan incessantly tried to subvert the True Church, was now represented by popery, and that the 'semi-reformed' Elizabethan Church could not be purified of this infection until all its members completely obeyed God's commands revealed in the history of the True Church. This required a standard of behaviour qualitatively different from that sanctioned by the Natural Law.

Harrison's 'Chronology' by its very nature and content militated against any connected discussion of the relationship of the Natural Law to unchanging true doctrine. Yet he may have found such ideas irrelevant, for Melanchthon's *Loci communes* (1521) suggest that concentration on the pattern of the Two Churches encouraged a tendency to diminish the importance of Natural Law for fallen man, and to emphasise instead the need for faithful obedience to that original corpus of doctrines revealed to the covenant line and historically expressed in their godly actions. Melanchthon argued that in addition to the Natural Law imprinted on all human minds 'God also made known to Adam certain laws', for sin blinded humankind to the Natural Law. In his revelation to his Elect God 'restored the knowledge of the natural law by a constant proclamation...so that I may almost call the law of nature not some sort of congenital or innate judgement engraved by nature on human minds, but merely laws accepted by the fathers. These laws were passed along forthwith to posterity' within the covenant line. Only within the context of the True Church did natural law have anything to do with salvation, for the covenant line retained the prerogative of faithfully expounding it and determining its place within the boundaries of saving knowledge.[80]

The general formulas of the Natural Law found amongst the Gentiles had to be distinguished both from the 'ius gentium' and the 'ius civile' since the latter represented the faithless distortion of Elect knowledge transmitted to the Gentiles, for 'very many of their common judgements imitate the depraved affections of our nature and not our laws'. The inability of the Gentiles to apply basic Natural Law precepts to the whole of their experience merely underlined the limitations of human reason and emphasised that uncorrupted Natural Law could only be found in the Scriptures, where the covenant line penetrated to its deepest meanings under the influence of grace. For although the Decalogue merely summarised the Natural Law, including

79 Bale attributed to Sir John Oldcastle the view that 'Rome is the very nest of antichrist...and those pilled friars are the tail which covereth his most filthy part... Not only is it my saying, but also the prophet Esay's, long afore my time. The prophet (saith he) which preacheth lies is the tail behind' ('A Brief Chronicle', in *The Select Works of John Bale*, ed. H. Christmas (Parker Society: Cambridge, 1849), p. 36).

80 *The Loci Communes of Philip Melanchthon*, ed. C. L. Hill (Boston, 1944), p. 145.

the fundamental principle of the love of God, 'these affections are not in our power', pointed out Melanchthon, 'so that no one knows except the spiritually minded, what is the trust of God, the fear and love of God'. Thus the Protestant emphasis on fallen man's inability to keep the Decalogue undercut any pretensions which the Natural Law might have to provide an autonomous source of saving knowledge. In fact such knowledge had been imparted only to Adam and his successors in the covenant line, and re-published in the Decalogue.[81]

The example of Noah showed Melanchthon that within the covenant line of the 'spiritually minded', fear of God's threatenings and total reliance on His promises constituted a qualitatively different kind of knowledge from a bare recognition of God, and even from the idea that He punished the wicked and saved the good. Completely dependent on grace, individual actions had to be intimately obedient to God's will. Even when he gave greater emphasis to the rational bases of faith in a later edition of the *Loci Communes*, Melanchthon restricted the natural light, the 'legal understanding of the law' in fallen man, to the regulation of 'external civil life'. He still maintained that God had upheld his law against such blindness 'since the time of Adam in his Church, and has given public testimony to this' in the events of the Old Testament. The proclamation at Sinai also delineated God's nature and established 'a positive distinction between God and devils', which revealed the limitations of a legalistic knowledge of the Natural Law, for 'it is not enough', insisted Melanchthon, 'that man know that he is not to kill other innocent men, nor rob others of their wives and goods'.[82] For the emphasis on Natural Law fundamentally implied salvation through good works, and that was impossible.

Melanchthon's fellow humanist-trained reformer, Heinrich Bullinger, took this concentration on Elect godly models a stage further. Bullinger exerted a dominant influence over English nonconforming clergy during the vestiarian controversy of the 1560s, the period of Harrison's most intensive theological studies. In an early polemical work, *Der alt gloub*, translated by Myles Coverdale in 1547 as *The Olde Fayth*, Bullinger showed in broad and sweeping terms how, within the conflict of the Two Churches, the covenant line encapsulated the only proper understanding of Natural Law. Reliance on anything but their interpretation and example, and the Scriptural account of God's law, led headlong into Satan's Church. Like Harrison later on, Bullinger argued that after the Flood Noah received from God the same laws 'as he had geven to hys forefathers and written in their hertes',

---

[81] Ibid., pp. 116–17, 118, 189.
[82] *Melanchthon on Christian Doctrine. Loci Communes 1555*, ed. C. L. Manschreck (New York, 1965), pp. 128–9.

including 'whatsoever concerned to love God and their neighboure', the summation of Christian doctrine. Similarly the Decalogue merely renewed and summarised 'the lawe that he hytherto had wrytten in the hartes of holy men' and which they had 'perfourmed thorow true fayth in Christe' since the beginning of the world. Clearly Bullinger believed that only within 'the holy genealogie of the true belevers' could one find 'men of ryght understandynge' who discovered Christ in the Natural Law, and that the Scriptures provided the only necessary examples of obedience to that law written by God in the hearts of men, but which only this minority properly understood. The Scriptures set the parameters for the interpretation of Natural Law, the Natural Law did not provide the criteria for Scriptural interpretation. To put it another way, while all the Natural Law might be in the Scriptures, not all Scriptural teachings conformed to the Natural Law. In a similar, intensely evangelical, context Harrison emphasised that, in comparison with the Scriptural ethical model, Platonic virtue was only 'as the gentiles measured the same'.[83] Only divine grace could rekindle the true spiritual understanding of the Law in fallen man, so that while all men might agree upon the Natural Law, its proper commands could be found only in the eternal doctrine of the Elect covenant line. Human reason could not be the _a priori_ source of such saving knowledge, for that depended _a posteriori_ upon the Scriptural definition of virtue.

Calvin also used an analysis of the Two Churches to bolster his contention that a fundamental antipathy existed between what the flesh conceived and what God commanded.[84] For although he believed that 'God doth never so regenerate his children in this world, that they doe perfectly serve him', yet the best way to obey Him was 'for godly minds to be kept under the order of preaching and the obedience of the scripture, that they may not seek the worde of God in erronious speculations'. For 'the light of understanding being extinguished', said Calvin, the natural man 'is not capable of reason',

---

[83] Bullinger, _The Olde Fayth_, sigs. C8v–D1r, D6r–v, E4v, C7r, E5v, and TCD MS 165, fo. 110v. Aquinas saw no contradiction between the idea that 'a virtuous person, through the disposition given by virtue, has a right judgement about what is in keeping with his virtue' and the way that a Christian 'through the light of faith divinely infused, gives assent to what is of faith and not to the opposite' (_Summa Theol._ 2a, 2ae, 2, 3), but Bullinger required a kind of obedience outside rational criteria, for 'yf we beleve and do as Abraham dyd, then are we Abrahams chyldren', and will inherit the kingdom of God, that is if we are 'obedient to the voyce of God...willyng and content to leave our frendes, to forsake oure owne wylles, our owne landes and gooddes at Gods callyng, and dwell in a straunge countre, to do goddes pleasure as Abraham dyd', for we must 'suffre adversitie with the people of God' (_The Olde Fayth_, sig. D2r). Harrison noted that Noah did not leave the Ark when the earth dried out, as one might rationally assume, but when God commanded him to – such was his 'holy fear of obedience of faith' – a significant conflation of ideas (TCD MS 165, fo. 25v).

[84] 'For al those things which do delight us under the colour of vertue, are like unto wine corrupted with the mustie caste', since 'the verie affections...of nature which are of themselves commendable, are notwithstanding defiled with originall sinne, and...degenerate from their nature: suche are mutual love betweene man and wife, fatherly love towards their children' (_Commentarie...upon...Genesis_, sig. O3r).

'untill he begin to be spirituall, through the grace of regeneration':[85] Calvin further underlined that history, not Nature, gave the clearest revelation of the divine law, for Isaiah taught that Nature teaches God; 'Yet suche is the dulnesse and grossenesse of our witt' that the idolatrous misinterpreted Nature. Only distant echoes of God's revelation of Himself could be heard in creation, for fallen man's corrupted judgement discerned only vague knowledge of God, knowledge whose limitations were clearly revealed in the erroneous discourses of Gentile philosophers on God's nature. God had revealed his counsel precisely and uniquely in the Scriptures, and unregenerate man's recourse to Nature could not enliven the vestigial remains of his pristine knowledge of God, nor provide another source of saving knowledge.[86]

Therefore like other Reformers, and like Harrison subsequently, Calvin emphasised that the contemporaneity of the Elect covenant line since Adam put merely contemporary assessments of honest conversation in their proper light. Indeed 'carnall men are oftentimes of a civil disposition', warned Calvin, but 'we have a race set before our eyes, as it were in a glasse, wherein we ought to runne with the holy Fathers'. The conventional image of the mirror of history here becomes a great confirmation of true faith: 'that we are followers with the patriarchs', unto whom God had revealed Himself and in whose worship 'the proper exercises of the church show foorth them selves' for our emulation. For since Adam 'the everlasting succession of the Churche sprang from this founteine, that the holy Fathers imbracing one after an other through faith the promise offered unto them, were gathered into the housholde of God'. The repeated renewals of the covenant 'which the Lorde had made with their fathers', reaffirmed Israel's election and showed that there was 'no other true faith'. Scriptural godly models were therefore normative for all times in the Church, for 'whosoever will woorship God aright, and will be counted members of his Church, must follow no other way than this which is here shewed'. The covenant made all men contemporaneous, for regarding the covenant with Noah, others 'may take holde of his testimonie by faith, which were to be borne afterwards, and might assure themselves that it is the very same to them, which was promised to the sonnes of Noah'.[87]

[85] Ibid., sigs. I1v, I3r; 'The Philosophers transferring that to a habite or qualitie, whiche God here ascribeth to nature, bewray their ignorance. And no marvell: for we please and flatter ourselves: so little we perceive how mortall the sickenesse of sinne is, and how great wickednesse possesseth all our senses' (sig. O3r).

[86] *Institution* (1561), I.xiv.1, fos. 43v, 44r–v; *cf.* Richardson, *History, Sacred and Profane*, pp. 78–90. See also I. McPhee, 'Conserver or Transformer of Calvin's Theology? A study of the Origins and Development of Theodore Beza's Thought 1550–1570' (unpublished Cambridge Ph.D. dissertation, 1979), pp. 177–8, 183–4, 186, 192–6.

[87] *Commentarie...upon...Genesis*, sigs. O3r, O8v. Thus 'Caine...in outward shew lived a well ordered life, as one which shewed himselfe dutifull towardes God in the workes of Godlinesse, and whiche got his living and his families with honest and upright labour, as it became a

Harrison does not fit into a neat 'Calvinist' box, however, for there were two important differences between Calvin's and Harrison's views on the Two Churches, differences which reflect their differing temperaments. Calvin insisted on a praeterist interpretation of Revelation, whereas, in common with many English 'Calvinists', Harrison believed that the recent history of the papacy fulfilled many of Revelation's obscure prophecies; he also found apocalyptic meaning in chronological patterns. This difference of temperament partly explains why Calvin's denunciation of the papacy in his *Institutes* is curiously lifeless, lacking the gut feeling generated in Harrison and other Englishmen such as John Bale by an examination of the mysterious rise of the papacy through prophetically determined time. Yet this lack of colour may also reflect Calvin's intention to present in the *Institutes* a careful, logically argued statement of Protestant beliefs, for by contrast he appears in his *Commentary on Genesis* far more spiritually involved in the grand sweep of history as the Two Churches fought out their cosmic struggle. In the *Institutes*, however, Calvin based his identification of the Pope with Antichrist on the dehistoricised general characteristics of the 'mystery of iniquity' which had been identified by Daniel and Paul, precepts unconnected with those historical papal actions which other commentators interpreted as fulfilling apocalyptic prophecy. Since 'this calamitie was neither to be brought in by one man, nor to be ended in one man', Calvin analysed the contemporary papacy to show that it was 'directly contrary to the true order of a Chirche'. He did not investigate the fulfilment of Daniel's and Paul's predictions, but tried to convince a learned audience with a calm and clear demonstration of papal iniquities. This militated against the excited sense of contemporaneity with all the Elect covenant line evident in Harrison and other Protestants and indeed present in Calvin's *Commentary on Genesis*. These differences in temperament between Calvin and Harrison, and the tension within Calvin's thought, are important. For although Calvin in his *Institutes* was relatively less absorbed in the details of the Elect's universal struggle, according to some modern commentators the conception of time which he expounded in the *Institutes* should have made those historical details much more immediate for him.[88]

Previous attempts to explain the sense of contemporaneity discussed above have fixed on the idea that the earliest events seemed adjacent to sixteenth-century men because the whole of history comprised only five or six thousand years. This very chauvinistic explanation depends on our notion of astronomical time, unknown in the sixteenth century. F. C. Haber has

thriftie and modest housholder', yet 'in the person of Caine we have an image of a wicked man painted forth to us, who notwithstanding his wickednesse will be counted iust, and arrogateth to himselfe the chiefe place among the Sainctes'. Yet this only underlined the character of his hypocritical Church (ibid., sigs. H8r, I2v).

[88] *Institution* (1561), IV.vii.25, fos. 45v–46.

asserted that although the six thousand years of the earth's existence were known to be brief, any number was simply insignificant in comparison with eternity. Yet this argument conceives eternity as an inexpressible number, while the sixteenth century still accepted Augustine's conception of eternity as an expression of God's nature in which 'all is at once present', a state of being antithetical to the nature of time in the created world where events are perceived sequentially.[89] For sixteenth-century thinkers to realise the narrow limits of created time, eternity had to be measurable, which was clearly impossible for them. Quite simply, the six thousand years of the earth's history appeared to Harrison as an enormous length of time because he did not recognise endless millennia before recorded history with which he could compare them. He was not unique in holding this view. On the other hand, pagan concepts of eternal time insidiously influenced those who attempted to refute them, so that Calvin came to perceive salvation history from the outside and took a coolly objective view of the six millennia. Harrison viewed recorded time from the inside, and was consequently awed by its immensity and its mighty evidence of God's power. In his subjective perception, time ceased to be merely the objective phenomenon we know, which exists merely as the period of Nature's demonstration, and took on a dynamic character.

Calvin's detachment from historical detail in his prophetic interpretation contrasts with Harrison's search for the divine majesty in the most intricate and confused series of events.[90] Harrison's immersion in the sequential historical fulfilment of prophecy seems relatively more constant than Calvin's. Calvin derived his conception of historical time in relation to eternity directly from Augustine's discussion of time in his *Confessions*, and especially Augustine's refutation of idle speculation about God's actions before the Creation. Yet in reiterating the perpetual boundaries of legitimate speculation set down by Augustine as a member of the covenant line, Calvin's discussion of God and eternity fails to match Augustine's clarity, and Calvin's mental imagery betrays the greater influence of the pagan speculations which his argument claimed to refute. Against the impious 'full of their old leaven', Augustine had vigorously argued that the Creator existed before all times, and that there could be no innumerable ages before God's first creation 'For there was no then, when as there was no time'.[91]

[89] *St Augustine's Confessions with an English Translation by William Watts 1631* (2 vols. London, 1961), p. 233. F. C. Haber, *The Age of the World, Moses to Darwin* (Baltimore, 1959), p. 25, See also Bale: 'Like as he aforetime both taught and promised by his peculiar chosen servants the prophets. No time shall be after this, but that which will be of all time the end' (*Image of Both Churches*, ed. Christmas, p. 374).

[90] Calvin, *Commentaries on the Book of the Prophet Daniel*, trans. T. Myers (London, 1852–3), ii, p. 16; and see below, pp. 74–6 for Harrison's interpretation of Daniel.

[91] Augustine, *Confessions*, pp. 229, 281, 235.

Although Calvin also dismissed the 'evile and hurtfull speculations' of the ungodly, since 'For why God so long differed it, is neither lawful nor expedient for us to enquire', here the question is already transmuted. For Calvin obviously had some grasp of a time before recorded history, a conception resembling ours and one which only served to emphasise for him the test of faith in God's concealment of His will. He deplored the 'wantonesse' of those who 'quarrel wyth God for that the emptynesse wherein nothyng is conteyned, is a hundred tymes more'. The six thousand years of history contained sufficient examples of God's providence, 'wherof our myndes may be exercised', so 'Let us therefore willingly abide enclosed within those bounds wherewith it pleased God to environ us, and as it were to pen up our mindes that they sholde not stray abroad with liberty of wandryng'. In the different context of his discussion of the covenant line, Calvin appears much closer to Harrison in his remark that God 'revealed himselfe a great while ago unto them', although he was concerned to show that despite this, 'we are fellowes with the patriarches'.[92] Contemplation of the covenant line therefore introduced a certain tension into Calvin's thinking about time, but clearly he felt closest to past generations of the Elect not when he perceived time from the outside as a limited period, but when he felt immersed in its immensity.

Harrison's own intense interest in the covenant line had to overcome an apparently far steadier awareness of his ignorance in the face of an immense time-span. His struggles with the confused historical data of the fourth century BC forced him to accept that few 'can safely deale with things of suche antiquitie and determine of anything exactly'. Long periods of time had so corrupted the 'histories' of the Greek gods that 'who is able now to seperate ther acts and of things so farre passed what man can geve any sound judgement?'.[93] So vast were the millennia that even the Scriptures had suffered. Harrison felt constrained to excuse the confused succession of the Judges, for 'you must not blame me, sithe it is impossible for me living in these late times to discusse these thinges wherof antiquitie stoode in soche doubt'. The errors and misapprehensions of ancient authorities showed that even the mightiest rulers could become 'in longe tract of time growen quite out of remembrauns'. Even the details of the twelfth century AD appeared remote to Harrison, for 'who can now discusse these matters of soche antiquitie?'. Other industrious defenders of Scripturally-prophesied chronology found the period of the world's existence equally immense.[94]

92 *Institution* (1561), I.xiv.1, fo. 44r; *cf. Commentarie...upon...Genesis*, sig. B3v. J. C. Scaliger had revived the notion of infinite time, but Bodin roundly condemned his ignorant impiety (*Method*, tr. Reynolds, p. 314).

93 TCD MS 165, fo. 45r. He found the years since the foundation of Carthage 'an huge nomber' (ibid., fo. 81r).

94 Ibid., fos. 62v–63r. The chapters of the Book of Judges had become disordered, see below, pp. 80, 220–1. Ibid., fo. 282r; and see Bodin, *Method*, tr. Reynolds, pp. 317, 328; Raleigh, *History*, sig. A3r.

Those who closely identified with significant moments in the history of the covenant line did not necessarily feel chronologically close to those moments but discerned an unchanging underlying meaning within diverse actions in widely different periods. For believers this inner congruence derived from the fact that those moments and those actions fulfilled divine prophecies about the fate of the True Church, and therefore showed the regenerate how significant actions contributed to the movement of history towards its End, when all events would truly become contemporaneous, in the eternity of the fulfilment of God's purpose. In the meantime before the achievement of this final insight, prophecy directed the interpretation of events. This assumption that the historical process produces little qualitative change does not require a belief in the brevity of historical time, for that is an equation which we make in a different time-scale. In fact it depended upon the belief that God had kept His promises to His Elect in the past, and that He would keep those same promises in the present and in the future. As John Bale insisted, the perpetual and certain covenant ensured that 'it worketh even now as it did in the primitive church'; that Rome will fall as Jerusalem did, 'both are of one certainty, though the one be past and the other yet to come'.[95]

In Harrison's thought the certainty of the covenant seemed not only to demand that the past must condition the interpretation of the present, but also to require him to determine the meaning of a given event, which might not be specifically prophesied, by reference to a comparable moment in the history of the True Church. What had happened to 'men of like condition' could be used outside the strictly Scriptural context to discover the complete meaning of the revelation given by the Holy Ghost in the Scriptures. This subjective historical interpretation therefore dissolved the boundaries between Scriptural and secular history, so that Harrison applied what he conceived to be Scriptural criteria to later history, where all events could be interpreted so as to elucidate the central mysteries of salvation history. In accordance with Harrison's concept of the *a priori* authority of the Scriptures, facts were not allowed to supplant the organising authority of prophecy but were made subordinate to prophecy in order to give it greater clarity. Where they apparently failed to do this, they became irrelevant. Harrison therefore broadened the Pauline interpretation of the Scriptures, that 'whatsoever things were written aforetime were written for our learning' (Rom. 15.4) into the confident opinion that all history existed for this precise purpose.[96]

One example shows that without reference to any specific Scriptural text,

---

[95] *Image of Both Churches*, ed. Christmas, pp. 336, 517.
[96] *A Disputation on Holy Scripture, Against the Papists, especially Bellarmine and Stapleton. By William Whitaker.*, tr. and ed. W. Fitzgerald (Parker Society; Cambridge, 1849), pp. 648–9. See also T. Cooper, *A briefe exposition...of the olde testament* (Henrie Denham for Rafe Newbery: London, 1573), which quoted Rom. 15.4 on the title page. J. Ponet, *A short Treatise of politike power* ([Strasbourg], 1556), sig. H2v.

Harrison's interpretation of an event could be suffused with an apocalyptic awareness that he was describing actions of universal meaning for the Church. A great famine in Italy in AD 1084 'I take no doubt to be a ponishment sent of God upon that ungodly country', pronounced Harrison, 'for her abusing of her sovereine Lord themperor and so treading downe the imperiall majesty under her feete whome God commaunded all men to obeie and fere'. This general appeal to Rom. 13 should not overshadow the fact that for Harrison the historical actions of the Elect provided the real points of comparison, summarised in images of righteous behaviour which he felt did not require exposition. He therefore asked, 'Did Paule procede in this order against Nero, Peter against Herod, or Christ against the Scribes and Pharisees?'. Harrison measured the thoroughly degenerate papacy of the eleventh century against these Scriptural models, and found it wanting, for it did not seek the reformation of heresy, or of manners, or to punish any crime of the Emperor. Even if this had been the case, in the context of the Scriptural models 'is this the right order of proceding in redresse therof?'. Harrison saw papal aggrandisement in the light of relatively corrupt Apostolic actions, which revealed the lurking presence of Satan behind this whole process, perpetually attempting to undermine the True Church and to set up his own, antichristian structure. For, Harrison argued, 'this contention now reigning in the churche...is nought els but a renewing of the contention which beganne in christes time amonge his disciples wherin thei contended which of them should be the greatest'. This use of history, reminiscent of prophetic reasoning, allowed him to conclude his analysis in terms perpetually relevant for the Church, including the Elizabethan Church. Comparison with the Scriptures reveals that 'this strife is not for god but for the world, not for heaven but temporall authority, with what colour of justice can the pope then follow it as he doethe'. For Harrison the fundamental pattern of the conflict of the Two Churches provided a universal reference point for the interpretation of any event, even though that event may not have been specifically prophesied.[97]

Contemplation of the conflict of the Two Churches generated intense excitement which could distort individual assessments of contemporary problems; it could lead to correspondingly unworldly solutions drawn directly from the experience of the True Church and applied without adaptation to sixteenth-century conditions. The various solutions seized upon by Protestants reflect the circumstances through which this common idea was filtered. Yet from the evangelical point of view, this acceptance of Scriptural solutions merely exemplified godly obedience, a proper fear of God's threatenings amidst temporal felicity. This way of thinking seems particularly characteristic of those who emphasised the oppressions by which

[97] TCD MS 165, fo. 272v.

the True Church was tested, for then its recoveries appeared specially relevant to periods of upheaval and peril. The Scriptures offered an invincible historical pattern as a solution to the contemporary predicament, for the predestined sufferings of the True Church had also provided an equivalent remedy. Harrison found in Theodore Bibliander's work, support for the notion that in times of crisis caused by man's turning away from God prophets were sent to reiterate the eternal promises of Christ's kingdom. He quoted Bibliander on a crucial moment at the very foundation of the Church of Cain, when the future conflict was prophetically foreshadowed. For 'when Cain builded his Citie Henoch and erected his kingdome', Bibliander stated, 'God set up the Prophet Henoch who published a boke of the celestial decrees, wherin he foresheweth evidently a discourse of the kingdome of christe and the regiment of Antechrist'.[98] Those divine promises fully explained the predicament of sixteenth-century Christians, and some of the consequences of this contemporaneous reasoning for perceptions of contemporary social and political problems can be seen in Bibliander's *Godly consultation...By what meanes the cruell power of the Turkes bothe may and ought for to be repelled of the Christen people* (1542). In that work Bibliander saw the contemporary apocalyptic threat of the Turk against the background of other antichristian threats to the True Church, which had been repulsed by a return to faithful obedience.

The fervency of Bibliander's argument reflects less his fear of the Turk than his certainty that what God has threatened, He will accomplish in the present as He has in the past. True obedience and fear of God required that the present crisis should be seen within the historical pattern of the Two Churches. For the same threatened punishment for apostasy could be traced throughout time under different guises; the Turk simply represented the latest instrument of God's wrath. Bibliander felt confident that he correctly understood the nature of this threat because he saw complete congruence in the successive prophecies of Ezekiel, John and Methodius, who at different times had identified the same kind of attacks upon the true faith by the members of Satan. Therefore the Turks were 'kynred with Gog and Magog', and allied with Antiochus Epiphanes, who 'dyd scourge the Jewes according to the prophecy of Ezechiell', and in that conflict, at a time of near-extinction for the True Church, 'the warre of Antichrist was greatly fygured'.[99] Under divine instruction Ezekiel had revealed the meaning of this scourge at the divine command, and John's Revelation promised the

---

[98] Ibid., fo. 4r. Harrison owned Bibliander's chronological treatise *De ratione temporum* (Basileae ex officinae Ioannis Oporini, 1551), now Derry shelf-mark E.f.12, but wrote no significant marginalia in it.

[99] *A godly consultation unto the brethren and companyons of the Christen religyon* (n.p., 1542), sig. L6v. Bibliander thus relied on the covenant line's depiction of the threat and the remedy, as Bale noted (*Image of Both Churches*, ed. Christmas, pp. 260–1).

same conflict, for 'Gog and Magog be put as for the aydes of Antichriste', characteristics which Methodius reiterated when he prophesied four centuries before Mahomet 'that these borderers of the mountaynes of Caucasus sholde invade the Christen domynyons' as part of Antichrist.[100]

These insights derived from divine illumination, not rational processes, and Bibliander quickly pointed out that his conclusion that the Turk would come was not a prophecy of that order. The era of revelation had ended. Rather he reached his conclusion by a process of regenerate reasoning strictly limited by Scriptural criteria, influenced not by the contemporary fact of Turkish advances so much as by the past fulfilment of prophecy in the punishment of disobedience. Therefore he interpreted the present according to God's eternal will revealed in the past, in the same way as 'certen godlye men' prophesied the death of Julian the Apostate after 'consyderinge with them selfe what fortune evermore is wonte for to folowe the persecutors of the church'. Bibliander's study of the past was geared to a prophetic explanation of the present, so that he quoted Platina on the corrupt ministry and congregations under Sixtus IV specifically so 'that you may perceyve in the meane season ower tyme also for to be paynted'. Just as God had brought calamities on the degenerate Romans, so contemporary greater sins will be punished, for 'Beleve me, the Turke wyll come, wolde to god I were a false Prophet, yea he wyll come in ded a more vyolent enemye of the Christen name then Dioclesiane and Maximiniane. Even now he knoketh upon the walles of Italye'.[101]

An examination of the assumptions behind Bibliander's arguments reveals that his proposed remedies were not simply an abstract condemnation of the sins which had brought the Turks upon Christendom. Relying on the unchanging essential features of the historical encounters between God and His covenant line, Bibliander felt encouraged to follow their example of setting out a godly plan of action and threatening punishment for disobedience. The unchanging character of God and the internal harmony of the Scriptures set out the limits of legitimate thought and behaviour, for 'This is also the disposition of god and his perpetual custome, as the divine scryptures wyth a greate consente, and the hystoryes of thynges done, bereth recorde: that he dothe open unto men the pleasure of his eternall wyll and doth monyshe them in tyme what is to be done and what is to be avoyded'. Indeed there existed a direct model for emulation, and Bibliander consciously followed the example and renewed the counsel of Jerome who had had to deal with a Turkish invasion of Asia Minor, also caused by 'the synnes of

---

[100] *A godly consultation*, sigs. L6v–L7r; cf. Ezech. 38 and 39, Rev. 20. Harrison identified the Turks as a punishment for the idolatry of the Latin Church, first seen in AD 585 (TCD MS 165, fo. 192v).

[101] *A godly consultation*, sigs. L5r–v.

the Christen people'. Jerome had made manifest the will of God which remained unchanged in contemporary Europe, and Jerome's remedy, a return to virtue and righteousness, also had to be applied now.[102]

The very simplicity and apparent lack of sophistication in this reasoning betrays the apocalyptic pressure behind Bibliander's demands for reform. He did not advance what many contemporaries would have recognised as practical solutions, for he felt convinced that victory would not be determined by astrology or achieved through the advice of experienced soldiers, but must be given by that God whose prophetic pronouncements determined the rise and fall of kingdoms. This conviction derived just as much from his understanding of history and his role within it as from biblical precepts, for they simply provided complementary methods of expressing the same truth. The doctrines taught by the covenant line provided the criteria to interpret not just Scriptural but all history, revealing the most fundamental knowledge. Bibliander's argument rested upon the foundation stone of God's unchanging mercy and justice, described in the precepts of Exodus 34.6–8, 'But that the same thinge also is perfourmed with dedes that this description teacheth to be in the nature of god, bothe the holy scriptures and the Ecclesiasticall hystoryes do sufficientlye beare recorde, that we may passe over and speake no thinge at all of other strange and prophane matters, and how easye and gentle the lorde is to them that repente'.[103] Therefore Bibliander's historical interpretation contemporaneously illuminated his criticism of Europe's present ungratefulness in persisting in sin in spite of clear historical evidence of God's mercifulness.

This prophetic reaction to crisis affected Bibliander's attitude towards the secular powers, and a similar effect can be seen in William Harrison's thought. Both men believed that Antichrist could only be repulsed by the preaching of the oppressed minority of true believers, not by magistrates who persistently neglected the requisite reforms. In Bibliander's experience reform had come 'only by the prescription of the holy scriptures', an example of godly obedience which the 'superior magistrates wente aboute to kepe backe very obstinately'. In the 1570s Harrison maintained a similar sense of apocalyptic crisis by deliberately focussing on the advances of Antichrist along a broad front. From that perspective he also saw that the rulers of Christendom had made no attempt at necessary reforms, being distracted by the papal schisms, 'about the resolution of which brabling questions when our kings and princes have bene most occuped then hathe the Turk bene most busy to abridge them out of ther segnories and possessions'. Bereft of proper Scriptural guidance, the princes' adherence to worldly 'policy' had

---

[102] Ibid., sigs. J1r–v, A3v, B4v.
[103] Ibid., sigs. J6r–v.

resulted in their being led by the nose to 'become the onely mainteiners of the develles title in the pope'.[104]

Harrison drew a lesson from princely failings which Bibliander also found particularly exemplified in the German cities to which he addressed his *Godly consultation*. Bibliander argued that those cities secure in their present possessions ignored God's commands evident in history, and only a few poor cities followed the Scriptural remedy, because their very weakness made them more aware of God's mighty power. Yet richer cities who complained of difficulties 'in renewinge of religion and righteousnes' had no excuse, for 'the lorde hath set forthe' an historical model describing what they should all do. They should contemplate the history of 'Ninive the cheyfe cyttye of the Assyrians kingdome...a worlde with all hyr malice brought within the precincte or bridgement of one wall', which after twelve hundred years of prosperity and security was transformed by Jonah, an unknown stranger who had failed to convert the Israelites. By bringing the Ninevites to repentance Jonah averted the terrible fate that God had threatened for them. Bibliander confidently expected that evangelical action like Jonah's would bring the same miraculous result, for history showed the inevitable consequences when men turned to the Scriptures for the necessary programme of reforms.

To describe the way in which these reforms might come about and the aims which they should have, Bibliander used a striking and dynamic historical image in the manner of the Hebrew prophets. Since princes enjoyed the privileges of their office but neglected their godly function of administering justice equitably and without corruption, 'Doth not that troublesomenes of thinges and extreme ungratiousnes requier that Nabuchodonossor cummynge with Nergall and Sacasar may set his throne in the gates of Hierusalem and teache them to execute judgement and righteousnes?'. This dramatic action clearly meant more to Bibliander than any amount of words, but it does not represent merely a surrender to vague messianic hopes in the face of insuperable difficulties. For it conveys Bibliander's trust that God never deserts His people in their time of greatest need, that he will provide a solution which will confound worldly understanding. For the example to follow is already written and confirmed by the historical experience of the True Church, God is present in the Scriptures not just as *ratione scripta* but in the events themselves; a godly solution exists because the present witnesses the same struggle as the past in which a solution was provided.[105]

John Bale's writings show how in the English context such beliefs could lead to a radical disaffection from existing institutions. Essentially Harrison and Bale both approached history from a point of view opposed to the

[104] Ibid., sig. Lir and TCD MS 165, fo. 327v.   [105] *A godly consultation*, sigs. G3v–G4r.

current dispensation and found in the perpetual conflict of the Two Churches ample justification for their radical criticisms of the present. Like the later Puritans, Bale argued that our actions should not be guided by worldly considerations, but by the living past which demonstrates the meaning of all present occurrences. Most of Harrison's references to Bale are to the *Scriptorum illustrium maioris Brytannie catalogus*. In his copy, which survives at Derry, Harrison chose to write his 1565 autobiography, which reveals his awareness that he was caught up in the struggle of the Two Churches.[106] Harrison's other uses of this scholarly catalogue also reveal his general agreement with Bale on the necessity to reinterpret the papist account of history by a time-scale which reflected the fluctuating fortunes of the True Church under the persistent attacks of Antichrist. In this context the notion of anachronism depended upon the apparent fulfilment of prophecy in the decline of the Church. Thus Harrison denounced a reference to ember days in AD 220 as a forgery 'invented long sins by some zealous Prelate', particularly since it flattered Heliogabulus, 'the most bestly monster of the world'. Moreover, 'if any imber daie had bene now talked of should it not thinke you have bene spoken of in the Counsell of Nice [Nicaea] wherein Jezebelles Bedde was made as Bale saith'.[107]

The fact that Harrison recognised Bale's picture of the primitive church reflects a more fundamental congruence in their thought, summarised by the title of Bale's *The Image of Both Churches*. For Bale's clear challenge to contemporary believers that 'either we are citizens in the new Jerusalem with Jesus Christ, or else in the old superstitious Babylon with antichrist the vicar of Satan' expressed his conviction that 'Since the world's beginning hath the mystery of iniquity wrought in Cain and his posterity, and so continued in the beastly members of antichrist, and so shall do still to the latter day', whereas the True Church 'had Christ in her womb since the beginning'.[108] Paul Christianson has claimed that Bale gave the pattern of the Two Churches new and cosmic importance by using it to interpret the Book of Revelation, and that his English disciples added this component to the European Protestant outlook during their Marian exile. Yet while this may have contributed to the formation of Harrison's outlook it should not be allowed to devalue the importance of Continental interpreters and indeed the rest of the Scriptures in persuading him that the struggle between the Churches would last to the end of time. The consequences rather than the causes of their agreement were anyway more important for Bale and Harrison.

Both chose to identify with past examples of godliness in the covenant line rather than accept what reason perceived to be good in the present,

[106] Derry shelf-mark D.ii.d.7.   [107] TCD MS 165, fo. 153v, and see fo. 290r.
[108] *Image of Both Churches*, ed. Christmas, pp. 252, 450, 405.

because the Two Churches were always locked in conflict. There existed
no basis for rational agreement or common ground with the popish church,
for the recurrent pattern of persecution throughout time reinforced the
prophetic command to come away from Babylon. Bale felt unable to
compromise about the eternal doctrine of the True Church, regularly
reiterated by the covenant line. In an attack remarkable for its subjective
fusion of several tenses into one status, its sense of contemporaneity with the
whole history of the True Church, Bale decried popish ceremonies because
'With these abhominable wayes and soche other was Christ yet never
acquainted. But he demaundeth of yow this question by his holy sprete in
Esaye, who hath required these thinges at yowr handes?'. Bale did not
question popish practices by comparison with a general principle drawn
from a rational study of many examples, but by comparison with a doctrinal
truth, taught at one specific moment by the covenant line, but held to express
an eternal truth by that very special context. Such knowledge could be
utilised by present members of the True Church, but they could not derive
it from the rational study of mere human experience.[109]

Bale's identification of the antichristian characteristics of the papacy
reveals the ability of this contemporaneous way of thinking to condition
individual interpretations of both past and present. For reference to the true
prophets of the earlier covenant line enabled him to identify characteristics
now manifested in the papacy as those of the perpetual enemies of the True
Church. Neither the passage of time nor the movement of history
established the real satanic nature of the papacy for Bale, although in his
judgement both time and history fulfilled canonical prophecy. Rather, a
recurrent image used by a succession of prophetic witnesses encapsulated the
essential principles of Antichristian behaviour. Divine revelation had made
these witnesses contemporaneous with, and had given them full understanding of, all events. By aligning himself with their interpretation Bale participated in this divine knowledge and perceived the inner nature of the
papacy. Therefore he understood the present state of Rome and Italy not by
reference to their own secular histories, but by the image of Gog in Rev.
20.8, and linked himself with the covenant line by following Augustine's
equation of Gog with the glorious hypocrites of this world.

Further enlightenment came from Ezekiel's identification of Gog (Ezek.
38.2) as the chief prince of Mosoch and Tubal, 'whom some expositors take
for Cappadocia and Spain. But...the Hebrews do take this Tubal for Italy,
which is much more agreeable to this purpose'. The Elect interpretation

[109] J. Bale, *A mysterye of inyquyte* (Michael Woode: Geneva, 1545), sig. I3r. Thus 'Who seeth not
now-a-days that hath light in the Spirit the malignity...in certain false prophets at Paul's
Cross in London, and in other places else?' (*Image of Both Churches*, ed. Christmas, p. 437.
P. Christianson, *Reformers and Babylon*, pp. 13–21).

guided Bale's apparently highly subjective use of evidence, for the rise of the papacy had been revealed to the covenant line from the beginning: 'Now mark this wonderful mystery, and consider therein both the time and story. So shall ye well perceive the Holy Ghost to meane none other here by this Gog…but the Romish pope'.[110] The consistency of the divine revelation behind its different manifestations underlined the continuity of the covenant line despite its apparent diversity; this consistency and continuity allowed no other interpretation of the present, no other programme of action, than had been revealed in the Scriptures.[111]

Bale admirably expressed the sense that the Elect at all times faced the same opponents when he proclaimed that the Book of Revelation provided the surest guide for contemporary actions: 'A perfect preparation is it to a constant soul, when the battle is seen afore, the end thereof known, and the remedies learned'. This conviction rested on the previous experience of the Elect in similar circumstances, for 'Much less harm felt they of Antiochus Epiphanes, that had read Daniels prophecy afore, and marked it, than they which knew it not when that tyrant came upon them'.[112] John's Revelation gave the most comprehensive explanation of the teleological movement of history, which demanded that the godly succour the oppressed True Church. In Bale's view Revelation most fully expressed the divine knowledge given partially and obscurely to the succession of prophets, for 'The very complete sum and whole knitting up is this heavenly book of the universal verities of the bible'. Bale evidently discerned these 'universal verities' in the historical experiences of the True Church, for where all other prophecies merely repeated God's promises for the future of His Church, 'this mystery declareth effectuously fulfilled' what had been promised, and revealed the historical realisation of God's will. Revelation's most important function was to restrain corrupt human reasoning, and not unnaturally Bale felt its apparent obscurities only reflected our stubborn refusal to enter whole-heartedly into the inner meaning of the past and to find that same meaning revealed in the present. Although the truth expressed in the obscure imagery of Revelation 'be shut up from the untoward and wicked generation for their unbelievers' sake; yet will it be plain enough to the faithful believers' who applied the prophecy to their own experience.[113] Harrison also came to emphasise that the Scriptures delimited the area of legitimate reasoning and thought. Bale consequently argued that obedience to the divine will came through reading the proper significance into events, so that 'he that will be

---

[110] *Image of Both Churches* ed. Christmas, pp. 570–1.
[111] Thus Bale's interpretation of the Turkish Antichrist drew together the various prophecies of Isaiah, Ezekiel, Daniel, Zachariah and John's Revelation to show their fundamental agreement on that threat (ibid., pp. 261–2).
[112] Ibid., p. 261.   [113] Ibid., pp. 252, 260–1.

strong when adversity shall come, and avoid all assaults of antichrist and the
devil, let him give himself wholly to the study of this prophecy'.[114]

The same kind of reasoning is evident in Harrison's anxiety to interpret
his experiences at Oxford as fitting the pattern of persecution which identified
the True Church, just as Bale found the eternal experience of the Elect
repeated in his own life. Trying to reinterpret the bare events in the light
of this myth, Harrison insisted that as a result of his conversion to
Protestantism under Mary he 'would not, perhaps, have escaped harm if that
Jezebel had reigned longer'. Moreover the coincidental deaths of Mary and
Reginald Pole, 'whom the Almighty Father wonderfully carried off',
showed once again that the chastisement suffered by the True Church for
its disobedience often gave way to miraculous recovery, so that in his view
those two sudden deaths were 'to the solace of the whole church'.[115]
Harrison therefore continued a persistent English tradition, in which the
experiences of exile and persecution that marked the English Reformation
were believed to confirm the contemporary relevance of prophecy, especially
the Revelation of John. This interest in the prophetic meaning of past and
present, which went deeper than in some continental Reformers, owed much
to Bale. His identification with the primitive church rested on Revelation's
depiction of what 'the church suffered in the primitive spring, what it
suffereth now, and what it shall suffer in the latter times' at the hands of
the members of Antichrist. Bale's innovative interpretation of Revelation
decisively influenced the English apocalyptic interpretation of the past, thus
eventually helping to overcome earlier doubts about its canonicity, but his
grasp of the importance of present actions directly reflected his subjective
identification with the experience of John.[116]

Just as William Harrison eventually recognised that he had been 'a shaven
worshipper of Baal', when he interpreted his apostasy as a continuation of
the idolatry encountered by the True Church in the Old Testament, so also
Bale rediscovered an eternal truth about persecuting Babylon in his own life.
Bale's perception of his historical role confirmed the contemporary relevance
of Revelation, for 'At the writing of this prophecy felt John of their cruelty',
being exiled for his faith, 'And so did I, poor creature, with my poor wife
and children, at the gathering of this present commentary, fleeing into
Germany for the same'. Bale felt that God's grand design for His Church
had brought about this deliberate parallel, for 'The forsaken wretched sort
hath the Lord provided always to rebuke the world of sin for want of true
faith... for nought is it not therefore, that he hath exiled a certain number

114 Ibid., p. 252, citing Ephes. 6.10–20.
115 Edelen, 'William Harrison', p. 258.
116 *Image of Both churches*, ed. Christmas, p. 253; and see R. J. Bauckham, *Tudor Apocalypse*
    (Abingdon, 1978), pp. 41–5, 48–9, on how the Marian Exiles' enthusiasm for the prophecy
    brushed aside the cautious approach of Calvin, Peter Martyr and Bucer.

of believing brethren the realms of England', amongst whom Bale counted himself.[117] From such electrifying short-circuits in time flowed both his understanding of the present and the vehemence with which he expounded that understanding. For his well-known 'biliousness' merely reflected his obedience to Christ's command in Revelation, to those 'whom he hath called of mercy from their wretched beggaries, to spare no rebukes, but to pour out double upon that bloody bawd and malicious mother of theirs'. Bale's experiences since his own conversion made it obvious that 'Never was this commandment more effectually to be followed than now'. He asked critics of his sharp language to 'consider I pray you the huge tiranny of this most wicked Viper of the world, whose destruction according to Gods promises is at hande'. To temper his argument would implicitly deny the past and present fulfilment of God's promises; only by exposing the utter corruption of Babylon could Bale align himself with this perpetual truth, and make men abandon Babylon and bring it down.[118]

Harrison's insistence that the present merely formed part of the prophetic continuum of events explains why his attitude towards the medieval scholastic interpretation of the Scriptures shows important continuities with John Bale's. For Harrison was reacting against a radically different view of history and of the meaning of the Scriptures. The medieval lack of historical perspective reflected not a prophetic sense of the continuity between past and present but the real historical continuity between the ancient past and many aspects of medieval life. Harrison had lost this assurance of continuity, for he perceived medieval society as 'antiquity', and his *Description* reveals his profound awareness of the rapid changes taking place in English society in his lifetime. The fact that generally he considered those changes to be for the worse merely emphasises his growing sense of separation from the immediate past and his reliance on a prophetic sense of continuity in diversity.[119] A more fundamental contrast between Harrison and some medieval thinkers concerned the very notion of 'the present'. Like early Christians in their conflicts with pagan notions of eternalism, Harrison struggled to keep the past alive, to stress the relevance of Christ's example for the contemporary world. Born in a hostile climate and propagated in a period of persecution and turmoil, such an interpretation prospered in times of dislocation and crisis, when it could be used to make dramatic and disturbing events less alarming by indicating their necessary place in the

---

117 *Image of Both Churches*, ed. Christmas, pp. 494, 254. Bale's *Vocacyon* interpreted his Irish experiences in terms of Old Testament models, and portrayed his flight to Germany in the light of St Paul's journey to Rome (T. B. Blatt, *The Plays of John Bale* (Copenhagen, 1968), pp. 44–5, quoting Bale's *Vocacyon* (1553), fos. 6r–7r).
118 *Image of Both Churches*, ed. Christmas, p. 260; *The Pageant of Popes* (Thomas Marshe: London, 1574), sigs. *e3v, *e3r.
119 *Description*, ed. Edelen, pp. 195–204, on the qualitative changes in English rural life.

apocalyptic scheme. Since such events did not need to be studied as independent phenomena, for their significance lay elsewhere, there was no period that could be distinguished as the present.

In contrast, by the twelfth century monastic historians found it possible to believe that their present world differed from the violent and bloody past, and therefore began to treat that past as a *fait accompli*, with little relevance to their own condition. Therefore they gave up historical research in favour of numerous compilations from which they drew their own abridgements. They developed a notion of the present as something worthy of study in itself, neither continuing the programme set out by the past, nor bringing about an imagined future.[120] Thus in Harrison's eyes they committed the error which typified Gentilism. This medieval view of past and present survived in Holinshed's *Chronicles*, which also digested previous compilations and devoted most attention to contemporary journalism. Holinshed happily included contrary opinions about the past for his readers to resolve for themselves, for he saw no overwhelming relevance for the present in the larger issues of history. The few occasions on which Holinshed quoted Harrison's 'Chronology' as an alternative interpretation stand out from the *Chronicles'* essentially medieval approach because the 'Chronology' under-lined the way in which events fulfilled the prophetic purpose of history, usually by taking a sinister view of clerical actions as the mystery of iniquity developed to the full flower of evil in Antichrist.[121]

At the same period when journalism replaced history in the concerns of medieval chroniclers, the scholastic theologians developed a method of drawing propositional truths from the Scriptures by rational means, without reference to the prophetic movement of history. Nature appeared to them to reveal divine knowledge.[122] In rediscovering a sense of contemporaneity with Scriptural history through his membership of the covenant line, Harrison became aware of this medieval misinterpretation, which had robbed the Scriptures of their contemporaneous role as a guide to right actions. He found Satan at work in this erroneous emphasis on human reason. For those who thus misunderstood the Scriptures sought righteousness through participation in ritual which in all its details manifested propositions derived solely from the defective processes of human reasoning, without reference to Scriptural criteria. Essentially Harrison preferred the Augustinian approach to the Scriptures as living examples, rather than the Thomist

---

[120] R. W. Southern, 'Aspects of the European Tradition of Historical Writing. 4: The Sense of the Past', in *Transactions of the Royal Historical Society*, 5th ser., vol. 23 (London, 1973), p. 248. Thus medieval intellectuals had a very modern view of contemporary prophecies – if they did not work, they abandoned them, because they did not consider that the past had fulfilled them in order to produce the present (B. Smalley, *Historians in the Middle Ages* (London, 1974), p. 183, on this type of reaction to Joachimist ideas).

[121] Parry, 'Harrison and Holinshed's Chronicles', pp. 791, 807–8.

[122] Richardson, *History Sacred and Profane*, p. 78.

'Schole theology...grounded upon logique with whose precise rules the scripture is not acquainted'. This intuitive insight into the mentality behind the Scriptures Harrison believed had been shared in the medieval period by John Wyclif, a member of the covenant line 'very moche beloved of the nobility and people for that in his lectures he touched alwaies the sens of the text and spent not the time in allegories, schole points and workes of merite as other did'.

Not only contemporary Protestants but the covenant line at all times therefore appeared to Harrison to reject the spiritual, allegorical and anagogical interpretations of the Scriptures beloved of popish scholastics, in favour of the literal sense of the Scriptures which in turn recounted the historical fate of the covenant line. The Scriptural account of the True Church and its doctrines provided the criteria by which to judge scholastic teachings, which indeed did not always seek to bind the Scriptures *a posteriori* to rational categories. For example, in Harrison's opinion Nicholas Goreham's scholastic Scriptural commentaries 'are not without diligent choise or judgement to be embraced or receaved considering' that he taught when 'it was lawful quidius ex quinis inferre whereby the simple and plaine meaning of the scriptures was often times wrested into a contrary sense'. The literal interpretation of the Scriptures as an historical account of the Two Churches, which also prophesied their future struggle, had to prevail over rival scholastic interpretations, for the former reflected Elect knowledge and by its propagation would defend the True Church, while the latter represented the pollution of truth by Gentile reasoning which perpetually enhanced the power of the Church of Cain. The medieval liturgy and theology of the degenerate popish Church seemed to prove this point to Harrison, for whereas Scriptural ceremonies outwardly represented the inner spiritual doctrines transmitted by the covenant line, he perceived the continuation of the Church of Cain in the succession of men who had argued for the 'bestly doctrine' of transubstantiation.[123]

Bale had earlier seen that differences over the meaning of the Scriptures themselves had always been central to the conflict between the Two Churches. Antichrist's supporters had attacked the Elect interpretation of the Scriptures as prophetic history with contemporary relevance precisely because the Bible taught that Gog and Magog, 'the two horns or beastly kingdoms of the great antichrist, or whole body of the devil', would rise up 'by the earthly studies and devilish devices of wicked men'.[124] Satan relied on scholastic theology to obscure the true meaning of the Scriptures and to keep individuals in ignorance of the conflict of the Two Churches going on around them. Thus Bale set the precedent for Englishmen in

---

[123] TCD MS 165, fos. 334v, 346v, 350v, 213v.
[124] *Image of Both Churches*, ed. Christmas, pp. 571–2.

rejecting the errors of 'Thomas Aquinas, Joannes Scotus, Occam, Gerardus Bononiensis, Aegidius Romanus, Magister Sententiarum, with other like subtill schoolemen and Sorbonistes, who with their glosses, allegories and distinctions, corrupted the true sense of the Scripture, and in maner toke it cleane awaye'.[125] Harrison also recognised this deadening interpretation of Scripture as antithetical to the True Church of right actions. The scholastic reliance on the satanic corruptions of the Gentiles had led to the rejection of the true knowledge transmitted by the Elect, and to the rise of Antichrist. As Bale summarised the process, 'By the doctrine of Aristotle, Plato, Porphyry, Avicenna, Averroes, Avenzoar, and such other, became the Romish pope Christ's vicar, and head of the universal church'. Harrison's 'Chronology' demonstrated that by a false interpretation of both the Scriptures and history the Schoolmen closed the eyes of the people to the true meaning of the Bible and prepared the way for Antichrist, thus confirming Bale's contention that 'Petrus Lombardus created him a new divinity, so did Gratianus Monachus a new canon law of decrees to establish the same, beside that was done then by Petrus Comestor [author of a scholastic history], the third brother. For all they were the children of one adulterous mother'.[126] They so polluted the living stream of revealed godly knowledge as almost to stop it flowing.

Harrison saw the scholastics as false prophets, because they did not create in their audience that heightened awareness of the prophetic importance of the present which devout Protestants believed would galvanise individuals into godly actions. Rather the scholastics created a false sense of security in the present, which allowed Antichrist to usurp power by deceiving the corrupt natural reason of fallen man. Harrison believed that Antichrist could only be kept at bay if the regenerate refused to trust in the things of this world. Therefore Bale's spirit of uncompromising opposition to prevailing orthodoxies, fostered by times of real hardship and persecution, still seemed relevant to radical Protestants in the less fraught atmosphere of the Elizabethan Church. Men in Harrison's position felt a deep need to maintain their self-perception as an oppressed minority, despite much evidence to the contrary, in order to confirm their connection with the True Church. When Antichrist had seemed to dominate England, Bale had found it self-evident that 'to be marked up for the servants of God is not only to believe, after the mind of Ezekiel, but also to lament the abomination and bewail the wickedness that is done here'. Bale saw the contemporary representatives of the Church of Cain, opposing the true prophetic interpretation of events, in 'such like moody prelates resisting the truth to this present day'. These

---

[125] *Pageant of Popes* (1574), fo. 113v, and see fo. 17v.
[126] *Image of Both Churches*, ed. Christmas, pp. 871–2; cf. TCD MS 165, fos. 179v, 183v, 213v, 277r, 318v, 328v, 334v, 350v.

persecutors of the true interpreters, such as Thomas More, were motivated by the desire of worldly fame, argued Bale, and therefore they refused to acknowledge that Roman iniquities had aroused God's wrath. The papists sought 'to crepe into the faver of those that the worlde fawneth upon', yet 'Wo be unto you false prophetes (sayth Ezechiel) that sowe pyllowes undre mennys arme holes, and bolsters undre their heades, to catche sowles with all for lucre'.[127]

George Withers, Harrison's friend and superior as Archdeacon of Colchester and a one-time presbyterian critic, also refused to accept the status quo on its own terms. In *An ABC for layemen*, a short but remarkable work of Scriptural interpretation, Withers set out to apply the prophetic meaning of numerous Scriptural images to the everyday experience of Elizabethans, to condition their interpretation of their daily environment. He included the same references to Ezekiel among the lessons to be drawn from visual phenomena interpreted strictly according to Scriptural criteria, so that 'When we see men sowing soft Pillowes and cushions for men to leane on...then are we to remember to be headefull, that we be not perswaded by false and lying Prophetes, to looke for at the hands of God, peace and prosperity, when our contemptuous and obstinate sins deserve the contrary'.[128] Harrison's 'Chronology' shows that he understood that this deluded majority who would persecute the godly minority, included the magistrate. Even under Elizabeth he found great contemporary relevance in the stoning of the son of Jehoiadiah 'at the commandment of the king' because he had attacked popular nature cults. Royal sanction for the stoning of Jeremiah in Egypt because he had prophesied the overthrow of that kingdom also showed the 'common reward of the faithfull true and zealous preachers of the worde of god'. Such vicarious participation in the sufferings of the Elect reflects Harrison's willingness to discover the incipient encroachments of Antichrist in many aspects of Elizabethan England, not just in the 'semi-reformed' Elizabethan Church.[129]

The intensity of Harrison's prophetic insight and the thoroughness with which he applied Scriptural remedies to contemporary ills naturally varied over time. Like many other Elizabethan Puritans, he could often find enough evidence of continuities between Scriptural and contemporary institutions to alleviate his profound unease about encroaching Antichristian forces, and to

---

[127] *Image of Both Churches*, ed. Christmas, pp. 333, 345, 395–6; *A mysterye of iniquyte*, sig. G8v. Paul Christianson points out that *The Image* expected reformation through the efforts of the oppressed Elect rather than the godly prince, an accurate reflection of the situation in the 1540s, but an attitude which it carried into the entirely different situation under Elizabeth (*Reformers and Babylon*, pp. 20–1).

[128] *An ABC for layemen...delivering unto them such lessons as the Holy Ghost teacheth them in the worde, by things sensible* (Robert Waldegrave for Thomas Man, and William Brome: London, 1585), sig. H8v.   [129] TCD MS 165, fos. 77r, 91v.

encourage his wavering hopes that a complete reformation might yet be built upon incomplete foundations. Yet his 'Chronology' and *Description* both show him to have been more consistently aware of the necessity for Scriptural revelation to govern his thinking, as we shall see in subsequent chapters. His responsiveness to the Scriptures never allowed him completely to accept inherited institutions at face value, for Scriptural criteria set definite limits to what he could recognise as legitimate knowledge and behaviour. Such a heightened awareness consequently made him quicker to recognise periods of apocalyptic crisis, which in turn served to reaffirm the value of those criteria and those limits. This sensitivity to the prophetic meaning of contemporary events not only emphasises his connection with the European Protestant tradition, and with the English tradition represented by Bale, but also helps us to place him against the background of Elizabethan Protestantism. For some of his godly colleagues and contemporaries put forward historical interpretations similar to that which informed Harrison's worldview, but it required sudden and immediate perils before they expressed those ideas with the heightened prophetic awareness more constantly evident in Harrison's 'Chronology'.

Alexander Nowell, Harrison's old teacher, friend and patron, exemplifies this difference. Nowell's homily on the plague of 1563 reflects the same Pauline understanding of the Scriptures that we find in Harrison, focussing as it does on the words of Rom. 15.4, that the Scriptures were 'written for our doctrine and consolation' for they described the experiences of God's Elect in all periods. Nowell argued that the 1563 plague shared common characteristics with many examples of divine retribution for disobedience in 'the holy scriptures and histories ecclesiastical', in which God 'dealt with his people of all ages'. For just as Harrison believed that the Holy Ghost 'doth often by later examples...set furth such thinges as passed before time' in men of the same condition, so Nowell claimed that 'the whole writings of the prophets, and universally of the scriptures, be nothing else but like callings to true obedience...by like promises and threatenings'. The same immutable God who had sent preachers and prophets throughout history to recall his people and threaten punishment remained at work in the present; 'And hath he not now at the last, after almost twenty years patience and forbearing of us, sent us this pestilence?'. Nowell acknowledged that the fulfilment of God's threatenings in the plague had proved more effective than decades of preaching precepts against the love of this present world 'which we yet could never hitherto by hearing believe' but which 'are now put in practice in deed', and could be sensibly perceived. Edmund Grindal, who commissioned this homily from Nowell, also believed that the Scriptures provided the proper framework through which to interpret the present, and argued that a public fast to appease God's wrath, following the example of Israel and the primitive church, seemed especially relevant 'in this our time, wherein many things have been reformed according to the doctrine and examples of God's word and the primitive church'. From this perspective the Scriptures appeared to be a complete model for living.[130]

The next two chapters will explore Harrison's historical vision in greater detail and show how it was intimately related to his opinions on contemporary issues of religious, political and social reform. The fourth chapter will then return to the examination of how these historical assumptions, shared with other members of the Elizabethan Church, coloured radical Protestant attitudes to ecclesiastical reform.

[130] TCD MS 165, fo. 6r; and *The Remains of Edmund Grindal*, ed. W. Nicholson (Cambridge, 1853), pp. 107, 97–100, 93.

2

A reformed chronology – patterns and parallels

Harrison's obsession with 'the exact correction of the time' in his historical studies reflects his belief that the apocalyptic conflict of the Two Churches provided the backbone for his 'Chronology'.[1] For the True Church suffered and prospered in accordance with God's predestinate will, expressed through his prophets in their calls to obedience. Time therefore played a dynamic role in fulfilling the prophecies concerning the True Church, and Harrison felt that in studying the mysterious patterns and symmetries of chronology he participated in a divine revelation whose enormous contemporary significance could be dimly apprehended, but which would only be fully explained at the end of history. For to his way of thinking the past fulfilment of divine prophecy confirmed its contemporary relevance; the present merely continued the irresistible working-out of the majestic divine plan.

Harrison's confidence in the historical and chronological evidence for the existence of this predestined continuum of events allowed him to gloss over internal discrepancies in Scriptural prophecy and chronology which later commentators came to find increasingly disturbing. In turn his unclouded trust in the authority of the Scriptures further encouraged his interest in the assumed prophetic patterns of chronology. What he imagined to be Scriptural criteria always directed his interests in such fields, enabling him to reject or adopt current historical patterns and prophecies by reference to the shared experiences and teachings of the Elect covenant line. Eventually this secure vantage point allowed him to extend the canon of legitimate prophecy to areas where other prophetic interpreters felt unable to follow. Indeed careful study of the arcana of Harrison's chronological thought is more rewarding than one might initially assume, for in the process of tracing the habits of mind and patterns of thinking revealed in Harrison's treatment of history and chronology wider issues emerge. These include Harrison's attitude to important religious, political and social issues in Elizabethan England, which will be discussed in subsequent chapters. This present discussion and the next chapter introduce these subjects in their proper

[1] TCD MS 165, fo. 170v.

58

context, as part of the general framework of Harrison's thought, and demonstrate their relationship to his Protestant, or in the English context Puritan, interpretation of history.

The work of Philip Melanchthon again provides our starting point and helps to throw Harrison's ideas into sharper relief. Melanchthon stressed the religious importance of believing and proving that God had predestined the rise and fall of nations, which especially intrigued contemporary readers of history.[2] While bowing to the convention that princes could discover God's will in past successes and failures, he emphasised the more fundamental lesson to be drawn from a proper understanding of chronology. For the fulfilment of 'al maner of prophecyes of exterior kingdomes' proved 'that our worde is come of God, and that none other faith save ours is true'. To follow any but the Scriptural chronology would rock the foundations of the Christian faith, for that alone shows 'whan Christe muste come, and whan the ende of the worlde is to be loked for'. Scriptural prophecies found exact fulfilment in both Gentile and sacred history, so 'it shall be very expedient to know the success and alteracion of the monarchies and kyngdomes, with the computacion and noumbre of the yeres'. Such knowledge 'is necessary for christians, that they maye the better understand the prophecies, and of theym the more certainly iudge', for the covenant line's success in predicting the course of events through divine grace also confirmed the truth of the doctrines it transmitted.[3]

Perhaps for this reason Harrison emphasised his concurrence with Melanchthon's general chronological calculations from the Creation to the building of Solomon's Temple. Indeed he believed that until the Delivery from Babylon in 2453 AM, 'there is not one monethes differens betwene my positions and those of Melanchthon'.[4] Like Melanchthon, Harrison saw God's imperturbable will resplendently demonstrated in the necessary order of events, but he devoted more time to emphasising that all the resources of human wisdom were simply impotent against that will. Harrison's more doctrinaire acceptance of contemporary predestinarian theology also led him to give greater prominence to individual examples of disobedience, where the unregenerate exercise of free will not only disobeyed God's commandments but threatened to prejudice the precise, deliberate arrangement of all events in chronological sequence. Harrison's intense respect for this prophesied order shows in his interpretation of Isaac's twenty-year wait for children, which demonstrated 'that the godly often times do not obtaine

---

[2] L. B. Campbell, *Tudor Conceptions of History and Tragedy in 'A Mirror for Magistrates'* (Berkley, 1936), p. 2.

[3] Melanchthon, *Carion's Chronicle* (1550), sig. *6r, reprinted in the popular *Cooper's Chronicle* (1560 and subsequently).

[4] TCD MS 165, fos. 44v–44ar, 67r and 255r. Their reckonings differed by four years by the time of David, and by two years at the Incarnation (ibid., fo. 44ar).

there cheef desires here in this world at the first untill god by his Divine providens have appointed ther time and season'.[5] To us this may appear a hackneyed idea, but we need to recapture its freshness and importance for Harrison, since for him it underlined the inability of unregenerate reason to fathom the purposes of God's will and his minute care for the covenant line. Thus Rachel's use of the mandrake to help her conceive only emphasised the limitations of human reason not sanctioned by divine revelation, for 'notwithstanding her vaine practizes' she 'spede not of her desire till god sawe his time and brought his purpose to passe upon her as he had erst determined'.[6] Similarly when Sara gave Hagar to Abram 'she offended in that she sought by unlawfull meanes to prevent the time that god erst appointed' for Isaac's birth, and God punished her disobedience with Hagar's insolence.[7]

Harrison's 'Chronology' in its detailed survey of the prophesied historical continuum thus illuminates a previously neglected aspect of contemporary concepts of predestination, grace and free will. Not only the number and identity of the Elect, but every incident of their historical experience had been determined before the Creation. Harrison developed this notion into a rigorous insistence that it was not enough simply to believe God's promises and to obey His will, but that individuals had to surrender completely to God's commands in every aspect of their lives, that all thoughts and actions had to have Scriptural sanction. In the history of the slaughter of the sons of Ephraim when they attempted to enter Canaan, for example, 'we maie learne what it is to attempt any thinge of our owne heddes without goddes warrauntise or expectation of the time which he hath appointed unto us'. Harrison's chronological studies opened his eyes to the temporal dimensions of the familiar Protestant insistence that all actions should be ordered in complete conformity to God's commands, and that insistence in turn served to justify those studies. Detailed examination of prophesied chronology showed him that confident belief in God's promises did not by itself prevent ungodly actions, for the sons of Ephraim 'reposing a confidens in goddes promises, applied the same sinisterly', 'Loth as it shold seme to abide the time which god had appointed for the returne of ther lignage into Palestine'.[8] Godly obedience also involved a proper understanding of the place of contemporary actions in the unfolding drama of history.

---

[5] Ibid., fo. 27v.   [6] Ibid., fo. 33r.

[7] Nor did God will 'that the figure of his sonne' – Isaac for Christ – should be base born, alleged Harrison (ibid., fo. 24v).

[8] Ibid., fos. 37v–38r. John Coolidge's otherwise perceptive comment, that to Puritans directions discovered by reason were no more equal to Scriptural direction than a good map of the country could have replaced the guiding pillar of cloud in the Exodus, misses this chronological dimension which gave godly actions their importance (see Coolidge, *Pauline Renaissance*, p. 11).

Harrison applied this tough-minded predestinarianism to larger historical movements, again stressing that apparently autonomous human actions in fact intimately obeyed prophecy and therefore gave a special resonance to chronology. We have already noticed Harrison's view that when Antipater received the governorship of Palestine, 'the providens of god beginneth to worke' to fulfil Jacob's prophecy of the Incarnation, the fulcrum of history 'which could not ere this time be worthily fulfilled'. Indeed chronology seemed vital to sixteenth-century prophetic interpreters, for, as Bale pointed out, 'Howe shall a man apply' the apocalyptic 666 prophecy 'if he have not the certaine time when Pompeie toke the scepter from the Jewes' and appointed Antipater?[9]

This approach to time has two important consequences. In a spirit of complete prostration before God's majesty, men such as Harrison could insist that history was not primarily a series of examples for the edification of successful politicians. Renaissance humanist historians, of course, had equally strong motives for proclaiming that the past did not differ from the present, since without that suspension of disbelief their historical *exempla* of virtue and vice became irrelevant. Yet to Protestants the humanist contribution to human wisdom sometimes threatened to free rulers from the necessity to act in accordance with God's will, most notoriously in Machiavelli's *Prince*, where the very practicality of Machiavelli's precepts tended to obscure his own belief in teleological historical cycles.[10] Protestants preferred to emphasise the potential for conflict between human wisdom and the inexorable working out of God's will, a latent contradiction which did not simply sanction the actions of earthly powers, but judged them according to the unchanging criteria of God's plan for His Church. For from this perspective the mightiest powers had been merely instruments in the fulfilment of the divine plan, so that no worldly political wisdom could be drawn from the self-justifying historical sequence, but only the theological truths which Protestants found revealed in historical and chronological patterns. Political wisdom had never deflected the necessary unfolding of events in the prophetic continuum. Another order of knowledge must be drawn from history, for the downfall of princes reflected their failure to direct their actions by that theological truth, confirmed by history and therefore relevant to the present.

Such ideas still seemed important long after Harrison's death. Indeed to men of religious conviction like Sir Walter Raleigh they justified a damning indictment of the humanist historians' bland assumptions about the didactic value of a purely secular interpretation of political history. The relentless surge of prophesied history 'purswaded me to fetch my beginning from the beginning of all things', acknowledged Raleigh, for only the minute

[9] TCD MS 165, fo. 130r; Bale, *The Pageant of Popes*, fo. 37v, and see below pp. 71–4.
[10] H. Baker, *The Race of Time* (Toronto, 1967), p. 62.

demonstration of God's omnipotence, as in *The History of the World*, could bring home to princes their own impotence. For the humanists had overlooked the psychology of contemporary politicians, which Raleigh knew so well, namely that 'wee are content to forget our own experience and to counterfeit the ignorance of our owne knowledge, in all things that concerne ourselves; or perswade our selves, that God hath given us letters patents to pursue all our irreligious affections, with a non obstante'. Misled by the inability of unaided human reason to appreciate the real lessons of history, politicians regarded themselves as free agents in a random universe of unbounded opportunities, but in such present-mindedness 'wee neither looke behind us what hath beene, nor before us what shall bee'.[11]

Similarly the German chronologer Henry Bunting emphasised that actions should be oriented to accord with prophecy, for success depended upon obedience to the predestined order of time. Bunting believed that the experiences of the Emperor Julian displayed the ability of prophetically organised time to defeat human reason. Julian, 'that he might frustrat the prophecy of our Saviour, that Jerusalem should never be built againe', assisted the Jews in restoring their city. An earthquake followed by fire from earth and heaven twice destroyed their efforts, 'and that the Jewes nor any Philosophers might impute it to a naturall cause', supernatural crosses appeared, so that they were forced to abandon their task 'and to acknowledge that Christ whom their forfathers had crucified in that place was the true Messiah'.[12] Only by such painful lessons could natural man's stubborn, unregenerate reason be forced to obey irresistible revelation.

As part of his own attempts to assess all actions according to Scriptural criteria, Harrison also dwelt upon historical evidence of the failure of human wisdom to distort that necessary order of events, in which he detected significant patterns. In contrast to current humanist historiographical theories, his type of history, which concentrated upon God's judgements upon the nations, offered few worldly political precepts. For example, the Romans had installed Perseus as the last king of Macedonia, although 'His father intended in his lives time to have transferred the crowne from him' because he foresaw that he would ruin the kingdom. However, Harrison believed that 'goddes appointment surpassed his devise, so that Perseus enjoyed it, maugre all his fathers attempts and practizes to the contrary'. To Harrison this episode merely demonstrated the limitations of conventional political wisdom, especially Perseus' assumption that his enormous wealth would sufficiently

---

[11] Raleigh, *History* (1614), sigs. D2r, C2v, A2v–A3r, which descant on the utter erasure of the mightiest empires in history; and sig. D1v, which stumbles over the contradiction implicit in a predestined history, where human impiety is still somehow to blame, although 'God, who is the author of all our tragedies, hath written out for us, and appointed us all the parts we are to play'.

[12] H. Bunting, *Itinerarium totius sacrae scripturae*, tr. R. Brathwaite (A. Islip: London, 1619), p. 51.

defend his kingdom; Harrison believed that the Scriptures encouraged princes to rely on a numerous population, an insight into God's will which he applied to the Elizabethan commonwealth.[13] In their turn the Romans fell foul of this perceived prohibition against worldly ambition, for Harrison willingly accepted the story that unfortified Numantia had withstood their siege for forty years, because 'soch successe god geveth often unto unjust quarrelles for the Romaines had no cause in the world to make warre against the Numantines'.[14] The final ruin of Rome also had its allotted place in the apocalyptic scheme, and could only be completed after the accomplishment of the necessary preliminary events in the prophetic continuum. Therefore when Harrison argued that Henry IV failed to raze Rome in AD 1083 'and leave that sinke of Sodome an irreparable heape of stones', because 'god would not suffer it as yet to come to passe because the time thereof was not come', he was not simply indulging in pious casuistry but expressing his fundamental beliefs about the course of history, and consequently the meaning of contemporary events.[15]

Harrison's endearing lack of political sophistication should not distract us from appreciating the importance of his strenuous efforts to maintain that state of mind. For like other clerics he saw that worldly 'policy', often opposed and at best indifferent to God's commands, hindered the complete reformation of the contemporary Church and society. He wanted to achieve a steady sense of confident submission to God's will and of kinship with the covenant line, which had never allowed worldly considerations to deflect it from carrying out the divine will. We should not expect practical political thought to emerge from such an obsession. As Henry Bunting put it, from the mutation of states 'such as have any small knowledge of the graces of the spirit, may draw such comfortable resolutions that neither povertie can subvert them, nor riches and honour exalt them'.[16] We must further recognise that for many of his contemporaries Harrison offered an entirely valid explanation of events. Abraham Fleming, who edited the second edition of Holinshed's *Chronicles* in such a way as to bring out more forcefully the providential significance of events, endorsed similar views. He felt it essential for Christians to recognise that 'God is omnipotent, all princes are impotent, he immortall, they mortall, he above, they below: he Creator, they creatures: finallie, he a cleare fountaine of all goodnes, they filthie

---

13 TCD MS 165, fo. 123r, and see below, pp. 128–30, 283–9.
14 Ibid., fo. 124r. 15 Ibid., fo. 272r.
16 'Since neither the prosperitie of the world is permanent, nor the adversitie therof intollerable', and 'by comparing the actions of men with the beginnings and endings of cities' not only divines but 'such as are at all toucht with a true sence of worldly affaires', 'might the better understand the Prophets' and the power of divine Providence. (*Itinerarium*, sig. ¶4r, and see pp. 413–14). See also P. Collinson, *Archbishop Grindal* (London, 1979), pp. 89–90, on the godly mistrust of 'policy'.

puddles of wickedness'.[17] Similarly Raleigh pointed out that the dark deeds of subtle politicians in contemporary France, Burgundy and Spain had merely provoked divine vengeance, 'and seene an effect so directly contrarie to all their own counsailes and cruelties, as the one could never have hoped for themselves, and the other never have succeeded, if no such opposition had ever bene made'.[18]

The Protestant reliance upon Scriptural chronology as a fundamental guarantee of the prophetic continuity of past and present had a second consequence, which only really appeared towards the end of Harrison's lifetime. The selective criteria which made time and history seem to conform to prophetic expectations provided a visionary framework within which the authority of prophecy could not be undermined simply by the failure of the present to agree with it. For the simplified history presented by prophetic interpreters naturally confirmed prophecy, and while this selective view of the past remained unchallenged, the failure of present events to bear out prophecy could always be attributed to erroneous interpretation. Not until the past could be objectively seen not to conform to prophecy could the present and future be freed from its influence. Only when deprived of this basis in known 'historical facts' could prophecy be discredited by the complex reality of current events. For many Protestants their sense of insecurity in the present encouraged the belief, evident in previous times of dislocation, that most prophecies had been accomplished, and that the future would be not only simple but short – Harrison expected that the end would come before 1700.[19]

Therefore not the failure of the future to materialise as promised but an increasing sense of security in the present transformed the prophetic interpretation of past and future. The surprising defeat of the Spanish Armada in 1588, interpreted by many as an act of divine intervention, created a wave of worldly optimism throughout England which for many individuals made redundant the older view that only the Gospel would be effective against Antichrist. Now it seemed increasingly obvious that the temporal power should help the Church under the Cross to go on Crusade, while the notion of England's special role against Antichrist gained new relevance. These ideas required a more militant version of the past enactment of prophecy, which

---

[17] A. Fleming, *The footepath to felicitie, which everie Christian must walke in, before he can come to the land of Canaan* (Henrie Denham: London, 1586), sigs. A4v–5r, and see p. 31.

[18] Raleigh, *History*, sig. C2r.

[19] Bauckham, *Tudor Apocalypse*, p. 40, and see *Description*, ed. Edelen, p. 390. The Tudor Welsh poets also abandoned secular prophecies of a violent restitution of native rule once their patrons had been absorbed into the Tudor political system, since they no longer required a violent past which could justify future political upheaval (G. Williams, 'Prophecy, Poetry and Politics in Medieval and Tudor Wales', in *British Government and Administration: Studies presented to S. B. Chrimes*, ed. H. Hearder and H. R. Loyn (Cardiff, 1974), pp. 104–16, at pp. 106–8, 113–16).

the traditional interpretation simply could not deliver, so that early seventeenth-century prophetic interpreters laid increasing emphasis on the future enactment of prophecies previously applied to the past.[20] The change finally undermined the authority of prophecy and left Scriptural chronology open to objective interpretation, because the prophetic interpretation of the past no longer supported that chronology. This change in attitudes gave new significance to the internal discrepancies of Scriptural chronology and the accumulating evidence supporting rival chronologies, although not until Hobbes did anyone overtly challenge the Scriptural version of the early history of man.

Consequently by the time that Hugh Broughton published his detailed interpretations of canonical prophecy in the 1590s, the natural harmony between sacred and profane chronology which Harrison had confidently assumed, had become a loud discord. By then the increasing problem of discrepant interpretations of Scriptural chronology had provoked laborious and intricate attempts to rescue the authority of the Scriptures which only seemed to multiply the evidence in favour of profane chronologies. The problem was that Protestant chronologers who had nailed their colours to a prophetically determined chronology as a confirmation of their doctrines could not face the challenge which rival chronologies posed to the authority of the Scriptures. A stark choice confronted prophetic interpreters. One could follow the Oxford don, John Rainolds, who denied the precise fulfilment of Daniel's seventy weeks and added seventy years to the prophesied 490 between Daniel and the Incarnation, or one could believe with Broughton that to do so 'shaketh Gods word, whereby prophanesse only will beare sway, and the Gospell shall be nothing worth'. In Broughton's view 'the holy story is disturbed by seeking helpe' from profane chronologies, but re-establishing its sole authority would 'lighten all the glory of the Gospell, to skatter all Antichristian clouds'.[21]

To Broughton the bewildering contradictions emerging from chronological studies already threatened the prophetic interpretation of history, precipitating his withdrawal within the bastions of Scriptural inerrancy. Thus Broughton provides an early example of the seventeenth-century attempt to circumvent increasing doubts about the possibility of any true human knowledge by disallowing any human failings in the Word. For in answer to those authorities who implicitly challenged the Scriptures he re-emphasised the special significance of Scriptural chronology and chronological patterns,

---

[20] Bauckham, *Tudor Apocalypse*, pp. 173–7; K. R. Firth, *The Apocalyptic Tradition in Reformation Britain 1530–1645* (Oxford, 1979), pp. 252–4; Christianson, *Reformers and Babylon*, p. 11, and see below, pp. 130–1.

[21] H. Broughton, *An apologie in briefe assertions defending that our Lord died in the time properly foretold to Daniel* (William Kearney: London, 1592), sigs. A1v–A2v; and *A Seder Olam* (1594), sig. *2r.

by restricting both to the shaping of divine history, where 'tymes have more use then for human affayres; no lesse then heavenly thinges overmatch earthly'. The simplified components of the Scriptural historical pattern were still 'deepe in signification, to be carefully studied', but in contrast the rise and fall of secular commonwealths had multiplied chronological patterns to the point where they had become utterly meaningless to Broughton, 'For the Lord, who altereth times and seasons, changeth states in such varietie, that the true report of theyr memory perished with them'.[22] The mounting evidence against the prophetic interpretation of time had devalued secular history for the devout Broughton, and had shaken his confidence in the value of chronology as a universal interpretative tool in history.

In a less polarised atmosphere Harrison did not have to defend the Scriptures from entrenched positions. He foresaw no major difficulties for the authority of the Bible in answering Melanchthon's call for the integration of secular and sacred history into a common chronology.[23] He felt correspondingly less defensive about the Scriptural text, and did not claim that every word breathed God's inspiration. On the contrary, like Luther he admitted human characteristics and even flaws in the text. Harrison believed that Esdras had edited much of the extant Old Testament, epitomising earlier books of 'the Jewish historie conteined in the bokes of Kinges and Chronicles of the auncient seers and prophetes...though these bokes are now quite perished and lost'. More importantly for a chronology directed by prophecy, Jonah 'prophecied moch more then is extaunt in the Scriptures, where he entreateth only of the affaires of Ninive', while the Bible displayed many chronological contradictions.[24] By comparison with Luther, however, Harrison appears closer to the later Protestant insistence on the inerrancy of every Scriptural detail, although the constant development of Luther's position makes this a slightly artificial contrast. Luther only concerned himself with discrepancies in the Scriptures when they affected the fundamentals of the Christian faith. Harrison wrestled with details that had little relevance to saving knowledge as defined by Luther, but which satisfied his need to find expressed in every facet of history the kind of truth defined by the Word. To a certain extent this concentration on detail became an end in itself, but on the other hand Harrison deeply regretted his failure to clarify

---

[22] H. Broughton, *Sundry workes, defending the certayntie of the holy chronicle* ([R. Watkins] London, 1591–4), sigs. A2r–v.

[23] Melanchthon, preface to *Carion's Chronicle*, and Fraenkel, *Testimonia Patrum*, pp. 52–5. Harrison completed a work integrating sacred and profane chronology, which 'being conferred together it shall hereafter be easie for the reader of the scriptures to discerne the true time of ech incident whose daie and yere is noted in the volume of the bible and whereof hetherto no one man hath made any sound delivery and report', but though listed on the title-page of TCD MS 165, it is not extant.   [24] TCD MS 165, fos. 101r, 79v.

the catalogue of High Priests from Herod to the Fall of Jerusalem, for, as we have noticed, he ranked 'the certeintie of the historie' second only to his preaching vocation. Most significantly, Luther found errors in those prophecies which Harrison believed both set out the temporal framework and pointed to significant events within the chronological system which so obsessed him. If Luther felt that the divine purpose involved only some events, to which other occurrences had only limited relevance, Harrison by contrast appears more adamant about the prophetic determination of all events.[25]

Placing Harrison in the context of Reformation prophetic historical interpretation reveals that even in the 1570s he could still utilise a traditional method of interpretation which managed to juggle with several chronological contradictions at once without letting one fall to the ground. He was aware, however, that the monumental labours of busy chronologers attempting to defend the Bible threatened to upset his juggling act by throwing in new and heavily weighted interpretations of the Scriptural text. In principle he had no objection to 'the diligent serche of the botomes of things used in my daies', which had renewed almost moribund Christian learning, but the few valuable corrections that had been made could not persuade him to 'condemne and alter the whole course of [my] the ancient Chronology'. Harrison's revealing alteration emphasises his subconscious identification with sacred chronology as an essential part of the Scriptures and saving knowledge. Thus he feared to innovate not only because once started the process threatened to be never-ending, but also because it might undermine his own confidence in his ability to understand and obey God's will. Perhaps therefore it was more than a literary conceit when Harrison stressed the implications for his mental stability of what to us appear totally inconsequential matters of minor chronological detail, for 'wold not my readers thinke me more then half frantike trowe you to remove the birth of Christ to the last daie or middest of September, to place the begining of the wekes of Daniell at the first of Cyrus, and to add 60 yeres to the time of Thera before the birth of Abraham'. Perhaps no other statement reflects so clearly the importance to Harrison's thought of an agreed chronology. For when he wrote in the 1570s it was becoming increasingly necessary to defend 'an olde receaved error, not yet confuted', against 'a new invention not yet fully concluded upon', because the weak and fallible human understanding which had initially caused this confusion, if not quickly restrained by the Word, would go on to question all of the Scriptures.[26]

This incoherence appeared particularly unsettling in the context of

25 By this catalogue, Harrison dated the Crucifixion to AD 35 (ibid., fo. 138v). On Luther: Reid, *Authority of Scripture*, pp. 67–9, 71; and J. M. Headley, *Luther's View of Church History* (New Haven and London, 1963), p. 110.   26 TCD MS 165, fo. 117r.

Harrison's belief that the correct interpretation of time and history had been transmitted by the covenant line as an integral part of true faith. His attempt to resurrect this knowledge in his 'Chronology' reaffirmed, in his view, his connection with the covenant line. Any discovery by ever-busy human intellects of irreconcilable contradictions in this received history and chronology therefore struck at the very roots of his sense of corporate membership of the True Church. For nothing better demonstrates the importance of chronology to Harrison than the seriousness with which he laboured to resolve its contradictions. His painstaking efforts to define the chronological sequence as comprehensively as the internal meaning of events reflects his belief that both these aspects of history revealed something about the covenant between God and the Elect. He believed that the Patriarchs and prophets had been made intensely aware of the way in which the workings of history would lead inexorably to the Incarnation, and that his 'Chronology' recorded the same prophesied continuum of events that had been shown to them, with the added burden of divine promises confirming that events after Christ contributed to the final End of history. Thus it appeared vital that on every page of his 'Great English Chronology' God's mysterious will should not merely be shown to be working itself out, but that its fulfilment should be accurately recorded. For the correct interpretation of the past was one of the mutual safeguards of true doctrine.

Harrison assumed that a correct historical understanding was inextricably bound up with true faith and the good works which confirmed that faith. Proper godly teaching about God's mighty works in history gave insights into the present human condition, and this information had been deliberately preserved by God within the covenant line, for example through the longevity of the Patriarchs, especially Methuselah. He 'became disciple unto Adam and teacher unto Noah', so that 'the memory of thinges done was as yet kept sounde and voide of error forasmoch as the rehersall of them was not very farre derived from the originall hedde'. Thus Harrison did not restrict the meaning of true doctrine to theology alone, for true faith had a necessary corollary in true knowledge. The corpus of inherited doctrine therefore defined the limits of regenerate knowledge, of what could be legitimately accepted by those justified by their faith in Christ. That knowledge included exact chronology, for Cainan, who 'wrote of the true relligion and service of god, also of the motions of the sterres' according to the 'doctrine' of Adam, also 'wrote of the true quantity of the yere', and his teachings on the lunar calendar 'his successors did follow'. Disciples trained in this 'perfection of knowledge' emulated Cainan, 'a Prophet of great sanctity and knowledge'.[27]

---

[27] Ibid., fos. 2r–v.

By placing chronological studies in this context Harrison gave them equal importance with more obviously beneficial knowledge. For we have already noticed his belief that different facets of this shared corpus of knowledge could be discerned in the varied histories of the Elect, and that the true believers revealed this fundamental insight under different forms. Noah, for example, taught this perfect knowledge of divine and human things to his posterity after the Flood 'whereby thei became expert both in the true relligion and also in the direct administration of justice', another distinguishing feature of that just godly commonwealth which in its fully realised form represented the complete application of all aspects of the covenant line's legacy of true doctrine.[28]

Harrison accepted that a proper understanding of the past could only exist within the boundaries of regenerate, legitimate knowledge, and disagreements over chronological points, like other forms of unrestricted enquiry, threatened to blur the clarity of those boundaries. Therefore the unregenerate could be defined as those, whether in the time of the Patriarchs or the sixteenth century, who distorted the historical record, those who failed to interpret it according to Scriptural criteria. Disobedience in this apparently minor area could betray greater errors, therefore Harrison believed that one had to strive as he had 'to be exact even in the smallest things'. The Scriptures defined that chronological exactness which formed part of regenerate understanding. For in Harrison's view the pagans received all their true knowledge from the covenant line, where faith perfected human understanding and revealed the true meaning of history. When deprived of this godly influence, the pagans fell back on their own unaided reason, and errors consequently multiplied. For example, the fact that the pagan Abydemus agreed with Cyril of Alexandria on the dates of the antediluvian Patriarch Lamech confirmed this diffusion of true knowledge from the Elect 'which neverthelesse in processe of time grew so gretly to be corrupted that it was a hard matter for the paganes to find out the true discourse of thinges', warned Harrison.[29] The Gentile account of history indirectly illuminated the symbiotic relationship between true doctrine and a correct historical interpretation, for wherever the Gentiles appeared to echo godly doctrine they also demonstrated some understanding of the prophesied course of history. Indeed, 'the divine poete' Orpheus had not only read the Pentateuch and encountered Hebrew theology, but just as importantly he had seen 'sondri Prophecies of Christ and soch other treatizes as his predecessors had written before touching the knowledge of god and creation of the World'. Yet Orpheus lacked the gift of faith which would have enabled him to purify all his knowledge by reference to the doctrines received from the covenant line, and consequently he 'very often stumbled upon the errors of the

---

[28] Ibid., fo. 5v. [29] Ibid., fos. 170v, 4v.

gentiles, and such corrupted doctrine as he was trained up in'. His prophetic writings gave only a garbled version of history.[30]

For these reasons Harrison feared that airing doubts about the established Scriptural chronology only encouraged the atheistical opponents of true religion, while he could already foresee the deceptively easy option of asserting the absolute inerrancy of the Scriptures, a temptation which we have already noticed involved its own problems. Thus while he pointed out that 'if we mistrust the certaintye of the letter, upon just cause other will therby quickly take occasion to reiect the authority of the whole', he still felt able to leave open the specific textual discrepancy at issue, for on that 'I cannot as yet find out any constant assurans except the letter of the later do faile me in this behalf, which were very moche to affirme'.[31] Harrison's focus on the doctrinal and pastoral message of the Scriptures allowed him to broach such a possibility, whilst avoiding the dangerously rigid positions of later Protestants. This doctrinal confidence appears in his insistence that if the archetypical atheist tolerated current cosmological disagreements, 'moche lesse then ought he to take offens at or refuse to hearken unto the worde, for that all men either understand not every pointe, or do not exactly agree in the interpretation therof to the satisfaction of his humor'. The perceptible note of irritation in this comment derived not from the intricacies of Scriptural chronology but from the weakness of human understanding.[32]

Harrison asserted that the Scriptures did not have to give way to human reason, nor to justify themselves according to rational criteria. On the other hand he felt that an important part of the Scriptural message would be lost by an uncompromising and unreasoning insistence on the verbal inerrancy of the text. More could be learnt from the Scriptures by concentrating upon their description of the changing fortunes of the True Church and the experiences of the Elect under God's care, and by showing how that story displayed deep contemporary relevance at moments of prophetic and chronological significance. This approach could not dissolve the problems inherent in the text, but it could shift the emphasis towards the notion that the Scriptural account of Elect knowledge within the covenant line determined the *a priori* limitations to the rational interpretation of Scriptural mysteries. The consequences of this approach can be seen not only in Harrison's chronological interpretation of Daniel and of Revelation, but also his statements about the relationship between sacred and profane chronology and the internal problems of Scriptural chronology.

Harrison remained within the mainstream tradition of apocalyptic interpretation which had been popularised in England by Bale. For Harrison the

---

[30] Ibid., fos. 56r–v.
[31] Discussing the contradiction between 2 Kings 8.26 and 2 Chrons. 22.2 on Ahaziah's age at accession (ibid., fo. 76r).   [32] Ibid., fo. 117r.

millennium of Satan's bondage ended in AD 1001, although by AD 961 in his view Rome had become 'knowen for the second babilon, seat of Antechrist, and the pope the same sonne of perdicion of whome the prophete [Daniel] speaketh'. With the Lateran decrees of 1215 which made the papacy arbiter over kings and princes 'we see how no more the mystery of iniquity but rather wickednesse herself beginneth to work to the great reioysing of Sathan and overthrow of the gospel'.[33] Harrison seems never to have followed John Foxe's innovatory interpretation of the Apocalypse, and indeed, although chiefly concerned in his 'Chronology' with the correct order of events, Harrison contented himself with applying a consistent prophetic yardstick to historical events and resisted the temptation to interpret apocalyptic texts in the light of history and chronology, to tie a particular text to a particular event, as Foxe did. Harrison therefore appears to have been more impressed by Bale's demand for that subservience which would 'let the text be a light to the history and not the history to the text'. For, said Bale, 'The fearful judgments of the wrath of God which are infinite, and can neither be numbered nor yet measured of the creatures' vitiated any human attempt to dictate that the prophecies should display in series the course of history as understood by men.[34]

Harrison's application of the 666 prophecy demonstrates this contrast. Foxe seems always to have thought of 666 as referring to one historical date, a conviction which eventually led him to view the Apocalypse as a sequential foreshadowing of the history of the Church. Yet this approach contained a fundamental weakness, for it could be outflanked by the progress of historical research. Thus initially Foxe applied 666 to the effective beginning of Mohammedan power, an inspired reading of prophecy which swept aside alternative dates. But he later discovered that both the order of the text and the historical evidence pointed towards a new interpretation, towards *Lateinos* and Rome.[35] Foxe's many followers found themselves trapped in an endless series of such revisions, which eventually undermined the credit of the prophecies as the basis of historical explanation, when history and chronology could be shown to disagree with the text at all points.

Harrison escaped such embarrassment, for like Bale he sought prophetically significant periodisations which recurred throughout time, thus confirming the accuracy of his chronology rather than reflecting upon the

---

33 Ibid., fos. 247r, 239r, 305v. Foxe announced in 1583 that the millennium had run between Constantine and Wyclif (AD 324–1324) (V. N. Olsen, *John Foxe and the Elizabethan Church* (Berkeley, 1973), p. 71).

34 Bale, *Image of Both Churches*, ed. Christmas, p. 371, expounding the sealed prophecies of Rev. 10.8. Bale's reticence reflected his difficulties in fitting existing, popish historical interpretations into his apocalyptic scheme (Christianson, *Reformers and Babylon*, pp. 15–16).

35 *Actes and Monuments* (1583), p. 124, and see the discussion in Firth, *Apocalyptic Tradition*, pp. 96–8.

authority of the prophecies. Both Harrison and Bale regarded 666 not as a period of years which occurred only once in history, but as a measuring rod which, placed at various points alongside the chronological continuum, would bring out the true nature of disparate actions which manifested 'the number of the beast'. Bale believed that in applying this Scriptural vision of history in opposition to human traditions, he had aligned himself with the consistent doctrines of the covenant line, 'For not unlike is it to the time, times and a half time of Daniel and John, and to the years, months and days of Elias, and John also'. Like the later Puritans, Bale stressed that the conformity of the true prophets to this inherited doctrine established a kind of obedience which took precedence over contemporary demands for another type of conformity.[36] We have already noticed Bale's statement that this inherited truth included an exact knowledge of chronology, whose importance was underlined by prophecies such as that of 666 for 'howe shall a man apply it, if he have not the certaine time when Pompeie toke the scepter from the Jewes'? Only such godly knowledge could reveal the importance of the fact that Phocas established the papacy in AD 606, for that occurred 666 years 'from the consulship of M. T. Cicero, and Antonius, as Bibliander, Functius and other do evidently recken it, at whiche time the Jewes (while their bishops iarred for supremacie) lost their libertie' to Pompey. Bale obviously felt that he had recovered a significant mystery which had been entrusted to the covenant line, for he went on to argue that the rise of the beast through the destruction of the Christian commonwealth could be traced by applying 'this misticall number of 666 containing highe wisedom in it' to various periods 'from the time of Christes birth, or from the tyme of his passion, or from the XV yere of Domician' when John wrote, for at 666 years after each of these events 'ye finde some monstrous thing wrought in the church'.[37]

Harrison applied the 666 prophecy in a similar way, and again like Bale he believed that English as well as world history conformed to an apocalyptic mould which directed both towards that time when all earthly kingdoms would pass away.[38] Therefore Harrison discovered apocalyptic patterns in English historical chronology. Similarly, by emphasising the Samothean

---

[36] Thus John's reed (Rev. 11.1), like Ezekiel's measuring wand and Zachariah's measuring line, taught that 'the administration of God's heavenly verity is secretly of him committed unto them which have afore received it, and in faith digested it, that they should therewith rightly measure, discerne and judge all things. None other is it to prophesy again in this sixth age, but thus to mete the temple, the altar and the worshippers therein, and to prove them in length, breadth, height and depth' (*Image of Both Churches*, ed. Christmas, p. 383).

[37] Bale, *Pageant of Popes*, fos. 37r–v, especially Augustine's persecution of the British Church and the removal of the archiepiscopal see from London to Canterbury, on which see below, p. 137.

[38] Katherine Firth believed that no other sixteenth-century interpreter followed Bale's very convoluted investigation of the 666 prophecy (*Apocalyptic Tradition*, p. 52).

settlement of Britain, Harrison connected the British with the covenant line (Samothes being grandson to Noah), rather than with classical Troy via Brut, although the true religion established by Samothes had degenerated in Britain.[39] He continued to identify with the relative doctrinal purity of the British Church and the secular achievements of the Anglo-Saxons, excluding the Danes and Normans, who were 'scourges of god sent into this Ile for her revolture from his truthe and admission of error and ungodlynesse of life'.[40] Augustine initiated this apostasy, but it increased at prophetically portentous dates, thus demonstrating the fulfilment of apocalyptic prophecy in English history. Just as Harrison's sense of spiritual genealogical connection with the True Church encouraged his prophetic interpretation of contemporary actions, so did he believe that the apocalyptic content of English history had great relevance for contemporary Englishmen.

Harrison's perception of a prophetic connection between the history of the True Church in England and its contemporary condition did not lead him to give England a unique apocalyptic role, in the sense that William Haller claimed to have discovered in Foxe's *Actes and Monuments*. For like Bale (and indeed Foxe) Harrison claimed only that England provided localised examples of general developments in the Church, for example when English events in AD 666 seemed especially relevant to Rev. 13.18. For as Bale had pointed out, 'Not only in England is healed the beast's wounded head' in that year, 'but also in other certain regions'. Bale's sources limited his choice of examples, and he chose English illustrations in deference to his audience.[41] Harrison also used English events to illustrate the importance of prophesied chronology because writing for English readers 'I regard not gretly to dele in thantiquities of forren nations', not because he believed in a special national destiny. Indeed, while his examples were especially meaningful for Englishmen, the whole Church could learn something from the fact that because Aidan, the first Bishop of Lindisfarne, 'was the first of that kingdome that admitted the Romaine rites or had his crown shaven' he 'therefore died of the plage 666'. This and other events of that year might well bring home to Englishmen the wider consequences of their actions, but the farthest point of Christendom had also witnessed the intrusion of new ceremonies in AD 666. When England exchanged vernacular for Latin services, 'the masse also and variety of musike came into Grecia' under imperial patronage. 'Thus we see', observed Harrison, 'how nere the nomber of the best was fulfilled here in England and how many

---

[39] Parry, 'Puritanism and History', pp. 118–19, and see below on Harrison's use of Bodin's numerology, pp. 110–21. *Description of Britain* in Holinshed's *Chronicles* (1577), fos. 7r–8v.

[40] TCD MS 165, fos. 226v–227r.

[41] Christianson, *Reformers and Babylon*, p. 41, Bauckam, *Tudor Apocalypse*, p. 86, and Firth, *Apocalyptic Tradition*, pp. 106–9, effectively dispose of Haller's thesis in *Foxe's Book of Martyrs and the Elect Nation* (London, 1963). See *Image of Both Churches*, ed. Christmas, p. 450.

things were receaved in other places at one choppe together from the see and Bishop of Rome Apoc. 13. verse 18'. Yet he knew only the results in England – human and animal plagues, crop failure, death and devastation.[42]

Like Bale, Harrison did not believe that the 666 prophecy pointed to a single event. He used the text repeatedly because it not only reassured him that his general chronological research was worthwhile, but also because it confirmed his particular conclusion that Christ had died in AD 35. Rome's apostate ministry infected the Irish as well as the English, and rather ironically on a matter of chronology. The Irish received the Roman use and calculation of Easter 'as their histories note it...668 of the passion of Christ' in AD 701. Here emerges the temptation inherent in all this number manipulation to make the facts conform to mythical patterns, for since Harrison argued that Christ died in AD 35, not AD 33, 'the writer might so well have put in the 666 after the passion of Christ complete which is the number of a man and nomber also of the best that raged also upon the Irish by the admission of this constitution'.[43]

Harrison's approach to the Scriptural text therefore largely bypassed mounting evidence against the precise prophetic arrangement of time and history, which by the seventeenth century would make it increasingly difficult to align the Scriptures with the historical evidence. Then interpreters found it necessary to show 'that a unitary but progressively more detailed revelation' bound together the true prophets.[44] In this more polarised atmosphere Raleigh had to argue that 'the Revelation is wholly an interpretation of Daniel's visions', in order to defend Daniel against the latest revival of chronological evidence, first presented by the Neoplatonist Porphyry (AD 233–304), which purported to show, 'that these prophecies and visions remembered by Daniel, were written long after his death, and at, or neare, the time of Antiochus Epiphanes'. Stripped of Raleigh's pious gloss, this argument struck at the very roots of Daniel's authority and resembles the modern scholarly conclusion, that Daniel is an historical account of events down to Antiochus which then attempts an apocalyptic

[42] TCD MS 165, fos. 23v, 198v, 202v–203r. One of Harrison's lost works listed on the title page of this manuscript epitomises his spheres of interest: 'An historicall Calendar wherin the beginnings and endes of the kinges of England are principally sette down with the times of soche emperours and forren princes as are mentioned in our histories and finally the exact observinges of soche daies as were given us in the Scriptures'. Whether the latter refers to a chronological or apocalyptic conclusion unfortunately remains unknown.

[43] Ibid., fo. 212r, which notes that the British Church also followed the Apostolic calculation of Easter and rejected the Roman innovation. Brightman's *Revelation of the Revelation* (Amsterdam, 1615) owed much to Foxe, but much more narrowly saw events and individuals of the English Reformation as fulfilling apocalyptic prophecies (e.g., pp. 503–4, 388, 510–11).

[44] 'Prophecyes in every age, the first larger, the later narrower, all briefly told, all for event fully recorded: these shewe the constancy of this trueth', insisted Broughton (*A Concent of Scripture* (Gabriel Simson and William White: London, 159–), fo. 1r).

prediction of the future.[45] By the 1590s such disturbingly rational interpretations provoked either Hugh Broughton's dogmatic assertion of Daniel's
divine illumination, or more often the beginnings of a more reasoned
defence. Joseph Mede spoke for the majority of such interpreters when he
attempted to save Daniel's authority by contending that the last and most
troublesome of his seventy weeks did not end with the Incarnation, but like
the last of Daniel's Four Empires, would continue to the end of the world.
Mede went a stage further than Raleigh, arguing that Daniel learned in
general what John later received in detail. For many interpreters this
appeared to be the only way to retain Daniel as a weapon against the
papacy.[46]

Harrison did not regard Revelation as a fuller account of Daniel, for
Daniel's place in the covenant line ensured that his prophecy remained
perpetually relevant for the Church. In the same way that Harrison regarded
all the Scriptures as various expressions of the same truth, so he used both
prophecies as complementary explanations of the rise of Antichrist. When
Gregory III clashed with the Lombards in AD 732 'the Pope himself made
small resistens because that as yet he maintained no Armies but trusted to
other mens strenght according to the saieng of Daniell cap. 8'.[47] Harrison
realised that Daniel posed serious problems, but in a more sanguine
atmosphere he felt able, with the Fathers, to allow faith to gloss over textual
discrepancies. For he clearly recognised that Daniel forged another link in
the covenant line and continued the constant stream of revelation since Adam
by the correct application of canonical prophecy to his present circumstances.
Because Daniel had encouraged Cyrus in his wars against Cyprus 'out of
the prophecie of Esaie'.[48] Daniel had not rationally determined to apply
Isaiah, for God had merely used him as an instrument 'to bring the purpose
to passe whiche he before had determined' – the release of the Jews. This
allowed Harrison to believe that not the superfluity but the deficiency of
historical evidence accounted for the contradictory interpretations of Daniel's
prophecy after Antiochus Epiphanes, a fact which merely strengthened his
confidence in Daniel's outline of historical events. The later success of
historians in remedying this deficiency made it more difficult to blame human
ignorance for conflicting interpretations. For the moment, and despite
Harrison's concern for chronological accuracy, his belief that Daniel's
seventy weeks began with Cyrus's command to Nehemiah to repair the walls

---

[45] Raleigh, *History* (1614), III. i. 2. Porphyry's temerity in treating the Bible as an historical
document and checking it by other sources had earned Bale's censure, as the origin of the
scholastic interpretation of the Bible (*Image of Both Churches*, ed. Christmas, pp. 571–2).

[46] Eventually the failure of the present to conform to his expectations undermined Mede's
interpretation (Firth, *Apocalyptic Tradition*, pp. 224–5).

[47] TCD MS 165, fo. 212r; *cf.* Dan. 8.24.   [48] TCD MS 165, fo. 94r.

of Jerusalem 486 years before the Passion, sufficiently confirmed Daniel's prophecy of the Messiah.[49]

In effect, Daniel's place in the covenant line made it unnecessary to prove to human reason by the detailed study of chronology and history that his seventy weeks had been exactly accomplished; instead it required faithful acceptance of this as a fact. Further, to Harrison Daniel's election restricted the legitimate interpretation of his whole prophecy. Consequently Harrison refused to go beyond such faithful understanding when he encountered the transition from history to prophecy marking the period just after the death of Antiochus Epiphanes when the Book of Daniel had been written. Where Raleigh felt it necessary to make some reasoned denial of Porphyry's criticism at this point, Harrison simply refused to speculate, and regarded the difficulty as a reflection on the limitations of human understanding rather than on the divine origins of the prophecy. His sequential exposition therefore ended at 183 BC; until which time Dan. 11 'is equally and uniformly expounded by all the writers' because it corresponded to the historical record, 'but from hensfurth it is not plainely left, and therefore I cannot ascribe eche incident unto his due time as before wherefore I am constreigned to geve over'. Harrison may have reached the conclusion that further speculation went beyond the bounds of legitimate knowledge only after considerable soul-searching, for in a heavily amended marginal note he conceded that he stopped because 'some ascribe it to antiochus and some to be spoken [of] his people or of Antechrist'. Such contradictory opinions threatened Daniel's integrity, and ideas which did not contribute to the certainty of the Scriptures were better left uninvestigated.[50]

Harrison's desire to establish 'the order of the chronology' as an expression of prophecy which delimited time and its content is therefore evident in the minute care with which he arranged his 'Chronology'.[51] As

---

[49] Ibid., fo. 103r, and recall his opinion at fos. 13r–v that he would appear 'more then half frantike' if he placed 'the begining of the wekes of Daniell at the first of Cyrus'. Foxe shared Harrison's starting point, but somehow he ended up at AD 70 (Olsen, *Foxe*, p. 56). See L. Lloyd, *The consent of time* (George Bishop and Ralph Newberie: London, 1590), p. 77, for various attempts to make the prophecy fit the historical facts.

[50] TCD MS 165 fo. 122v, a torn and heavily amended marginal note. Edmund Livelie agreed with Broughton that Daniel's prophecy was 'a mightie upholder of the providence of God against all the Atheistes and Epicures of the world', but that did not stop him bitterly attacking Broughton's chronological works in his Cambridge lectures (*A true chronologie* (F. Kingston for Thomas Man, etc.: London, 1597), pp. 26–7).

[51] TCD MS 165, fo. 17v; and, for example, with the Babylonian Captivity, 'I translate the times of Nabonassar and Rome to the 4th [dating] columpne, and here also the yeres of the Transmigration till I come unto the captivity ended, setting them over the yeres before Christ as using them still because their remembrauns bringeth gret light to the prophecie of Ezechiell, for the times I mean…albeit they stand somewhat higher than their true seate requireth, by almost 3 monethes' (ibid., fo. 93r, and see Parry, 'Puritanism and History', pp. 412–15).

a divine creation the necessary historical sequence was an explanation in itself, but its details had to be drawn from profane as well as sacred authorities. Harrison could afford more leniency towards the histories of the nations than Hugh Broughton. Not only did pagan histories continue the Scriptural account of time, but pagan chronology could confirm sacred, and profane histories could even supply details of Elect history lacking in the Scriptures.[52] For although in 'the order and succession of time…the holy scriptures are by the divine providens of god sufficient guides and lodesmen', yet they 'conteine not a farder remembrauns of the particular times then unto the reigne of Cyrus' – in Harrison's calculations 537 BC. However, in common with other chronologers of his generation, Harrison believed that without the Scriptures the 'continuauns of the world itself hitherto' from the Creation, a vital part of Elect knowledge, would have been unknown, and that Daniel's prophecy provided the connection between sacred and profane histories, enabling a universal chronology to be developed from the Scriptural.[53]

Harrison's perception of time as a unique continuum of events also emerges in his list of preferred profane authors, whose calculations and accounts usually bolstered the Scriptural version of history, therefore making them 'true and infallible'. Here again he worked outward from the Scriptures and applied their criteria, so that from 537 BC 'we have the helpe, first of that excellent historie of Herodote…after whose boke ended, Thucydides continueth the discourse of time most exactly, then Xenophon, after him Pollybius, Pletho Gemistius, Diodorus Siculus, Pausanias, Strabo, Atheneus, Livie'. Harrison felt confident that only a perverse imagination could find discrepancies between 'the observation of time' in these writers and Scriptural prophecies. Prophecy therefore provided a chronological context which gave added significance to the actions described by these historians, 'if with any thoughe but meane diligens, thei be considered of by the diligent reader, and their writinges conferred with their owne intentes and meaninges'.[54] Examined under the magnifying glass of this prophetic context, profane histories could also demonstrate the workings of Providence.

During the decade in which he compiled TCD MS 165, Harrison needed to make many critical judgements about this mixture of sacred and profane material, applying to it balanced judgement, imagination and wide learning,

---

[52] From Macrobius he discovered that Orus Dionysius had been the Pharaoh responsible for the persecution of the Israelites (TCD MS 165, fo. 41r).

[53] Ibid., fos. 13r–v, 96v.

[54] Ibid., fos. 96v, 13r–v. James Ussher, who owned and used TCD MS 165 in the seventeenth century, also believed that a minute study of the historical sequence would produce edifying warnings about contemporary behaviour (R. Buick Knox, *James Ussher, Archbishop of Armagh* (Cardiff, 1967), p. 106).

the whole always being directed by his constant 'lodesmen', the Scriptures. The Bible offered the safest way of resolving Harrison's greatest and most frequently encountered problem, the great diversity of opinion on 'the observation of true yeres', a problem compounded by errors in transcription, which 'I accompt...almost infinite'. Harrison's methods of dealing with this chaotic material are more important and interesting than his conclusions. For not only did he change his mind – for example, offering different ideas about the Spanish era 'whose remembrauns...by reason of interposition of Times in writing of this treatize may grow quite out of my memory' – but also his use of profane chronologies emphasises the firmness of his trust in Scriptural chronology.[55] If we accept that Broughton and Raleigh roughly represent the opposite poles of faith and reason in these chronological studies, we can see that the freedom with which Harrison used profane chronologies to support the Scriptures counterbalances the incipient movement towards Broughton's rigid dogmatism in Harrison's interpretation of Daniel. His assessment of doctrinal orthodoxy in the 1570s still allowed him confidently to work outwards from the Scriptural centre of history, forcing him neither to withdraw baffled within fixed positions, nor to subordinate his Scripturally-informed judgement to what he perceived to be rational criteria. To avoid tedium, this approach will be illustrated by only a few examples.

Harrison accepted as radices for his calculations significant events in pagan history, such as the fall of Troy, the accession of 'Nabonassar' and the foundation of Rome, because they synchronised with, and did not compromise, sacred chronology. Where later interpreters found Scriptural chronology dangerously undermined by increasingly impressive historical evidence for the greater antiquity of the Egyptians and Chaldeans, Harrison could still draw upon Patristic arguments, skilfully elaborated in the sixteenth century, which explained away Egyptian claims of a history long before the traditional Christian date of Creation. Thus by an impressively sophisticated use of lunar cycles he briskly dismissed preposterous assertions about immense periods in ancient history.[56] Harrison's desire to emphasise the substantial concurrence of chronologers within these Scriptural limitations reflects the still relatively undisturbed contemporary confidence in the Bible's ability to explain both sacred and profane history. He could therefore depend upon his dating of the Flood of Ogyges as 'an infallible pitche', because 'so many without controversy do agree and their conclusions fall out in so good

55 TCD MS 165, fos. 209v, 248v.
56 'By their divisions into 135 (*sic*) which is the exact number of mones in every cycle of 19 yeres, for if you multiplie 19 by 12, and then adde 7 embolismes or odde mones (for so many yeres in eche cycle have 13 changes), you shall produce 235 and for the remaines of yor division you maie with like ese find out their iust proportion' (ibid., fo. 36v).

order' on the period between this event in early Greek history and the Olympiads. To wish that Harrison had been more profoundly original and critical than this is to miss the point that in defending the authority of the Scriptures there was greatest safety in numbers. Prevailing social and intellectual pressures demanded uncritical rather than critical approaches to this special source of authority.[57]

The Olympiads themselves offered an established system which promoted concord, once interpreters had surmounted the awkward problem of their precise date of origin, which established their connections with other dating systems. Only worried extremists like Broughton gloomily concluded that 'the holy story is disturbed by seeking helpe at these forlorne Olympike records'.[58] Bodin confidently asserted that the games put Greek chronology on a surer footing than Egyptian, Persian or Jewish civic calculations, which 'had no certain epoch or initial point of time' but measured time by regnal years, over which authorities squabbled endlessly. Raleigh realised the importance of finding agreement on the inception of the Olympiads, for 'The certaintie of things following the Olympiads, muste teach us how to finde when they beganne'.[59]

Harrison calculated that Iphitus had revived in 778 BC the Olympiads briefly instituted by Hercules in 1203 BC. The first games in 773 BC provided the radix for his calculations 'upon the first of [the month] Hecatombeon, and entrauns of the sonne into the crabbe'. Although he used eight other dating systems to fix the event exactly, he knew that others differed on the day and even the year.[60] Nevertheless he felt confident enough to continue the cycle of the games beyond their desuetude at the end of the first century AD until AD 519, when they made way for the regnal years of the West Saxons.[61] Harrison could see no irreconcilable differences between pagan and sacred accounts of time, and had no compunctions about using pagan evidence to pinpoint the holiest moments of Christian history, where that evidence did not challenge the autonomy of the biblical story. Accordingly even 'Christes Nativity is infallibly set downe, and therunto sufficiently confirmed by the Olympiades'.[62] Harrison, like Ludowick Lloyd, made 'the Sacred Histories the Centre and grounde of all beginnings, and the onely proofe of all antiquities'. Yet in pursuing this godly task at the end of

---

[57] Ibid., fo. 31v.
[58] H. Broughton, *An apologie in briefe assertions*, sig. G3v.
[59] Bodin, *Method*, ed. Reynolds, p. 326; Raleigh, *History* (1614), II. xxiii. 5, p. 576.
[60] TCD MS 165, fo. 82v; Raleigh agreed on 778 BC but relied heavily on the idea that Cyrus had acceded to the throne in the first year of the 55th Olympiad, while Harrison opted for the second (*History* (1614), II. xxiii. 5, p. 576; TCD MS 165, fo. 95v). Edmund Livelie (*A true chronologie*, p. 30) and Ludowick Lloyd (*The Consent of Time*, p. 66) assured their wider audience that the Olympiads began in 775 BC.
[61] TCD MS 165, fos. 185r, 143v.
[62] In the third year of the 194th Olympiad (ibid., fo. 136r).

Harrison's lifetime, the derivative chronologer, Lloyd, argued that the Olympiads 'made all Greeke and Latine writers to go farre amisse, and to faile in consent of time' by as much as twenty or thirty Olympiads, so 'I use them as little as I may'.[63]

Chronologers increasingly had to choose between faith and reason, between sacred and profane chronologies, as disquieting anomalies emerged within that unified world-view in which faith did not oppose but perfected reason. Eventually those anomalies would require integration into a new world-view which had no place for Harrison's Scripturally-inspired historical interpretation, and which thus undercut a fundamental part of his Protestant faith.

In the earlier, more relaxed atmosphere, Harrison could frankly admit, without prejudice to the Scriptures, that 'the five last chapters of the Boke of Judges are wrong set and shold immediately follow the second chapter', for such errors reflected the flaws of human transmission. He regarded it as unimportant that on this point he disagreed with what he loyally called 'our Geneva boke (the very best that we have in English)'.[64] However, even in this climate of undogmatic scholarly disagreement, prevailing in the 1570s, internal discrepancies in Scriptural chronology posed a more insidious threat. One of the points on which Harrison thought he would be 'more then half frantike' to abandon received opinions for new inventions was 'to adde 60 yeres to the time of Thera [AV: Terah] before the birth of Abraham'. The significance of deciding whether Terah was 70 or 130 years old at the birth of Abraham may now escape us, but as Raleigh later pointed out, for contemporary chronologers, 'Abrahams age beeing made uncertaine, all succeeding times are thereby without any perfect rule or knowledge'. Such uncertainty provided no solid basis on which to construct a faithful understanding of the world – and while Raleigh believed that Terah was 130 at Abraham's birth, Harrison supported the alternative calculation. By the 1570s these two rival interpretations of Gen. 11.26,32, and Gen. 12.4 had already created disturbing conflict. Harrison argued that these texts meant that Abraham had been born in Terah's seventieth year, and that Terah lived a further sixty years in Haran after Abraham left it, aged seventy-five. He thus followed, though not slavishly, the tradition of the Hebrews and Josephus, which Augustine and Bede had continued, and which several contemporary chronologers supported.[65]

Harrison accepted this interpretation despite the fact that many leading

---

[63] Lloyd, *The Consent of Time*, sigs. A2r–v.

[64] First suggested by Gilbert Genebrard, *Chronographia in duos libros distincta* (Paris, 1567), sig. A3v (TCD MS 165, fo. 58v); ibid, fo. 22r, and see *The Geneva Bible, A facsimile of the 1560 edition* (Madison, Wisc., 1969), fo. 116v, marginal note to Judges 17.1.

[65] Including David Chitraeus, Functius, Joseph Scaliger, Bucholzerus and Seth Calvisius, to Harrison's knowledge (TCD MS 165, fos. 17r–v); Raleigh, *History* (1614), II. i. 5, p. 223.

Protestants, including Peucer, Calvin and Beza, accepted the modern and contradictory interpretation, which Harrison attributed to Mattheus Beroaldus. In England Hugh Broughton made this new calculation, that Terah had been 130 years old at Abraham's birth, one of his four conclusive arguments to 'ende the endless controversies' on the whole of chronology. By the time that Raleigh had settled upon this latter date, an increasing minority had accepted the novelty. Yet this superficial agreement hid very different motives. Where Broughton insisted that this dating proved the veracity of Scriptural chronology in all its majestic symmetry, unimpeached by petty problems of detail, Raleigh addressed a more sophisticated audience, and sought by every means possible to silence rational doubts that the world could have been repopulated and civilisations have arisen so quickly after the Flood. Therefore he used the sixty extra years with other calculations to extend the time between the Deluge and Abraham, since 'they which shorten the times make all the ancient stories the more unprobable'.[66]

Harrison's argument differs in its assumptions from both these positions, and, although he shared Augustine's and Bede's conclusions, his reasoning also contrasts with theirs. His argument further reveals the character of his Puritanism, for he tried to preserve the authority of the Scriptures not by taking up a rigidly dogmatic position, but by emphasising the historical reality of the covenant line and its importance for the very processes of Hebrew thought which he found revealed in the text. Harrison felt it important to share this insight, to emulate the nuances of Elect thinking implicit in the text, in order to achieve a sympathetic, faithful understanding of the Scriptures. For 'in defens of the lettre of the Scripture which Beroaldus impugneth' he did not make it more acceptable to reason as Raleigh did, nor ignore reason altogether as Broughton did, but he brought both common sense and a faithful psychological insight to the text. He realised that the text described human actions, which therefore on one level could be interpreted by human reason, but he also knew that Moses in recording them gave a divine interpretation of their meaning, and that that kind of understanding could only be shared through faith.

The supporters of both calculations criticised Augustine and Bede for following the Hebrews, who in Raleigh's words vainly 'sought to make Abraham the first borne: as if God had respect to the eldest in nature'.[67]

---

[66] See M. Beroaldus, *Chronicum*, III. 2, in G. Mercator and M. Beroaldus, *Chronologia* (Basle, 1577); Broughton, *A Seder Olam*, sigs. A1r–A3r; Raleigh, *History*, II. i. 7, p. 226; and see E. A. Strathmann, *Sir Walter Raleigh, A Study in Elizabethan Skepticism* (New York, 1973), pp. 207–9. Everyone agreed (including Harrison, TCD MS 165, fo. 20r), that only 292 years could have elapsed between the Flood and the birth of Abraham if he was born in Terah's seventieth year, and 352 otherwise.

[67] 'I reverence the iudgements of the Fathers, but I know that they were mistaken in particulars' (*History* (1614), II i. 7., p. 226).

Harrison also emphasised that the rehearsal of Terah's offspring in his seventieth year named Abraham first only to show 'the order of the divine election' in 'the line of Christ', 'that only stocke unto godes promises and covenant'.[68] Raleigh and Broughton both used this notion to support their calculation that Abraham's birth occurred after this notice, when Terah was 130 years old. In contrast Harrison argued that the time of Abraham's birth chiefly concerned Moses, because 'Nachor and Aram were to be no partakers' of the covenant, and that therefore Abraham could easily have been a third son born after Nachor and Aram in Terah's seventieth year, for 'Neither is it likely that he lived 70 yeares, and begate neither sonnes nor daughters'.[69] An instructive contrast with Calvin's stricter interpretation of the text can be made at this point. Calvin accepted that Moses gave Abraham priority because of his membership of the covenant line, but insisted that Moses also meant that Terah was seventy years old 'before he begate those three sonnes', that Gen. 11.32. and 12.4 proved that Terah was 130 years old at Abraham's birth, and that he died at Haran aged 205 when God called Abraham into Canaan.[70] One could not reasonably assume, as Harrison did, that Terah begat other sons before he reached his seventieth year.

The interpretation advanced by Beroaldus and Calvin claimed powerful support from the statement in Acts 7.2–4, attributed to Stephen, that 'God removed Abraham from Charan after his fathers death', as Broughton paraphrased it, insisting that it 'may not be excused as though he had spoken negligently...but requireth beliefe in the simple sence of his wordes'.[71] Broughton's clear determination to stake everything on the verbal inspiration of the Scriptures here contrasts with Harrison's willingness to admit human failings within the text. Harrison believed that a narrowly literal interpretation could only really be true on the level of human reason, and ironically that such an approach merely reproduced the flaws of unaided Hebrew thought. For Stephen 'being a learned Hebrue', Harrison argued, like all his race read the text very scrupulously, and therefore because Gen. 11 and 12 mentioned the death of Terah immediately before the Calling of Abraham into Canaan, Stephen concluded, erroneously, that Abraham left only after his father's death, when Terah was 205 and Abraham 75. Harrison contended that Stephen's rationally correct interpretation failed to take account of the spiritual fact that Moses, enlightened here as elsewhere by the Holy Ghost, and 'hasting to the story of Abraham doth breefly (as by the waie) declare what came of his father and kindred', discontinuing his relation of them as irrelevant to his purpose. For Harrison discerned divine inspiration not in

---

[68] TCD MS 165, fos. 20r, 8r, and see the similar point in Broughton (*Seder Olam*, sig. A1v), who however uses it to support his alternative calculation.

[69] TCD MS 165, fo. 20r.   [70] Calvin, *Commentarie on Genesis*, sigs. Q8v–R1r.

[71] Broughton, *Seder Olam*, sig. A1v.

each word of Moses' account, but in the fact that Moses 'cheefly intended to intreat of the line of Christ, as I said, according to the flesh'. To say that Terah lived sixty years in Haran after Abraham departed did not endanger the Scriptures, for those years had no relevance to the history of the covenant line, in which Terah played no part.[72]

Harrison here found that a narrowly literal interpretation of a particular text fell far short of the interpretation which could be drawn from the rest of the Scriptures. Each text could not be considered in isolation but had to be viewed in the light of the Holy Spirit's overwhelming concern to portray the history of the True Church in the Scriptures. By drawing attention to this meaning within the Scriptures, Harrison believed that he demonstrated their relevance to his own time, where the spiritual members of the covenant line could see in their lives the fulfilment of God's promises and the accomplishment of his plan, in which the birth of Abraham had taken its predetermined place. He found that that spiritual interpretation provided a far more flexible and thus stronger defence against rational interpretations of the Scriptures than did a rigid insistence on verbal inerrancy, which only highlighted problems in texts such as those under discussion. His interpretation also allowed him to stress the organic connection between the Scriptures and the rest of history, and therefore to interpret all knowledge according to Scriptural criteria, a task increasingly difficult for later commentators such as Broughton, who were driven into an increasingly rigidly defined and narrow area of thought and were forced, as we have seen, virtually to abandon any attempt to interpret secular history.

Examination of Harrison's view of the historical content of time, and of the chronological and historical patterns which he discerned within that content, shows why he believed that he could use the Scriptures to interpret all his existential experiences. For Christian historians lacked any comparative scale by which to measure their meagre and distorted knowledge of history, and consequently that history assumed cosmic importance. This lack of a proper perspective accounts for Harrison's obsession with the prophetic continuum of events, it explains why he felt it possible to find confirmation of the Scriptural account of the Two Churches in all of history, and why in consequence he believed that historical patterns and parallels not only actually existed but had great importance for the present. Basically he saw

---

[72] Harrison capped his argument with a complex chronological proof showing how the complementary calculations of ancient pagans 'conspire against the assertion of Beroaldus, and utterly exclude those 60 yeres which he casteth in the waie as a bone for...Chronographers to gnaw'. He traced Beroaldus's calculation back through Nicholas Lyra's commentaries on Gen. 12 to a rabbinical opinion which however asserted that Terah 'abiding in Haran with Nachor his sonne' after Abraham's departure 'revolted unto or rather continued in his old idolatry' (TCD MS 165, fos. 17r–v). Harrison was of course unaware that Stephen was a Greek convert.

greater meaning than we can in a limited amount of information, which he found extremely relevant to his own situation by a process of 'reasoning' that we probably find irrational. Harrison believed that salvation came through the gift of a regenerate understanding obedient to revelation, which not only accepted the Scriptures' explanation of themselves, but used this framework to interpret the past and condition the perception of the contemporary world. Perverse and limited as this framework might appear, we shall see that what really confirms its vital importance for Harrison, in the case of chronological patterns, is not so much that he accepted certain patterns but that he very carefully rejected others. For in this rather abstruse field of thought as in every other, Harrison believed that he could simplify, select from and organise the multifarious data of his everyday experiences, including his encounters with the past, according to extremely selective Scriptural criteria which he accepted had been set down at the beginning of the world, had been confirmed by the historical experiences of the Elect, and remained completely relevant to Elizabethan England. Subsequent chapters will show how the application of this very different scale of values in other areas of Harrison's thought accounts for his 'unworldly' fixation on certain aspects of contemporary England, to which he attributed another significance from that which we might accord them.

Therefore to understand the nature of Puritanism in Elizabethan England we need to appreciate this way of thinking, in which an individual's basis for selection from the past not only reflects his perception of present realities, but is also to a large degree conditioned by the selective criteria already deployed in the Scriptures. For it reminds us that much of mainstream English 'Puritan' thought merely represented the application of a common European Protestant response to the Scriptures to the exceptional conditions of the 'semi-reformed' Elizabethan Church.[73] Many Protestants used the Scriptures as a critical tool to interpret the present in the light of the True Church, although really their sense of contemporaneity with the True Church depended upon extrapolating into the present some extremely poor data about the past. Postponing to subsequent chapters an examination of the way in which Harrison applied those data to his contemporary Church and society, we concentrate here on the way in which he perceived chronological patterns in a simplified past, for that attempt to organise the past also reveals the criteria which he applied to more obviously important contemporary phenomena.

The Old Testament offered the model for this selective treatment of data, for it sought to clarify the essential truths in human encounters with God, and especially to establish God's character by demonstrating His care for

---

[73] Ibid., fo. 201v.

Israel. To achieve this end its authors omitted certain facts, raised others from minute to cosmic significance, and arranged them to conform to a previously promised pattern. This process established the history of Israel, interpreted in the prophetic manner, as both an epic source of religious truth and the means by which that truth was taught.[74] Primitive Christianity showed no more respect for objective facts: like many contemporary religions it constructed a mythology to meet its apologetical needs, and one which outraged the Graeco-Roman sense of historicity. The New Testament distorted or invented details in the history of Jesus to conform to Messianic prophecies and explain away the scandal of the crucifixion, thus setting precedents for *a priori* selections from limited data.[75] A similar lack of knowledge allowed later interpreters to believe that historical reality conformed to vague eschatological promises, thus giving the millennia concrete reality and deep significance in their eyes. For the Hebrews, and those Christians able to respond to their complex vision, time appeared to be distinguished by its historical content. Thus the meditation on time in Ecclesiastes 3.2–8 deals symbolically with every human experience, and portrays time as composed of divinely given opportunities which the godly will utilise within the limits set by God, by limiting their reason and will through their fear of God, rather than exploiting the situation through human reason or free will.[76] God hid the full meaning of those periods from natural reason, for He 'hath set the world in their heart, so that no man can find out the work that God maketh from the beginning to the end'. The contemporaneity of all believers when confronted by God's unchanging nature, wherein 'That which hath been is now; and that which is to be hath already been', made it vital to respond correctly when called, and enhanced the importance of past Elect experiences, which formed much of the content of time.

Since believers held that history inevitably accomplished the divine purpose, the content of time had to be shown to reflect this purpose. The Hebrews therefore emphasised their communal beginning, and the fact that their historical destiny had found fulfilment in stages differentiated by their contents. The prophets constantly emphasised the contrasts between Israel's patriarchal genesis, her nomadic exodus and her kingdom of cities. Harrison's knowledge of Hebrew allowed him to grasp this fundamental contrast between periods by directly following the Hebraic tradition which reckoned the time of the Prophets from Samuel's Judgeship, so that 'the Bokes of the kinges in the Hebreue tongue are called the greater prophetes for in them

---

[74] Brandon, *Time and Mankind*, p. 62; Boman, *Hebrew Thought*, p. 201; Butterfield, *Christianity and History*, p. 73.

[75] Brandon, *Time and Mankind*, pp. 168–9, 172, 163.

[76] Wilch, *Time and Event*, pp. 118–28.

we shall finde moch more of the Propheticall then regall regiment'.[77]
Bearing in mind the importance of the covenant line in Harrison's thought,
we can see that this view follows a reading of the evidence which oriented
history towards its prophetic destiny and diminished the importance of
Israel's kings. The character of any given Scriptural period derived from the
actions it contained and thus expressed something about the accomplishment
of God's purpose. Yet Harrison often could not resist the lure of a scholarly
electicism and he also accepted periodisations which contributed only
tangentially to the godly understanding of the past.[78]

Harrison's views on the content of history thus perpetuated the habits of
those primitive societies which gave meaning to the past by characterising
and distinguishing periods of time, so that for example the Anglo-Saxon
Chronicle began as a means for the survivors of campaigns and battlefields
to recollect shared experiences.[79] This particular reading of the Chronicle
depended on personal experience and the oral transmission of that experience,
but learned Christians could rely on a prophetic framework to define the
contents of all time in apocalyptic, not historical, terms. For example, the
combination of formidable chronological learning, a powerful historical
imagination, and the inspiration of the Book of Revelation led Bede to see
distinctive content in each of the six ages of the world, which, in a tradition
deriving from Augustine, many believed had been foreshadowed in the six
days of Creation. Within each age Bede found a consistent pattern of
restoration followed by degeneration leading to disaster, clearing the way
for fresh restoration. Yet history did not consist of sterile repetition, for each
age, in parallel with the actions of a day of Creation, demonstrated a fundamentally different character and had a distinct result. The six ages would
accomplish God's purpose as surely as the week of Creation had done.[80]
However, Harrison apparently did not respond to Bede's particular detailed
periodisation, for the meaning of such briefly expressed but potent patterns
would appear only to those who shared practically identical assumptions
about the past.

Harrison's reactions to the prophecies of Joachim of Fiore reinforce the
notion that the attractions of particular patterns seemed obvious only to those

---

77　TCD MS 165, fo. 65r, which followed the Hebrews more closely than Alan Richardson
　　(*History, Sacred and Profane*, p. 58), who pointed to the contrasting contents of Genesis, Exodus
　　and Kings.

78　See below, pp. 96–101 on the prophecy of Elias.

79　*The Anglo-Saxon Chronicle*, tr. and ed. G. N. Garmonsway (London, 1977), p. xviii.

80　R. W. Southern, 'Aspects of the European Tradition of Historical Writing 2: Hugh of St
　　Victor and the Idea of Historical Development', in *Transactions of the Royal Historical Society*,
　　5th ser., 21 (1971), pp. 159–79, at pp. 161–3. Harrison felt that the historical content of Church
　　history condemned Bede: 'Certes if this man had lived in the purer time wherin Augustine,
　　Jerome and Chrysostome flourished I doubt not but he would have been comparable in fame
　　and judgement unto the best of them' (TCD MS 165, fo. 204v).

who shared certain concepts. Joachimist works, in which historical and chronological knowledge reached a nadir and imagination enjoyed a free rein, provide extreme examples of the prophetic characterisation of historical periods. Joachim rejected traditional pessimism by juxtaposing the period of greatest tribulation for mankind under Antichrist's rule with its moment of highest triumph. These two last ages dramatically differed in their qualities and the character of their events, but within the Joachimist context the assumptions of this scheme were sufficiently expounded by intimating that the life designated in Peter must give way to that designated in John. Joachim's three-fold division of time also gave each age a dominant character which showed how it fitted into the divine plan. The Old Testament became the Order of Wedlock, when the Patriarchs married according to God's command to people the earth; the New Testament represented the Order of Clerks, while the Third Age would be the spiritual Order of Monks. Joachim used images to represent complex prophetic ideas, and his disciples popularised his theories through ideology, trading upon the ambiguity of the images.[81]

Harrison's attitude to Joachimist prophecies demonstrates how he applied Scriptural criteria to assess the validity of human interpretations of the content of history. While he appreciated the Hebrew description of the Book of the Greater Prophets, as a contribution to the regenerate understanding of the movement of history, he obviously did not see the content of time as Joachim had, for he completely ignored his revolutionary reinterpretation of history. Proceeding *a priori* on the basis of Scriptural prophecy, what really interested him *a posteriori* in Joachim's work was a prophecy depicting what he could recognise as the true content of time, 'that the 6 seale [Rev. 6.12] shall be opened with thentrauns of the 1300 after the death of our saviour wherin the working of Antichrist shall openly be receaved'. For the iniquities of that period, such as the papal assumption of temporal lordship, could be understood by reference to the portrayal of Antichrist in Revelation. Here again the perpetual doctrine of the True Church provided Harrison's fixed reference point, allowing him to select from the knowledge he encountered, and by applying Elect doctrinal criteria to discover the exact limits of the legitimate understanding of history. For only the correct historical interpretation could contribute to the proper interpretation of the present – in this case the looming figure of the antichristian papacy which Harrison discovered and emphasised in Joachim's work.[82]

Harrison's historical understanding differed from the medieval outlook in other important ways. The sixteenth century inherited the medieval

[81] M. Reeves, *The Influence of Prophecy in the later Middle Ages* (Oxford, 1969), p. 506; B. Smalley, *Historians in the Middle Ages*, p. 182.

[82] TCD MS 165, fo. 296v.

cosmology which assumed, by analogy with the human body, that the whole of creation decayed through time. When Harrison wrote, however, the general lament for the decay of the world had to contend with a new interest in history as a source of positive knowledge, and an outlook which attributed important meaning to periodisations which did not suggest decay. Harrison expressed more interest in deciphering the chronological patterns created by the rise and fall of kingdoms than in deciding whether those changes warned of the mutability and degeneracy of all human things.[83] He could not rule out the possibility that sincere repentance and obedience to God's will would bring about an actual improvement in human affairs, for the unchanging, invincible truth given at the beginning of time offered a way out of the penalties of sin. This may explain why he did not pursue the progressive historical degeneration of mankind according to the pattern of the four metals. Although he calculated that the period from the Flood to Nimrod, and thence to Belus and the death of Ninus, 'make up 250 the continuauns of the golden world, wherof the old writers do make so often reporte', he did not remark on the other metallic ages; here he spent far more time in pointing out that the end of the Assyrian monarchy fulfilled the Platonic Great Number of 1728 years, the cube of twelve. Even outside such distinctive chronological periods, decay did not dominate Harrison's thought. Over half-way through the age of the world as he calculated it, he claimed that 'you shall not rede of anyone age hetherto, wherin was greater nombers of wise men living then in this'.[84] Melanchthon similarly found the degenerative implications of Daniel's idol symbolising the four empires mitigated by the realisation that although 'it was prophecyed before it was the pleasure of god that the monarchies shuld finally decay', yet God sometimes provided such a powerful emperor 'that the maiesty of the empire may be conserved' to support religion and international concord. As in Melanchthon's survey of Church history, the situation of the observer often precluded a subjective assessment of decay.[85]

Harrison and his evangelical contemporaries had no reason for dissatisfaction with their simplified view of history while that interpretation served their main purpose of demonstrating the constancy of God's justice and mercy. So long as history apparently revealed the unchanging divine character, there existed no great pressure on such historians to develop a sophisticated, rational concept of causation, although under this providential heading individual examples of rigorous historical thinking did develop. Yet in Harrison's thought these few examples never challenged the dominance

---

[83] See below, pp. 110–21.

[84] TCD MS 165, fos. 18r–v, 90v. Ludowick Lloyd only used the concept of decay when he wanted to score points off the pagan Greeks (*Consent of Time*, sig. A3v, pp. 12, 16).

[85] Melanchthon, *Carion's Chronicle*, 'The use of readying hystoryes'.

over his historical explanation of the biblical account of God's judgements on Israel, a dominance which as it reduced the amount of relevant information to that which could depict divine justice, consequently enhanced the importance of historical patterns. He therefore claimed that the apparent diversity of history in fact exhibited a rhythm which testified to the constancy of divine justice and the permanence of the cosmic order. From that fixed point derived patterns in the rise and fall of kingdoms, in the periods and numbers of time, around which the simplified contents of history could be arranged. At some points historical patterns appeared to connect with the movements of the heavens, further encouraging Harrison's obsession. Yet we shall see that some contemporary historians, less convinced about the mystical verities hidden in time, did not find historical patterns so absorbing.

Harrison's historical interpretation presented a myth, and myth depends largely on stressing the underlying symmetry of disparate events, on making any particular event more intelligible as an example and component of a universal pattern.[86] Thus pattern acquired doctrinal significance when Harrison presented the fluctuating fortunes of Israel as the most instructive pattern in history. Her apostasy under Eli reached such extremes as to provoke God to leave them 'to ther owne divises, a manifest token no doubt of some notable alteration to come upon that nation and people whom he dothe so reiect'. This event taught that all nations would suffer God's wrath 'only for the contempt of his worde and none obediens of his commandements'.[87] Lutheran historians had first introduced this extremely limited historical interpretation.[88] Their prophetic interpretation ignored historical developments, but appeared particularly persuasive to evangelical Protestants who sought to show that only faith led to salvation, and that to refuse the offerings of divine mercy would have dire consequences. In Harrison's thought this Lutheran notion became linked to chronological parallels and patterns, drawn within his narrow vision of the content of history.

While the predestined rise and fall of commonwealths established clear-cut patterns beyond human interference, Harrison saw that this also served to enhance the importance of those diverse human actions which contributed to the accomplishment of the predestined pattern. Thus the troubled reign of Eldred of Northumberland (765–72) intrigued him as 'a manifest token that some great alteration was very nere unto it for continually before a kingdome falleth downe right it first stagereth after releth and finally tombleth hedlong into the bottome of ruine'.[89] While hardly the most

---

[86] Firth, *Apocalyptic Tradition*, pp. 19–20, on how Lutheran historiographers used mythical history; also Butterfield, *Christianity and History*, pp. 81–2, and the important discussion in L. White, 'Christian Myth and Christian History', in *Journal of the History of Ideas*, iii (1942), pp. 145–58.   [87] TCD MS 165, fos. 64v, 163v.

[88] Firth, *Apocalyptic Tradition*, pp. 11–22, reviews Lutheran prophetic historical interpretation.

[89] TCD MS 165, fo. 216v.

penetrating of historical insights, this should remind us that what we regard as distinct historical processes appeared to Harrison to have contributed towards a teleological and chronological plan. The see of Canterbury, for example, 'grew unto a monstrous Synagoge, and the prelates therof almost matched the kinges of this land in port and princely countenauns', but both this increase and the subsequent royal diminution of its revenues acquired wider relevance through Harrison's observation that 'as it had a time to rise so had it a time to fall', time delimited not by objective historical causes but by God's predestination.[90]

Consequently although the structure of the 'Chronology' militated against extended discussion of causation, Harrison stressed the recurrent patterns of behaviour behind the downfall of kingdoms. The fact that 'niceness and voluptuous behaviour' no longer in themselves constitute valid explanations of political decline takes nothing away from Harrison's conviction that such actions were 'often knowen to be the onely cause of the ruine and alteration of thestate', since they provoked divine punishment 'as shall likewise appere hereafter in the processe of this boke'.[91] This consistent theme reflects his need for a myth which justified a chronology already assumed to reflect the divine will in its patterns, but Harrison's selective views on historical causation also mirror his contemporary preoccupations. Prominent amongst these stood the characteristic Protestant stress on godly learning, for as we noticed in the previous chapter, a decadent kind of education and the resultant spread of ungodly ignorance allowed antichristian superstitions to proliferate in the Church, while stubborn, ignorant popery seemed to mock that earnest, godly understanding which Protestant pedagogues sought to inculcate in Elizabethan Englishmen. Variations on this theme naturally emerged. Melanchthon, the foremost educator of his day, stigmatised the barbarian invaders of the Roman Empire as the destroyers of all learning, who prepared the way for Antichrist to foist his errors on the ignorant. Harrison saw the barbarians from a perspective less concerned with 'Imperial' ideals, for 'the wise Goths in Spaine' laid the foundation of Spanish resistance to papal encroachments. On the other hand, amongst his first actions in England Augustine suppressed 'the old universities of Stamford Legion', in order 'utterly to extinguish lerning in all places of England (saving in Monastereries)', so that the spread of barbarism would enable the papacy to introduce 'what mangled rites and ceremonies' it liked.[92]

---

[90] Ibid., fo. 195r, and see *Description*, ed. Edelen, pp. 41–2, which emphasises its remaining wealth, perhaps to reveal how far it still had to fall.

[91] TCD MS 165, fo. 34r; and fo. 217r, which promises that 'what mischief issued' from clerical celibacy 'shall not be omitted in this boke'.

[92] Fraenkel, *Testimonia Patrum*, p. 82; TCD MS 165, fos. 163v, 194v–195r.

Harrison imposed upon his simplified historical account patterns of causation which he believed had important lessons for his contemporary audience, but he also found those mysterious warnings confirmed by what were to him equally real and important chronological patterns, themselves geared to the workings of divine justice upon mankind. For example he believed that the fall of Constantinople not only signalled a significant advance of antichristian power, but also occurred in direct chronological parallel to the fall of Troy. Harrison's acceptance of such data as 'true' influenced his reading of the whole of Byzantine history and helped to underline the spiritual threat which the decline of learning posed to both the True Church and the magistrate. Harrison believed that Justinian, despite his immense efforts on behalf of the true faith, sowed the seeds of Antichrist's triumph when he diverted imperial revenues previously devoted to learning, under pressure from his avaricious nobility, 'who supposed knowledge and learning to be nothing beneficiall to a comon welth'. Through this ill-advised action, however, 'barbarisme and incivilitie in behaviour, error in doctrine and ignorauns in regiment crept in so fast among the Greciens that thempire never staied long in any one estate till it fell hedlong into the Turkish subjection'.[93] Without godly teachers to propound that regenerate understanding of history which directed proper actions in the present, religion became idolatrous and the magistrates followed short-sighted worldly 'policy'. From the time of Justinian the Empire declined into ignorance and impotence, a prophetic process in which Harrison's obsession with a powerful myth transcended conflicting evidence which now forms our interpretation of Byzantine history.

A whole cluster of historical patterns around the fall of Constantinople not only emphasised the significance of this decline in learning but in themselves provided supra-historical information. For, Harrison argued, as Carthage survived until another Dido ruled, and the Spanish Visigoths prospered until the second Alaric, 'so did Constantinople prosper till another Helene the mother and Constantine the sonne had the governauns of the same'. Moreover, this apocalyptic punishment created a portentous chronological symmetry, not simply because the Turkish victory somehow compensated for the sack of Troy by the Greeks, but because 'in the same nighte wherin Troie was wonne it was full mone, as was also a litle past at the losse of Constantinople 1453 of Christ which is 2635 after this iourney [the sack of Troy] and just so many daies before the summer solstice'.[94] Harrison also pointed to the connection between these patterns and God's displeasure

---

[93] Ibid., fo. 186r.

[94] Ibid., fo. 61v. Harrison vaguely recalled finding this pattern of rulers in 'sondry other kingdomes now out of my memory' (ibid., fo. 236r), but rejected attempts to make 'Romulus' Augustulus the last Emperor of Rome (ibid., fo. 180v). See Bodin, *Six Bookes of the Commonweale*, ed. McRae, p. 464.

against idolatry, so that the Turks 'justly also prophaned all the reliques and superstitious monumentes' on which the Greeks had relied. It could be argued therefore that at various times Harrison sought to explain the past by reference to different combinations of these meaningful patterns which existed beneath his over-arching interest in the rise of Antichrist. For all these particular patterns in Byzantine history were linked by the fact that with the Turkish conquest 'the grettest Empire of the world became the nest of an Antechrist and infidell'.[95] Other forces worked within the broad apocalyptic movement of history, and the whole displayed patterns which testified to a steady guiding hand in all earthly events.

Harrison's treatment of English history also shows how these beliefs helped him to select from and organise evidence which in turn confirmed the historical patterns that he sought. His explanation of the Danish hegemony over England eventually combined an apocalyptic theme with the most intricate chronological and numerological pattern-making, as we shall see in the next chapter. He attributed much of the blame to the atmosphere of ignorance deliberately cultivated by Augustine, and his 'Chronology' persistently savages 'the huge swarmes of idle monkes that raunged abrode (and as flieblowes were buzzed and blowen about by sathan every where)', especially during the Saxon era, when the idle and gluttonous religious neglected learning.[96] Indeed the nightmare growth of monasticism chiefly explained the Saxon defeats, the nobility being seduced into that luxurious profession so that in addition to the rise of Antichrist 'soche a security grew among the Saxons that the discipline of Mars was sone laid aside', attracting predatory peoples 'but chefly the nedy Danes...Thus we maie see how by means of Monkery the nobility and defens of the realme decaied both altogether'.[97] God used the Danes to punish a society already disobedient to His ordinances, most strikingly so in the great numbers of princes who entered monasteries, for 'to be a king is the ordinauns of god in whose hand his harte remaineth but to be a monke is only the invention of man'. Fundamentally this pattern of degeneration made secular history reflect the condition of the True Church in its struggles with the Church of Cain, and out of that struggle emerged other important patterns.[98]

Harrison's search for symmetry attributed quasi-doctrinal importance to historical patterns as evidence of the providential control of history. The Scriptures underwrote this procedure with the symmetrical conflict of the

---

[95] TCD MS 165, fos. 55r, 163v. Note that Harrison perceived the Empire in prophetic terms, without relevance to its actual condition in 1453.

[96] Ibid., fo. 267r.

[97] Ibid., fo. 211v; and see Bale, *Image of Both Churches*, ed. Christmas, p. 283, for similar sentiments.

[98] TCD MS 165, fo. 212v, and Bale, *Image of Both Churches*, ed. Christmas, p. 30, relating this development to the opening of the Fourth Seal. See below, p. 117, n. 62, on the Danes.

Two Churches, but within this framework other patterns could be discerned, especially typology. Since the first centuries, Christian interpreters had claimed that the Old Testament typologically prefigured the New, but Harrison applied this venerable principle in order to elucidate the cosmic struggle portrayed in the Scriptures. For example, at the birth of Isaac 'Saruch dieth in 231 of his age wherof I have to note that as the first instrument and setter forth of Idolatry ended his life with the birth of Isaac...so Sathan the originall author of that error was overcome and vanquished at the comming of Christ whom the said Isaac did prefigurate and represent being borne also by promise'.[99] Harrison used such insights as we would use more objective historical evidence, because he recognised that true doctrine compelled him 'to note' this type. Indeed he found support for typology in the earliest Christian tradition, and therefore used it with confidence, especially an epistle from Liberius of Rome to the Eastern Church which made the 318 trained servants of Abraham [Gen. 13.14–15] a type of the bishops at the Council of Nicaea. This provided sufficient evidence for Harrison to plump for this total amongst conflicting reports of the number of bishops present at Nicaea.[100]

Perhaps more importantly, Harrison's labours on Scriptural chronology enabled him to add a chronological aspect to traditional typology. This gives a rabbinical tone to some of his pronouncements, although as we shall see he had little time for cabalistic speculations. Thus chronology seemed to offer a mysterious intimation of the relationship of the Elect to the secular power, and reaffirmed God's control of earthly kingdoms, when Harrison found that 'as Abraham was borne about the 42 of Ninus the beginner of the Assyrian Monarchy, so Christ was borne about the same yere of Augustus, the first founder of the Roman Empire'.[101] The fact that the complete meaning of this pattern escaped Harrison merely reminds us that Protestants often resorted to an obscure mysticism when forced to confront God's refusal to completely reveal Himself to human reason. Such an outlook found constant encouragement in historical events that had no rationally discernible role within a framework which nevertheless offered no place for the purely random. Harrison could therefore point to some hidden facet of God's control of history in the notion that Herod won Jerusalem 'on the same daie (note the mistery) after the course of the yere wherin Pompey wonne it 27 yeres before and...that Moises brake the Tables upon the foote of the mount Synai'.[102]

At his most subjective Harrison could use chronological typology to

---

[99] TCD MS 165, fo. 25r. Melanchthon believed that the Testaments mirrored each other (Fraenkel, *Testimonia Patrum*, pp. 70–1).

[100] TCD MS 165, fo. 163v.   [101] Ibid., fo. 20r.

[102] Ibid., fo. 132v. Harrison felt that the timing of the Incarnation also involved Pompey's seizure of Jerusalem – see above p. 11.

discover historical 'truth' – perhaps the clearest evidence of his desire to impose providential order on the chaos of history. Here also his search for pattern has obvious bearing on the history of the Two Churches. Hebrew tradition held that Cain killed Abel when he was 60 'albeit that I receive not this assertion as an infallible verity', said Harrison, 'sith I thinke that he killed him either in the 30th or within a few yeares after, grounding my coniecture upon the age of christ of whom this Abel was a type and figure'. Elsewhere he applied a more detailed chronological frame to a decisive but undated moment in the True Church, dogmatically asserting that because Christ died at 35, Isaac had been offered by Abraham at that age.[103] Just as Harrison saw the conflict of the Two Churches continuing from the Scriptures into his own times, so did he extend to contemporary events the patterns set out in the Scriptures, for both had a sure foundation in the divine character. Bale displayed the same prophetic sensitivity to emerging symmetries, for in 1563 he expected Matthew Parker to accept such an explanation of the Marian persecution. Mary's excesses paralleled Augustine's murder of Dionotus and twelve hundred of his British clergy 'at the first entraunce of the Popes religion into England' under Ethelbert and Bertha. Bale urged Parker to compare all this with events at 'the departure of the same false religyon' under Philip and Mary, when 'our seconde Dionotus, blessed Thomas Cranmer', suffered martyrdom with many others, for 'I could prove that commynge in and thys goynge out much to agree, both in tymes and in nombre of martyrs that were slayne'. Surely, asked Bale, such chronological and numerical parallels had some mystical significance?[104] Whatever Parker made of all this, within a few years John Foxe popularised a similar approach, assuming that his audience would accept that chronological patterns between events partly explained their prophetically identical character.[105] Harrison used the same reasoning to give a Scriptural gloss to an essentially commonplace historical pattern. He had no evidence to support the common story that Thomas Mowbray had been banished exactly twelve months after the day when he secretly murdered the Duke of Gloucester, 'yet I denie not but by the word of god it is evident that with what measure a man doth mete to other with the like it shalle afterward be moten to him againe'.[106] Ignoring the obvious naivety of Harrison's historical interpretation at this point, we can see that it defers less to poetic justice than to God's immutable law, for Harrison accepted the suggestion of a chronological

---

103   Ibid., fos. 1v, 27r. Ludowick Lloyd also detected a guiding hand behind the 'fact' that Christ died on Friday, the same day that Adam sinned (*Consent of Time*, p. 8).

104   Letter to Matthew Parker, 30 July 1560, in *Cambridge Antiquarian Communications*, iii, 1864–76 (Cambridge, 1879), pp. 157–73, at pp. 164–5.

105   Firth, *Apocalyptic Tradition*, p. 95, citing *Actes and Monuments* (1583), ed. J. Pratt (8 vols. London, 1877), iv, p. 93.   106   TCD MS 165, fo. 350r.

parallel without clear historical evidence, simply because the incident conformed to Scriptural doctrinal criteria.

At one point Harrison's trust in the divine justice exemplified by historical patterns and parallels powerfully overcame the objective lack of sufficient evidence and encouraged him to pronounce a remarkable prophecy about contemporary France. In the usurpation of the Capetians upon the race of Pepin, himself a usurper, 'we see the just judgment of god how it rewardeth every man according to his dedes... There is also great likelyhode in my time that the Guizes shall re expell the Capetes for the scope of such a practize is already conceaved as most men gather', a conclusion which seemed probable to Harrison on the basis of previous patterns revealing God's unchanging character, 'although as yet there be no soche act put in apparaunt execution'.[107] Objectively, of course, this merely rationalised the events of the French Wars of Religion, but Harrison's confidence in his own reasoning here reflects his belief that he had made his reason subservient to the Scriptural framework as he perceived it, just as Bibliander had promised the coming of the Turk for the sins of Europe by reference to previous punishments. No practical political lessons could be drawn from the secret political manoeuvres in France, but rather the futility of using worldly 'policy' to forestall the working-out of God's will. In other words, Harrison interpreted contemporary events according to Scriptural criteria. Not all history could be made to conform to those criteria, and Harrison's prolonged study of the rise and fall of kingdoms made him conscious of empirical patterns which appeared to be religiously neutral, or at least for which he could discover no doctrinal significance. Thus he concluded that 'There is a certeine period of kingdomes, of 430 yeares, in which commonlie they suffer some notable alteration', but a commonwealth that survived 500 or 530 years 'is one of the rarest thinges that happeneth in the world'.[108] Yet the study of these innocuous chronological patterns brought him into contact with other chronological schemes which he felt it necessary to approach with greater care because of their implications for the true faith, and we now turn to consider some of those patterns.

---

[107] Ibid., fo. 244v. See S. Baldwin, 'Jean Bodin and the League', in *Catholic Historical Review*, 23 (1937–8), pp. 160–84, for Bodin's attempt to impose some sort of pattern on the chaos of French politics during the Wars of Religion.

[108] TCD MS 165, fos. 65v–66r, which shows Harrison's abiding interest in chronological periods and patterns.

ᴥᴥ

A reformed chronology – interpreting the prophecies

Harrison expected to find significant meaning in history, for he approached it with the same scrupulous care for the limits of regenerate understanding which he observed in the most important spheres of human knowledge, such as theology. More precisely, his caution in dealing with historical and chronological patterns and periods testifies to their importance in his thought, for he only accepted those which he believed conformed to Elect doctrine. Any periodisation which did not originate in what Harrison regarded as Elect prophecies, or which did not conform to the knowledge transmitted by the covenant line, had to be rejected. Therefore, the periodisations which Harrison rejected only serve to emphasise the importance of those patterns that he accepted as part of Elect knowledge. The following discussion also illustrates the individuality of his vision within this general framework, for the boundaries of legitimate knowledge which he recognised emerged through a process of constant interaction between his contemporary circumstances and his response to the particular Scriptural interpretation of history. Indeed those boundaries could shift under the changing pressure of circumstances. These various and variable influences led Harrison to some strikingly original conclusions on the chronological questions which absorbed the energies of sixteenth-century intellectuals, but the ways in which he arrived at those conclusions have wider implications for his thought.

Thus, much can be learned about Harrison's way of thinking by examining his attitudes towards the prophecy of Elias. Harrison's confident assurance that Creation had occurred 3966 years before the Incarnation complemented his calculation that Christ died aged 35 at the very end of the fourth millennium.[1] This calculation highlighted the pivotal position of Christ's life in Christian chronology, but it also confirmed the prophetic pattern hidden in significant events, and especially the framework of time provided by the prophecy of Elias, or Elijah. The Old Testament Elijah, an

[1] TCD MS 165, fos. 67r and 138v

extremely important member of the covenant line, had been rewarded for his complete obedience when God translated him to heaven as He had translated that godly Patriarch and true prophet, Enoch.[2] The prophecy of Elias limited the duration of the world to six thousand years, divided into three equal periods, although to save the remnant of true believers at the end the latter period would be shortened.[3] Harrison followed the traditional designation of these three periods as 'without the law', 'under the law', and 'under grace', although he knew that the essence of the law had been revealed by grace to Adam together with the Christian faith.[4] This prophecy shows how extreme could become the desire to impose a rigid symmetry and simplified content upon history. It had been taken up by early Christians and enjoyed great authority in the sixteenth century, whether as a product of the 'house' or 'school' of Elijah, or especially when directly attributed to the Old Testament prophet. Eventually Harrison accepted this latter and more extreme attribution, propagated by Melanchthon and Andreas Osiander.[5] The prophecy particularly attracted the more mystical and chronologically obsessed interpreters, while few agreed with Bodin that these periods were purely imaginary, and that 'to investigate more subtly these matters', which surpassed human wit and could neither be rationally proved nor justified by divine prophecy, 'seems not less stupid than impious'.[6]

Melanchthon certainly felt that Elias had prophesied concrete and definite periods, though not even he demanded exact fulfilment in equal millennia. He publicised the prophecy by using its framework to give a universally acceptable and coherent structure to Carion's *Chronicle*, putting it at the beginning 'that it myghte be commytted to every mans hearing'. Like Harrison, Melanchthon believed that a correct understanding of chronological pattern constituted part of true doctrine; indeed, he used the prophecy partly to broadcast its 'many notable doctrines'.[7] Elias, said Melanchthon, had clearly foretold 'both the moost alteration of thynges in the world, and order of the tymes', and he had been almost exactly verified by the date of

---

[2] Ibid., fo 5r.
[3] Ibid., fo. 130r, in parallel to the early appearance of the Flood (ibid., fo. 8r).
[4] Ibid., fo. 5r.
[5] Osiander, *The Conjectures*, tr. George Joye (1545), sigs. A4v–A6r, and Melanchthon, *In Danielam prophetam*, fo. 145v, cited in Bauckham, *Tudor Apocalypse*, p. 165, and Firth, *Apocalyptic Tradition*, pp. 5–6, 62–3.
[6] Bodin distinguished this Elias from the Old Testament prophet (*Method*, tr. Reynolds, p. 333) and felt that calculating the age of the world was more difficult than it seemed (J. L. Brown, *The Methodus ad Facilem Historiarum Cognitionem of Jean Bodin. A Critical Study* (Washington, D.C., 1939; repr. 1969), p. 79).
[7] Melanchthon was attempting to remedy the chaos caused by differences over the seven ages, devoting his first book to the 2000 years from Adam to Abraham; the second covered Abraham to Christ, the third began at the Incarnation (*Carion's Chronicle*, 'The use of readying hystoryes', sig. *7r).

the Incarnation.[8] Harrison generally accepted this viewpoint, and eventually interpreted time in the light of Elias, but he managed both to be one of the first Englishmen to dismiss the prophecy and yet be more rigid than Melanchthon in applying it.

The manuscript 'Chronology' gives very few physical clues about this change of mind, and there is no conclusive proof about what prompted it, but it appears to reflect the development of Harrison's thinking towards a more rigid periodisation, and especially towards the conviction that prophecies similar to that of Elias could be found in the covenant line. Melanchthon conceded that Elias was only approximately correct in his prophecy of the end of the Law, because the Incarnation abrogated the Old Covenant in 3944 AM. Harrison, with a stricter eye to the parallel of sacrifice demanded of Abraham, postponed the end of the Law to the Passion. This had obvious advantages, for several prophetic patterns coincided at that momentous death, so that 'The 81 Sabaoth after Gerardus doth enter in the yere of Christes passion and concurreth with the 13 of the 81 Cicle of the Jewes, the entrauns of the 4th yere of the 70 weeke of Daniell, the beginning of the 53 of the third Temple and 4000 of the worlde', all dates confirmed 'by testimony of the Scriptures'. Such a mysterious nexus at the end of the fourth millennium emphasised the recondite significance of the Passion, for the end of the eightieth sabbath and beginning of the eighty-first, together with the end of Daniel's seventy weeks, 'is not without gret mistery', insisted Harrison, 'if it be applied to the ceremonial law, and ceasing of the sacrifice'.[9]

This symmetrical neatness encouraged Harrison to consider the different contents of Elias' dramatically distinct periods, which contributed to the consummation of history but also showed that 'tempora mutantur et nos mutamur in illis'. He did not consider this a gradual historical process, for in the first two thousand years 'men gave their mindes for the most part to sounde religion, wisdome and knowlege of the celestiall motions', a generous interpretation of patriarchal influence over the earliest commonwealths. However, in the next two millennia, 'men are no lesse occupied in building of cities making of lawes, studieng of philosophie, leading of Colonies, and maintenauns of Idolatry'. This highly selective review makes the conflict of the Two Churches implicit rather than explicit, but it is still discernible in Harrison's equation of the period 'without the law' with

---

[8] Melanchthon placed the Incarnation at 3944 AM, but did not 'counte the yeares exactly, and narrowly', for 'the prophet sayd moreover that God wold prevent and come spedely before the tyme of hys comminge, because the end of all thinges myght be more neare' (ibid., fo. 87v).

[9] At 3997 AM he had noted the beginning of Daniel's 70th week, 'in the middest wherof christ our saviour suffred his passion...whereby the...acceptation of the Jewish sacrifice doth cease', referring to Dan. 9.27 (TCD MS 165, fo. 138v).

'sounde religion', implying that the philosophy and idolatry of the second age represents a degeneration from the pristine dispensation. The building of cities, which had originated with Cain, and the spread of human law in the second age, also recall Harrison's belief that the Gentiles corrupted truth first given to the Hebrews. This struggle remained unresolved in the last two thousand years, when 'we are diligent in the invention and perfection of sondry artes, continually exercised with warres, and contentious about religion'.

Despite the freedom with which he characterised the periods attributed to Elias, however, at this point in the manuscript Harrison denied the canonicity of the prophecy, for the period of the world was only 'supposed to conteine 6000 yeres after the opinion of some of the hebrues, grounded upon the coniecturall assertion of one called Helias', whom he originally stigmatised as 'a Rabbine', and after second thoughts left unidentified. Harrison's discovery that the Talmud cited Elias tainted the prophecy for him, for he distinguished sharply between the divine insights conferred on the Hebrews while they held the true faith, and the unfettered ramblings of the Jews after their final apostasy. Thus he condemned Elias as a Rabbinical speculation, 'wherof the Jewish nation hath great nombers as men delited with frutelesse allegories and Pythagoricall suttleties'.[10] He quarrelled not only with the Talmudic context of the prophecy, but its origin, 'as the Jewes talke' in a disciple of Rabbi Elias, allegedly the son of the child restored to life by the Old Testament Elijah. Harrison concluded after reading conflicting authorities that this prophecy degenerated from the original spring of true revelation, for 'the [best but] new writers conclude that it beganne but of late to speake of by one Rabbi Helias a Talmudist', and that no one of credit would ascribe it to the prophet Elijah. One of the major authorities to reject the prophecy as a mere Jewish speculation was Theodore Bibliander, whom Harrison cited on the True Church's earliest struggles to preserve the truth.[11]

The physical evidence of his 'Chronology' does not allow us to put Harrison's struggles with this cosmically important prophecy in chronological order of writing. However, his most extensive treatment of Elias, which rehearses all the major authorities in favour of the prophecy (authorities rejected by those who objected to its uncanonical origins), finds a way out of his dilemma by putting the prophecy alongside canonical patterns which allowed similar interpretations. Eventually he felt able to justify the prophecy by reference to Scriptural criteria and to identify Elias with Elijah. Examining Enoch's translation into heaven, he mentioned 'some' who say 'that as the

---

[10] Ibid., fos. 22v, 75v, which shows that Harrison's suspicions were originally aroused by the reference to Elias 'in the 4 part of the Talmud second boke and chapiter Helec'.

[11] Ibid., fo. 75v, and see Bauckham, *Tudor Apocalypse*, p. 165, on Bibliander, who thought Elias encouraged chiliasm. See above, p. 43.

first 6 patriarches died, and the seventh was taken up unto God', so death will reign in the first six millennia 'and in the seventh the godly shal reigne and dwell with Christ in the heavens'. Since Enoch disappeared before 1000 AM (Harrison reckoned in 990 AM), by analogy the last millennium will not be finished. By using the traditional equation of a prophetic day with a thousand years, Harrison made the six days of Creation an image of the millennia, 'allowing the seventh unto the everlasting Sabaoth', and thus opened the way for introducing 'the Hebrues' who 'have soch an other coniecture, which thei ascribe unto one Hely as appereth in ther Talmud'.[12] Harrison now faced the major problem of purifying this tainted source, and he quickly showed that the 'conclusive sentens' of this prophecy, that 'for our sinnes...the later 2000 shall be abridged' seemed 'not discrepant from the wordes of our saviour Christ' in Matt. 24.22, that 'for the chosens sake those daies shold be cut off'. At the same time he carefully avoided making the prophecy depend upon the dubious authority of 4 Esdras 4, which Sheltco à Geveren, following Bibliander, had described as canonical. Harrison reported Sheltco's claim that 4 Esdras prefigured the 6000 years by 'the vision of a burning furnace and watry clowde', but warned 'herein he wadeth farder then any other or at the lest wise I my self can gather to be aptly applied'.[13]

The other authorities which Harrison cited at this point in his argument reveal his desire to prove that Elias belonged to the covenant line of true prophets which he traced from Adam. He attributed greatest importance to the disciples of the true doctrine, and cited others merely as second-hand retailers of this truth. Thus not only Augustine, Melanchthon and Peucer gave valuable support to Elias, but also, along the subordinate genealogy of Gentile knowledge, echoes could be found in Orpheus, whose own debt to Hebrew mentors we have already noticed, and Plato, who quoted the verses of Orpheus 'as Peucer also noteth them'.[14] In a different context, when later the prophecy of Elias became fashionable as a precise instrument for dating

[12] Mystical chronologers like Sheltco à Geveren, Andreas Osiander and John Dove found this equivalence perfectly plausible. See ibid., pp. 165–7, on its popularity in Tudor England, although Harrison had to contend with some who held it a merely Jewish speculation, since it 'appereth in ther Talmud Ordinatione seu parte 4. lib. 2. Sanhedrin, cap. 14 and lib. 5 cap. 1'. (See *Babylonian Talmud: Sanhedrin*, tr. and ed. H. Freedman (London, 1935), ii, p.657, Sanh. 97a–97b.) He relied on Heb. 4.3–4, Ps. 90.4 and 2 Pet. 3.8 to establish its canonicity.

[13] Although Harrison regarded Esdras as an important Reformer, and contemporaries believed that he had edited much of the Old Testament, 'of his 2 later Bokes I meane those which are intituled the third and 4th...there is some suspicion' (TCD MS 165, fo. 101r). Geveren's *Of the ende of this worlde, and seconde commyng of Christ* (T. Gardner and T. Dawson for A. Maunsell: London, 1577), fo. 2r, cited Bibliander in support of 3 and 4 Esdras, including the 'Ezra Apocalypse', which the Geneva Bible rejected as apocryphal. (*The Oxford Dictionary of the Christian Church*, ed. F. L. Cross (Oxford, 1958), pp. 462–3 discusses the problem.) Harrison considered the Geneva Bible 'the very best that we have in English' (TCD MS 165, fo. 22r).   [14] Ibid., fos. 56r–v.

the Last Judgement, William Perkins branded Elias as a 'fond Jew', and criticised his supporters' reliance on sources of authority in natural reason such as Plato and Orpheus. Yet Harrison just as firmly denied that Plato was 'a Moses speaking greke', and merely used his approval of Elias to show the indebtedness of Gentile philosophers to the prior and purer Hebrew revelation.[15]

For Harrison felt compelled to establish that the true faith had been revealed to the Elect before its partial and distorted reception by the unregenerate, and to ensure that this fact put Jewish speculations into the proper perspective. Therefore, perhaps equally as important as the confirmation of Elias by members of the covenant line, Harrison discovered historical evidence for the existence of this prophecy before the creation of the Talmud in AD 411, as he dated it.[16] By establishing Elias' connection with the oral and written stream of prophecy since Adam, Harrison could rest 'persuaded that this prophecie is more auncient than all the Rabbines and therto than their aforesaid Helias who was one of the most dere prophets in the sight of the lord that ever lived on erth as maie also appere by his translation into heaven and other points set doune in the scriptures'.[17] This radical argument thus circumvents theological criticisms of the prophecy because of its Rabbinic origins by presenting Elias as a prominent member of the covenant line who merely repeated a prophecy which had been entrusted to the Elect at the Creation. Harrison regarded his prophecy as canonical not only because he could trace his teachings to Adam, but also because God blessed him by translating him to heaven as he had the true prophet, Enoch.[18] This revelatory action occurred at a chronologically significant moment, as Melanchthon noted, 'even in the myddes of the worldes age, that the word and promise of Christ might be sometime renewed'.[19] Harrison also noted that 3000 AM was famous for the prophecy, but tried to avoid any disturbingly uncanonical speculations which could undermine his new-found certainty. Therefore he rejected Functius' calculation that Elijah and Elisha were born about the date, since 'as he hath no Scripture to prove it, so I yelde not somoch credite to the Jewish writers that I will avow his note to be sound without Scruple'.[20] Having shifted the boundaries of Elect knowledge far enough to incorporate Elias, Harrison was determined that they would remain clearly drawn in the future.

[15] W. Perkins, *The Workes* (3 vols. John Haviland for J. Boler: London, 1631), iii, 2nd pagination, p. 469; TCD MS 165, fo. 117r.
[16] Ibid., fo. 173r.
[17] Ibid., fos. 5r–v, and Bauckham, *Tudor Apocalypse*, pp. 165–7.
[18] TCD MS 165, fo. 5v, and see below, p. 105, on Satan's riposte.
[19] 'Incontinently after happened moost greatest and sodayn chaunges in all kyngdomes...for the last tyme of the worlde dyd drawe on' (*Carion's Chronicle*, fo. 15r, 14v).
[20] TCD MS 165, fo. 73r.

Harrison's perception of the limitations imposed upon regenerate understanding reflected his assessment of his own situation in Elizabethan England, as we have seen in the differences between his own and Melanchthon's views on Augustine. Essentially that contrast derived from Harrison's more persistent identification with the oppressed Elect, and his distaste for worldly success can also be seen in his interpretation of the Four Monarchies prophesied by Daniel. This major pattern in traditional Christian historiography had begun with Jerome's detailed historical interpretation of Daniel's four beasts, but that approach lapsed in the twelfth century when the relegation of history to the status of a sterile source of examples for scholastic dialectic deprived Daniel of any relevance to the settled present.[21] In the sixteenth century, however, German Reformers took up the pattern of Four Monarchies, for it showed them that the structure of history made Germany the divine instrument which would preserve Europe against Antichrist and his minions. Harrison encountered the interpretation as popularised in Carion's *Chronicle*, but he found it far less interesting than the concept of the Two Churches, and only mentioned as an afterthought that the *Chronicle* contained 'a description of the 4 monarchies of the worlde'.[22] In fact the Two Churches provided the context for his interpretation of the Four Monarchies, and just as Melanchthon assessed the Fathers by reference to the continuous doctrine of the covenant line, so Harrison assessed Melanchthon's Monarchies against the perpetual voice of the True Church. Generally, he concluded that they were not a major phenomenon for Christian chronologers, nor a justification for German claims for political dominance in Europe. This much of his argument reveals a patriotism shared by other English interpreters, but Harrison's dislike for the Four Monarchies also reflects a more fundamental disagreement about the historical relationship between the Elect and worldly power. Harrison's views on this relationship and their influence on his political outlook will be discussed more fully below, but here we need to establish the firm roots of that outlook in the teachings of the covenant line, against which standard of judgement he measured the Four Monarchies and found them wanting.[23]

Harrison's patriotic reaction against German claims of prophetic sanction for their imperial dignity reflected both sixteenth-century conditions and his interpretation of English history, in which he firmly identified with the ancient Britons against the Romans. Melanchthon eulogised the Four Monarchies as the fulfilment of God's will that the world should be 'maintened by a certaine gouvernaunce in hys place, that a certen means of

21 R. W. Southern, 'Aspects of the European Tradition of Historical Writing. 3: History as Prophecy', in *Transactions of the Royal Historical Society*, 5th ser., 22 (1972), pp. 159–80, at pp. 162–3.
22 TCD MS 165, fo. 219r.
23 Firth, *Apocalyptic Tradition*, p. 185, on British versions of the Four Monarchies.

shame and honesty might be conservid', and the wicked punished. The German Empire inherited the status and power of the Roman Empire as a buttress to civil order. This did not impress Harrison for he followed the traditional English interpretation of British history, arguing that after initial heavy defeats the Romans had only conquered Britain by subterfuge, while the arrival of Caesar marked the beginning of 'our servitude and miserable thraldome to the Romans'. He rejoiced at the Britons' casting off 'the Roman yoke in the 500 after the coming of Caesar'.[24]

More importantly, Harrison diminished the importance of the Four Monarchies because he disagreed sharply with Melanchthon on the origin and true nature of German rule. Consequently Harrison used the images of the four beasts (Dan. 7.4–7) rather than the image of four metals (Dan. 2.31–5), thus avoiding Scriptural sanction for the transfer of the empire from Rome to Germany in the feet of iron and clay, which Melanchthon interpreted to mean that the Empire 'is much lesse and weaker, than it was wont to be'.[25] Melanchthon defined empire as 'a monarchy...of so great puissance, that the exterior [power] of foren kings, could not withstande or oppresse it', and claimed that 'to the honor of such an empire or superiorite hath God exalted the Germanes before other nations in these latter times'. Harrison saw through such inflated claims – Flavius Maurilius Augustulus was 'last Emperor of Rome that Italy ever saw for those Emperours that succede him even to my time are but counterfectes only bering a name and not exercising the authority that belonged to ther title'. Even this diminished power only indirectly devolved upon Germany, which therefore had no exclusive claim upon it, for by the coronation of Charlemagne 'was the empire translated to the French', said Harrison. Only at the death of Arnulphus in AD 899 did 'the line of Charles and empire of the French' cease, and 'the dominions of the Germanes entreth' with Conrad.[26] Even so it did not remain an entirely German possession, for with the death of Henry IV in AD 1106, 'the empire ceased to continue among the Gibellines', a family whose French origins Harrison had discovered from Carion's *Chronicle*.[27]

Harrison and Melanchthon also used different criteria in assessing the

---

[24] Melanchthon, *Carion's Chronicle*, 'The use of readyng hystoryes'; cf. TCD MS 165, fo. 131r. Harrison considered the Romans 'wofull ghests to this our Iland', their legions brought 'all maner of vice and vicious living' (*Description* (1577), fo. 2v; (1587), p. 5). Similarly J. Ponet, *A Treatise of Politike Power* (1556), sigs. K3v–K4r; and Lloyd, *Consent of Time* (1590), p. 77.

[25] *Carion's Chronicle*, fo. 5v. Harrison gave orthodox identifications for the four beasts – the Babylonian, Persian, Greek and Roman empires – but identified Rome with an eagle, whereas Daniel and Melanchthon only referred to the 'Fourth Beast' (TCD MS 165, fos. 12v, 96r, 112r, 131v).

[26] *Carion's Chronicle*, 'The use of readyng hystoryes', sig. *7v; TCD MS 165, fos. 180v, 221v, 261r. Melanchthon regarded Charlemagne as German, and Conrad I his last descendant and the eighth German Emperor (*Carion's Chronicle*, fos. 127r, 137r).

[27] TCD MS 165, fos. 278r, 252v.

German emperors. Despite the fact that he placed the history of the Empire in the larger prophetic matrix of the history of the True Church, Melanchthon managed to assess each emperor by his contribution to the worldly prosperity of Germany. For although 'It was prophecyed before it was the pleasure of god that the monarchies shuld finally decay', nevertheless God sometimes raised up 'an Emperour of such power, that the maiesty of the empire may be conserved'.[28] In contrast Harrison judged the emperors by a prophetic yardstick, and only adopted a position resembling Melanchthon's when he wanted to condemn the papacy's arrogant treatment of the secular power by contrast with the Apostolic example. Only in this indirect light did Harrison speak of the 'imperiall majesty' of the papacy's 'soveraine Lord themperor...whome god commaunded all men to obeie and fere'. Applying the criteria of the interests of the True Church, not Germany, Harrison believed that the Emperor who had most vigorously opposed the papacy deserved greatest praise, and had best served the Imperial interests by obeying the injunction to come out of Babylon (Rev. 18. 4-5).[29]

The fact that Henry IV had suffered the greatest papal persecution therefore explains Harrison's eulogy on his virtues: 'There was never Emperor more valiaunt and noble then this prince, more goodly of person, more happy in the warres neither more prudent and pollitike in the imperiall affaires if he might have borne the swaie'. Melanchthon in contrast argued that with Henry IV 'dyd not onely the vertue of suche kynde of Emperours fayle, but the empyre of whole Germany began so to decaye' through internal dissension that it never recovered its former strength. In Harrison's view Rudolf of Habsburg, divinely appointed to restore an empire 'well nere come to the uttermost ruine and confusion', obeyed the apocalyptic command to avoid Babylon by refusing to enter Italy, and by surrendering the imperial possessions there to the papacy. Harrison assessed this policy by the same apocalyptic terms, since 'in mine opinion he did wisely for as harlottes will no longer bere a man good will then he is able by new giftes to continue the same among them no more will the pope...and therefore is that sie worthily liked to Babylon as the cheefe prelate therof to a famous strompet'. Melanchthon did not consider Rudolf a divine appointment, but was anxious to stress that he reasserted his authority in Italy through a lieutenant, pacified Germany, 'and dyd in a maner set up the decayed empire'.[30]

Most fundamentally, the fact that Harrison applied unworldly standards

<hr />

[28] Carion's Chronicle, 'The use of readyng hystoryes', sig. *7v.
[29] TCD MS 165, fos. 272v, 290v, where 'the sacred authority of the empire' appeared in the special context of a contrast to 'the Romish sie'.
[30] Ibid., fo. 278r; cf. Carion's Chronicle, fos. 151r, 154r. TCD MS 165, fo. 319v; cf. Carion's Chronicle, fos. 169r–v.

where Melanchthon applied worldly ones to the German Emperors reflects not only Harrison's antipathy to German self-aggrandisement but also a much more basic disagreement about the essential character of imperial rule. For just as Cain's murder of Abel revealed the nature of the contemporary struggle between the Two Churches, so Harrison perceived worldly dominion in the light of the same contrast between the covenant line and the descendants of Cain after the Flood – especially Ham. Melanchthon stressed the benefits to be gained from a continuous and strong Empire, and found in the example of Joseph 'that rygour is most nedeful to entertayn the people in there office or duety, and alowed of God. For the comon people is comonly destroied by lybertie'. Melanchthon admitted that in the first Empire, established by the Chaldeans, 'the successors of Cham rayned fyrst', including the tyrant Nimrod, although (as Raleigh later drily commented) in contrast to the Fathers, Melanchthon 'conceived not amiss' of Nimrod's tyranny. Melanchthon argued, however, that when the Assyrians under Ninus conquered the Chaldean Empire, God had clearly vindicated such rigorous rule for contemporary Europe, for Ninus was descended from the righteous Sem.[31]

Suspicious of the worship of naked power, Harrison emphasised that Nimrod had been a creature of Satan, who used him, as he used the unregenerate throughout history, to create a satanic parody of the True Church. God had translated the patriarch Enoch into heaven, therefore 'we finde that Sathan (imitating in all his doings to be like unto his creator) bare awaie Nimbrote, the first monarche of Babilon after the floode'. This corrupt action revealed the true nature of Nimrod's Empire, although Harrison admitted 'that god brought this man and his authority at the first upon the people as a scourge unto them for their sinne and wickednesse'.[32] However, this did not perpetually excuse severe government, for the basic question concerned whether the first monarchy represented the eternal pattern of the ungodly persecuting the Elect, or encapsulated the virtues of the posterity of Sem, keeping evil in check.

We should note therefore that Harrison deliberately chose to contradict Melanchthon on this point, for both men shared a particular view of history which made their reactions to the earliest types of authority vitally relevant to their contemporary political outlook. Consequently Harrison felt it important to argue that the Church of Cain had triumphed at the very beginning of imperial rule. By the same reasoning which made the conflict of the Two Churches fundamental to his judgement of the contemporary Church, Harrison saw that the victory of the ungodly in the earliest empire required the godly to distance themselves from contemporary worldly

[31] Ibid., fos. 6r, 7r, and see Raleigh, *History*, I.x.1., p. 186.
[32] TCD MS 165, fos 5v, 12v.

power, whose original corruption manifested itself in actions such as the Roman oppression of Britain. Therefore it was exceptionally significant that he disagreed with Melanchthon's assertion that after about 200 years the empire passed from the Chaldeans to Assyria under Ninus, who 'shold come of the race of Sem so that the posterity of Cham lost ther holde (saith he) of the Monarchy begonne'. Harrison could not accept that the covenant line in the person of Ninus had defeated the race of Ham, the reviver of Cain's church, and had thus justified worldly, oppressive authority, for 'this agreeth not with the assertion of all other writers who make Ninus to be the sonne of Belus'. This descent put Ninus back in the Church of Cain and made Melanchthon's insinuation that the victory of the righteous posterity of Sem blessed contemporary imperial rule totally unacceptable to Harrison, who made clear that 'in mine opinion Ninus, who cam of the posterity of Cham usurped upon the race of Sem in Assyria'. This victory by Ham's posterity meant either that Melanchthon had to agree that the Assyrians ignored the authority of their new ruler and 'became the cheefe people of the Empire under Ninus with out respect of the language of the said Ninus' (that is, they continued to speak Hebrew while he spoke a degenerate tongue), or that he had to admit that worldly, imperial rule reflected the vices of Ham's posterity.[33]

Harrison's reluctance to emphasise a periodisation which expressed the power of the Church of Cain has two important implications. Most obviously, it underlines his underlying suspicions about worldly rule, which have already been noticed and will be examined in more detail below. More importantly for our present purposes, his reaction against the pattern of the Four Monarchies suggests by contrast that the chronological and historical patterns which he did accept were in his mind connected with the True Church. In his dogmatic historical interpretation the very existence of such Elect periodisations made them part of God's injunctions set out in the necessary course of time. He felt more secure, for example, in accepting Augustine's division of the six ages of the world, for that pattern reflected Elect knowledge and commemorated the struggle of the Elect in this world, than he did in dealing with the Four Monarchies, which epitomised the worldly ambitions of the Gentiles. The genealogy given in Matt. 1.1-17 and Augustine's secure place in the covenant line gave the six ages definitive authority and a prophetic dimension for Harrison, who saw the fourth age of the world begin with David's kingdom in Hebron and continue to the captivity of Babylon, 'that is 471 complete yeres'.[34]

---

33 Ibid., fos. 15r–v; *cf. Carion's Chronicle*, fo. 6r. Harrison's attitude to Nimrod had important implications for his view of Constantine; see below pp. 237–43.

34 TCD MS 165, fos. 67r, 8v, and see *De civitate Dei*, XXII, xxx, on how the patterns of the generations of the Elect fitted into the ages of the world. See G. R. Driver, 'Sacred Numbers and Round Figures', in *Promise and Fulfilment*, ed. F. F. Bruce (Edinburgh, 1963), pp. 62–90, at p. 84.

On another flank, Harrison's allegiance to the knowledge transmitted by the covenant line excused him from wasting time on the 'great matters Michael Eitzinger doth dreame of in his Cabalisticall pentaplon', although he did warn that Eitzinger's strange interpretation of Daniel's seventy weeks would hopelessly confuse accepted chronology and that his innovative demarcation of only four ages of the world contradicted Elect knowledge and merely perpetuated Gentile errors.[35] Eitzinger's dubious chronology represented a particular aspect of the complex occult and mystical theories generally described as the Hermetic philosophy, and Harrison's reactions to that interpretation of the world will be examined below. Here we need only to notice Harrison's emphasis that Eitzinger's chronological errors reflected his inheritance of a degenerate tradition outside the limits of regenerate knowledge. He took considerable pains to refute Eitzinger's detailed chronological calculations, but rejected out of hand his claim that seven planetary angels governed the world's history for set periods, for that denied to Scriptural prophecy and God's providence their proper authority, and endangered the many who from Harrison's apocalyptic viewpoint 'incline already toward Atheisme'.[36]

This same distinction between Elect knowledge perfected by faith and Gentile knowledge corrupted by infidelity, based on the Scriptural depiction of that contrast, also determined Harrison's attitude to the Cabala and helps to introduce the subject of numerology. We have already seen that at a period when he rejected the prophecy of Elias, Harrison believed that the Jews fruitlessly delighted in allegorical chronological and historical interpretation. Even though he revised his opinion of Elias, he remained convinced that the Jews misplaced their confidence in 'the common Cabala'. Harrison claimed to have no time for their gematria, a system wherein the total numerical value of the letters spelling a word was held to convey hidden information. He argued that no proper information could be 'gathered out of the positions and significations of numbers and letters which are for the most parte more curiously then [wisely and] profitably invented'. This tone also appears in his comment on the fact that out of the 6476 verses of the Pentateuch, 'the Cabalists gather moch touching the continuauns and ages of the world'.[37] Yet his perception of the limitations of gematria and mystical numerology as a lever on cosmic powers may not always have been so clear. Harrison rejected the Hermetic philosophy, and its emphasis on the power of number as the common element throughout the hierarchy of worlds comprising the cosmos, only after he had initially accepted its interpretation of Nature and had read widely in Hermetic literature. His reference to the

---

35 TCD MS 165, fos. 8v, 101v–102r; *cf.* M. Eitzinger, *Pentaplus regnorum mundi* (Antwerp, 1579), pp. 35–6.
36 TCD MS 165, fos. 17v–18r, 61r, 2v.
37 Ibid., fos. 75v, 46v, and see Driver, 'Sacred Numbers', p. 68.

'common' Cabala shows that he had sufficient knowledge of the study to distinguish between the Jewish and Christian versions, and indeed he had read Pico della Mirandola's commentary on the Cabala, which introduced it to Christian readers in the more acceptable context of the magical Hermetic philosophy.[38] Harrison's 'Chronology' also demonstrates his familiarity with the influential treatise *De occulta philosophia* by the arch-magician Henry Cornelius Agrippa, which dilated on the correspondences between numbers and the powers of the cosmos.[39]

After his conversion to Protestantism, and as a result of his self-conscious attempts to correct his understanding by reference to the doctrines trans-mitted by the covenant line, Harrison became a profound critic of the Hermetic philosophy.[40] Hermes retained his authority with other historians such as Raleigh, who praised the Hermetic philosophy 'which bringeth to light the inmost vertues' of Nature, but Harrison adopted an uncompromisingly evangelical stance. Now it mattered little that number manipulation had formed part of ancient Babylonian astrological lore, or ancient Greek Pythagoreanism, for both could be dismissed as typically degenerate Gentile forms of knowledge. More complex problems emerged when the Fathers found Scriptural warrant for the use of numbers to convey instruction under figures. Thus Harrison could cite Ireneus 'being immediately after the Apostles' in support of the interpretation of 666 as *Lateinos*, which promised 'surely Antechriste should be a Latin and in the Latin churche'.[41] Once more the line between regenerate and unregenerate knowledge seemed to dissolve, and Harrison evidently found himself drawn more and more into manipulating numbers to uncover the divine order in history, before recalling himself and retreating within more secure boundaries. For his psychological need to discover order in the cosmos, and justice in God's dispositions, sometimes inclined Harrison to make events conform to patterns of dubious origin. For instance, AD 197 was 'the fatall yeare of Rome according to the proportion of her Numericall letteres' as written in Greek in the Sibylline prophecies, though whether any calamity occurred then 'as yet I do not find althoughe I must nedes graunt' that her decay began to gather pace from that date. The prophecy might even refer to the expulsion of the kings, although many prognosticated the fall of Rome after a thousand

[38] TCD MS 165, fo. 75v, and see below, pp. 315–16.
[39] TCD MS 165, fo. 26v; and C. A. Patrides, 'Approaches to Numerology', in *Premises and Motifs in Renaissance Thought and Literature*, ed. Patrides (Princeton, 1982), p. 70, which lists more examples.
[40] See below, pp. 309–21.
[41] Raleigh, *History* (1614), I.ii.2 and II.vi.6.; TCD MS 165, fos. 42r, 144r; Bale, *Pageant of Popes*, fos. 42r–43r; and see above on their chronological use of the 666 prophecy. Patrides, 'Numerology', pp. 67–70, cites Patristic support for numerology, including Augustine.

years. Harrison's words might be variously interpreted as either a search for confirmatory evidence or ironic ridicule of the prophecy, but if they reflect his indecision between these two alternatives then he did not always resolve his inner debate in favour of orthodoxy, for 'the like I may gather by the numerall lettere which is M in the word Roma as the latines wrote it. But what shall I stand longer in thes trifles'.[42] Clearly the contempt which Harrison sometimes summoned up for such equivalences barely matched the seductive appeal which they held for him. The Puritan self-consciousness betrays itself in such tension, and we shall see that only within the doctrinal inheritance of the covenant line could that tension be released.

Another reason why number appeared so full of mystery to Harrison was his relative ignorance of simple arithmetic. Like many of his contemporaries he used tools he did not fully understand to deal with the unknown, and consequently found it easier to overestimate the significance of the apparently inaccessible and esoteric. Yet he appears to have been better trained than most numerological commentators. Simple arithmetical instruction was rarely offered outside the universities, and the quadrivium and trivium emphasised the speculative over the practical uses of number to students whose limited grasp of the subjects would make the superficial connections of proportions and symmetries more potent. So perhaps because of this academic background, practical mathematicians like Leonard Digges had to deny the popular belief that mathematics was necessarily an evil and dangerous form of magic.[43] Giordano Bruno's almost total ignorance of basic mathematical procedures led him into extreme Hermetic raptures, while a little mathematical learning could lead into the unfathomable chronological waters traversed by John Foxe, despite his inability to do simple multiplication.[44]

Harrison may have been rather better prepared for his chronological labours. The evidence strongly suggests that he encountered the mathematician Robert Recorde while at Oxford under Mary, and he later knew Thomas and Leonard Digges, but there remains no evidence about how he learned to calculate in arabic numerals. Before the mid 1560s he seems to have gained a grounding sufficient for him to claim later that university mathematical teaching had declined after the new statutes of 1564–5 altered

[42] TCD MS 165, fo. 152r.
[43] M. Feingold, *The Mathematicians' Apprenticeship* (Cambridge, 1984), pp. 24–5, 35–40, shows the considerable provision for arithmetical and general mathematical teaching at the universities, and (ibid., pp. 1–15) suggests the context in which it was taught. For more on the latter see E. G. R. Taylor, *The Mathematical Practitioners of Tudor and Stuart England* (Cambridge, 1954), pp. ix, 4–9, 18. Feingold, *Apprenticeship*, pp. 17–18, stresses the rigour and dedication required for a proper understanding of mathematics in the sixteenth century – perhaps requiring too much from most students.
[44] F. A. Yates, *Giordano Bruno and the Hermetic Tradition* (London, 1964), pp. 306–24; Foxe, *Actes and Monuments* (1583), pp. 100–1, for circumstantial evidence of his arithmetical limitations.

the curriculum.[45] Even so, his additions and subtractions scattered throughout
the margins of TCD MS 165 and in his books at Derry, appear extremely
laboured. He never seems to have acquired the habits of mental arithmetic,
for even the simplest calculations had to be written out. There survives no
example of multiplication or division of even the simplest numbers, both
procedures fundamental to many prophetic and other periodisations. Harrison
must have taken a lot of such notions on trust, while he no doubt dwelt
on the patterns which emerged so laboriously from his own calculations.
Anything so deeply hidden in time must have seemed pregnant with that
divine symmetry which Harrison was already seeking in history. Yet when
he encountered similar ideas in Jean Bodin, Harrison was once more
reminded of the need for caution in such interpretations.

The Scriptural account of the covenant line set the boundaries of legitimate knowledge which helped Harrison to reject some historical patterns,
and more importantly emphasised the importance of those periodisations
which he accepted. Yet his thought also shows that contemporary changes
decisively affected Harrison's response to the historical interpretation put
forward in the Scriptures. The boundaries of legitimate knowledge which
he identified constantly shifted as current intellectual movements, and even
social and economic developments, subtly modified Harrison's reading of the
Scriptures and thus of all history. This refinement in our approach does not
diminish the central importance of the Scriptures in Harrison's thought, for
they remained for him the *a priori* source of interpretation. Yet Harrison
eventually persuaded himself to approach Elect knowledge by means which
he had previously considered improper when he achieved heightened
awareness of the apocalyptic significance of changes occurring in English
society in the 1580s. Much of the remainder of this chapter will be concerned
with this interaction between Harrison's thought and his environment.

Early in his chronological studies Harrison discovered significant periods
in the rise and fall of kingdoms, but it seems that Jean Bodin's *Methodus ad
Facilem Historiarum Cognitionem* first caused him to consider the mysterious
numerological patterns within those periods, and within individual lives.[46]
The fact that he ignored Bodin's political thought but seized upon his
numerological speculations, which only indirectly dealt with politics in the

---

45   On Harrison and Recorde see TCD MS 165, fos. 212r, 302r; and below, pp. 306–7 on Recorde
     and Digges père et fils. On the decline of mathematical teaching, see *Description*, ed. Edelen,
     p. 72, ignored by Feingold, *Apprenticeship*, p. 27, who not unnaturally preferred more
     anodyne comment. J. W. Shirley, *Thomas Harriot* (Oxford, 1983), pp. 43–4, discusses the
     revised Oxford curriculum.
46   Bodin's *Methodus* first appeared in 1566, then 1572, 1583 and in *Artis historicae penus* (1577 and
     1579). It is not clear which edition Harrison used; neither *Methodus* nor *Republique* survive
     in Harrison's library at Derry, although Bodin's *De magorum daemonomania* (Basle, 1581), is
     Derry shelf-mark J.i.b. 42.

context of cosmic forces, epitomises Harrison's desire to find in history a constant divine justice and order rather than worldly political wisdom. His many references to Bodin in the 'Chronology' are among the earliest known in England, two important citations in the hand of Harrison's amanuensis suggesting a date *c.* 1575 when he was most heavily engaged on TCD MS 165.[47] It is unclear whether Harrison or Holinshed was the first to alert the other to Bodin's *Methodus*, for they used it in similar ways, although Holinshed steered clear of Bodin's numerology.[48] Harrison's 'Chronology' reveals his dislike for Bodin's whole attitude. A difficult conflict existed between Bodin's analytical and rationalist approach to history as a source of political wisdom and Harrison's search for the historical evidence of God's will, which demanded a different response from his contemporaries. Furthermore, Bodin started from the premise that the Golden Age was in the present, while Harrison trusted those closest to the original fount of truth, criticising Bodin and others who 'to insinuate their workes and bring the same in credite do utterly condemn the most part of soche as have written before them, althoughe few men except thei shew better reason will be over hasty to beleve them'.[49] To cap it all, many of Bodin's novel opinions reflected on the majesty of the traditional British history, so 'How he accuseth and rageth against Paulus Jovius, Frossard and other also that have written of our country, I pass over to declare', said Harrison.[50]

Therefore the fact that Harrison overcame his deep distrust of Bodin's ideas to meet him more than half-way in speculation reveals the true depth of his fascination with chronological pattern and symmetry. Harrison's contemporaries saw nothing inconsistent in using material from an author they otherwise condemned, particularly not from the encyclopaedic *Methodus*, but Harrison took up the most dubious of Bodin's notions, his application of numerology, and applied it to the known facts of British history, where the Frenchman had already aroused Harrison's xenophobia.

---

[47] TCD MS 165, fos. 34av, 55r. See Parry, 'Puritanism and History', pp. 412–16, on the construction of the manuscript. William Fleetwood, who collaborated with Holinshed, cited the *Methodus* in a treatise completed in July 1575 (Trinity College Cambridge MS O.10.11, fo. 60r).

[48] Holinshed, *Historie of England*, in *Chronicles* (1577), p. 4, *cf. Description of Britain* in Holinshed's *Chronicles* (1587), p. 3, and TCD MS 165, fo. 34av; *Historie* (1577), p. 4, and *Description* (1587), p. 13. L. F. Dean overlooked these references in his survey of Bodin's influence in England, which contends that the publication of the *Republique* first attracted attention to the *Methodus* (L. F. Dean, 'Bodin's *Methodus* in England before 1625', in *Studies in Philology*, 39 (1942), pp. 160–6).

[49] *The Letter-Book of Gabriel Harvey, AD 1573–80*, ed. E. J. L. Scott, Camden Soc, new ser. xxxiii (Westminster, 1884), p. 86; TCD MS 165, fos. 11r–v.

[50] E.g., deriving 'Albion' from Olbia in Languedoc, a 'fond and [cocbrained] rashe assertion' (ibid., fo. 34av); *cf. Description* (1587), p. 3, and other criticisms, TCD MS 165, fos. 93v, 134v. But see Parry, 'Puritanism and history', pp. 136–8, which shows Harrison to have been less xenophobic than some in his defence of the 'British' Samothes against Bodin.

Harrison's application of Bodin's theories demonstrates the tremendous intellectual attractiveness of chronological symmetry for an even more profound reason, for at first he had fled in horror from the dangers of investigating such mysteries. This important change of mind emerges when we compare a lengthy discussion of Bodin's numbers in the 'Chronology', written *c*.1575, with its substantially revised version printed as an Appendix, 'Of the manifold conversions and alterations of the estate of the common-welth of Britaine sithens the time of Samothes', added to Harrison's *Description* for the second edition of Holinshed's *Chronicles* (1587), but which Harrison had written by 1585 at the latest.[51] The manuscript and printed versions differ only slightly up to the point in the Appendix where Harrison began to apply Bodin's theories.

Harrison's discussion of Bodin's numerology in the 'Chronology' begins by deliberately putting the whole question into a providential context, for Harrison claimed that 'god by his divine providens doth as it were prefixe in the begining of thinges how long their state shall continue, which being fulfilled an alteration ensueth though comonly into worse'.[52] This explains the transfer of the kingdom of the Argives to the Mycenaeans, 'whereby the Periode thereof is justly said to be come about'. In the Appendix Harrison began with a more overtly numerologically based observation, that 'There is a certaine period of kingdomes, of 430 yeares, in which commonlie they suffer some notable alteration', which however reflects his earlier interest in chronological periods rather than the stimulus of Bodin's ideas.[53] Both versions point out that these periods include both increase and decay, but more importantly that God sends tokens of His wrath before executing His purpose. The tone of Harrison's interpretation of those tokens changed over the years. In the 'Chronology' they warn that 'he is displeased with us and ere long he will visit our continuous contumacy with his rodde of [alteration] correction', but the later Appendix stresses that those tokens provide opportunities for repentance. Harrison supported both interpretations with the same quotation from Joachimus Camerarius, giving examples of such divine warnings from pagan history.[54]

---

51 TCD MS 165, fos. 54v–55r, where Harrison inserted a marginal instruction to his amanuensis: 'set this in my description lib. 1. cap. 8', although in fact it was appended to chapter nine, 'Of the Ancient Religion Used in Albion' (*Description* (1587), pp. 28–9). Abraham Fleming cited this Appendix in 1585 (Holinshed's *Chronicles* (1587), p. 202).

52 TCD MS 165, fos. 54v–55r.

53 Ibid., fos. 54v–55r, and fos. 65v–66r, the latter prompted by a notable exception to the rule, the end of the Sicyonian kingdom after 962 years.

54 Although he found his work 'sometimes mere superstitious', since Camerarius was a leading humanist advocate of the occult sciences (TCD MS 165, fos. 54v–55r, 65v–66r; *Description* (1587), p. 28; F. Baron, 'Camerarius and the historical Doctor Faustus', in *Joachimus Camerarius (1500–1574)*, ed. F. Baron (Munich, 1978), pp. 200–22, at pp. 202–15). See Camerarius, *Norica sive de ostentis libri duo* (Wittenberg, 1532), vol i, which elaborated on the malevolent significance of cosmic phenomena in reaction to the appearance of Halley's comet, August–September 1531.

Harrison then examined Plato's theory of the divine force within numbers which determines the alterations of commonwealths, agreeing 'that God created all things in number, weight and measure', but 'after an incomprehensible maner unto our fraile and humane capacitie'. God had obscured his purposes from fallen man's enfeebled understanding, but Harrison confidently rejected any idea that these proportions were primary causes in themselves, for God 'appointed not these three to have the rule of his works'. By virtue of their fear of God rather than numbers men could free themselves from bondage to these worldly elements, once they realised that change occurred not through numerical destiny but 'the divine providence and appointment of God, which onelie may be called destinie as S. Augustine saith'.

Having disposed of Platonic numbers by this reference to the eternal doctrine of the covenant line, Harrison contended that the precedent causes for the extinction of commonwealths were not those listed by Aristotle, but sin. Human sinfulness caused kingdoms to rise and fall, for the turmoil that surrounds their births and deaths sufficiently punished the iniquities of the nations, 'whiche being suffred till it come unto the fulnesse is then cut downe at the appointed season as corne is in harvest by the Justice of god the cheefe cause of all'. This uninspired but orthodox argument establishes the importance of the patterns discernible in chronology, and Harrison then links the two explicitly, making God's foreknowledge of sin the reason why He 'doth constitute such a revolution of things in their beginnings, as best standeth with the execution of his purposes', so that Aristotle's causes were in fact God's means. Again in the manuscript God has a less benevolent purpose, 'the performance of his will in ponishing our transgressions', than the 'correction of our errors' promised in the Appendix. Both accounts stress, however, the enormous latent power behind the predestined order of events not only for individuals but for the rise and fall of commonwealths which Tudor readers found so fascinating, and the importance of those chronological patterns which indirectly testified to God's power.

Having thus established the importance of chronology, Harrison turned to Bodin's use of numbers in his *Methodus*, pointing out Bodin's contradiction in applying his theory despite his initial denial of the force of number.[55] The manuscript made this appear a more covert and sinister contradiction than the Appendix, which now begins to ameliorate Harrison's original condemnation, in order to allow him to apply Bodin's system. Both versions claimed that Bodin's fatal numbers, six for women and seven and nine for men, had proved equally dangerous in the lives of commonwealths, whether

---

[55] Bodin began by criticising the Platonic notion that numbers had inherent powers, and claimed to show 'that human things are governed not recklessly and by chance, but by the majesty and providence of Almighty God' (*Method*, tr. Reynolds, pp. 223, 225), but he soon lost sight of this distinction. TCD MS 165, fos. 54v–55r.

multiplied together or used to divide greater numbers. At this point in the manuscript Harrison, who frequently thought out his ideas on paper, saw the abyss at his feet and quickly retreated from such external limitations on God's will, for although he admitted 'that in these odde yeres great alterations do often happen' to individuals and commonwealths, he felt it a great impiety to believe 'that thei should in any wise depend upon these proportions or that god should be delited with these odde numbers and direct his purposes after them'. He therefore began to set out the limits of legitimate knowledge, constructing defences against his own unvoiced speculations, noting that 'rare thinges' also occurred in even numbered years, 'wherof divers are remembred of set purpose in this treatize'. Trying to reassure himself that 'ther is no soche but by some meanes and from some entrauns may be brought unto an odde proportion', he concluded that 'if a man shold addicte himselfe to the serching out of these thinges', then apart from wasting his time 'he shold shut himselfe into soch a mase as hath neither botome to finde, nor yet profite to be reaped by all his curious travaile'. Such endeavours contributed nothing to the stock of edifying godly knowledge, and he concluded the manuscript discussion by reiterating that the real lesson in the fall of kingdoms was the execution of God's wrath upon the nations.

Within a few years of thus narrowly delimiting the Elect use of numbers in this eminently sensible argument, Harrison abandoned his objections to Bodin's impiety in order to utilise his theories. Often such a change represents an aspect of the act of thinking which is beyond historical explanation, but there are other features of Harrison's thought which help to explain his increasing willingness to seek occult meaning in events. In particular his developing interpretation of Christian liberty and his views on the prophecies relating to 1588 seem relevant to this change of mind, and these aspects of his thought are examined below. More immediately, new influences appeared within his intellectual milieu. Harrison may have been encouraged to enter the 'mase' of Bodin's numerology by Abraham Fleming, editor of the 1587 edition of Holinshed's *Chronicles*. Not only did Fleming share Harrison's confidence in God's providential control of all events, but he appears to have been more determined to make the reading public understand the reality of this providential power and accept the gift of Christian liberty which it bestowed on true believers, freeing them from the fear of worldly powers.

A comparison of the two editions of the *Chronicles* confirms that Fleming edited the 1587 *Chronicles* so as to make explicit the historical evidence for Providence, where Holinshed had left the workings of Providence implicit. Holinshed did not ignore Providence, but he did not apply his general and inarticulate belief in God's control of history as precisely as Fleming did, nor did he find an expression of the divine will in the chronological patterns created by the rise and fall of kingdoms.[56] This contrast appears particularly clearly at the end of the *Historie of England* in the *Chronicles*, where Holinshed concludes with a brief note on the four conquests by the Romans, Saxons, Danes and Normans which refers back to his 'preface to the Reader' for an explanation of the significant causes 'in everie of which alterations of the state'. Holinshed's preface, which makes typically bland reading, ascribes the Roman success to faction amongst the British princes, while attributing the eventual fall of the Empire to popular disaffection towards the 'insufferable tiranny' of the Emperors, together with civil discord over the imperial office itself. Not until the pagan Saxons defeat the Christian Britons does he make the point, from Gildas, that 'the wicked sinnes and unthankefulnesse of the inhabitants towardes God' are 'the chiefe occasions and causes of the transmutation of kingdomes'. Even so, in explaining the Norman Conquest he gives prominence to 'the insolent dealings' of the Saxon ruling elite, which alienated the King from his people, although this merely represented God's punishment for 'their sinnes and contempt of his lawes'. Primarily, however, the title to the English crown had been brought into dispute through spite and envy.[57]

In the second edition Fleming replaced Holinshed's conclusion and its emphasis on secondary causes with a much longer 'notable advertisement' on the four conquests, written in 1585, which took pains to establish the duration of each period. Fleming insisted that 'these alterations of regiments be remembred', and referred his readers to 'a notable animadversion in the description of Britaine, pag. 28, 29', that is Harrison's Appendix. Fleming's 'advertisement' demonstrates that he was not simply concerned with the punishment of sin, but with the mysterious aspect of chronological pattern in the successive conquests, which 'teach us that therein the iudgements of God revealed themselves to speciall purposes'.[58]

The Appendix to which Fleming referred differs markedly from Harrison's earlier criticisms of Bodin in the 'Chronology'. Here the boundaries of legitimate investigation into God's mysterious will are less distinct, and involve far more subtle differentiations, which Harrison sometimes found difficult to maintain. Rather than dogmatically refusing further to investigate such matters, Harrison now merely states that Bodin had revived 'an old

---

[56] S. C. Dodson, 'Abraham Fleming, writer and editor', in *Studies in English*, University of Texas, 34 (1955), pp. 51–66; and especially R. M. Benbow, 'The Providential Theory of Historical Causation in *Holinshed's Chronicles* 1577 and 1587', in *Texas Studies in Literature and Language*, I, no. 2 (1959), pp. 264–76, at pp. 265, 267. See A. Fleming, *A treatise of blazing starres* (London, 1618), which emphasises his confidence in Christian liberty.
[57] *Historie of Englande*, in Holinshed's *Chronicles* (1577), p. 289 and the Preface, sigs. 4v and 5r. Parry, 'Harrison and Holinshed', pp. 807–8.
[58] Holinshed's *Chronicles* (1587), p. 202.

kind of arithmancie fathered on Pythagoras, yet never invented by him'. This important distinction reflects Harrison's belief that Pythagoras's works revealed his indebtedness to Hebrew mathematicians, whose true faith directed their scientific investigations.[59] The boundary at which Harrison had previously insisted we must restrain our vain curiosity now becomes the starting point for numerological interpretation. He reiterates that 'we Christians...have not to leane unto these points in any wise as causes: for we know and confesse that all things depend upon providence', yet, by a distinction between cause and effect which in practice became rather blurred, he allowed himself to examine Bodin's theories, 'so long as we use them rather as Indices than Causas mutationum'. This definition epitomised an important contrast in approach, for where Bodin used his numbers six, seven and nine to produce significant periods which he sought to impose upon the historical evidence, Harrison tried to divide known historical periods by these numbers, and consequently felt rather puzzled when history refused to conform to pattern. The point of Harrison's investigations had been succinctly expressed by Bale in the course of his similar endeavours, that 'No man ought in this heavenly work superstitiously to observe the number, but rather to seek diligently to understand the godly mysteries that they comprehend'.[60] In contrast, Bodin's arguments betray his increasingly superstitious attitude to numbers, his weakness for mistaking the means for the end, and although Harrison went some way along that path he retained a fairly clear perception of the point of no return.

Harrison examined two series of events in his Appendix: British history from the Flood to his times, and the course of religion from Christ to the accession of Elizabeth, 'but still protesting in the meane season that I utterlie denie [these numbers] to be any causes, or of themselves to worke any effect at all in these things, as Bodinus would seeme to uphold'. Perhaps he protested too much, for although he felt able to enter the maze only because he saw the flaw in Bodin's reasoning, the very use of these numbers seems to have diminished his consciousness of that error. He became so convinced as to refer his readers to Aristotle's *Politics* and Plato's *Republic* for similar observations on foreign histories, despite his previous scorn for their reliance on second causes. Eventually he felt constrained to explain why a period did not reach the full limit demanded by the theory.

Harrison had no compunctions about using whichever of the three numbers fitted the particular case under investigation. Thus he divided the interval between the Creation and the Flood by nine, that between the Flood and the division of tongues at Babel by seven (being universal these both

---

59 Harrison claimed that Pythagoras's 'divinitie...he brought to perfection by conferens with the Jewes' (TCD MS 165, fo. 96v).
60 Bale, *Image of Both Churches*, ed. Christmas, p. 601.

related to Britain), while he divided the period from thence until the arrival of Samothes in Britain by both nine and seven, although to make them just fit he ended the period with Samothes' promulgation of laws in his second year, which 'maketh much for this purpose'. The majestic symmetry of such calculations helped to suppress any suspicion that this might be devilish knowledge, for 'where shall a man find a more precise period after this method or prescription, for manie and divers considerations' than in the 630 years between the arrival of Brute and the extinction of his posterity, which divided by nine gave the mystically significant number of seventy.[61] Again, forty-eight 'septenaries', or 336 years, had elapsed between the rebellion of Brennus against Beline and the coming of Caesar, 'than the which concurrences I know not how a man should imagine a more exact'. Furthermore, 'these numbers do hold exactlie' in the periods of the Saxons, Danes and Normans.[62]

In his eagerness to emphasise the divine mystery behind these patterns, Harrison not only distorted the evidence but also more revealingly altered information drawn from his 'Chronology'.[63] However, he came nearest to admitting that numbers might be causes in themselves in a reference to the period of Norman rule ending with the accession of Henry II, which Harrison believed had restored the Saxons. This contained eighty-nine years rather than the more exact ninety, but this discrepancy 'is a small thing, sith upon divers occasions the time of the execution of any accident may be prevented or proroged, as in direction and progression astronomicall is often times perceived'. The comparison with astronomical direction suggests the power that Harrison attributed to numbers at that moment, but it also recalls that numerical power, like that of the heavenly bodies, only indirectly reflected that divine providential care which dominated all creation. The planets exercised no power over those who lived in Christian liberty, for the godly appreciated that they merely acted as God's agents, and planets should not be feared as though they enjoyed power in their own right. Harrison's confidence in this liberty even allowed him in his 'Chronology' to advocate a pious, non-demonic astral magic which he held was consistent with Elect knowledge and did not compromise an individual's free election.[64] In the Appendix he placed the same limitations on the force of numbers, for his

[61] *Description* (1587), p. 28. See Patrides, 'Numerology', p. 79, on the significance of 70.
[62] E.g., 'in the 43 novenarie or 387 after the comming of the Saxons, the Danes entered' (*Description* (1587), p. 29). See above, p. 92, *n.* 98.
[63] In TCD MS 165 Dunwallon reigned for only 40 years, not the more convenient 49 (TCD MS 165, fo. 104r; *cf. Description* (1587), p. 29), the time between Brennus and Bellinus and Caesar's arrival, originally 335 years (TCD MS 165, fo. 131r) became 336, while to make the time between Henry II's accession and John's surrender of the kingdom to the Pope more easily divisible, he brought the latter event forward to 1210 from 1213 in the 'Chronology' (ibid., fo. 350v). Bodin treated Roman history similarly (Brown, *The Methodus*, p. 138).
[64] *Description* (1587); p. 28; TCD MS 165, fo. 160r; and see below, pp. 320–3.

application of Bodin's numerology to the changes of religion in Britain concluded 'that if there be anie hidden mysterie or thing conteined in these numbers, yet the same extendeth not unto...the gift of grace and free mercie unto the penitent'. The change in Harrison's attitude to numerological interpretation of history, from fascinated horror to appreciative understanding, reflects the clarity with which he eventually grasped this limitation on the power of numbers.

Despite Harrison's evident enthusiasm in the Appendix, other limitations on numerology prevented him from following Bodin uncritically. Indeed, this discussion does not revolve around questions of intellectual 'influence', for Harrison really only found Bodin's ideas acceptable where he could adapt and apply them within the framework of his pre-existing set of ideas. It is therefore enlightening to see where Harrison openly rejected Bodin's arguments, and also to discover those less obvious points where Bodin's ideas ran counter to Harrison's fundamental beliefs. Both the passage on numerology in Chapter VI of Bodin's *Methodus*, 'Conversiones rerumpublicarum ad numeros collata', and the fuller discussion in the *Republique* (Book IV, chapter ii), listed examples of commonwealths that had perished at the expiry of their divinely predestined periods.[65] Harrison's Appendix shows that he accepted Bodin's dictum that 'God who with wonderfull wisdome hath so couched together the nature of all things, and with certain their numbers, bound together all things to come: to have also within their certaine numbers so shut up and enclosed Commonweales, as that after a certaine period of yeares once past, yet must they needes then perish and take end, although they use never so good lawes and customes'.[66] Since these limiting numbers began with the Creation, however, its precise date had an important role in Bodin's calculations, 'for that it hath great force for the discerning of the ruines of commonweales'. Yet Harrison differed on this vital radix, and following Gerardus Mercator began his 'supputacions of the yeres of the worlde' with the first moment of the astrological sign Leo, while Bodin specifically rejected Mercator's calculations and concluded that the world had been created in September.[67]

Bodin's approach also contravened Harrison's delimitation of legitimate knowledge in another fundamental and revealing way. Harrison accepted empirical evidence that commonwealths altered about every 430 years, 'but if it come to 500 or 530 it is one of the rarest things that happeneth in the world'.[68] Historical experience provided Harrison with a rule of thumb, but

---

[65] Note that the deterministic fatalism about celestial influences in the *Methodus* (tr. Reynolds, p. 226), is moderated in the *Republique* (tr. as *Commonweale* and ed. McRae, p. 438).
[66] Ibid., p. 457.
[67] Ibid., p. 439; TCD MS 165, fo. 1r; *cf. Method*, tr. Reynolds, p. 325.
[68] TCD MS 165, fos. 65v–66r.

Bodin found this unsatisfying and wanted instead to apply a 'scientific' law which would have general, if not universal validity. We have seen that Harrison deplored Bodin's arrogant attitude towards ancient authorities. Amongst other numbers Bodin settled on 496, which 'consists of the number of Daniel, which becomes a perfect number by the addition of the perfect number six'. 'This quantity', announced Bodin, 'is the one which the ancients meant to indicate when they said that the cycle of empires is five hundred yeares', a challenge to experience and received wisdom which insisted that 'they had no skill in these matters', for five hundred was neither a perfect nor a square number, nor derived from nine or seven, and therefore inapplicable to human or natural cycles. Already Bodin's devotion to numerological systems appears to outstrip Harrison's. Apart from the weight of historical evidence against Bodin, Harrison could hardly concede imperfections in Daniel's prophesied seventy weeks, interpreted as the 490 years between his prophecy and Christ.[69] Essentially Bodin wanted to trim history to fit his theoretical framework, while Harrison remained content to let history delimit periods which could be searched for internal numerical mysteries. He did not insist that Henry II had acceded a year too soon, for such speculations implied rebellion against the divine ordinance.

Bodin's obsession with his numerological system appears most tellingly at the very moment when he acknowledges God's power to rearrange events 'at will, and sometimes arbitrarily', for he chose the example of the Flood, which at God's command 'gathered sooner [in 1656 AM] than in the order of nature the great number could have been completed'. Bodin considered that Platonic Great Number, 1728 or the cube of twelve, fatal to all states, for none had exceeded it. While Harrison accepted that God had shortened the time before the Flood for the Elect's sake, thus typologically foreshadowing the second destruction of the unregenerate, no Scriptural warrant existed for the idea that God had originally predetermined that the Flood would occur in 1728 AM. In Bodin's view this proved 'that God is bound by no number'.[70] From Harrison's standpoint Bodin's fixation on the Great Number limited God's will and introduced dangerous speculation about matters which God had seen fit to hide from human reason. Harrison avoided the impiety of using this rationalist method of discerning the divine will, and confined himself to seeking the will of God as revealed in known historical events.[71] In contrast, Bodin proudly boasted that his numerological system could accurately prophesy the future, that those with sufficient leisure could study the pattern of past changes and learn 'to prophesy more truly

---

[69] *Method*, tr. Reynolds, p. 299. Bodin's *Republique* (tr. as *Commonweale*, ed. McRae, pp. 462–3) was more respectful towards antiquity. On Harrison and Daniel's works, see above, pp. 74–6, 98.

[70] *Method*, tr. Reynolds, p. 236.   [71] TCD MS 165, fo. 9v.

and better those to come (although known to God alone)', than by astrological guesswork. Bodin later attempted to predict the course of French politics according to his numerological patterns, while as we have seen Harrison's belief in God's immutable justice led him to prophesy that events in France would follow an historically based pattern of usurpation.[72]

Yet this important disagreement did not prevent Harrison from delighting in the precise correlation between the periods of kingdoms and the completion of the Platonic Great Number where that phenomenon helped human reason to some limited perception of God's precise control of historical events. Therefore although he would not alter the predestined order of time to make it conform to *a priori* numerological theories, where the evidence allowed Harrison went further than Bodin in emphasising the force of Platonic numbers. Like most chronologers, Harrison counted 1728 years from the foundation of the 'Assyrian' monarchy by Ninus to its collapse with Alexander's victory at Arbela. Bodin considered that Alexander's victory 'completed this number to a nicety', and cited in support Philo Judaeus and 'all the learned' including Melanchthon, but without mentioning Plato.[73] Harrison explicitly described Alexander's victory as 'the conversion of which Plato speaketh de Rep. Lib. 8 sub initio', the cube of twelve 'is the time of the continuauns of this monarchy...an observation worthily to be noted because it conteineth so exact a confirmation of the time here alledged'. Where divinely predestined historical events apparently confirmed that Plato's number contained hidden divine meaning, then Harrison willingly acknowledged the mysterious import of chronological pattern, for here the *a priori* criteria emerged from God's revealed will, not the Platonic Great Number.[74]

Bodin's concentration on numerological systems led him to apply this pattern where Harrison could not. Not only did Bodin transgress the boundaries of legitimate knowledge as Harrison perceived them, but also he attempted to subordinate the history of the True Church to the limiting power of the Great Number. Philo Judaeus had counted 1717 years from the Flood to the destruction of Solomon's Temple, but Bodin thought that eleven years should be added to this total, so that the result would make the cube of twelve. He argued 'both from the truth of history and from the excellence of the great number itself', but there seems little doubt which carried most weight for him.[75] Certainly Harrison had no doubts, for he

---

[72] *Method*, tr. Reynolds, p. 232; and Baldwin, 'Bodin and the League', p. 176; *cf.* TCD MS 165, fo. 244v.

[73] *Method*, tr. Reynolds, p. 227; *cf. Republique* (tr. as *Commonweale*, ed. McRae, p. 463).

[74] TCD MS 165, fos. 18r–v.

[75] *Method*, tr. Reynolds, p. 227. Reynolds's Introduction tries to explain away Bodin's deterministic numerology, insisting that 'he dismissed as erroneous Plato's belief that the ruin of a state is brought about by mathematical forces', yet admitting that Bodin allowed no empire to last longer than 1728 years and had produced a long list of illustrations, fiddling the figures

noted that Marsilius Ficino, the leading populariser of Hermetic number manipulation, had made the same claim. Harrison found the clearest evidence of God's character in His dealings with His chosen people, and he would have none of Bodin's attempt to apply rational and profane criteria to the unique history of the True Church. In his 'Chronology' he coolly dismissed 'some, who intreating of the conversion of Emperes do recon 1728 yeres from [the Flood] to the overthrow of the Jewish commonwealth', but in fact only 1706 years had elapsed. Harrison attributed special importance to Israel's uniquely direct experience of God's care, where, as in the Church generally, 'the gift of grace and free mercie' was not bound by numerological patterns. The Scriptures provided the *a priori* criteria by which all knowledge could be assessed, and that process could never be reversed.[76]

The care with which Harrison distinguished between the proper and improper uses of numerology further testifies to the importance which he attached to the proper understanding of chronological patterns. His willingness to adopt and apply Bodin's numerology within strict limits also partly reflects his mystical approach to history. However, while Harrison personally found mysterious forces a sufficient explanation of the past, proper historical explanation demands that we do not rely on occult causes but must attempt to solve the mystery of his change of mind, and seek explanations beyond Abraham Fleming's personal influence. Essentially we are confronted by the central problem of Harrison's criteria of true and false prophecy, of proper and improper explanations of past, present and future. His attempt to understand the present under the tutelage of the covenant line was perhaps the most important source of these criteria, for his sense of connection with the line of Elect prophets fundamentally depended upon his ability to perceive present social and economic dislocations in their terms. Like the Old Testament prophets, Harrison continually pondered the prophetic meaning of all aspects of his contemporary world. Some of his contemporaries failed to see this universal significance in present actions or deliberately tried to minimise that significance; others needed to experience dramatic and portentous events before they achieved a similar prophetic insight. Harrison seems to have lived on this higher plane of prophetic excitement even amongst the most mundane happenings. This heightened sensitivity consequently made him more receptive to apparently dubious prophecies which echoed what he considered to be the Elect interpretation of the present, thus enabling him to justify his partial acceptance of what some contemporaries insisted were non-canonical prophecies.

where necessary. Reynolds also claimed that Bodin used the biblical account where authorities differed (ibid., pp. xix–xx), but here Bodin refused to be bound by the Scriptures.

[76] For example, Bodin held that the Egyptians and Chaldeans taught Israel mathematics (*Republique* (*Commonweale*), ed. McRae, p. 438), but Harrison claimed that this only revived 'those observations which the Patriarchs had left' (TCD MS 165, fo. 7v).

This historical dimension underlying Harrison's interpretation of contemporary England, which helped to establish his criteria for true prophecy, emerges most clearly in contrast with William Perkins's poised, logical and detached analysis of true and false prophecy, which enabled Perkins to reject 'the prophesies of Merlin...the prophesies of those that tearme themselves Elias...Anabaptisticall revelations...dreames...these flying tales of the second comming of Christ', as well as the 1588 prophecy.[77] Perkins directed his criticisms at over-enthusiastic contemporary prophets and tried to limit the encroachments of their deluded carnal reason on God's hidden and mysterious will. Perkins identified carnal reason as the fundamental characteristic of Satan's parody of the True Church, and emphasised its utter opposition to the unchanging inspired doctrine transmitted by the covenant line. Perkins assessed contemporary behaviour according to this dualistic model, so that a merely 'civil conversation' was insufficient for salvation, only obedience to the Scriptures offered an alternative to perpetual decline, and Perkins believed that he perpetuated Elect doctrine. Yet while Perkins, like Harrison, discerned ethical norms in the Scriptural picture of the Christian community, his temperament disposed him to accept only a small corpus of true prophecy, which would not 'make disquietnesse in the Church and Commonwealth'.[78] Thus, although Perkins is often uncritically described as relying exclusively on the Bible, his fear of socially disruptive prophecies prevented him from aligning his criteria of true prophecy according to the godly models provided by Scriptural prophets. Instead he framed logical criteria which effectively (though not deliberately) ruled out many Scriptural prophets whose example Harrison found relevant to later times.[79] Therefore, in comparison with Harrison, Perkins displayed a relatively weak sense of connection between past and present; his definition of true prophecy derived little inspiration from the history of the True Church and allowed it only strictly limited influence on the present.

When compared with Harrison's views, Perkins's caution dangerously resembles that of those false prophets who allowed their audience to luxuriate in secure enjoyment of the present. Harrison envisaged a Church in which the members of the covenant line distinguished themselves, and were able to distinguish each other throughout time, by their refusal to pander to contemporary prejudices and their determination to reiterate the message of history and to suffer the consequences.[80] Perkins established a different standard by excluding certain types of prophets through a logical process of

---

[77] Perkins, *Of the ende of the worlde* (1587), in *Workes* (1631), iii, 2nd pagination, pp. 468, 469.
[78] I. Breward, *The Work of William Perkins* (Appleford, 1970), pp. 32–60, 88–9; and *Workes* (1631), iii, 2nd pagination, p. 468.
[79] This contrast had wider consequences for their views on Church reforms, see below, pp. 196–7.
[80] See above, pp. 31–4.

elimination, which essentially assumed that only wise old men well-versed in canonical Scriptures (that is, learned Cambridge divines) could prophesy in general terms about the Church. In effect their prophecy would be the product of reasoning conditioned by long study of the Word, but Harrison accepted the very different criteria provided by the concrete historical examples of spiritual illumination. These did not always coincide with Perkins's academic categories.[81] Unlike Perkins, Harrison could not bring himself to reject some prophets simply because of their obscure speech, especially if he found their prophecies agreed with his own chronology. In more direct contrast with the Scriptures, Perkins believed that Satan prevailed most in the weakest sort and therefore denied that any woman could be a true prophet. Harrison found at least five female prophets mentioned in the Scriptures including Olda, who 'notwithstanding that divers Prophetes lived in her time was singularly indued with the gift of prophecie', and was consulted by the King of Judah and the High Priest on the Book of the Law.[82] In Harrison's thinking this example powerfully supported the authority of Catherine of Sienna, who was further excluded by Perkins's rule that notorious vice in the prophet vitiated the prophecy. Aware of the frequent unworthiness of the recipients of divine illumination, Harrison minimised Catherine's alleged immorality and held it immaterial 'by what spirite she shold prophecie sins god often times even by the wicked (as we see in Balaam) doth manifestly revele his holy will and purpose'. Catherine's congruence with the general criteria established by the Scriptures in Balaam's example persuaded Harrison to accept her prophecies, but even more importantly her alignment with Scriptural criteria appeared in her criticism of contemporary laity and clergy and her description of the glorious reformation to come 'which in mine opinion is not to be omitted and passed over in scilens'.[83]

The contrast between Harrison's and Perkins's definitions of true prophecy underlines the need to recognise the influence of character and environment upon the individual Protestant response to the Scriptures. Harrison did not share Perkins's desire to temper prophetic enthusiasm with some awareness of contemporary political and social reality. Consequently, while Perkins's ideal prophet stood as a type of spiritualised worldly perfection, and his

---

[81] Common ground remained: both rejected 4 Esdras in support of Elias (TCD MS 165, fo. 191r (cf. Perkins, *Workes* (1631), iii, 2nd pagination, p. 469)), but crucially, while both made chronology the test of Elias's canonicity, Perkins showed that chronology did not obey his prophecy as Harrison believed (ibid., p. 469; cf.TCD MS 165, fo. 22v).

[82] Ibid., fo. 324r, on Thomas of Erceldoune, and ibid., fo. 90r; cf. Perkins, *Workes*, p. 468. One could argue that Joachim of Fiore fitted Perkins's categories – see the description of Joachim in Southern, 'Aspects 3: History and Prophecy', pp. 173–4.

[83] TCD MS 165, fo. 343v, although generally he agreed that 'you shall seldome see a good spirite appere in the likenesse of a woman nor an ill in the similitude of a man' (ibid., fo. 86v).

prophecy a product of sustained intellectual endeavour, Harrison's greater detachment from contemporary reality prevented him from limiting the divine choice. He only had to contemplate the examples in the covenant line to find different categories set out in the Scriptures. The wilder prophecies troubled Harrison less than they did the austere, scholarly Perkins because the covenant line had never enjoyed the settled circumstances and complete orthodoxy upon which Perkins insisted. His assumption that the Elect could attain doctrinal purity reflects the growing self-confidence of established Protestantism, but Harrison was more nervously aware that even the members of the covenant line after Christ, for all their trenchant criticisms of Antichrist, espoused suspect doctrines and 'clogged the lordes people with frutelesse and unnecessary ceremonies'.[84] Again Harrison appears much closer to the earlier generation represented by Bale, who also denied that prophecy could be deduced through a form of scholastic exercise and derided those who 'think that they can of their own wit and industry declare such causes, unless God openeth unto them by his word or some evident sign, as he hath done in this age most plenteously to many'. Naturally Perkins insisted that he subordinated reason to revelation, but reason had a larger part to play in determining his criteria of true prophecy than he acknowledged, and he gave less room to illumination.[85] Two different appreciations of the impact of spiritual forces on human thought processes can be seen in Perkins's assertion that the mentally ill could not prophesy truly, and Harrison's observation that madness 'worketh not upon the godly after their visions' but resulted from the visitations of evil spirits.[86]

Perkins required an external standard of holiness which, while firmly based on the true faith, appears superfluous in the light of Harrison's belief that Satan's distorted parody of true religion often manifested itself in hypocritical external holiness. This external formalism could even outdo the covenant line, where 'All was not without superstition, though they lived in much pureness of life', as Bale conceded. Harrison discovered in the covenant line's faith in Christ a more essential criterion for assessing true prophecies. For example, this demonstrated that the outwardly holy Appollonius of Tyre had received instantaneous revelation about Domitian's death from an evil spirit, since Appollonius 'wanted faith in Jesus Christ, and surely I am persuaded that he was an instrument set up by Sathan, the comon enemy of the regenerate, onely to deface the preaching of the gospell and workes of our Messias'. For his holiness so impressed some contemporaries

---

84 Perkins, *Workes*, p. 468; TCD MS 165, fo. 71r. Harrison's former popery no doubt gave to this added personal significance.

85 Bale, *Image of Both Churches*, ed. Christmas, p. 372; Breward, *Perkins*, pp. 37–40, 48–9, acknowledges that reason played a larger part in Perkins's thought than he himself believed.

86 In Perkins's thought the diseased intellect produces the prophecy, in Harrison the disease reflects the source of the prophecy (Perkins, *Workes*, p. 468; TCD MS 165, fo. 86v).

that they 'were not abashed to preferre him moch lesse to compare him with our saviour and redeemer'.[87] By shifting his focus from external social behaviour to inner spiritual illumination, Harrison achieved a more subtle appreciation of the Scriptural criteria of true prophecy than did Perkins, whose blanket rejection of any prophecy that contradicted the Word 'or any circumstance of it' also acknowledged the force of contemporary circumstances.[88] Harrison adjudged Appollonius a false prophet because as Satan's instrument he failed to see Christ's ministry in the proper context of prophesied history. False prophecy established false history and blurred the distinction between the Two Churches, attempting to reduce the prophetic significance of the present by tempting men away from the true faith through worldly prosperity.[89]

The individual's perception of the relationship between past and present, and the conformity of any prophetic historical interpretation to that perception, drew the dividing line between true and false prophecy, between the correct and incorrect interpretation of past, present and future. Therefore Harrison could redefine that dividing line when he encountered prophecies about the year 1588 which enhanced his already well-developed receptiveness towards mystical interpretations of time. This new element in his thought in turn helped him to accommodate Bodin's numerology within the boundaries of legitimate knowledge, sometime between 1576 and 1585, in the way discussed above. The 1588 prophecies, which John Harvey complained were 'now so rife in every mannes mouth', appeared so compelling to Harrison that he rewrote parts of his *Description* to illustrate their contemporary significance and deliberately arranged the second version of his 'Chronology' in order to put them on a par with canonical prophecies in their influence on history and chronology. This lost second version of the 'Chronology' filled three volumes, the last 'containing the periode of time from the comming of the Normans until the year of expectation which is of grace 1588 expired, wherein the age of the world runneth all by fire'.[90] These excitedly confused images reflected the fact that Harrison followed the most

---

87 Bale, *Image of Both Churches*, ed. Christmas, p. 347. As with Nimrod and Enoch, Appollonius and Christ revealed that the Church of Cain was only a satanic parody of the True Church, Appollonius himself being 'forged by the Devell to steine the doinges of christ', with whom he was favourably compared (TCD MS 165, fos. 144r, 301r).

88 Perkins, *Workes*, p. 468.

89 Satan published a false prophecy to end the persecution of Christianity and achieve by worldly blandishments what he had failed to do by bloodshed, argued Harrison (TCD MS 165, fo. 145r). Bale also saw that the decline of the True Church had begun with the end of persecution and the loss of the prophetic sense that this world was only a temporary phenomenon (*Image of Both Churches*, ed. Christmas, pp. 316, 319–20).

90 *Harrison's Description*, ed. Furnivall, iv, Appendix I, p.xlvii. This second version of the 'Chronology' was at one time in Derry Diocesan Library, but is now lost. R. Harvey, *An astrologicall discourse upon the great and notable coniunction* (H. Bynneman: London, 1583), p. 44.

fervent interpretations of this warning. Kasper Brusch had first prophesied catastrophe for 1588 in verses published in 1553. Brusch enhanced their authority by ascribing them to the famous mystic and mathematician Johannes Regiomontanus; Cyprian Leovitius later paraphrased and widely disseminated them. Harrison quoted both versions on the title page of the Derry 'Chronology', but gave even greater authority to the prophecy than had Brusch, claiming 'these verses [were] written in older times, and brought to light by ' Regiomontanus.[91]

Richard Harvey had made the same claims in his *Astrologicall discourse* (1583), which had excited interest in the 1588 prophecy by associating it with a sinister conjunction of Saturn and Jupiter predicted for 28 April 1583. Harvey promised catastrophes leading to the End about 1588, in itself not an astrologically significant year.[92] Opponents of the prophecy included the prominent and respected academics William Fulke and William Perkins, who attacked it as blatantly non-canonical and possibly devilish. In the event, 1583 failed to meet expectations, merely providing easy meat for Perkins in his *Foure Great Lyers* (1583). Yet its vagueness enabled the tradition to survive, despite disparaging comparisons with the prophecies of Merlin and Elias.[93]

Indeed not every evangelical figure expressed dismay at such connections. Supporters of the prophecy drew comfort from the interest displayed in many non-canonical prophecies by the charismatic John Foxe. Like Harrison, Foxe included Sibyl, Merlin and much other medieval divination in the canon of true prophecy. Recent attempts to consign the enthusiasm of men like Foxe and Harrison to 'less strict theological circles', and to prefer the intellectual rigour of academic theologians who disparaged such prophecies, overlooks the fact that these non-university commentators systematically analysed all such prophecies according to Scriptural criteria.[94] It might be more profitable to abandon our twentieth-century preoccupation with rational distinctions between canonical and non-canonical prophecies, and instead to concentrate on the fact that men like Harrison believed that they were proceeding on the basis not of rational but Scriptural criteria, for, as we have seen, Perkins gave reason a greater role in determining true

---

[91] Bauckham, *Tudor Apocalypse*, pp. 168–77, on the debate over this prophecy. See also Firth, *Apocalyptic Tradition*, pp. 151–2. *Harrison's Description*, ed. Furnivall, iv, Appendix I, p. xlvii. Geveren, *Of the ende of this worlde* (1577), fos. 15r–v, gives an English version of Leovitius's prediction for 1588.

[92] Harvey, *Astrologicall discourse*, pp. 44–5 and *passim*. Bauckham, *Tudor Apocalypse*, p. 168, claims that Harvey translated the prophecy in his *Discourse*, but he did not (*Astrologicall discourse*, p. 45).

[93] Perkins, *Of the end of the worlde* (1587), in *Workes* (1631), iii, 2nd pagination, pp. 468–9. See below pp. 134–7 on Merlin.

[94] Bauckham, *Tudor Apocalypse*, p. 169. Such categories can be too rigid – where does Harrison's rejection of the apocalyptic prophecies in 4 Esdras leave him? (see above, p. 123, *n*. 81).

prophecy than did Harrison. Perkins certainly appears more theologically rigorous to us, but one could argue that Harrison's use of dubious prophecies was in sixteenth-century terms more thoroughly Scriptural, in that he took less notice of contemporary social and political *mores*. Such an approach not only informed Foxe's and Harrison's radical outlook but allowed them to see how contemporary events fitted into a universal framework. For what Foxe discerned in the sufferings graphically depicted in his *Actes and Monuments*, Harrison discovered in the less dramatic but far more wide-ranging social upheavals lamented in his *Description*.

These social changes partly explain the transition in Harrison's thought which allowed him to accept the 1588 prophecy, to utilise Bodin's numerology and perhaps also to change his mind about Elias. In their turn such disturbing historical patterns helped to make him more sensitive to the prophetic significance of contemporary changes. More obvious facts also predisposed him to accept the 1588 prophecy, especially that cosmology and true prophecy combined to mutually enhance each other's importance. The conjunction of the superior planets in 1583 paralleled a similar conjunction five years and 320 days before Christ's nativity.[95] This cosmic parallel suggested that the second Advent would occur in 1588. Harrison accepted this use of judicial astrology only because it conformed to the Revelation of John. Indeed, astrology remained 'one of the good giftes of god' only so long as its predictions confirmed God's will revealed in Scriptural prophecy. The destruction promised to false prophets in Jer. 14.13–15 taught a universal lesson against the 'impudent audacitie' of those astrologers who 'preferre the second causes' and dare to contradict canonical prophecies. Astrology could interpret the real effects of the heavens only as 'the handywork of god'.[96] The heavens could direct worldly events only in accordance with God's prior determination, they could only promote the fulfilment of Scriptural prophecies. Thus Harrison dismissed Cyprian Leovitius' sinister interpretation of a great conjunction in AD 293 because the Elect had been liberated from fear of the threatening heavens, since God had revealed His will in the Scriptures and removed the need to 'seeke for thexecution of the purpose of god out of the heavens and sterres'.[97] Consequently Harrison accepted Leovitius' prediction that the 1583 conjunction would make 1588 a climactic year only because it chimed with apocalyptic prophecies of global destruction by fire. The 1588 prophecy by its agreement with the Scriptural projection of history and its connection

---

[95] TCD MS 165, fo. 135v. Harrison dated the conjunction at 14 February, 5 BC, so that the Incarnation occurred on 31 December, AD 1, a year later than the Church generally held (ibid., fo. 136r).

[96] Ibid., fo. 90v.

[97] It was senseless for astrologers to 'set up their observations against the purpose of the first declared by his word' (ibid., fo. 91v); ibid., fo. 160r.

with cosmological observations thus confirmed its place in the unbroken stream of true prophecy since the Creation. This explains Harrison's insistence that the 1588 prophecy had existed long before Regiomontanus published it. Once again he equated eternal true doctrine with the correct interpretation of past and present.

However, Harrison also approached the 1588 prophecy in the context of two contemporary occurrences which assumed major importance for him – the increasing threat of Spanish invasion, and rising rural unemployment. While we can assess these phenomena separately and objectively, Harrison perceived them within an apocalyptic framework which demonstrated their related importance throughout history, and which therefore linked them together in Harrison's prophetic assessment of the contemporary English commonwealth. That framework increased Harrison's prophetic awareness of the dangers inherent in both the external threat of antichristian Spain and the internal threat of economic imbalances. The 1588 prophecy further contributed to Harrison's generally heightened sensitivity about apocalyptic threats, and thus confirmed its own authority while encouraging his subjective interpretation of Elizabethan England in the 1580s. Once he had applied this prophetic yardstick, he could see only one correct course of action against Satan – that which the Scriptures provided. Important changes in the *Description* between the editions of 1577 and 1587 demonstrate Harrison's developing recognition of this antichristian subversion at work in England.

In 1577 a chapter 'Of Provision made for the Poor' discussed the problem of those made 'idle beggars' by enclosures, as distinct from those 'sturdy beggars' whom the Word condemned. The area around Radwinter experienced enclosure 'even in the time of our most gracious and sovereigne Ladie Elizabeth' according to Harrison, considerably later than the rest of Essex. Seeing the process actually under way in his own locality perhaps deepened Harrison's appreciation of its evils.[98] The central question concerned whether enclosures caused depopulation, or whether they reflected the pressure of a growing population on nearly static resources. Promoters of overseas colonising ventures and their courtly patrons, including Harrison's scholarly acquaintance Sir Thomas Smith, insisted that England's population had outstripped her resources.[99] Objectively this seems nearer the truth, but we shall see that Harrison demanded that the evidence be read through a Scriptural model, which proved to his satisfaction that when individuals

---

[98] *Description* (1577), fo. 106v; (1587), p. 112; H. L. Gray, *English Field Systems* (1915; repr. London, 1949), pp. 389–93, on local geological conditions around Radwinter which favoured enclosure; and see below pp. 279–89.

[99] D. B. Quinn, 'Sir Thomas Smith (1513–77) and the beginnings of English Colonial Theory', in *Proceedings of the American Philosophical Society*, 89 (1945), pp. 543–60, at p. 552; A. L. Rowse, *The Expansion of Elizabethan England* (London, 1955), pp. 136, 138–9.

followed their economic self-interest, as had enclosers, the population inevitably dwindled. This model had wider significance, as Harrison revealed in a paragraph added to the *Description* in the 1580s. Then he not only pitied the plight of those made 'idle' by enclosures, but also like an Old Testament prophet pointed to the fate awaiting those who blithely aquiesced in contemporary evils and who failed to see that Elizabethan enclosures fitted a prophetic historical pattern, in which nations depopulated by unbridled, self-interested economic enterprise fell easy prey to their enemies. Indeed, 'this misfortune hath not only happened unto our isle and nation but unto most of the famous countries of the world heretofore, and all by the greedy desire of such as would live alone and only to themselves'. Yet many refused to accept that Elizabethan enclosures fitted this prophetic historical pattern, for 'in some men's judgements these things are but trifles and not worthy the regarding', and consequently they 'grudge at the great increase of people in these days, thinking a necessary brood of cattle far better than a superfluous augmentation of mankind'. Such arguments merely reflected the kind of natural reason against which the covenant line had always preached.[100]

Yet in the 1580s England faced the most horrible foe of all – Antichrist acting through Spanish power. Therefore Harrison discerned two aspects to the need for increasing the population – first to increase the power of the Sword which would defend England against Spain, and secondly to evangelise as widely as possible through the Word, which alone could go on to the offensive against Antichrist. Both aspects required that instead of pursuing present economic gains, self-interested individuals should act in obedience to God's plan for mankind. Harrison perceived that plan in much the same terms as Jeremiah had preached to Israel in exile, and as Paul had written to the Ephesians. Harrison epitomised the devout Protestant understanding of the present as both a continuation of the past and a contribution to the future when he stressed with Jeremiah and Paul that the true believers in their godly actions constituted the living stones of Christ's spiritual Temple. For when conducted properly their lives would fulfil God's will and build up the True Church's defences against Antichrist. History properly understood revealed that as many human beings as possible should strive to emulate the godly actions of 'men of like condition' portrayed in the Scriptures.[101] In the social and economic conditions of Elizabethan

---

[100] *Description* (1587), pp. 193, 183. Harrison believed that manorial records would provide the statistics to back him up – a notable advance in argument since Latimer's sermons; he provided some general statistical evidence in ibid., pp. 192–3, 205.

[101] George Withers, Harrison's archdeacon and friend, pointed out that the dead 'cannot praise God, nor declare his name, nor the great thinges which he hath done for them to the sonnes of men...for to that end is their life given them' (*An ABC*, sig. D5r). Note Withers's emphasis on God's intervention in history, and see Coolidge, *Pauline Renaissance*, pp. 27–30, 36, on the living Temple.

England such notions might appear to be unworldly 'commonwealth' and Puritan fantasies, but Harrison's apocalyptic vision of the godly commonwealth allowed no compromise when he believed that England's population was declining. As for those who complained of over-population, 'I can liken such men best of all unto the Pope and the devil, who practice the hindrance of the furniture of the number of the elect to their uttermost', to maintain papal authority and to defer 'the locking up of the other in everlasting chains'.[102]

This eternal truth found particular expression in England's worsening plight in the 1580s, for, in the likely event of foreign invasion, those who now condemned the swarms of beggars 'should find that a wall of men is far better than stacks of corn and bags of money and complain of the want when it is too late to seek remedy'.[103] Harrison's 'Chronology' repeatedly laboured this traditional point, that a large population provided the best defence for a commonwealth. Yet in the 1580s this historical truism achieved new status for Harrison as part of an apocalyptic framework, and this emotionally charged atmosphere in turn gave greater authority to utterances such as the 1588 prophecy. This complex realignment in Harrison's thought also made Bodin's numerology more acceptable in the 1580s, and perhaps explains his changed attitude to Elias, for when the most mundane phenomena acquired prophetic significance such mysterious teachings achieved new relevance.

A similar but more belated and abrupt transition can be seen in William Fulke's thought in the 1580s. Only after the defeat of the Armada, when as Harrison put it, 'God himself...fighting for us' struck a blow for His Church, did Fulke abandon his previous opposition to extra-biblical divination. The climactic events of 1588 persuaded him to utilise dramatic prophecies to understand contemporary events, as Harrison had done since at least the early 1580s.[104] Harrison may have been more exposed than an academic like Fulke to the realities of rural employment, and more aware of the inadequate preparations against invasion. This context helped to intensify his already well-developed ability to 'historicise' the present, surely an accident of temperament compounded by his learning. For even before the Armada, Harrison appears to have been intensely conscious that the present was not independent of a 'dead' past, while it took the totally unexpected English victory really to bring this home to Fulke. Therefore perhaps not degrees of intellectual rigour but difference of temperament separated Fulke and Harrison before 1588. Nor did Harrison's acceptance of

---

[102] *Description* (1587), p. 183. This explains Harrison's obsession with the dolorous consequences of monasticism and clerical celibacy, above, pp. 90–2.

[103] *Description* (1587), p. 183; and ibid., p. 194, on Harrison's fears about England's defences.

[104] *Harrison's Description*, ed. Furnivall, iv, Appendix I, pp. lviii–lx; *cf.* Bauckham, *Tudor Apocalypse*, pp. 173–4.

the prophecies of Sibyl and Merlin, the sort of extra-biblical divination which Fulke originally rejected, reflect a less evangelical outlook. On the contrary, Harrison's judicious treatment of those utterances only emphasises his commitment to the covenant line and its doctrines, and demonstrates that that commitment provided a viable alternative to both uncritical acceptance and dogmatic rejection of non-Scriptural prophecies.

As early as the 1570s, Harrison accepted certain parts of the non-canonical prophecies attributed to Sibyl and to Merlin, because he considered that those parts conformed to the doctrines transmitted by the covenant line and recorded in the Scriptures. Therefore we need to distinguish between Harrison's approach and the views of those who wholeheartedly accepted Sibyl and Merlin as well as those who routinely condemned them. He found truth in those parts of the prophecies which reiterated Elect doctrines and which consequently revealed some of the true historical sequence and correct chronology. He saw these prophecies as specific but complex examples of that general historical pattern in which truth originally, completely and purely revealed to the Elect, was corrupted by the unfaithful Gentiles, but where careful comparison with Elect teachings often revealed some remnant of true knowledge.

In the sixteenth century, the corpus of Sibylline writings consisted of an eclectic mixture of pagan and Christian enigmatic divination, greatly indebted to Hellenic Judaism. Scholars erroneously identified it with the classical Sibyls, although it had been created in the late fourth century AD, when Christianity was already the official religion of the Empire. Therefore the Sibylline prophecies put the life of Christ in an eschatological context, and this apparent 'prediction' excused for otherwise intelligent commentators the Sibylline prophecies' ludicrous, eclectic conflation of heterodox and orthodox data. Originally the prophecies had attempted to relate the triumph of Constantine and Christianity to their eschatology, but their vague eclecticism allowed constant reinterpretation to match historical developments. This reinterpretation developed in two different directions, neither of which Harrison found congenial. First, medieval scholars, ambitious to integrate Hebraeo-Christian and pagan learning, insisted that the Sibyls (in their classical guise) echoed rational scriptural precepts and confirmed the unity of Creation at work in history. Harrison discerned no break in the chain of revelation, while the very narrowness of the covenant line demonstrated its uniqueness as a source of saving knowledge.[105] Secondly, sophisticated and cultured humanists, who ruthlessly exposed the

---

[105] P. J. Alexander, *The Oracle of Baalbek, The Tiburtine Sibyl in Greek Dress*, Dumbarton Oaks Studies, X (Washington, D.C., 1967), pp. 136–41; Southern, 'Aspects 3: History as Prophecy', pp. 166–7. Southern argued that Sibyl enlarged 'the otherwise intolerable narrowness of the stream of salvation', but for Harrison its very narrowness proved the truth of that way to salvation.

crudity of much medieval divination, were originally impressed by the Sibyls' classical connotations, and then in the case of Sebastian Castellio came to see the Sibylline corpus as the key to a golden future.

Like other prophetic exegetes, Harrison used Sebastian Castellio's 1555 Latin edition of the Sibylline oracles; his copy contains detailed marginalia on their predictions.[106] Castellio published the Sibylline Oracles as part of his programme of reform, an ecstatic vision of a *renovatio mundi*, hovering somewhere between Protestantism and Catholicism, and deeply indebted to current Hermeticism. Like that other product of late humanism, Guillaume Postel, Castellio sought the original germ of truth in all knowledge, which would help man to regain by his own intellect the lost golden age. The oracles' dubious numerological predictions further encouraged the Hermetic fixation on Pythagorean and Cabalistic number manipulation as a lever on cosmic powers. Harrison clearly disagreed with the Hermetic overtones of this approach, stressing that Castellio's 'learned annotations' on the Sibyls drew different conclusions from his own.[107] Harrison's sharp distinction between those parts of the Oracles that reiterated the true knowledge confined to the covenant line, and those that reflected the distorted inventions of the Gentiles, enabled him to avoid both the medieval and the humanist traditions.[108]

Indeed, only Harrison's commitment to finding this primal Elect revelation in the Sibylline Oracles prevented him from accepting evidence that pointed to the modern view of them as 'rather an enigmatic report of thinges passed than a direct foreshowinge of that which is to come'.[109] Yet although 'I am persuaded that I shold do them great injury if I did not yelde that reverens unto them that by right is due unto workes of soche antiquitie', and he knew that his doctrinal test partly contravened the accepted view, 'neverthelesse herein I must yet show mine opinion'. Therefore while his argument led him away from the modern interpretation it also forced him to reject much

[106] In *Orthodoxographia Theologiae sacrosanctae ac syncerioris fidei Doctores numere LXXXVI ecclesiae columina luminaeque clarissima* (Basle, 1555). Harrison's copy, now Derry shelf-mark A.i.g.2, acquired in 1571, contains his identifications of the succession of Roman emperors prophesied by Sibyl (pp. 1468–1522, esp. p. 1497). Alexander, *Tiburtine Sibyl*, p. 3, unaccountably claims that the prophecies were first published in 1563.

[107] TCD MS 165, fo. 5v. Postel's syncretist approach attempted to restore human knowledge to its primitive pristine state while minimising the Fall (W. J. Bouwsma, *Concordia Mundi: The Career and Thought of Guillaume Postel (1510–81)* (Cambridge, Mass., 1957), pp. 252–3). See Firth, *Apocalyptic Tradition*, pp. 147–8, on Castellio and Postel, and TCD MS 165, fo. 4r, for Harrison's use of Postel's work.

[108] Postel and Castellio regarded the truth which they discovered in the Sibyls as proof that all religions contained some true divine knowledge, which could therefore be conflated to achieve a fuller knowledge of God, but for Harrison the fragments of truth buried in the Sibylline writings only revealed by contrast the distorted Gentile understanding, which corrupted their religion (Bouwsma, *Concordia Mundi*, p. 255; McPhee, 'Beza', p. 150; TCD MS 165, fo. 5v).

[109] Ibid., fo. 63v; see above, pp. 74–6 for similar sentiments about Daniel.

of the Corpus. He argued that the Oracles consisted of a chaotic recension of numerous Gentile prophecies, within which he found truth severely limited to fragments derived from the Elect. The rest, ignorant of Scriptural prophecy, demonstrated all the flaws of natural reason in their erroneous guesswork about the shape of history and chronology.

Harrison reckoned that none of the Sibyls' utterances had been transmitted intact, for the woman who sold them to Tarquin 'was onely owner and not author of these bokes', which she had gathered from the works of nine previous Sibyls. To this corpus Tarquin had added other fragments gathered independently, and indeed all the oracles had later been repeatedly destroyed and then restored from memory, 'and this is the only cause wherfore the order of those two oracles yet remaining is so confused and inverted'. Here again appears Harrison's paramount concern with the order of time, but that was further complicated by the name 'Sibyl' being given to 'every skillfull woman which had the gift of Prophecieng' – Harrison listed sixteen in all.[110] From these women's writings ancient authors had 'gathered sondry testimonies of thincarnation birth and passion' of Christ. Yet while a Christian could see that those authorities had in fact prophesied the order of events leading to the Incarnation, Gentile interpretations only reflected their distorted picture of history, preoccupied with worldly consequences. They particularly misunderstood the significance of the Roman subjection of Egypt, after which 'by the Prophecies of Sybilla it could not be long ere the holy king and sonne of god shold be born', for these words 'the Romaines understoode of Cesar'. Such an erroneous historical interpretation further proved that this divine promise of Christ, embedded in the Oracles, did not result from the Gentile rational interpretation of history. That vision clouded without divine illumination, so that for example elsewhere in the Oracles the events of Babel could be found in garbled form, 'whereby it is manifest that the Gentiles had understanding of this division of the tongues, even as thei that lie bounde in spelnica Platonis have the divine similion of those thinges that perteine to true felicitie'.[111] Because their infidelity distorted the Scriptural truths they had received, the Gentiles had remained entirely unaware of the prophetic significance of the events occurring around them. Generally the Sibylline Oracles contained ideas drawn from human experience rather than God's wisdom, notions which resembled the Hermetic speculations which Harrison abhorred.[112]

[110] Harrison's inconsistencies in identifying the Sibyls reflect the length of time during which he worked on his 'Chronology'. He listed one 'otherwise called Sambethe', but elsewhere refused to accept this identification (ibid., fos. 63r–v; cf. fo. 5v).

[111] Ibid., fos. 133r, 10v. Significantly, the Sibyls gave more information than the Scriptures about the iniquities punished by the Flood (ibid., fo. 8r).

[112] For example, Sibyl prophesied calamities for Rome in AD 197 'according to the proportion of her Numericall letters' in Greek, but Harrison found no historical evidence to support

Early Christian authors had perceived these discrepancies, and had attempted to resolve them by making Tarquin's Sibyl a Jewess, but Harrison went further in tracing back to their proper place in the covenant line those parts of the Oracles which correctly recorded the divine will in history. Theodore Bibliander, and 'divers' others who shared Harrison's perception of time, had reasoned along the same lines, ascribing the correct prophecies to Noah's wife Noema, but Harrison could 'in no wise subscribe unto ther saienges'. He demonstrated from internal evidence that the true author was Noah's disciple in the perfect knowledge of divine and human things, his daughter-in-law Noegla. Consequently, 'that which is now extent of the Oracles is a collection of suche thinges as are remaining of hers and all the other Sybilles whereas the whole treatizes of each of them are consumed and lost'.[113] Within this mixed inheritance Harrison found truth severely limited, not disseminated throughout the corpus as the humanists believed, and he found most of the Oracles irrelevant to the correct understanding of history. Wherever those Gentile divinations seemed to accord with the Scriptural interpretation of time and history, he ascribed the coincidence not to the efforts of human intelligence rising to divine heights, but to the influence of divine revelation imparted to the Elect.

Harrison's discriminating approach to current prophecies, governed by the knowledge of history and time revealed to the covenant line, also appears in his interest in Merlin Ambrosius, 'a bastard borne between a Romaine and a Nonne as some write'.[114] He found enough congruence between Merlin's obscure images and true prophecy to counteract powerful criticism from two directions. Humanists of wide culture who appreciated Sibyl as a classical text with European relevance looked down on Merlin as a provincial barbarian, while not even Harrison could directly relate Merlin to the stream of true prophecy. For from the moment Geoffrey of Monmouth introduced this Celtic legend into fashionable intellectual circles in the twelfth century, authorities like William of Newburgh had accepted Merlin's historical reality but had denounced his prophecies as demonic in origin.[115] Geoffrey's first readers, preoccupied with contemporary politics,

---

this, although the Empire began to decay from that time, 'but howsoever the case standeth in the tenth centenarie or hundered of the age of this citie her decaie is generally prognosticated by many following another oracle of Sibyl' (ibid., fo. 152r; see above, pp. 108–9 for Harrison's other comments on such 'trifles').

[113] TCD MS 165, fo. 5v.

[114] Harrison distinguished Ambrosius from his Scottish brother Merlin 'Sylvestris' (ibid., fo. 180r).

[115] John Harvey combined both criticisms (*A discoursive problem concerning prophesies* (John Jackson for Richard Watkins: London, 1588), pp. 52–5). Southern, 'Aspects 3: History as Prophecy', p. 169. Geoffrey published his *Prophetiae Merlini* in 1134 and included them in his *Historia* of 1136. Further research into the numerous Merlin legends led to a revised *Vita Merlini* (c. 1148–50): A. O. H. Jarman, *The Legend of Merlin* (Cardiff, 1970), pp. 10–11, 24–5.

had sought in Merlin's prophecies explanations of the fortunes of contemporary English kings and their rivals, an approach which reflects the twelfth-century notion of the present mentioned above. Later medieval intellectuals tried to Christianise the prophecies in order to broaden the stream of divine revelation.[116] Harrison's interest in Merlin had a different objective; he found the necessary movement of time towards Doomsday partly forshadowed in Merlin's ludicrous animal imagery.

By the mid-sixteenth century, the avant-garde openly despised Merlin, while for influential Protestant prophetic interpreters such as Heinrich Bullinger, the increasing relevance of the Apocalypse made Merlin unnecessary.[117] However the new reading public, 'the simple and vulgare people', as Edward Topsell described them, 'imagine that there is no Scripture like to Merlins prophesie'. Perhaps to counter similar evidence of carnal reason amongst the commons, William Perkins emphasised the devilish origins of 'Merlins drunken prophecies'.[118] There is no evidence that Harrison shared the popular belief that Merlin correctly predicted the future, but even in his more cautious approach the need to confirm his chronological precision and the exact sequence of past events prevailed over his own suspicions. He became sufficiently absorbed to compile 'anotations' on Merlin's prophecies, a work which he apparently completed but which is not extant.[119] The context of this reference shows that Harrison's use of Merlin formed part of his search for pattern in the periods of time leading to the End, a search which reached a more exact conclusion in the Appendix in which Harrison applied Bodin's numerology. Harrison's calculations had changed, however. In the Appendix he claimed that the Danes 'miserablie afflicted this Ile by the space of 282 yeares or 46 septenaries' until the accession of Canute in AD 1016.[120] In the 'Chronology' he used Merlin to highlight the significance of the end of Saxon dominance, for from Aethelheared of Wessex 'to Canutus or deth of Edmund Ironside are those 300 yeres whereof Merlin speaketh verified', although 'the Saxons lived 150

---

[116] Smalley, *Medieval Historians*, p. 93; Southern 'Aspects 3: History as Prophecy', pp. 168–9; Southern 'Aspects 4: The sense of the Past', p. 248; and see above, pp. 52–3.

[117] H. Bullinger, *A hundred sermons on the Apocalips* (John Day: London, 1561), p. 12.

[118] E. Topsell, *Times Lamentations or an exposition upon the prophet Joel* (Edmund Bollifant for George Potter: London, 1569), p. 63; Perkins, *Workes* (1631), iii, 2nd pagination, p. 468, which put Merlin on a par with Elias and the 1588 prophecies.

[119] Not listed on the title-page of TCD MS 165, and therefore perhaps intended for separate publication like another lost work on the 'Antiquities of England' (Parry, 'Puritanism and History', p. 92). What text of the prophecies he used is unknown. He might have encountered them in the 'Chronicle' of Ralph of Diss which he used in St Paul's Cathedral Library (ibid., p. 9), now Lambeth MS 8, fos. 156 ff. (M. R. James, *A Descriptive Catalogue of the Manuscripts in the Library of Lambeth Palace* (Cambridge, 1932), pp. 20–2). He also consulted a history in Peterhouse Library, where Bale claimed that there was a 'Topographia Hyberniae [Giraldus Cambrensis?] cum vaticiniis Merlini' in 1560 (*Cambridge Antiquarian Communications*, iii, p. 166). [120] *Description* (1587), p. 29.

above the rest in the gretest troble with the Danes'. The attractions of neat chronological pattern overrode doubts about Merlin's orthodoxy, for 'there cannot any more precise accoumpt be made then that which the said lerned man doth here (thoughe I wote not by what spirite) conclude upon'.[121]

Harrison's 'anotations' on Merlin would be extremely interesting if they were extant, for he did not accept the prophecies uncritically. As with the Sibylline oracles he made some attempt to isolate the core of true prophecy in the Merlin corpus from what John Harvey called 'monstrerous heraldical blazonings', by applying Scriptural criteria to the prophecies. Harrison only accepted Merlin where he agreed with his own prejudices and preoccupations, although he did go to the extreme lengths of claiming that those prophecies which did not contribute to the Scriptural understanding of history had not been written by Merlin. Thus he noted the birth of Edward II, 'the gote of Car' and 'the third king in order of his prophecie Henry 3 being the Lamb of Winchester, and king Edward the first the dragon medled with mercy, but I do not take these to be Merlines prophecies but rather the dreames of some later writer moche of his spirite'.[122] Similarly, other wild imaginings from the Celtic fringe failed to deceive Harrison. He had seen some fragments of excellent Latin verses by Gildas which prophesied 'many things touching the state of that land to come', based upon the writings of 'Perdix a lerned Astrologien and famous wise hart'. Some Britons had used them as oracles, but Harrison agreed with the critics of these 'fortune tellers and wiseharts...sithe that of all men thei are the most miserable'.[123]

Merlin's agreement with Harrison's projection of Scriptural models onto the past raised him above such fortune-tellers. We have seen Harrison's dismay at enclosure of tillage which repeated a prophetic historical theme and established the relevance of the 1588 prophecy. Therefore the topic of enclosures bulked large in his critique of the Elizabethan commonwealth. Scripture showed there would always be only one correct attitude to enclosures – one which Harrison consequently made his own. He was quick to notice that King John's godly actions, which provided a model for Harrison's times, included his destruction of enclosures, 'for the benefit of his subjectes whome the welthier sorte had sore opressed by taking in of their

---

121　Merlin called Canute 'Aquilo or the northe winde...and saith that flores quos zephyrus procreant eripret which is meant that the goodes which the Saxons had gathered thei shold forgo thoroughe the cruelty of the Danes. But more of this in those anotations which I have written upon the said prophecies' (TCD MS 165, fo. 211r). In fact Harrison's 'Chronology' gives only 289 years to this period.

122　Ibid., fo. 322v. Harvey adopted a posture of languid humanist contempt for Merlin's 'few simple latin verses...smelling of that rude unlearned age', any commentary on which would be 'overtedious'. No proof existed for the fulfilment of Merlin's prophecies, dressed up in outlandish composite animal costumes, 'gewgawes to delight children, and very toyish crankes to mocke Apes' (*A discoursive problem*, pp. 54–5).

123　TCD MS 165, fo. 84r.

groundes and comons therof to make parks and forrestes. Of this Merlin said nemora in planiam mutabit etc.'[124] Here especially Merlin's utterances seemed congruent with the divine understanding of significant actions, but equally he could be discounted when he seemed to support the medieval veneration of relics. Thus a few folios later Harrison noted that 'some... interprete the saieing of Merline to be fulfilled' by the burial of King John between two bishops, wherto 'thei applie the wordes et inter beatos collocabitur to his aforesaid sepulture...which maie be so and yet the credite of the Oracle never a whit of the more value'.[125]

On the other hand, Merlin's predictions seemed more relevant to the history of the Elect when they pointed to the transfer of the archiepiscopal see from London to Canterbury by Augustine. This not only offended Harrison as a Londoner, but represented a significant step towards the revelation of Antichrist and the papal domination of England.[126] Only when Merlin's prophecies matched Scriptural criteria could they be safely used, but when they did they became infinitely more important as a reflection of the teachings transmitted by the covenant line. This not only outweighed the doubts expressed by Bullinger and Perkins, but in Harrison's interpretation showed that Merlin had wider relevance than the humanists asserted. For his prophecy clearly had some significance for the universal True Church when it correctly predicted the death of Louis IX after his failure to crush 'the silly Albigeois whose quarrel god defended'.[127] As always in Harrison's examination of the relationship between prophecy, chronology and history, the covenant line provided the reference point. The covenant line also provided the means to judge and attempt to reform more significant contemporary phenomena than Merlin's prophecies, as we shall see when we examine Harrison's attitude to the Elizabethan Church in the next chapter.

---

[124] Ibid., fo. 303v.
[125] Neither did he think much of John's nunnery built near Oxford 'for the soule of Rosamund', 'of which thei saie [Merlin] prophecied when he said Virgenea munera, virginibus donavit unde promerebitur favorem tonantis' (ibid., fo. 306v).
[126] 'For as yet London was the chief see but ere long (as Marlin said) dignitas Londoni adornabis Doroberniam, as Menevia urbis Legionum Pallio iam indicebatur etc.' (ibid., fo. 94v). This formed part of Augustine's imposition of antichristian Roman authority; see above, p. 72, *n*. 37.
[127] Louis died while returning home at Montpenser 'according to the prophecie of Marlin who said in monte vente morietur Leo pacificus' (ibid., fo. 308r).

PART II

A Protestant Vision of England

4

A reformed church

We have already seen that other prominent members of the Elizabethan Church shared Harrison's outlook on the world, and now we must examine the wider implications of this way of thinking. Harrison believed that the covenant line had transmitted through its historical experiences, both in the Scriptures and afterwards, the doctrinal criteria by which he could assess all human knowledge. The previous chapters examined his application of those Scriptural criteria to the arcana of prophecy, chronology and historical interpretation, and in passing pointed out the intimate relationship between his thinking on those matters and his notions about the nature and role of the Church, its relationship to the worldly powers, and the proper objectives of human society and human intellect. Now we can investigate Harrison's application of those same Scriptural criteria to these human institutions, and particularly the Elizabethan Church, while subsequent chapters will follow the same course through Harrison's thinking about political power, social organisation, and the investigation of Nature.

In this chapter we move away from the European sources of Harrison's developing ideas and relate his outlook more specifically to the experiences of Englishmen under Elizabeth. Here the 'Chronology' offers an unusually detailed insight into the historical assumptions behind Harrison's reforming ideas. For we can categorise Harrison's thoughts about the Elizabethan Church, and his activities within its institutional structure, as those of a moderate Puritan, in the descriptive sense in which modern historians use that term. Yet we can only fully understand those ideas and actions in the light of the historical interpretation of the Two Churches which simultaneously reflected and conditioned Harrison's interpretation of his contemporary world. The importance of his ideas derives not from their uniqueness – indeed, the more commonplace they appear the more this present argument acquires general relevance – but from the fact that he expressed them in a work of history which gives an unusual perspective from which to look into his historically minded perception of his present. Therefore we are concerned both with his individual adaptation of a common historical model and with its appearance in the thought of other Elizabethan Churchmen, or indeed their rejection of that model. Harrison applied it with exceptional fullness and complexity in his 'Chronology', but the fundamental continuity between that historical model and his rather familiar criticisms of the Elizabethan Church suggests a possible explanation for the distinctive way in which other Protestants perceived the defects in that Church and argued for specific reforms. This emphasis on the historiographical foundations beneath many structural criticisms of the Elizabethan Church avoids a confusing concentration on that perennial Christian asceticism which Puritans like Harrison shared with Roman Catholics. His devoted reformist Protestantism – his Puritanism, if one can use that term – really centred on those two obsessions which we have already seen emerged from his experiences of popery and his conversion to Protestantism under Mary. First, a conviction that preaching of the Word could transform individuals and thus human society, an end to which the entire energies of the True Church had always been and should always be directed, and secondly an obsession with the antichristian threat of popery, which continued the nature and policy of the Church of Cain, perpetually attempting to subvert this preaching function of the True Church.

Harrison applied both insights to the Elizabethan Church, calling for a return to that original pristine structure which best supported a preaching ministry, while combatting popery as far as the existing structure of the Church allowed, and sometimes beyond the legal limitations of that structure. However, he knew that his piecemeal efforts at reform could not prevail against natural man's weakness for idolatry and popery, until the Church was freed to preach that complete reformation which in the long term provided the only sure defence against subtle Satan and Antichrist. The general contours of his thoughts and actions therefore follow the underlying shape of his historical vision, although sometimes there was no precise correlation, for Harrison was not a monster of rectitude. This occasional discontinuity between thought and action only makes him appear more human and believable, and should encourage rather than dismay the historian who interests himself in historical figures as individuals and not types. It also makes those ideas and actions which are intimately connected to Harrison's historical interpretation doubly important, when we put him into the context of his parish, his archdeaconry and his diocese, and then assess his attitude towards the whole Elizabethan Church.

The fundamental tension between Harrison's visionary ideals for the Church and the social and political reality within which he had to live became at times of crisis an almost insupportable burden. We shall see that he wished to eradicate lay control over the appointment and promotion of ministers, for the laity had usurped upon that Scriptural organisation which had provided a preaching ministry for the True Church.[1] Yet while he advocated returning to the Scriptural structure and diminishing the traditional role of lay patronage, Harrison owed his first benefice to William Brooke, tenth Lord Cobham and Lord Warden of the Cinque Ports. For want of any firm evidence, we can only guess about the origins of this intriguing connection, but there existed powerful social and religious forces which might have brought them together. As a probationary fellow of Merton, Harrison had had first-hand experience of the interference of lay patrons in fellowship and scholarship elections, which perverted those stipends from their original function of providing for the higher education of poor scholars destined for the Church. Harrison's well-known criticism of the deleterious results of such practices, that 'he that hath most friends, though he be the woorst scholar, is alwaies surest to speed', is confirmed by Archbishop Parker's visitation to Merton in 1562.[2] Whether or not Harrison felt that his lack of an influential patron diminished his own prospects of a full fellowship, his resignation after his conversion to Protestantism, some time before the end of his probationary year in July 1558, enabled him to satisfy both his social and religious needs by finding a stoutly Protestant patron.

Harrison's new religious convictions probably carried greater weight, however, since in 1558 the Brookes were still clawing their way back from the edge of political ruin after unwisely politicising their religious affiliations by becoming involved in Wyatt's rebellion. George Brooke, ninth Lord Cobham, had been an early patron of advanced reformers, a protégé of Thomas Cromwell and a die-hard supporter of Northumberland's policies, as a Privy Councillor signing the instrument which limited the succession to Lady Jane Grey. He quickly made his peace with Mary, but John Ponet in his *Shorte Treatise of Politike Power* singled him out from the other Councillors for his constancy in not abandoning Northumberland immediately the Lord President left London. Ponet's praise perhaps reflected the prominence of the Brooke family in Wyatt's rebellion, in which Ponet also participated. His *Treatise* epitomises the religious motives behind the uprising, which undoubtedly influenced the loyalties of the Brookes when their allegiances were tested.[3] George Brooke equivocated when Wyatt sought his support, but William Brooke with two of his brothers joined

[1] Rome introduced impropriation of benefices in the eighth century, 'whereby true doctrine decaied and dombe dogges were fedde', as also in Elizabethan England (TCD MS 165, fo. 217v).

[2] *Description*, ed. Edelen, p. 71, perhaps a comment on a 1584 Bill to reform these abuses (J. Simon, *Education and Society in Tudor England* (London, 1966), p. 374, n. 2); Parker's Register, fos. 321r–325v, read in Cambridge University Library Microfilm MS 1846.

[3] D. M. Loades, *Two Tudor Conspiracies* (Cambridge, 1965), emphasises opposition to the Spanish Match rather than religious motives behind the rebellion, but see A. Fletcher, *Tudor Rebellions* (London, 1973), pp. 86–90. J. Ponet, *A Shorte Treatise of Politike Power*, esp. sigs. I5v–I6r, on George, Lord Cobham.

Wyatt, and spent some time in the Tower. They escaped with a pardon, since George remained indispensable to Mary as the leading magnate in northern Kent, and could point to his own refusal to aid Wyatt as an important contribution to the defeat of the rebellion.[4] Consequently in October 1558 William succeeded his father as Baron of Cobham and Lord Warden without mishap.

Harrison became William's chaplain, possibly in 1558, joining a household in which recent political events had given religious beliefs greater than normal significance. William Brooke had fought for Henry VIII's forces with the Schmalkaldic League, had been a squire of the body to Edward VI and was knighted in 1549. Under Mary, the Spanish Ambassador regarded him as a known supporter of Elizabeth, and as MP for Rochester in 1555 he had voted against Mary's restoration of tenths to the papacy. In Elizabeth's reign his political influence derived from his social position as the nearest equivalent to a county magnate that Kent possessed, as well as his close friendship with Cecil and the intimacy of his second wife, Frances Newton, with the Queen.[5] A Protestant by upbringing as well as a learned and cultured patron, like Cecil, Cobham initially sympathised with those who desired more reforms than had been achieved in 1559. He engaged the controversial presbyterian, William Turner, only recently returned from Genevan exile, to preach the funeral sermon for his first wife in October 1559. Thomas Tymme praised Cobham's 'godly zeale' and dedicated several Calvinist theological works to him. This background explains why Harrison found his way into the Brooke household, and perhaps damped down any incipient doubts about the role of the laity in the Church. Yet Cobham pursued a political vendetta against Robert Dudley from early in Elizabeth's reign, which gradually became fused with a growing unease about the godly cause, as represented by the more militant line against popery propounded by Leicester's supporters. Like other Cecilians, by the 1580s Cobham had moved so far as to throw his weight behind Whitgift's reaction, and at one time Harrison's fellow-chaplains included the crypto-Catholic Peter Hendley.[6] Therefore, although Cobham and Harrison enjoyed a relationship closer than the usual behaviour of patron and client, we should not assume an identity between their views. To a very limited extent Harrison followed his patron in turning against the kind of presbyterian extremism depicted in government propaganda, but the developing disparity between their views provides part of the background to Harrison's later opinions about the role of the laity in the Church. Harrison remained loyal to that radical spirit

---

[4]   P. Clark, *English Provincial Society from the Reformation to the Revolution: Religion, Politics and Society in Kent 1500–1640* (London, 1977), p. 95
[5]   D. B. McKeen, 'A Memory of Honour' (unpublished Birmingham Ph.D. dissertation, 1964), pp. 28, 35, 138, 82–4; Clark, *Kent*, pp. 128–9.
[6]   McKeen, 'Memory of Honour', pp. 913–38; Clark, *Kent*, pp. 129, 137, 174.

which seems to have prevailed in the Brooke household when he became Cobham's chaplain and when Cobham presented him to the Rectory of Radwinter, Essex, in February 1559.[7]

Harrison became a pluralist, holding three other livings in succession besides Radwinter from 1567 to 1587, but like other critics of the Elizabethan Church he felt that he was turning a scandalous imperfection to evangelical advantage by preaching to a wider audience. He defended his pluralism against extremist criticism of the Court of Faculties by emphasising the inability of the universities to provide enough preachers for all the cures in England, and advocated instead the merging of small, poor urban parishes which could never individually support a learned, preaching ministry.[8] This pastoral commitment enabled Harrison to establish a radical tradition at previously quiescent Radwinter despite his ministering to other parishes, but the shape which this local reformation took justifies the view that when Harrison became Rector of Radwinter he joined a network of godly Essex clerics whose ecclesiastical patronage advanced a 'Grindalian' vision of the Church. Perhaps just as importantly, Harrison's 'Chronology' reveals how he perceived that ingrained popery which the Grindalians sought to eradicate throughout England, and therefore may help to explain the vehemence of their opposition to the remnants of popery in the Elizabethan Church.

Edmund Grindal's concern to establish the Pauline ideal of pastoral care while Bishop of London from 1559 to 1571, was echoed at the furthest edge of his diocese, in William Harrison's Radwinter. Grindal did not ordain Harrison, but the latter anyway criticised those who tied 'the gift of the holly ghost unto... thimposition of handes', and he acknowledged a spiritual rather than sacramental connection with the covenant line.[9] More importantly, Harrison shared Grindal's suspicions about the malevolent influence of worldly 'policy', which inevitably produced a 'mixed' religion, degenerate from the doctrines and nature of the True Church.[10] Grindal tacitly supported moderate Puritan attempts in the Convocation of 1563 to revise the Prayer Book rubrics so as to remove those remaining popish ceremonies which epitomised the idolatry of this 'mixed' religion. Signatories of the important petitions on 13 February 1563 included Alexander Nowell,

---

[7] Bonner's Register, Guildhall Library MS 9531/12, fo. 481r, and see Parry, 'Puritanism and History', pp. 25–8, for more on their intimacy.

[8] Ibid., pp. 28–9, and *Description*, ed. Edelen, pp. 27–8. Both his London livings, St Olave, Silver Street (1567–71) and St Thomas Apostle (1583–7), were peculiars of the Dean and Chapter of St Paul's, noted for preferring zealous preachers to their City livings (Collinson, *Grindal*, p. 116), while Wimbish (1571–81) abutted Radwinter.

[9] TCD MS 165, fo. 154r.

[10] Collinson, *Grindal*, pp. 89–90, on 'policy', and *Description* (1587), pp. 139–40; see below on Constantine and mixed religion, pp. 241–3.

Harrison's former Headmaster at Westminster, his fellow scholar, and later as Dean of St Paul's patron of both his London benefices, and John Pulleyne and James Calfhill, successively Harrison's immediate superiors as Archdeacons of Colchester. Despite the narrow defeat of the reformers in 1563, Harrison like many other zealous preachers apparently put into practice their proposed revisions of the 1559 Act of Uniformity, and indeed went even further. Calfhill, Grindal's chaplain, appointed Harrison as an Official of his Archidiaconal Court before 1569. Calfhill had been Harrison's contemporary at Christ Church, Oxford. Harrison's appointment reflected his Protestant connections and his radical credentials as one who sought primitive simplicity in the Church, but perhaps the truest measure of their close relationship is that Calfhill lent Harrison money.[11]

Harrison's historical interpretation sheds fresh light on the scrupulosity of these men towards popish ceremonies and observances, by providing a more elaborate parallel to their arguments in the Convocation of 1563. Calfhill, Nowell and Pulleyne urged that 'ministers be not compelled to wear such gowns and caps as the enemies of Christ's gospel have chosen to be the special array of their priesthood'. Parker ensured that 'mediocrity' prevailed, and the Puritans reluctantly accepted the surplice alone, but there remained compelling reasons why convinced Protestants like Harrison could not accept a mixed liturgy, but only one absolutely distinct from the popish church.[12] The lawfulness or otherwise of popish ceremonies was irrelevant; the fact remained that God demanded that His people should be perpetually distinguished from the Church of Cain. Therefore Harrison perceived the remnants of popish ceremonies in the Elizabethan Church in the light of the eternal struggle of the Two Churches – as the gorgeous and pompous shows by which Satan had always seduced natural man's weak understanding, to entice him into idolatry. To countenance their retention now would allow Antichrist to continue to work his subtle wiles and to undermine the fragile, partial reformation which had been achieved. Such a perspective made popish survivals appear to be anything but 'adiaphora', for they expressed the satanic inspiration behind popery and its total opposition to the truth nurtured by the covenant line.

Not everything could be achieved at once. Although in the 1577 *Des-*

---

11 E.R.O. D/ACA 5, a note of borrowings at the end of the Act book of the Archdeacon's Court. Harrison obtained from Calfhill *Tomus secundus omnium operum reverendi domini Martini Lutheri* (Wittenberg, 1546), Derry shelf-mark B.ii.d.16. Parry, 'Puritanism and history', pp. 53–4, and A. J. Carlson, 'The Puritans and the Convocation of 1563', in *Action and Conviction in Early Modern Europe*, ed. T. K. Rabb and J. E. Seigel (Princeton, 1969), pp. 133–53, at pp. 145–50.

12 T. W. Davids, *Annals of Evangelical Nonconformity in the County of Essex* (London, 1863), p. 63; Strype, *Annals* (Oxford, 1824), I, p. 504; Collinson, *Grindal*, pp. 161–2; Carlson, 'Convocation of 1563', pp. 145–6.

cription Harrison indiscriminately lumped 'vestments' with copes, albs, tunicles and other popish 'trash', probably like Calfhill and Pulleyne in 1563 he grudgingly accepted the surplice, especially since Radwinter provided none of the pastoral reasons which Grindal allowed to excuse nonconformity in more radical livings. In the *Description* Harrison accepted that clerical apparel 'is comely, and in truth more decent than ever it was in the popish church', the familiar self-justification of those who rejected the extremist charge that even the plain surplice represented a remnant of idolatry.[13] Further evidence from the 1590s suggests that Harrison enforced conformity to statutory obligations which distinguished but did not justify religious observances.[14] Again, despite Calfhill's objections to it in 1563, Harrison's suspicion that outward 'precisenesse' often covered inner hypocrisy probably helped him to wear 'the long black gown' which had been used by the papists. Indeed he disliked over-precise austerity in apparel, 'for soch odde behaviour in attire maketh men to become but gasing stockes to the world'.[15]

Comparison of Harrison's thought with other reforms proposed in 1563, however, reveals more clearly that those mildly expressed complaints about externals masked deep anxieties about the need to obey God in the smallest things, to follow the example of the True Church in combating satanic practices. The petitioners asked that ministers should be compelled to face the people and say common prayers distinctly, an attack on the covert survival of popish ceremonies directed towards the east. While this would ensure that the people 'may hear and be edified' by the Word, as Harrison recognised, the popish practice of praying towards the east was also a sinister mark of Satan's success in corrupting the True Church. Harrison believed that popery represented the re-emergence of Gentile practices in the True Church and reflected the addiction to error 'in the corrupted minde of man'. The importance of the phenomenon of praying to the east was such that when Harrison discussed it in his 'Chronology' he considered inserting a discourse showing 'how the christians stombled upon so many of the errors of the gentiles', and although the structure of the manuscript prevented this, he did note the importance of the distinction between popish and godly ceremonies which the reformers attempted to establish in 1563. The Scriptural account of the True Church taught that 'god at the beginning and institution of his lawes did seeke by all meanes to plucke his people from the rites and

---

[13] Harrison's acceptance of the living of St Olave, Silver Street, in 1567, soon after Grindal and Parker's drive against nonconformity, proves nothing, since as a peculiar of the Dean and Chapter of St Paul's (like St Thomas Apostle) it was exempt from Grindal's ordinary jurisdiction (Collinson, *Grindal*, pp. 55, 116; *Description*, ed. Edelen, pp. 372, 36; G. R. Elton, *The Tudor Constitution*, 2nd edition (Cambridge, 1981), p. 437).

[14] Parry, 'Puritanism and history', p. 38.

[15] TCD MS 165, fo. 156v, criticising Novatian hypocrisy; *Description*, ed. Edelen, p. 237; TCD MS 165, fo. 122v.

Ceremonies of the gentiles' and so 'divised his ordinaunces quite contrary unto theirs'. It was not the prerogative of human reason to decide the relative merits of these ceremonies, but to obey the divine command to distinguish the ungodly from the godly. For the mere doing of ceremonies weighed nothing with God, unless they were done with that obedience and faith which always distinguished the covenant line – hence the frequent Protestant insistence that the genealogy of true believers had taught a spiritual interpretation of the ceremonial law of the Old Testament.[16]

Harrison considered that the True Church after the Apostles had lost this spiritual understanding, for human reason refused to be bound by the Scriptural revelation that God had not allowed His people to share Gentile ceremonies. Zealous bishops of Rome in the primitive Church had over-reacted against superstitious Jewish observances, and 'he thought himself the holiest man which might decree and divise orders in his churche most disagreing from theirs'. However, this erroneous use of reason caused them to lose sight of the spiritual meaning behind ceremonies, and 'thei returned again in many thinges to plaine gentilisme which god had condemned and abolished among his chosen people'. This constituted an important objection, for repeatedly in the 'Chronology' Harrison explained the corrupt nature of popish ceremonies by reference to their Gentile origins, including, as here, praying to the east. Harrison pointed out that the Gentiles sacrificed towards the rising sun, but God, 'desirous to withdraw his people from the superstition of the gentiles', decreed that in the temple at Jerusalem they should face west. Naturally the stubborn Jews failed to realise the importance of distinguishing themselves from the Gentiles, and many of them returned to their customary praying towards the east. The papists had also unheedingly reacted against God's ordinances, so that in their churches, 'soch as enter into them shall knele toward the est. I saie a toie learned of the gentiles as are many other used in the aforesaid religion'.[17]

Therefore Harrison could not have regarded praying to the east at Radwinter, or anywhere else, as a thing indifferent, for he attached fundamental importance to the distinctions between the Two Churches, Satan now sought to subvert the True Church through antichristian popery, just as in the Old Testament he had sought its destruction through seductive Gentile ceremonies. Therefore Harrison felt that the popish survivals in the 1559 Prayer Book could not be tolerated, for 'the consciences of the true and zealous christians are often miserably intangled' by the enforcement of popish ceremonies. These distorted parodies of a true form of worship masked satanic Gentilism, and Harrison sought to expose 'the filthinesse of the gentile relligion', which was only exceeded by that 'more ugly and lothsome matter',

[16] Ibid., fo. 69v.
[17] Ibid., fo. 69v, and Carlson, 'Convocation of 1563', p. 146, on the emergence of this point.

the 'bestly doctrine' of the papists.[18] His persistent harping on this subject throughout the 'Chronology' emphasises his fears about the worldly attractions of popish ritual. For only by interpreting their predicament according to the criteria of the Two Churches could contemporary Christians appreciate the dangers of the present struggle. Only by adopting this correct perspective would they realise that 'Sathan practized to reduce a christian gentilisme into the churche of christ' through Roman innovations, for the rational, human motives behind Israel's perpetual inclination to idolatry were 'even the same which move us to follow the papist religion and idolatry brought from Rome' – chiefly that idolatry ensured wealth, power and carnal liberty. In seeking a true form of worship the Elect had to abandon such rational criteria, for to leave any popish elements in the Elizabethan Church would allow Satan to prey upon natural man's weaknesses and ensure backsliding into idolatry.[19]

Harrison probably attempted to impose upon Radwinter a local version of that thoroughgoing reformation which Puritans vainly attempted to make the pastoral standard for the Elizabethan church, not only in communal acts of worship, but in those individual rites of passage which punctuated the life of small communities. In January 1563 Nowell led an attempt to remove the Prayer Book rubric which tolerated baptism by midwives, and although after some discussion the Puritans abandoned their hopes of ministers monopolising baptism, they did attempt to forbid the use of the sign of the cross in baptising, 'as tending to superstition'. Again Harrison's 'Chronology' provides a context which reveals this more clearly as a conscious blow against Antichrist, for baptism by midwives he considered not only heretical in origin but 'a matter most distant from Christes institution...sithens it is not lawfull for them so moche as to speake in the church'. Harrison's intimate associate George Withers cited private baptism to excuse his own nonconformity, and attacked its continued toleration by the Prayer Book even after he became Archdeacon of Colchester, and thus Harrison's ecclesiastical supervisor, in 1570. Despite the failure to reform the Prayer Book rubric, Harrison refused to tolerate private baptism, so that at least one child died unbaptised during his incumbency of St Thomas Apostle, London.[20] There is no evidence about

---

[18]　TCD MS 165, fo. 48v.

[19]　Ibid., fos. 253v, 59r. The 1563 petitioners also objected to the rubric enforcing kneeling during communion, and since Harrison noted the symbolic meaning of popish attempts to bind Christian consciences to 'knele towarde the est', he possibly allowed his parishioners Christian liberty on this matter (ibid., fo. 69v; Carlson, 'Convocation of 1563', p. 146).

[20]　Ibid., p. 42; TCD MS 165, fo. 149v; Collinson, *Grindal*, pp. 161–2, on Parker's resistance; Withers and John Barthelot, August 1567 in *Zurich Letters* (Cambridge, 1845), Second Series, p. 149; and to Burghley in 1583 in Strype, *Annals*, III, ii, p. 270. Guildhall Library MS 9009, Register of St Thomas Apostle, unfoliated, burial 14 August 1585. Whitgift defended private baptism against Cartwright (*Works*, ed. J. Ayre (3 vols. Parker society: Cambridge, 1851–3) ii, pp. 535–7).

Harrison's attitude to crossing in baptism, but although the fact cannot be directly attributed to him, in the 1640s some Radwinter parishioners violently objected to it as 'the mark of the Beast'. This despite the pressure after 1587 to make ministers conform to using the sign in baptism.[21] The 1563 petitioners also objected to the tradition of godparents responding for the infant, and although Harrison carefully chose substantial local figures as godparents for his own son, he presumably dispensed with the debased popish tradition of responding which had usurped upon the original godly function of spiritual parents.[22]

Already before 1563 many London parishes had defied the Act of Uniformity and the 1559 Visitation Injunctions on these and other matters, and notably the use of organ music and chant in services. Harrison believed that organs had been introduced into the Church in eighth-century Rome, and on the basis of their retention alone he felt able to argue that the Elizabethan Church was merely 'semi-reformed', mixing antichristian features with the lineaments of the True Church. The removal of organs had been demanded in the 1563 Convocation, and Withers complained bitterly to his mentors Bullinger and Gualter that although Grindal disapproved of organs and choral chant, the bishops 'all adopt them in ther churches', while Parker had even erected a new organ at Canterbury. Harrison's objections make it clear that not the thing itself but what it signified and what its implications might be for true worship worried him. He greatly appreciated music, and wrote knowledgeably about it, but the example of the True Church could not be ignored. Outside the Church, music could be legitimately enjoyed, but he knew from his Oxford years that Satan used the seductive beauty of organs and popish singing to pervert the true form of worshipping God. For 'with the noise of the instrument, voices of the singing men and partaking of the choristers the harmony is soche that it toucheth the ere with marvellous delectation', but to entirely the wrong end, 'moving rather the senses with a kind of admiration then sturing up of minde to devotion or any godly meditation'. Therefore when Harrison outlined Church ritual in his *Description* he used the occasion for some subtle Puritan propaganda, extrapolating from the simplified pattern of his own parish to the whole Elizabethan Church, blandly assuming that the complete reformation sought by the first generation of Elizabethan Puritans had actually been achieved. As with other, more obviously fundamental issues, he was no less radical for preferring positive encouragement to negative criticism. For

---

[21] B.L.O. MS Rawlinson D. 158, fo. 43v; and J. P. Anglin, 'The Essex Puritan Movement and the "Bawdy" Courts, 1577–94', in *Tudor Men and Institutions*, ed. A. J. Slavin (Baton Rouge, 1972), p. 197.

[22] Carlson, 'Convocation of 1563', p. 142; and E.R.O. D/P 313/1/1. Register of Wimbish, fo. 5r, entry for William, son of William Harrison, 7 October 1576.

despite Parker's lead at Canterbury, ideal had become reality at Radwinter, where Harrison's account mentions no organ and emphasises that the singing is so plain 'that each one present may understand what they sing', thus in theory encouraging godly meditation on the words and their significance.[23]

A working definition of Harrison's Puritanism therefore begins to emerge from the bare facts of his ministry. He simply refused to accept the 1559 rubrics as the last word on the daily working of the institutional Church, because the historical record of the conflict between the True Church and the Church of Cain demonstrated the dangers of such an equivocal distinction between truth and error. Fallen man's natural susceptibility to idolatrous blandishments made it vital to establish a clear distinction between the Two Churches, to prevent backsliding. Therefore, when the final attempt to reform from within the Church established in 1559 failed in 1563, Harrison simply instituted what reforms he could as his contribution to that necessary distinction, and preached and no doubt prayed for a complete reformation which would re-establish the True Church against Antichrist. Just as important as his actions, of course, was his manner, and again we should not underestimate his radicalism simply because he did not adopt the strident postures by which other Puritans positively invited that oppression which distinguished the Elect. Harrison's equally profound conviction that the Church achieved its greatest purity under the Cross of affliction did not lead him to jeopardise what had been gained, by intemperate attacks on the status quo. To that extent, like other moderate Puritans he had to play the increasingly elaborate game by which he suspended his growing disbelief in Elizabeth as a godly reformer, and 'abide till god by the magistrate shall execute his purpose'.[24] Equally, this act of intellectual self-denial forced him to employ more subtle means of furthering reformation than were advocated by extremists.

The first demand in the revised petition in 1563 had been that Sundays and 'principal feasts of Christ' alone should be kept as holy days, abrogating all saints' days.[25] Harrison tried to elevate the Sabbath and diminish the importance of the popish saints' days by associating the latter in his *Description* with 'the heathenish rioting' at the bride-ales, wakes, guilds,

---

[23] TCD MS 165, fo. 201v; Withers and John Barthelot, August 1567, *Zurich Letters*, Second series p. 150. Yet Withers, *An ABC for layemen* (1585), sig. F4r, advocated musical instruments 'to set out the praises of our God'. See *Description*, ed. Edelen, pp. 33–4.

[24] This reflected his sorrow at 'the inconsiderate zeale' of an early Christian bishop who provoked persecution, just as 'Some of my time are persuaded that perseqution is so necessary in the church of christ that it can not long flourish or reteine her integrity and fervent zeale, if it be absent but a little, and therefore thei not onely wishe for it but also to their power attempt sondry things therby to draw the same upon our neckes'. Harrison recognised the danger that prosperity posed to the True Church, but refused to sacrifice innocent blood (TCD MS 165, fo. 173v).

[25] Carlson, 'Convocation of 1563', p. 146; and see Elton, *Tudor Constitution*, p. 437.

fraternities and church-ales which had knit together the medieval community. Harrison claimed to have abolished all these, but he went further at a time when the neglect of holy days provided for in the 1559 Prayer Book was becoming a major charge against nonconforming ministers in the Archdeacons' courts of the diocese of London. He proposed consolidating the feasts of the apostles, evangelists and martyrs at Christmas, Easter and Whitsun (the periods advocated in 1563), and then, quite casually, that those of the Virgin Mary, 'with the rest' should be abolished 'as neither necessary nor commendable in a reformed church'. In keeping with this deliberately underplayed advocacy of radical reforms in the face of increasing pressure from the establishment for conformity, Harrison did not raise the wider issues involved in sabbatarianism, but rather ingenuously suggested that the abolition of saints' days was 'no great matter'.[26]

Harrison wrote the *Description* to a commission within a relatively short period, however, whereas he devoted years of studious labour to compiling the unpublished 'Chronology'. Therefore the latter perhaps better reflects Harrison's opinions, and more outspokenly faces major issues of importance to him, including the Sabbath. Thus the 'Chronology' observed that while popish festivals were being enforced by statute, Parliament failed to abolish Sunday fairs 'of soche continuauns are the wedes of vice and vicious dealing if thei ones take hold amongst us'. He digressed on one contemporary incident which highlighted this ungodly incongruence between divine and human law, for one Sabbath-breaker had argued that 'we have no more of goddes law to follow then the act of Parliament doth allow of'. This 'good gere', that 'in respect of mans law and friendship of the courts, the commaundementes of god are either made not lawfull or els of none effect', demonstrated the necessity for the complete reformation of society, which would bring it to that godly obedience which distinguished the True Church.[27] A society so distorted from the Scriptural model revealed Satan's success in corrupting natural man, particularly in that 'heathenish rioting' at quasi-religious celebrations which the deluded people preferred to a godly form of worship. George Withers also found the greater conflict of the Two Churches exemplified in the contemporary excesses of the unheeding masses, for 'when we see our Holidays spent and consumed in idle pastimes and belly cheare; then are we to remember that as the children of Israel tooke that corruption from the Egyptians, so to us it is come from popish idolaters and idolatrous Papists'.[28] As surely as the most obvious features of popery,

---

26 Anglin, 'The Essex Puritan Movement', pp. 194, 204; *Description*, ed. Edelen, p. 36. Can the silence of the court records on wakes and ales be taken to mean that they had been successfully suppressed? See F. G. Emmison, *Elizabethan Life: Morals and the Church Courts* (Chelmsford, 1973), p. 275.

27 TCD MS 165, fos. 323r, 122v, the latter a miller's reply to the commissary's complaint of Sabbath-breaking. Millers most frequently suffered prosecution for Sabbath-breaking.

28 Withers, *An ABC*, sig. F7r.

the observance of saints' days and their attendant feastings distinguished the Church of Cain from the True Church and reflected the appeal of satanic Gentilism to fallen human appetites.

Such an analysis not only illuminates Harrison's radicalism by comparison with men who had experienced greater persecution and exile, while providing a new perspective on their arguments, but also by comparing him with Withers reveals the underlying continuity between Harrison's brand of Puritanism and the presbyterians, a continuity which will be discussed more fully below. For not only did Withers come to bemoan the loss of 'many things of the greatest advantage of the church' in the defeat of the 1563 petitioners, but he also refused the vestments when pressed by Grindal and Parker, and became one of the original academic presbyterians. His outspokenness in the cause of complete reformation eventually brought him promotion to the Archdeaconry of Colchester under Grindal, and with the sanction of both Grindal and his successor Edwin Sandys he moderated a local prophesying which included Harrison amongst its members. There is evidence that this prophesying continued to meet in the 1580s, apparently because the clerics who attended valued the pastoral benefits of its mutual edification in Scriptural study more highly than Elizabeth's commands in 1576 to cease the prophesyings.[29]

Therefore Withers probably encouraged Harrison's attempts to further reformation at Radwinter, a process which simplified the familiar fabric of his church as much as its traditional liturgy. At Cambridge in 1565 Withers preached a rousing sermon advocating the immediate removal of stained-glass windows as manifest objects of idolatry. Much as he wished to achieve this, Harrison lacked the money and materials, and had to content himself with their gradual decay and replacement at Radwinter.[30] He certainly removed all 'images, shrines, tabernacles, rood lofts and monuments of idolatry', not merely as a restoration of primitive simplicity, but also as a rejection of the satanic Gentilism adopted by the papists. His *Description* blandly claimed that such iconoclasm was standard in the Elizabethan Church. Removal of the rood loft still left a screen of now uncertain symbolic meaning between the choir and the nave at Radwinter. Perhaps because his parishioners, whose responsibility the nave was, objected to the removal of the screen, Harrison fudged the issue in the *Description*, unable to claim more than that the former great screens were generally now 'very small or none at all', while still insisting that they were 'to say the truth, altogether needless'. For now the pulpit provided the focus for services, during which 'the whole congregation

[29] Collinson, *Puritan Movement*, pp. 110–11, 185; Davids, *Nonconformity*, pp. 73–5; J. and J. A. Venn, *Alumni Cantabrigienses* (Cambridge, 1922), I, iv, p. 61; and see below pp. 181–4.

[30] J. Strype, *The Life and Acts of Matthew Parker* (3 vols. Oxford, 1821), pp. 192–4. Withers earned suspension for this sermon. *Description*, ed. Edelen, p. 35. A few fragments of medieval stained glass survived the nineteenth-century 'restoration' of Radwinter Church.

at one instant pour out their petitions unto the living God'.[31] Whether or not this accurately depicted his success in eradicating traditional liturgical observances, Harrison certainly encouraged the process by replacing the altar with a communion table, which in the 1640s was alleged to have 'anciently stood above the Ascent in the Chancel', which in defiance of the Ecclesiastical Commission of 1561 had been on the same level as the nave.[32]

A similar tension between what Harrison considered to have been the practice of the True Church since Adam, and the stubborn refusal of carnal reason to abandon devices originally invented by Satan to pervert the truth, marked his reaction to another customary religious rite, that of churching women after childbirth. Again it united him with George Withers on an issue where zealous pastors isolated themselves by their refusal to accept the dictates of social custom. Fundamentally, the controversy reflected the contrast between the religious duty imposed upon the Elect to multiply their numbers, and Satan's attempt to divert humanity from this godly obedience by making virginity a religious virtue rather than a gift of grace. We have already noticed that the same requirement for a large population to withstand the wiles of Antichrist, and to build up a living Temple and godly commonwealth through their lives, informed Harrison's interpretation of enclosures under the aegis of the 1588 prophecy. Therefore it revealed Satan's purpose that the papists hated marriage, 'insomoche that they adiudged any woman with childe to be uncleane, naye not worthy to come into the churche after her delivery with out purification as if she had bene about some uncleane and abhominable businese'. In contrast Harrison's acceptance of the prophetic necessity to populate the world reveals itself in a typical comment that 'a goodly woman great with childe...is of all other in my judgement the most excellent sight in the world'. The potential for social conflict in such laudable notions surfaced in Withers's embarrassment in front of an amused congregation in 1587, when a husband and wife interrupted his sermon to demand that she be churched.[33]

Harrison's Protestant consciousness of his duty to obey God's commands rather than accept prevailing custom or acquiesce when human laws tolerated ungodliness, therefore marked him out as a Puritan in the English context. Yet his pluralism must have diminished his effectiveness in similarly evangelising his parishioners, and his desire to spread true doctrine wider may have been self-defeating, despite his typically 'Grindalian' conviction that

---

[31] Images were a mark of Cain (TCD MS 165, fo. 69v). *Description*, ed. Edelen, pp. 35–6. The screen survived into the 1640s (B.L.O. MS Rawlinson. D. 158, fo. 45r). See Collinson, *Grindal*, p. 118, on attempts to rid such screens of religious significance.

[32] In the 1640s the incumbent, Richard Drake, was accused of having elevated the chancel (B.L.O. MS Rawlinson D. 158, fos. 43r, 50r). Collinson, *Grindal*, p. 118, on the Ecclesiastical Commission of 1561 and its attempt to stop radical ministers levelling down the chancel.

[33] TCD MS 165, fos. 216r, 277r, and Emmison, *Elizabethan Life: Morals*, p. 160.

'preaching and teaching of the flocke…is the true imitation of Peter and Paule'. He held a second benefice in London between 1567 and 1571, and held preferments in Radwinter, London and Windsor simultaneously between April 1586 and September 1587, when he must have been over-stretched. He resigned the London living of St Thomas Apostle in September 1587, but until 1590 the statutes of St George's Chapel bound him to reside there for nearly the whole year. Therefore he employed one George Pomfret as his curate at Radwinter, who possibly preached, if we take at face value Harrison's attacks on those impropriators of benefices who contented themselves with 'dombe dogges' as curates.[34] Harrison took the opportunity to reduce his enforced absence from Radwinter when in 1590 he joined with the rest of the Windsor Chapter to secure a reform which freed them to feed their flocks for at least half the year. Soon after, Harrison carefully calculated that he had to reside at Windsor, remote from his pastoral calling, for 185 days every year. The very preciseness of this calculation reflects his scrupulosity, for he despised those who sheltered behind human law and 'thinketh it ynough to have a dispensation' to disobey God and neglect their cure of souls. Therefore his Will shows that he divided his time equally between Windsor and Radwinter, arranging for his burial in either place, 'where it shall please god to call me'.[35]

Harrison's willingness to forego the pleasures of the great royal palace at Windsor for his evangelical calling at obscure Radwinter, at least for half the year, explains his preference, along with other evangelical Protestants, for the title 'Pastor' as against the traditional names 'not yet abolished'. In the same spirit he went further than merely rejecting the popish elements in the 1559 Prayer Book and used the pastoral aids supplied by the English exiles at Geneva. His reference to metrical psalm singing suggests that he acquired a Genevan psalm-book, and instead of Alexander Nowell's two catechisms accepted by Convocation in 1563 he may have used the Genevan catechism which survives amongst his books at Derry.[36] Perhaps most importantly, like George Withers who criticised the Bishops' Bible, he proclaimed his loyalty to 'our Geneva boke (the very best that we have in English)'. This possessive

---

[34] TCD MS 165, fo. 217v, and Collinson, *Grindal*, pp. 94, 204. Anglin, 'Essex Puritan Movement', p. 190, claims that Harrison employed as curate in 1586 one Thomas Chaplain, detected by Aylmer's Visitation that year as preaching unlicensed, but the Visitation book, E.R.O. D/ACV 1, fos. IV, 56v, records Pomfret as Harrison's curate, listing Chaplain as curate of adjoining Hempstead.

[35] B.L.O. MS Bodley 613, fo. 53v; G. J. R. Parry, 'MS Bodley 613', in *The Bodleian Library Record*, X, no.2 (1979), pp. 139–40, describes this manuscript. TCD MS 165, fo. 227v; P.R.O. PROB 11/82, fos. 268v–269r.

[36] *Description*, ed. Edelen, p. 33; and *Catechismus ecclesiae Genevensis hoc est formula erudiendi pueros in doctrina Christi* (Geneva, 1560), shelf-mark C.i.c.16. The argument that wear and tear might account for the absence of Nowell's catechisms at Derry could also extend to other copies of the Genevan catechism.

tone presumably reflects Harrison's belief that the Geneva Bible with its marginal notes best suited his pastoral need to instil into his parishioners that awareness of the perpetual conflict of the Two Churches which conditioned his own perception of all created things. For Harrison considered 'the preaching of the worde' his chief vocation precisely because God had always used the covenant line to 'sture and wake up his drowsie people to the receiving and imbracing of the gift of the true faith which cometh as the apostle saith by hering and taking note in soch as are ordeined unto life'.[37] Leaving aside the predestinarian implications of this comment, we should note it as an important elaboration of his otherwise commonplace injunction that 'a precher must indeavour to edifie his herers and not curry their eres with a combe of vaine flowing eloquens'. For this typically Puritan encomium for plain preaching also reflects Harrison's attempt to apply to Elizabethan England his interpretation of the Scriptures, outlined in the first chapter.

The Scriptures in his view taught more than vain 'eloquens', a typical attribute of natural, carnal reason which inevitably led men to falsify the Scriptures and 'amend those thinges which the spirite of god hath set downe' but which eluded the application of rational criteria.[38] The refusal to accept that the Scriptures plainly described the Two Churches acting in history characterised the Church of Cain, which gained everything from obscuring this straightforward sense. Antichrist distorted the Scriptures through carnal reason, a latent threat always present as an essential part of man's nature. Therefore Harrison insisted that 'hering and taking note' of the godly models in the historical True Church formed the essential basis for his audience to understand their contemporary predicament, both as sinful individuals who could find justification solely through faith in Christ, and as members of a Church continually under attack from Satan through that antichristian popery which distorted Christ's significance as the seal of the covenant uniting all true believers. Therefore the content of Harrison's preaching also contributes something to the definition of his Puritanism, and while none of his sermons survives, we can at least gauge his intentions from his 'Chronology'. For we have noticed his special concern that his readers should closely examine the histories of Israel and the Gentiles, and 'applie ther errors and corrections with ther recoveries and returnes unto thy self' in order to discover what God's justice and mercy demanded that they do in the present. Not only the Scriptures, but, as we have seen, all history interpreted according to Scriptural criteria, demonstrated what it meant to obey God on one side, and serve Satan on the other. In the *Description* Harrison justified his historical research solely on this basis, for 'by this means

---

[37] Withers to Burghley, 19 February 1583, in Strype, *Annals*, III, ii, p. 271; and TCD MS 165, fos. 220r, 138v, 253r.   [38] Ibid., fo. 163r.

I have reaped some commodity unto myself by searching of the histories, which often minister store of examples ready to be used in my function'. The desire directly to apply Scriptural models to 'men of like condition' in contemporary religious, political, economic and social life, without reference to historical context as we conceive it, therefore distinguished Harrison's world-view as much as it characterised presbyterian propaganda.[39]

Therefore to establish why Harrison did not go on to advocate presbyterianism may tell us something important about Elizabethan Puritanism. Zealous pastors like Harrison consciously sought to expose the dangerous contrasts between the True Church and the Elizabethan Church as established in 1559, and to remove whatever maintained those contrasts. Those who accepted the Church as established preferred to emphasise the laudable contrasts between the Elizabethan Church and popery, and claimed to regard as indifferent what zealots believed to be essentially popish remnants, symbolising the corruptions which Satan had succeeded in introducing into the True Church via Gentilism and popery. To put it crudely, one could argue that the clarity with which they perceived the differences between the True Church and the Elizabethan church distinguished Puritans from conformists, a qualitative distinction manifested in a multitude of individual and contextual variations. For even more, presbyterians and later separatists differed from moderate Puritans in their ability to remain conscious of those contrasts between the True Church and the Elizabethan institution while being continually exposed to the obdurate conservatism and popery of the mass of the people, and in their ability to devalue the contrasts between popery and the 1559 settlement, which those pastoral experiences might tend to magnify. Harrison, for example, failed to maintain an intense consciousness of the remaining contrasts between the True Church and the Elizabethan Church when confronted by popery in his ministry, so that he remained a moderate Puritan. For while he accepted the theoretical truth of presbyterian arguments, he found them too idealistic to put into practice given the spiritual state of the vast majority of Elizabethan Englishmen. Doubtless such a broad framework requires qualification in details, but it certainly explains many of William Harrison's thoughts and actions.

Within the limited and particular context of the Elizabethan Church, the outlines of such distinctions emerge from the scanty evidence of the impact of Harrison's ministry upon the attitudes and actions of his parishioners. This evidence it still incomplete, but it bears out his major objection to presbyterian demands, that given present human resources it remained impossible 'to stir up such an exquisite face of the church as we imagine or desire, sith our corruption is such that it will never yield to so great perfection'.[40] Both the comparative lack of a godly, learned ministry, and

---

[39] See above, pp. 13–27 and *Description*, ed. Edelen, p. 293.　　　　　[40] Ibid., p. 98.

the reality of a people singularly lacking in the bonds of apostolic love and purity, made a presbyterian system unworkable in contemporary England. Regretfully rather than critically, Harrison concluded that presbyterian idealism did not match his daily experience of entrenched superstition and ignorance. The response of a few individuals may have made Harrison's thankless task more worthwhile. For example, the Will of Henry Browne of Radwinter leaves a remarkable impression of a substantial property-owner whose business failures had not only forced him to sell most of his lands but also left him in a state of shock and riddled with doubts about his election. Therefore he used his Will, written 'withe myne owne hande', to reassure himself, despite his worldly failure, of his membership of God's 'faithfull people' by an elaborate confession of faith. Writing in 1575, five years before his death, Browne reveals that years of Harrison's preaching about the application of Scriptural models had led at least this hearer to 'professe to serve the Lord oure god according to his holie worde'. Yet this example stands out from the generally formulaic Radwinter wills.[41] Indeed Harrison's apocalyptic sense that 'in my time here in England…the repaire to churche and zeale to devotion wexeth cold and is almost utterly like to be extinguished' reflects his somewhat over-sensitive reaction to his experiences at Radwinter.[42]

Of course, what we would regard as indifference Harrison perceived as atheism, but if we turn from considering faith to examining works, then the evidence of the Archdeacon's Court suggests that Harrison had his fair share of unregenerate parishioners at Radwinter. Yet since the archidiaconal records inevitably focus on wrongdoing, it would be unfair to allow the scattered evidence of theft and fornication at Radwinter to give the final verdict on his evangelising. Radwinter's moral tone may have been no worse, and perhaps even a little better, than that of most Essex parishes. Perhaps therefore we should refrain from generalising from the fact that William Sexton of Radwinter 'suspected to mayntayne bawdry', eventually owed the largest sum of unpaid fines to the Archdeacon's Court in this period, and in 1580 stood accused of absenting himself from Harrison's services for three quarters of the year.[43] At various times Thomas Sparke, Thomas Hyde, Alice Sexton and Margaret Croxall all stood contumacious or excommunicate for refusing to accept the censures of the Court upon their alleged moral failings.[44] Such entries probably indicate his parishioners' indifference to the

[41] P.R.O. PROB 11/63, fos. 8r–v; and contrast, e.g., the standard preamble to the Will of Thomas Mundeford in 1588, P.R.O. PROB 11/72, fos. 458r–460v.

[42] TCD MS 165, fo. 314v.

[43] E.R.O. D/ACA 3, fos. 59v, 74v, both before Harrison as Official. See also F. G. Emmison, *Elizabethan Life: Morals and the Church Courts* (Chelmsford, 1973), p. 77. In 1588 Sexton attacked Harrison's curate, George Pomfret (ibid., p. 209).

[44] E.R.O. D/ACA 3, fos. 12r–v, 23v, 77v; D/ACA 13, fo. 74r.

penalties rather than radical disrespect for the role of the 'bawdy' courts in a reformed Church. Two Radwinter men refused to attend the Court after a brawl in church in 1586, presumably during Harrison's absence in either London or Windsor, but on the other hand Henry Croxall and his wife purged their guilt in 1585, after a period of wilful excommunication, at a session of the Court which we know from other references that Harrison attended.[45] While men like Calfhill and Withers, who shared his anxieties about the Church, at least nominally controlled the 'bawdy' courts, Harrison personally found little to attract him in presbyterian criticisms that their unreformed procedures and profligate use of excommunication imposed ungodly restraints on the pastor's role as reconciler amongst his flock. Since Harrison, when an Official of the Court, occasionally disregarded its formal procedures and legal restraints, he may have managed to combine this godly role with his formal office, although of course such actions would leave no trace in the records.

While Harrison apparently did not have to contend with over-zealous laymen and women at Radwinter, his comments suggest that he did not have it all his own way with the conservative majority of his flock, who on certain issues perhaps only grudgingly accepted the novelties with which he confronted them. The immemorial disputes over tithes seemed part of the familiar social fabric,[46] but Harrison's marriage caused wider social reper- cussions, not only putting him on the defensive in his attitude to the legal establishment, but probably offending parochial prejudices against clerical marriage and thus making his evangelical task harder still. By 1570 at the latest, Harrison had married a Protestant from the Calais Pale, Marion Isebrande. In his eyes this union obeyed God's command to furnish up the number of the Elect, but even at the end of his life he felt the need to defend his marriage from both contemporary criticism and legal doubts, twice emphasising in his Will that Marion was 'by the lawe of gode...my true and lawfull wife'.[47] This issue continually reminded Harrison of the contrast between the divine injunctions and the traditions of carnal reason, formalised in popery, for in the 'Chronology' he had insisted that despite the Edwardine statute in favour of clerical marriage, it was totally unnecessary 'that our children should be made legittimate by mannes law'. Conservative common lawyers perpetuated this disobedience to God's commands, however. For example, Sir John Fitzjames 'being demaunded in open terme to saie what preestes wifes were he answered after his blockish manner concubines,

---

45 Emmison, *Elizabethan Life: Morals*, p. 120, and ERO. D/ACA 13, fos. 65v, 72v.
46 TCD MS 165, fos. 58r, 217v, grumbling about the slow payment of tithes. He sued at least once for subtraction of tithes, in 1578 (F. G. Emmison, 'Tithes, Perambulations and Sabbath-breach in Elizabethan Essex', in *Tribute to an Antiquary*, ed. Emmison and R. Stephens (London, 1976), p. 179).
47 Parry, 'Puritanism and history', pp. 29–32; P.R.O. PROB 11/82, fos. 268v–269r.

concubines', although, as Harrison pointed out, the common law had never made clerical marriage illegal.[48] Yet he could never silence those 'curious carpers of our time' who 'discommend' the chaste clerical wives 'in respect of the unchast whoredome of ther monasticall and professed votaries'; indeed clerical spouses could not be called wives.[49]

Another ingrained social prejudice, the common belief in the power of witchcraft, proved equally difficult to eradicate. Harrison's growing confidence that Christian liberty freed him from a fearful bondage to Satan's works allowed him to investigate Bodin's numerology within careful limits, as we have seen. This confidence also allowed him to practise a non-demonic, learned and intellectual astral magic. Yet he also displayed a superior contempt for 'the toies that superstition hath brought into our husband-mens heads' about the effectiveness of necromancy upon cattle. As vicar of Wimbish, adjacent to Radwinter, between 1571 and 1581 he conspicuously failed to convey this sense of freedom from satanic powers to his parishioners, most notably to John Cornell, who had presented him to the living. Cornell persistently persecuted one Margery Stanton and her family, whom he accused of bewitching his cattle. This prejudice gradually infected the whole parish, until in 1579 Stanton was indicted for killing two animals by witchcraft. Witnesses also deposed about a series of incidents in which we can see that guilt caused by refusing Stanton's requests for charity prompted hysterical illnesses in adults and fears that children had been bewitched. Harrison took a more detached view, however, and although his son allegedly fell ill after being touched by the disgruntled Stanton, he quickly recovered after Harrison's return. No other case of hysteria ended so quickly, suggesting that alone in his parish Harrison perceived his spiritual freedom from the fear of witchcraft.[50]

Harrison clearly attributed popular belief in necromancy to the influence of superstition and carnal reason, which he identified with popery. His encounters with papists at Wimbish, added to his experiences under Mary and his problems at Radwinter, demonstrated the tenacity of antichristian beliefs, and the difficulties that remained to be eradicated before presbyterianism could become a viable organisation for the Elizabethan Church. His parishioners at Wimbish included the Wiseman family, convinced recusants who sheltered many itinerant popish priests. Thomas Wiseman led local society, and by persuading him to conform Harrison fulfilled most expectations of government policy, which sought the purely political goal of

[48] TCD MS 165, fo. 275v, and *Harrison's Description*, ed. Furnivall, i, Appendix I, p. lii, reprinting part of the Derry 'Chronology'.

[49] TCD MS 165, fos. 34r, 222r.

[50] See above, pp. 114–21 on Bodin, and below, pp. 319–23 on talismans. *Description* (1587), p. 110; *A Detection of damnable driftes* (for Edward White: London, 1579), sigs. A6v, B1r; K. V. Thomas, *Religion and the Decline of Magic* (London, 1971), pp. 554–5.

securing outward conformity from the heads of popish households. Harrison's ability to persuade Wiseman to conform suggests that his radical distinction between the True Church and popery did not lead him to assimilate to irreconcilable antichristianity everyone who did not meet his exacting standards of godliness. Despite his fear that the satanic wiles of antichristian Gentilism could subvert the True Church, Harrison's confidence in the power of the Word enabled him to make allowances for individual weaknesses. Certainly he found more pastoral benefit in a sympathetic style of preaching and teaching than the aggressive, punitive anti-Catholicism that increasingly attracted evangelical Protestants exasperated by the sullen intransigence of papists and conservatives. Harrison followed the Pauline model and gave soft milk before strong meat, 'but my neighboures will not here on that side'; they complained about the incorrigible ignorance of their audience, 'saieng that it availeth not to preach grace where the herers are ignoraunt of the effect of the law'. Yet this attitude ignored 'the infirmitie of the weaker sort which I utterly mislike' said Harrison. His successor at Wimbish, Lancelot Ellis, perhaps did not follow Paul's precepts, for the Wisemans relapsed into recusancy almost immediately upon Harrison's resignation in November 1581.[51] Harrison may have just possibly been referring to George Withers, who, despite his emulation of the Pauline style of preaching, eventually concluded that 'there is no hope of the conversion of these obstinate wicked ones, who stubbornly refuse to here all wholesome doctrine'. Withers, like Harrison, identified contemporary papists with the perpetual opponents of the True Church – he could detect no differences between those who had stoned Stephen and 'the papists amongest us', who refused to hear the Word, and he used that comparison to explain his contemporary failure.[52]

Harrison's ability to discriminate in individual cases, even in times of growing apocalyptic crisis, did not amount to tolerance, but it does reveal a more sympathetic side to his Protestantism. This does not mean that he abandoned his belief in the reality of the struggle between the Two Churches – merely that individuals do not conform to type on all occasions. In 1585, for example, he agreed to compurgate for John Luddington, vicar of the adjoining parish of Great Sampford, that 'he is no defender of transubstantiation in the sacrament of the Lord's Supper'. Harrison, when

---

51 TCD MS 165, fo. 197v; H. M. C. *Tenth Report*, pt. IV (London, 1885), Appendix, pp. 478–90. Relations with Ellis became so bad that the Wisemans later asked Harrison to confirm the christening of Dorothy Wiseman by an itinerant popish priest (E.R.O. D/P 313/1/1, fo. 6r). John Foxe's unusual tolerance towards recusants also rested on his confidence in spiritual religion (Olsen, *Foxe*, p. 15 and *passim*).

52 Withers, *An ABC*, sigs. A5r, H3v–H4r. Withers's impatience with stubborn popery perhaps indicates his unease at the way in which it made the Elizabethan Church appear reformed by contrast, and thus hindered the argument for further reformation.

Official of the Archdeacon's Court, had censured Luddington in 1569 for neglecting his calling as preacher and teacher to his flock. This might have made him ultra-sensitive to the suggestion that Luddington was a papist, especially since Harrison regarded the 'bestly doctrine' of transubstantiation as the overt distinguishing mark of the Church of Cain since Christ. Yet Harrison probably acted on his intimate knowledge of the personality clash between Luddington and his fire-brand of a curate, John Knight, rather than allowing his apocalyptic theories to determine his interpretation of Luddington's status within the cosmic struggle. Knight's vehement refusal to subscribe to Whitgift's Articles of 1585 'but so as the same are agreinge to the word of god' establishes his position in the affair. Indeed 'he wold not be slandered to have simplie subscribed' and seemed to invite the Court's punishment of suspension by his obdurate tone. Even the dry formulas of the Court records cannot completely obscure Knight's zealous readiness to detect popery in Luddington's every remark. The churchwardens of Great Sampford were asked whether on Easter Tuesday they had heard Luddington and Knight 'reason upon transubstantiation', and their answers suggest that Knight had seized upon something in Luddington's reasoning which smacked of popery, and that hearsay quickly spread the accusation amongst the parishioners. Harrion's refusal to be panicked into distancing himself from Luddington's alleged popery infers that he maintained some sense of proportion despite his own fears and his knowledge of Luddington's inadequacies. Nor does it necessarily imply that Harrison now adopted a more lenient posture towards popery than Knight, for even Lancelot Ellis, no friend to the papists, found himself suspended for publicly describing the abrasive Knight as 'a sauce box'.[53]

While on the one flank the enduring problem of popery made idealistic remedies for the Elizabethan Church less immediately compelling to Harrison, on the other government actions against popery occasionally made him think better of the magistrate's role in the Church. Like other 'commonwealth' preachers he criticised the establishment's destructive self-interest, yet his ability to interpret existing institutions in the light of Scriptural godly models paradoxically saved him from impotent extremism. Sometimes, therefore, his actions modified the potentially alienating criticism divulged in his 'Chronology', referring to 'princes of our time of whom some canne dispense with ther subiectes either for frendship or gaine to use their [popery] idolatry still'.[54] A conformist like John Whitgift found it easier to accept the existing social hierarchy because he believed that while the Church provided an essential basis for society it 'giveth not the whole

---

[53] E.R.O. D/ACA 3, fo. 45r, on Luddington's deficiencies. D/ACA 13, fos. 72r, 74r, 75r; and see fos. 57v, 59v, for papists detected at Great Sampford. TCD MS 165, fo. 48v.

[54] Harrison's alteration; ibid., fo. 73r.

forme or fashion to that which is builded upon it'. Harrison's view, that Church and commonwealth had been founded together by the patriarchs and should now both be directed by the Word, contained greater tension and shows important continuities with the presbyterians. Yet Harrison could avoid most of the disruptive consequences of this ideology and 'abide till god by the magistrate shall execute his purpose' not only because he believed in the immense latent power of God's promises, but also because he interpreted Elizabeth's actions by a Scriptural model.

In July 1578 the Royal Progress halted at Audley End, near Radwinter, and besides the vital exchange of social pleasantries, diligent enquiries were made about local recusants. The new Jesuit missions made the reduction of socially important recusants to conformity imperative, and at Norwich on 22 August the Privy Council ordered the arrest of 'Rooke Grene, gentleman', 'to be conferred with all by Mr Lawson [Vicar of Saffron Walden] and Mr Harrison, preachers, to bring him to conformitie in Religion'. Evidently Grene proved less tractable than the Wisemans, for he later became a prisoner in Colchester Castle. Nevertheless, this appointment testifies to Harrison's local reputation as a godly preacher, and it also affected his perception of Elizabeth's role, as we shall see in the next chapter. For he identified the dispensing of justice and suppression of idolatry as the chief and comple- mentary functions of Israel's intermittent, itinerant Judgeship, which as a divine institution he felt obligated to prefer to continuous monarchy. There- fore when Elizabeth on her Progress appeared from his perspective to fill the place of an Old Testament Judge, his doubts about the establishment tem- porarily subsided.[55]

At the parochial level Harrison's pursuit of a typically 'Grindalian' vision of a pastorally centred church paradoxically helped to moderate his radicalism, as it did for so many other godly preachers. Yet even the limited success that he achieved showed that the complete reformation of the Elizabethan Church remained a possibility, and that much might be done to restore to its original, evangelical functions the legalistic apparatus inherited from degenerate popery, without destroying that structure altogether. This conviction involved a difficult suspension of disbelief, which can be seen in Harrison's work as an Official of the Archdeacon of Colchester's Court, and his reactions to that experience. His appointment dates from some considerable time before July 1569, when the extant records begin, for although 'no lawyer', he presided alone until July 1570, and then with others until January 1576, afterwards occasionally sitting as surrogate at Saffron

---

[55] J. Nichols, *The Progresses and Public Processions of Queen Elizabeth* (3 vols. London, 1823), ii, pp. 111–14. *Acts of the Privy Council of England*, new series, X, 1577–78 (London, 1895), pp. 313, 323–4, 327; XI, 1578–80 (London, 1895), pp. 174–5. John Lawson was Vicar of Saffron Walden, 1570–80. See below, pp. 233–5.

Walden until 1581.[56] Harrison clearly enjoyed the confidence of the 'Grindalian' group of reformers headed locally by Archdeacon James Calfhill, and of George Withers, who succeeded Calfhill in 1570. Two years previously, in a debate with Thomas Erastus, Withers had defended presbyterianism, thus adding to his previous reputation as one who favoured the kind of thorough reformation which he had promoted in the Palatinate. In 1584 he defended those clerics who refused to subscribe to Whitgift's Articles.[57] Not only did Calfhill and Withers actively seek to reform the Prayer Book along the lines suggested in the Convocation of 1563, but they appointed a succession of reform-minded Officials to their Courts. Therefore, despite the Archdeacon's official duty to enforce uniformity, those who practised a sincere obedience to God's Word rather than the 1559 Prayer Book rubrics went unmolested. Only after Aylmer's visitation of 1583 were the archidiaconal courts in Essex used against clerical non-conformity, and even then zealous pastors counter-attacked by using the courts to correct inadequate incumbents, when profitable testamentary business already clogged the system.[58] Consequently, under the kind of local regime fostered by Calfhill and Withers, Harrison could reconcile his desire for further reformation with the limitations imposed by the popish structure of the Archdeacon's Court.

This does not mean that Harrison accepted the legalistic institution as he found it, for he never reconciled himself to the contrast between ideal and reality which the Courts epitomised. Just as Grindal found his apostolic conception of his ministry at odds with the inherited mass of legal forms which had grown up around the office of bishop, so the traditional methods of the church courts and their inadequate punishments frustrated Harrison's desire thoroughly to punish sin. The courts depended upon the co-operation of parochial clergy and churchwardens for the effective correction of incontinence, and remained encumbered by an interminable legal process designed to give all parties a fair hearing.[59] Such scruples seemed superfluous to Harrison. His ideal remedy distantly echoes Bucer's civic Protestantism enforced at Strasbourg, and reveals some of the difficulties encountered by Grindal and his lesser officers like Harrison in applying such ideas in England. After years of presiding over impotent attempts to restrain sin, Harrison felt that the problem required two officers, with the summary powers of Roman censors, 'in every citie and incorporate town in England, for then Idleness, dronkenesse, swearing, whoredome, unchastity, gaming and lewde exercise should quickly be restreigned'. Harrison's censorious willingness to detect

---

[56] See E.R.O. D/ACA 3, D/ACA 4, D/ACA 5; and Edelen, 'William Harrison', pp. 265–6.
[57] Collinson, *Puritan Movement*, pp. 81, 96, 223–4, 256.
[58] Anglin, 'Essex Puritan Movement', pp. 191–7. See E.R.O. D/ACA 3, fos. 45v–46r, for Harrison's personal attempts to reform local deficiencies in 1569.
[59] Anglin, 'Essex Puritan Movement', p. 192; and Collinson, *Grindal*, pp. 108–23.

a deeper meaning in contemporary incontinence thus led him to envisage a return to the primitive pattern of the direct administration of justice, with which Grindal heartily agreed.[60] Harrison's awareness of the history of his office also contributed to his wish to see it swept away, for he claimed that it had a somewhat tainted beginning with Canute, who abolished ancient severe laws against sins such as adultery and committed the administration of a milder law to the clergy. Yet Harrison argued that the harsher punishment had shown the laity's estimation of marriage, while the medieval clergy had been more interested in punishing married priests than adulterers and fornicators, and consequently had provided insufficient penalties, 'For what great smart is it to be turned out of a hot sheet into a cold?'.[61]

The traditional penitential white sheet and taper, dismissed as 'toyish censures' by the presbyterians, too often provided an excuse for irreverence. Yet even Grindal, when he attempted to add a godly seriousness to the proceedings, retained the white sheet and sought no more drastic punishment for the sin. In contrast, the censorious Puritan regime at Bury St Edmunds imposed a much severer penal code in 1578, punishing fornication with prolonged whippings, a foretaste of the morally repressive magistracy which became increasingly common in England by the early seventeenth century. Harrison went even further and insisted that adulterers should lose their freedom. In the 1587 *Description* he advocated that 'adultery and whoredom' should be treated as theft, 'the parties trespassant to be made bond or slaves unto those that receive the injury, to sell and give where they listed, or to be condemned to the galleys'. This almost hysterical proposal reveals the dangerous gulf between Harrison's ideals and the reality in which he had to work.[62] On the other hand his frustration could find a more benevolent outlet when he purged the legal system of some of its worst abuses. Harrison roundly condemned 'caterpillars' who increasingly vexed the commonwealth by promoting discord in order to share in the fees charged for subsequent litigation in the church courts, and he dismissed one such grub, his apparitor Edward Birchemore, 'for sondry abuses and misdemeanours'. Birchemore got off lightly, for Harrison believed that such activities deserved banishment.[63]

The desire to reduce corrupted structures to their primitive purity

---

[60] TCD MS 165, fo. 104r. Note the urban bias, which would limit the scope of this censorship. Possibly Harrison aimed at adapting presbyterian deacons to parts of the English social structure. Collinson, *Grindal*, pp. 121–3; and for more on the direct administration of justice, see below pp. 211–12, 232–4.

[61] *Description*, ed. Edelen, pp. 189–90.

[62] *The Remains of Edmund Grindal*, ed. Nicholson, pp. 455–7; P. Collinson, *The Religion of Protestants* (Oxford, 1982), pp. 158–9; *Description*, ed. Edelen, p. 190.

[63] P.R.O. C 24/177/52; TCD MS 165, fo. 339v. Apparitors had been on the make since at least Chaucer's time.

necessarily ignores the inertial weight of an entrenched system, for too thorough a knowledge of the problems often makes idealistic solutions appear naive. Harrison's inability to ignore ingrained popery and opt for presbyterianism exemplifies this restraint, and at other times he reveals that very human common sense which he often deprecated as the obstacle of carnal reason in the way of proper reformation. Thus although Grindal insisted that the true doctrine of repentance needed to be taught through public acts of contrition, and later forbade any commutation of public penance into money payments in the northern province, Harrison undermined this godly policy at least once. Commutation of penance occurred very infrequently since it required episcopal permission and consequently larger fees, but Harrison allowed it to one George Slowman of Kelvedon, Essex, apparently without episcopal permission.[64]

Harrion's action may represent a painful coming to terms with reality, but if so that realism also eventually penetrated the assumptions of those Essex presbyterians who began to criticise the church courts from the early 1580s. They resented the courts' powers of excommunication and suspension, which interfered with the godly pastor's right to discipline his own congregation, and they sought to revive synodal congregations where archdeacons and zealous ministers could meet as equals to discipline the ungodly and insufficient clergy, thus abandoning the unscriptural 'bawdy' courts and episcopal visitations. Yet like Harrison they encountered the obdurate refusal of the unregenerate to respect the apostolic structure and discipline of the True Church, and had to fall back on the traditional weapons of detection by churchwardens and punishment by the Archdeacon's Court to control contemptuous parishioners, whose refusal to participate in primitive discipline had previously forced Harrison to reject presbyterianism as a practical alternative to episcopacy. Indeed, at this parochial level Harrison's commitment to combating the people's indifference by fervent preaching of the Word can be distinguished from the presbyterian recognition of that same responsibility only by Harrison's recognition of the limitations of the apostolic discipline. For Edmund Chapman, a member of the Dedham classis, also felt that God had imposed upon him the duty 'to bear up the scepter of His holy truth', for 'the zeal of many decayeth'. Yet Chapman still felt it possible to impose this discipline without the supervision of his Archdeacon, George Withers.[65]

The very narrowness and empirical basis of this distinction clearly indicates Harrison's position in the Elizabethan Church. For he accepted that

[64] E.R.O. D/ACA 3, fos. 56v, 71v, 79r, 91r, 101v, 110r and 112r, record the aptly named Slowman's glacial progress through the court procedure. Collinson, *Grindal*, p. 197; Emmison, *Elizabethan Life: Morals*, pp. 290–1.

[65] Anglin, 'Essex Puritan Movement', pp. 183–5, quoting Chapman at p. 185.

given the right pastoral circumstances, a presbyterian system of discipline could be made to work. More fundamental differences separated Harrison from the views of conformists like John Whitgift and Richard Bancroft, despite the fact that with many other moderate Puritans he echoed their criticisms of 'precisians'. Indeed Harrison's conception of history almost completely accepted the presbyterian case, a particularly important fact since that shared historical interpretation revealed the ambivalent nature of the Elizabethan Church. For both presbyterians and moderate Puritans like Harrison focussed their allegiance upon the True Church, not the particular society whose Church Whitgift and Bancroft defended. Harrison's belief that the present witnessed the continuation of the struggle between the covenant line in the Church of the Elect, and the Church of Cain now manifested in popery, showed him that God required an absolute dichotomy between true and false religion, and consequently heightened his fear of the infection of Gentilism, in the form of popery, within the Elizabethan Church. Harrison wrote his 'Chronology' depicting this cosmic struggle during the 1570s, when Thomas Cartwright was advancing a similar historical interpretation in the Admonition controversy, itself largely a debate about the shape of salvation history and its meaning for the present.

Essentially, Cartwright shared Harrison's belief that Gentilism, satanically inspired opposition to the Elect before Christ, had reappeared after the Passion in those satanic innovations which caused the Church's degeneration into popery and the rise of Antichrist. The fact that both Harrison and Cartwright independently concluded that popery represented the continuation of satanic Gentilism suggests that that connection may have been fundamental to Puritan sensitivity towards residual popery in the Elizabethan Church. Even more strikingly, Harrison's deep commitment to the creation of a pastoral ministry took the form of an insistence that the True Church, the sole defence against Antichrist, could be built up only by reviving those prophetic institutions depicted in the Scriptures, a way of thinking which justified the presbyterian programme. In this context Harrison could perceive dangerous contrasts between the True Church and the Elizabethan Church, contrasts which showed where Satan had broken into and laid waste the institutions of the True Church; his perception that those institutions must be rebuilt identifies him as a Puritan within the context of the Elizabethan church.[66] We should bear in mind this suggested relationship between Harrison's historical interpretation and his Puritanism during the

---

[66] The extant evidence leaves unresolved whether Harrison always opposed presbyterianism; he did not discuss it during the 1570s debate but in the polarised atmosphere of 1587. Furnivall's selections from the Derry 'Chronology' (*Harrison's Description*, Appendix I), provide the only evidence about Harrison's latest ideas, but reforms Harrison added to the 1587 *Description* are consistent with his 1570s historical interpretation.

following discussion, for it may have wider implications for our understanding of Puritan thought, especially since Harrison's rejection of presbyterianism on pastoral grounds can be traced in lesser contrasts with
Cartwright's historical interpretation.

Harrison's belief that advocates for presbyterianism underestimated the
problems presented by an unregenerate populace also had a theological
dimension. Harrison accepted the broad Calvinist consensus that the test of
effectual calling in 2 Pet. 1.10 offered certainty of election to all who rested
upon the security of God's promises and followed the godly examples of the
covenant line.[67] Although he did not over-react, he avoided the presbyterians' growing and pastorally difficult emphasis on the 'temporary' faith of
the reprobate, indistinguishable to human perceptions from true faith. This
interpretation would exclude many from the gathered congregation which
best suited a presbyterian polity.[68] Such extremism contributed nothing to
the solution of already difficult pastoral problems, and while mere tinkering
with episcopacy would not remedy 'the want of discipline in the church',
neither would presbyterianism, for human weaknesses demanded a complete
reorientation of the Church to its prophetic duty of creating 'lively stones'
to build up Christ's Church, before a presbyterian system could become
feasible.[69] Harrison suggested a programme of reforms which aimed to bring
about such a reorientation by returning inherited structures to the purpose
from which they had been distorted by Satan – the provision of a learned
preaching ministry.

Here we may add a further refinement to the distinction already drawn
between presbyterians and moderate Puritans, for Harrison was not an
'establishment' moderate Puritan. To a certain extent his pastorally centred

---

[67] Two fragments of a theological treatise in Harrison's hand which he re-used in TCD MS 165,
fo. 141r, emphasise the role of grace in this process and criticise those who denied the
importance of election 'as if his word shold speake of gret things...not possible to be atteined
or that no man in this life could be partaker of his spirite...which is contrary to his worde
wherin he hath freely promised that he will powre out of his [spirit upon] all flesh' (Joel 2.28).
Unbelievers who so little credit the truth cannot crave any divine mercy; 'can any man be
the lordes that is not after his callinge partaker of his spirite', citing John 3,24 (*sic*) and Gal.
4.6.

[68] This uncompromising idea developed from undercurrents in the thought of Calvin and Beza,
and particularly attracted William Perkins (R. T. Kendall, *Calvin and English Calvinists to 1649*
(Oxford, 1979), pp. 7–8, 25–6, 37, 51). Harrison was not completely put off, deriding
unnamed contemporaries 'that defend the truth when thei be yonge and in their age become
cold professors of the same' (TCD MS 165, fo. 154r). The former presbyterian William Fulke
similarly appeared theologically outmoded in the Cambridge of the 1580s (R. J. Bauckham,
'The Career and thought of Dr William Fulke 1537–89' (unpublished Ph.D. dissertation,
Cambridge, 1973), pp. 126–36).

[69] *Description* (1587), p. 213. The British Church had originally ensured that those who 'walke
in the spirit' were 'corrected by severe discipline', to stop individuals back-sliding into
'former wickednesse' or even becoming 'meere Atheists', but Satan and Antichrist had
destroyed this discipline (ibid., p. 24).

Church would have been recognisable to that Puritan establishment which complained in 1576 of the 'want of discipline', and earned Whitgift's splenetic opposition. Like those men, Harrison made no excuses for episcopacy but felt that the narrow divisiveness of the extremists could not contribute to the profound reformation which he sought throughout society, and in fact only weakened the godly commonwealth against the antichristian papacy.[70] Harrison also insisted that extremism hindered this reformation by undermining that social order and degree which provided an essential safeguard against anarchy and antichristian assaults. He echoed the current accusation that the presbyterians 'can abide no superiors'.[71] Yet Harrison's proposed reforms largely ignored any claims that the laity might have in a truly reformed Church, and in detail they overturned fundamental social assumptions about the necessity for lay patronage to support a preaching ministry. Nor did he regard bishops as mere royal appointees, in the manner of many Elizabethan Protestant laymen, but he emphasised that the history of the covenant line justified their pastoral pre-eminence. The intimate partnership between magistracy and clergy, of the kind which flourished during his lifetime at nearby Bury St Edmunds, never attracted him, for a comparison with the Scriptural godly society revealed too many serious failings in contemporary magistrates.[72] Therefore, although Harrison's *Description* apparently proposed a reformed pastoral ministry within the existing social and ecclesiastical order, his Scripturally-inspired reforms were as potentially revolutionary as the presbyterian system.

Harrison's dutiful subjection thus differed from the submissive conformity demanded by Elizabeth and preached by Parker and Whitgift. For the order which would come from universal obedience to the Word intrinsically differed from that which Whitgift defended, as we have noticed in Harrison's excited interpretation of Elizabeth's Progress in the light of the Old Testament Judgeship. Such an order had more in common with the godly discipline destroyed by the triumph of Antichrist.[73] Whitgift also encouraged a preaching ministry, but he accepted that it could be produced by those inherited institutions which Harrison believed encapsulated and perpetuated

---

[70] Collinson, *Puritan Movement*, pp. 161–3, 206, and p. 128, which describes this as an attitude common to Cambridge-educated Puritan clerics. See also Collinson, *Letters of Thomas Wood, Puritan, 1566–77*, B.I.H.R., Special Supp. No. 5 (November 1960), p. xxxi, for the similar opinion of Thomas Norton, a leading Puritan layman.

[71] *Description* (1587), p. 157, a chapter 'Of Degrees'. Other Cambridge Puritans, including presbyterians, assumed that their reforming ideas were congruent with existing social structures (Collinson, *Puritan Movement*, p. 128; P. Lake, 'The dilemma of the establishment puritan', in *Journal of Ecclesiastical History*, xxix (1978) pp. 23–35 at p. 25).

[72] P. Collinson, *The Religion of Protestants*, pp. 153–64. See below, pp. 259–69.

[73] Foxe found 'all order broken, Discipline dissolved, true Doctrine defaced, Christian Faith extinguished' by the time of Innocent III (*Actes and Monuments* (1583), sig. *4v); and see *Description* (1587), p. 24.

papist corruptions in their deformities, corruptions which would inevitably destroy any Church which tolerated them. Harrison and Whitgift also saw different purposes for a pastoral ministry, and these contrasting objectives conditioned what they believed should be the content of that ministry's preaching. Harrison struggled to interpret the present according to the Scriptural criteria laid down by the covenant line, and by this contemporaneous application of Scriptural knowledge sought to identify those popish remnants whose complete reformation would help to defeat Antichrist. Whitgift encouraged preaching which primarily defended the status quo as something validly distinct from popery in both doctrine and sacraments; it did not have to conform in its discipline to an alleged godly model of a completely reformed Church.

Harrison's historical interpretation enabled him to perceive existing institutions in the light of Scriptural godly models, and thus to preserve a sustainable balance between ideal and reality, by suggesting that the present order could be transformed by the Word. Yet while this saved him from impotent extremism, there remained underlying tensions, never totally resolved, in his view that the True Church and commonwealth had been founded together in Scriptural history, and that the teachings of the covenant line should direct both in the present. Therefore at times his outlook resembled Cartwright's claim 'that the commonwealth...should be framed according to the church' founded at the beginning of the world. Whitgift had fewer misgivings about the existing commonwealth because the Church 'giveth not the whole forme or fashion to that which is builded upon it'. Bancroft echoed this implicitly authoritarian view, comparing alleged presbyterian disorders with the time when 'there was no king in Israel...the magistrates did not their duties', the very period when Harrison believed that Israel's polity had been most obedient to the Word.[74]

An understanding of this fundamental point, that in Harrison's mind the eternal struggle of the Two Churches made specific demands on Elizabethan England, also helps to counterbalance his other conventional criticisms of presbyterian arguments. Like Bancroft he was put off by presbyterian contradictions about the details of their future ecclesiastical regiment, and he also agreed with Whitgift that the Genevan system could not be stretched to fit English society.[75] Like many moderate Puritans, Harrison abandoned a balanced appreciation of presbyterianism in the 1590s when exposed to

---

[74] J. Whitgift, *The Defense of the Aunswere to the admonition, against the Replie of T.C. by John Whitgift Doctor of Divinitie* (Henry Binneman for Humfreye Toye: London, 1574), p. 646, arguing that Cartwright's imagined godly commonwealth existed 'only among the anabaptists'. R. Bancroft, *A Sermon Preached at Paules Crosse the 9 of Februarie...1588* (for George Seton: London, 1588), sig. ¶ 4r, and see below, pp. 220–2.

[75] Bancroft, *Sermon*, sig. G3v; *Description* (1587), p. 157; Whitgift, *Defense*, p. 639.

virulent government propaganda against the classes, and he echoed Whitgift and Bancroft in his analysis of 'presbyterian' machinations in the Parliaments of 1589 and 1593. Now the unrealistic idealists had become dangerous extremists. He described the manoeuvrings of some radical MPs in the excited and polarised language of uncompromising conformity. He felt threatened by what he saw as their anti-clericalism, and bemoaned the disastrous effect which their proposals would have on the Church's wealth, an approach consonant with Whitgift and Bancroft's attempts to defend the integrity, dignity and financial independence of the Church according to the standards of the secular hierarchy, but contrasting with Grindal's earlier emphasis on the Church's pastoral status.[76] Again, however, this only emphasises Harrison's commitment to a clerically dominated, fully reformed Church, and his refusal to countenance any partnership with the laity, whose 'reforms' attempted in 1589 and 1593 masked a deeper purpose against all true religion.

Thus in 1589 Harrison described the Commons as packed with 'yong burgesses, picked out of purpose to serve some secrete turne against the state present of the clergy', laymen whose ostensible purpose of making the clergy share the burdens of heavy war expenditure really aimed at Cathedral incomes.[77] Harrison's comments on the 1593 Parliament seem to place him firmly behind Whitgift, especially because Harrison contradicts Sir John Neale's stress on the defensive aims of the Puritan lawyers and the weakness of a compliant House of Commons.[78] Harrison attributed aggressive motives to 'the precisians', who combined in 1593 to procure 'the overthrow of bishops and all ecclesiastical regiment, and erection of soch discipline as thei themselves have prescribed', a view reminiscent of Bancroft's both in tone and content. The fact that Harrison believed that 'there were more then 100 of the lower house returned for outlawes' in this Parliament made the extremist measures appear to be a plot by men who 'will obey no law at all'.[79] This dual threat to stability pushed the sick and aged Harrison into his most unquestioning identification with the status quo, for he recorded his relief at the passing of an Act to restrain 'the malicious dealinges...of the precisians, papists and comelinge [alien] provokers', an obvious reference

[76] *Harrison's Description*, ed. Furnivall, Appendix I, pp. lix–lx; *cf.* Collinson, *Grindal*, p. 286.
[77] J. E. Neale, *Elizabeth I and her parliaments 1584–1601* (London, 1959), pp. 222, 225, 238; *cf. Harrison's Description*, ed. Furnivall, Appendix I, p. lix; Bancroft at the opening of this Parliament on 'the hope which manie men have conceived of the spoile of Bishops livings, of the subversion of cathedrall churches', and havoc of all Church revenues (*Sermon*, sig. C4r). Neale's use of Harrison's account is highly selective.
[78] Neale, *Parliaments 1584–1601*, pp. 241–5; *cf. Harrison's Description*, ed. Furnivall, Appendix I, p. lx.
[79] Ibid., Appendix I, p. lx; Neale, *Parliaments 1584–1601*, pp. 313, 318, discussing a bill on outlawry in this session.

to a Bill against papist recusants which emerged as the only Elizabethan Act against extreme Protestants.[80]

Yet Harrison's uncompromising language did not mean that he had abandoned his pastoral aims. For where Whitgift suspected the egalitarian consequences of proposed measures against pluralism and non-residence, Harrison, true to his belief that pluralism spread true doctrine wider, complained that 'hereby most churches should quickly have bene without their pastor'. Clearly, even at this period he still chiefly concerned himself with the pastoral ramifications of presbyterianism.[81] We should also recognise that Harrison criticised presbyterianism in the context of a desperate war against the truly antichristian power of Spain, which required unity and stability in Christ's Church. For that context also intensified Harrison's scrutiny of the Elizabethan Church and commonwealth in comparison with the True Church. The first edition of his *Description* published in 1577 described England only very generally in the light of the True Church. He revised the *Description* in the deepening apocalyptic crisis of the 1580s, a predicament which demanded that the godly commonwealth must strengthen its defences against Satan and Antichrist by a return to its Scriptural organisation. Therefore he not only integrated the *Description* more closely with the 'Chronology', which described the experiences of the True Church, but also added radical reform proposals and used stricter Scriptural criteria to analyse the Church in England. These changes reflect his conception of history as an oscillating conflict between the True Church and the Church of Cain, now represented in aggressive popery. For essentially Harrison's Puritanism reflected his recognition that this process was partly working itself out in contemporary England, which had to be brought as close as possible to the model of the True Church in order to survive against Antichrist's assaults.[82]

---

[80] Ibid., pp. 286–7; cf. Collinson, *Puritan Movement*, p. 431; *Harrison's Description*, ed. Furnivall, Appendix I, p. lx.

[81] Neale, *Parliaments 1584–1601*, pp. 227–9; cf. *Harrison's Description*, ed. Furnivall, Appendix I, p. lix. In 1589 Harrison acquired the only two works extant from his library relating to presbyterianism, significantly concerning the pastoral ramifications of godly discipline; Thomas Erastus's *Explicatio gravissimae quaestionis utrum excommunicatio, quatenus religionem intelligentes et amplexantes, a sacramentorum usu propter admissum facinus arcet, mandato nitatur devino, an excogitata sit ab hominibus* (Pescara, 1589), later bound with his copy of Beza's reply, *Tractatus pius et moderatus de vera excommunicatione, et Christiano Presbyterio* (Geneva, 1590), as Derry shelf-mark H.ii.c.44.

[82] Without the 'Chronology', the prophetic dimension of the *Description* has been overlooked by A. B. Ferguson, *Clio Unbound: perception of the social and cultural past in Renaissance England* (Durham, N.C., 1979), pp. 91–6; H. C. Porter, *Puritanism in Tudor England* (London, 1970), p. 176; P. Collinson, 'Episcopacy and reform in the later sixteenth century', in *Studies in Church History*, iii (1966), pp. 91–125 at p. 103; *The Description of England by William Harrison*, ed. G. Edelen (Ithaca, NY., 1968). See Parry, 'Harrison and Holinshed's Chronicles' pp. 796, 809, on the closer connection between the 'Chronology' and the 1587 *Description*.

We have already noticed that Harrison perceived popery in the light of the Two Churches, as a continuation of the idolatrous errors of Gentilism, summed up in the figure of Antichrist. For 'Sathan practized to reduce a christian gentilisme into the churche of christ' by appealing to natural man's weaknesses through Roman innovations. The human motives which had corrupted Israel through idolatry were 'even the same which move us to follow the papist religion and idolatry brought from Rome', warned Harrison, so the Elizabethan Church had to be purified of popery because it represented the infection of satanic Gentilism whose poison had almost destroyed the True Church and might do so finally by working through human appetites.[83] Thus, despite his doubts about presbyterian theories, Harrison still accepted in 1587 that the Scriptures demanded an unequivocal contrast between the godly and ungodly societies. Like the presbyterians, he believed that this distinction between truth and error could only be achieved by 'men of like condition' following the revealed godly models of the covenant line, the sole defence against Satan and the attractions of Christian Gentilism. For Thomas Cartwright shared Harrison's fundamental belief that Gentilism continued in antichristian popery. Therefore they both argued that the New Testament described Christ's perfect reformation against Gentilism, that it detailed at a decisive moment in the history of the covenant line those perpetual institutions in the True Church which provided the godly remedy for the present danger. Yet although Harrison went so far as to acknowledge that a presbyterian ecclesiastical polity constituted this perfect pattern, and that the development of an ecclesiastical hierarchy reflected the infection of Gentilism, he still found justification for contemporary episcopacy in a godly hierarchical model.

The familiar features of Harrison's account of Church history after Christ do not constitute the whole story, therefore. They represent only fragments of his overall concept of the Two Churches in existence since the beginning of time, and acquire different meanings when seen in that context. Like other radicals he believed that the primitive church ended with the first century AD; his concentration on persecution and the connection between early heresies and popery also fit a familiar pattern. His general comments on Antichrist appear unexceptionable.[84] In the context of the Two Churches, however, the details of Harrison's view of Antichrist reveal his ambivalence towards contemporary episcopacy. Satan used disorder and schism to achieve the destruction of the True Church, yet not only heresy but humanly devised

---

[83] TCD MS 165, fos. 253v, 59r.

[84] The 'Romaine Antichrist' released from bondage in AD 1000 usurped 'all power in heaven and yerth' as 'the best who hath made all the princes of the world dronke with the wine of her fornication' (TCD MS 165, fos. 270v–271r, 339v). His general church history was recently mis-attributed to the radical William Fulke (Bauckham, 'William Fulke', pp. 239, 242–4, 255).

authority paved the way for Antichrist. For in the True Church the origin, style and purpose of authority was always a central issue.[85]

Harrison's acceptance of presbyterian theories about ecclesiastical polity is evident in his use of Jerome's Commentary on Titus, an epistle which provided a litmus test for Elizabethan views about the primitive church. He argued that Jerome confirmed the apostolic constitution which Harrison had discovered by 'conferens of writers', namely that until the end of the first century 'the offices of bishops and elders were not distinguished in the [churche] congregations'. Only after the apostolic age were 'many schisms and heresies...daily stirred up by Sathan', forcing the appointment of superintendents. This marked the end 'of the first primitive churche' about AD 100, yet another in the cyclic declines of the True Church. Yet this superintendency still constituted a godly, spiritual authority, for 'in every citie one elder was appointed by general order out of the rest, to whom the name of bishop was only applied thereby to remove farder inconveniens'.[86] The ultimate contrast to primitive humility could be seen in the papacy, but even a reformed hierarchy was compromised by the consequences of this well-intentioned innovation. For the primitive superintendency 'proved in time a cause of gretter troble' than the schisms it was intended to control, since it opened the way for Antichrist.[87]

The primitive presbyterian organisation, which conformed itself to the differing gifts of grace, had survived in some places until nearly the end of the third century, when, Harrison claimed, a satanic hierarchy replaced it. In the same way that Satan had used Gentilism to prey upon the weaknesses of human reason and undermine the True Church in the Old Testament, so was this godly polity subverted when Rome decreed that ecclesiastical offices previously 'belonging to distinct persons' should now be held in succession.[88] This apparently laudable attempt to raise the status of the ministry according to rational criteria decisively diverted it from its pastoral aims and prepared the way for an exalted episcopacy which mocked the apostolic institution, after Rome established its hierarchy throughout the Church. For it was a Gentile innovation. Numa's seven-fold Roman priestly hierarchy provided the model, rising from the 'curiones' comparable to

[85] Cartwright could accept paternal rule over single congregations, Whitgift thought that English bishops sought the same jurisdiction as 'the olde Bishops' (*Defense*, pp. 417–21, 418). See Collinson, *Grindal*, pp. 126–52, on paternal episcopacy.

[86] TCD MS 165, fo. 144r. The Apostles only appointed 'elders and deacons locally in the severall congregations to see to the flocke'. Early bishops, identical with elders, were popularly elected. Roman corruption gave bishops the nomination of elders (ibid., fos. 138v, 169v). Whitgift cited Jerome on Titus for Apostolic episcopacy over many parishes (*Defense*, pp. 304, 318, 369, 377, 385, 390); Cartwright held with Harrison that Jerome meant that 'in every town there was a Bishop', pre-eminent only in his power of ordination (ibid., p. 385).

[87] TCD MS 165, fo. 144r.

[88] 'As dore keeper or reader, exorcist [benet collet], subdeacon, etc.' (ibid., fo. 159r; *cf.* Cartwright, *Defense*, p. 444).

contemporary 'parsones and vicares', to the 'pontifices or as I may call them Archbyshopes', endowed with papal powers in religion.[89] Harrison further detected the roots of the popish hierarchy in 'the originall of all vilenesse', in Ham and the priapic rites of Cain which he revived after the Flood. For 'as in the late popishe churche...benet and colet' were prerequisites for higher orders so none could serve the pagan gods who 'had not first bene a servant unto Priapus'.[90] In many places presbyterianism resisted 'the Romish order' until the mid-fifth century, but Antichrist's path to power was finally opened when this human invention became a part of saving faith, taking precedence over evangelical preaching early in the sixth century. Consequently the Pope 'is enemy to christ and utter adversary to the churche of god', the complete antithesis of truth, for whoever sat 'in the seate of Antichrist' became 'steigned with wickednesse'.[91]

Harrison thus shared the presbyterian belief that popery's pompous, lordly hierarchy betrayed its fundamental Gentilism, and that the Scriptures provided a godly, apostolic antidote in the shape of presbyterianism. Given his fear of Gentilism and antichristian subversion, what prevented Harrison from fully accepting the presbyterian programme? Why did he feel it possible to find 'true discipline' in the Elizabethan Church, a discipline which could be impeded by extremist demands for 'the satisfaction of their curious humours'? In fact, as we have seen, many of Harrison's experiences militated against the restitution of apostolic presbyterianism, and deterred him from emphasising the antichristian nature of English episcopacy. His experience of popish persecution under Mary put the Elizabethan Church in a better light – here the contrast with popery again worked in favour of the 1559 settlement. His limited success in overcoming stubborn carnal reason and outright popery amongst his parishioners also served to emphasis by contrast the pastoral dimensions of the established structure. Equally, the survival of recusancy and 'atheist' indifference also showed that the apostolic state of spiritual fellowship required for presbyterianism was beyond the present resources of both people and ministry. On the positive side, legally at least the Elizabethan Church had not made its hierarchy an article of faith binding conscience. Officially, the bishops were not a separate order within the ecclesiastical polity, though in a society so reliant on social deference even Harrison found this difficult to accept.[92] More importantly, the continuing

---

[89] Altering rites and ceremonies at will, controlling the entry of foreign superstition into Rome, dedicating temples and protecting 'the immunity of preestes and maintenauns of their estate'. Satan inspired Numa to create religious customs (TCD MS 165, fos. 88r, 253v). See Cartwright on the archbishopric, below, p. 189.

[90] TCD MS165, fo. 18r; and *cf*. note 88. Hence Harrison's dismay at his papist ordination.

[91] Ibid., fos. 177r, 183v, 327v. Roman aggrandisement followed and distracted Christian princes, letting in the Turk and advancing Antichrist. Ibid., fos.184v, 196r, 328r, 249v.

[92] Ibid., fos. 160v–161r. Bishops were 'accounted honourable', said Harrison, and ranked after barons (*Description* (1577), fos. 102r–v; (1587), p. 157).

attacks of the Church of Cain disposed him to interpret English episcopacy through a godly pastoral model. For in the face of Satan's furious onslaught there was no breathing space to reform fully. All energies had to be committed to preaching, and Harrison willingly accepted evidence of his pastoral ideal in operation, in the hope that human discipline could be completely transformed into godly discipline under the rule of the Word.

Harrison's Puritan vision of episcopacy was no less radical for preferring positive encouragement to negative criticism. He recognised the contrast between apostolic ideal and tawdry reality, but seized upon those elements which conformed to the dimensions of his prophetic Scriptural model, to create a contemporary godly example which true pastoral superintendents could emulate.[93] By this emphasis he sanctified episcopacy in an entirely different way from later *iure divino* apologists, retaining the freedom to censure bishops for more significant pastoral failings. This accounts for Harrison's tone in his defence of episcopacy added to the 1587 *Description*. Like Whitgift, Harrison agreed that the eldership was 'equallie distributed' between bishop and minister, though the bishop received greater secular power from the prince, in order to ensure uniformity. By 1587 Whitgift's interpretation of this episcopal function had begun to reaffirm the wider political responsibilities of the hierarchy as an end in itself, but Harrison concentrated on the pastoral aspect, perpetuating Calvin's distinction between 'godly' and 'bastard' bishops, which presbyterians had abandoned in the 1570s.[94] Perhaps influenced by his experience of Grindal's episcopacy, Harrison believed that unlike the papists, most Elizabethan bishops 'every Sunday or oftener...expound the Scriptures with much gravity and skill' somewhere in their dioceses. Previously this seemed improbably idealistic, but now it appears that some at least of Elizabeth's appointees spent much time in the pulpit both before and after their election.[95] Yet Harrison's vision of episcopal preachers in his *Description*, while it reflected reality, selected from that reality what conformed to the prophetic criteria delineated in his 'Chronology', a contrast to both 'Erastian' apologies for episcopacy and Whitgift's wider claims.[96]

Harrison's reasoning at this point reflects his subjective perception of the contemporary Church in terms of the True Church, a perception which

---

93 This overcame the contrast between Apostolic ideal and grubby reality which was as obvious to Harrison working in the Church courts as to Grindal on the episcopal bench, but to Cartwright Harrison's refusal to apply the presbyterian interpretation in the present would have resembled the papist 'historical' or 'dead' faith.

94 *Description* (1587), p. 157; Collinson, *Letters of Thomas Wood*, p.x.

95 *Description* (1577), fo. 76r, adding in 1587 that Bishops preached 'not without the great misliking and contempt' of the unregenerate who 'hate the Word' (*Description* (1587), p. 135). Collinson, 'Episcopacy and reform', p. 103; and see now Collinson, *Religion of Protestants*, pp. 49–51.

96 Collinson, *Puritan Movement*, pp. 101–6, on pragmatic defences of episcopacy.

circumvents anachronism. He asserted that it best fulfilled a bishop's calling 'to see him in his pastorall rochet looking out of a pulpet'.[97] Yet he did not quarry the Scriptures unimaginatively in search of a proof-text to support this argument, for the previous discussion has demonstrated that Harrison considered that the Scriptures taught a single story from many different aspects. Like other Protestants he believed that the interpretation and use of any single Scriptural text had to conform to this overall context, which the Scriptures consistently revealed to the regenerate reader. The recorded conflict of the Two Churches provided this context, but a considerable effort of imagination had to be made to recreate mentally the historical experience of the True Church and perceive the relevance of any part of that experience to the present. This sophisticated, learned and devout approach to the Scriptures should be distinguished from our modern attitude to the Bible, especially because in this instance Harrison concerned himself with the geography of Israel, not England, and by allowing the former to predominate in his thoughts creatively applied it to the existing institution as a universal prophetic model. Thus the bare mention of Melchizedeck in Gen. 14.8 provided an example of episcopal rule which allowed Harrison to accept episcopacy in the entirely dissimilar context of Elizabethan England. For Melchizedeck was also Sem, the member of the covenant line who had taught Abraham 'to walk upright in the waies and states of the Lorde'. Sem passed on through his preaching 'the some of true and undefiled religion', and reformed the True Church which had been subverted by Satan.[98]

Harrison emphasised that Sem accomplished reform by preaching within a compact diocese, the model for his interpretation of English episcopacy and a limited jurisdiction which remained the ideal of many English reformers. For 'as Abraham dwelt in Hebron so Sem inhabited that citie which was afterward called Jerusalem and is distant not fully 20 miles. Loth also and Abimelech of Geron were not passing 10 miles from Hebron', with other true believers, 'so that it is a goodly consideration for a man to weigh how the Church of god flourished under so good a Bishope as Sem'. Superior spiritual knowledge and the faithful teaching of true doctrine made Sem a bishop, a type of pastoral authority evident at the end of the first century AD, and its only justification in Harrison's time.[99] We should note

---

[97] TCD MS 165, fo. 208v.

[98] Melchizedeck stood in contrast to the Levitical priesthood, his unknown generation 'a figure of the eternity of Christ', Heb. 5–7 showed that his pastoral ministry prefigured Christ's, superior to the Levitical priesthood (TCD MS 165, fos. 31r, 24r). Christ bodily descended from Sem (Luke 3.36).

[99] *Cf.* Foxe, *Actes and Monuments* (1583), pp. 19,17, on spiritual pre-eminence and episcopal accountability for 'all soules in his dioces'. *Cf.* Collinson, 'Episcopacy and Reform', p. 95. Note that Harrison used human knowledge about the geography of Palestine which did not contradict Scriptural teachings but helped to establish the context of the actions they described, and thus to eludicate their meaning.

that Harrison found only an imperfect reformation as the true parallel for England, for the superintendency represented a degeneration from the apostolic
presbyterian constitution. Yet until the Church returned to that apostolic
state of harmony which Satan had subverted in the first century AD, a
pastoral episcopate represented an acceptable alternative to religious anarchy.

Harrison's view of the Two Churches presented in his 'Chronology' thus
provided the interpretative model for his account of the Elizabethan Church
in his *Description*. His sense of the interpenetration of past and present recalls
his debt to Melanchthon's 'examples' for his understanding of the True
Church, and thus indirectly to the humanist historiographical tradition,
which regarded both the historical text and its imagined social context as
a comment on the present. For Harrison. like other moderate Puritans and
the presbyterians, the experiences of the True Church provided both the
content and the context of the Scriptures, and his proposed reforms
consequently went some way towards fulfilling the presbyterian demand
that the present copy 'the manner of governinge the church which the story
of the primitive church rehearseth', although Harrison realised that 'our
corruption is such that it will never yeeld to so great perfection'.[100]

Harrison's ideology trapped him in a world which had never existed, and
he could not make his aspirations amenable to his lay contemporaries
without losing sight of his ideal commonwealth, for the prophetic covenant
line dominated his ideals. Thus his predicament demonstrates the difficult
consequences of adhering to continental Protestant ideas about the Two
Churches, for in the particular circumstances of Elizabethan England such
ideas could become stigmatised as 'Puritan'. Harrison's allegiance to the True
Church prepared him for the inevitable opposition of the unregenerate, but
it also made it impossible for him to remain silent. An examination of the
reform proposals which Harrison added to the 1587 *Description* reveals this
inner tension.

Realistic reformers co-operated with the ruling elite in programmes
tailored to social reality, accepting the need to inculcate obedience and
deference towards the self-image projected by powerful lay patrons.[101]
Harrison appears less worldly, for in his projected reforms his regenerate
understanding ignored the social and economic self-interest of lay patrons.
His prophetic historical interpretation of inherited institutions persuaded him
that they could be purified of their antichristian accretions and distortions
and returned to their original functions within the True Church – chiefly to
create a pastoral ministry. History showed that the True Church had always

---

100 *A full and plaine declaration of Ecclesiastical Discipline out off the word of God, and off the declining
     of the churche of England from the same*, trans. T. Cartwright ([M. Schirat: Heidelberg], 1574),
     p. 119; *Description* (1587), p. 158.
101 Collinson, 'Episcopacy and reform', pp. 118–21.

been a preaching Church, for that had been the chief function of the covenant line. Indeed the Word was so powerful that in Harrison's lifetime parts of England had been recalled from popish barbarousness to godly civility by preaching alone. The alternative could be seen in the rapid decline of the Byzantine Empire and Anglo-Saxon England through the spread of ignorance and the disappearance of a preaching ministry, as we noticed in the second chapter. Therefore Harrison believed that preaching could and must recreate the godly order, which was not simply social discipline but a new obedience in ruler and ruled, the best defence against Antichrist as he redoubled his efforts in the 1580s.[102]

Here again the 'Chronology' reveals that in its description of existing institutions the *Description* was less an accurate depiction of the Elizabethan Church than a subtle attempt to encourage further reformation by emphasising the potential for much-needed reforms inherent in current structures. This particularly applied to the provision of that learned preaching ministry which alone could reform and rescue England. For, writing in the 'Chronology' in the 1570s, Harrison claimed that 'zeale to devotion wexeth cold' because of 'the patching that is about many of our benefices...I am compelled to thinke that horses have the gift of them and asses serve the cures'. In contrast to the deliberate blandness of the *Description*, these are Harrison's real feelings on a matter of central concern to him. Thus, counterbalancing his admiration for episcopal preachers in the *Description*, in his 'Chronology' he attacked episcopal laxity in admissions to benefices, failings which merely compounded the carnal weaknesses of the laity. A decade after Parker and Grindal had abandoned their ill-advised attempts at mass ordinations, Harrison still had to ask that 'some of our bishoppes of England did not admitte soch as could hardly reade english moche lesse than a number of lewd pedlers, wevers and serving men that are voide of all piety, making accompt of the ministry as of the last refuge to avoide beggery and thereto have no more skill nor zeale to relligion then Hob my horsse'. Thus of the two characteristics of the 'Bischofsideal' current in this period, the indefatigable preacher and the scrupulous ordainer, Harrison could recognise only the former in the English episcopate.[103]

This did not prevent Harrison, when answering presbyterian accusations

---

[102] Harrison believed that Northumberland was largely civilised through the preaching of Bernard Gilpin and other learned men (*Description* (1587), p. 91), but see D. Marcombe, 'Bernard Gilpin: Anatomy of an Elizabethan Legend', in *Northern History*, xvi (1980), pp. 20–39, for a more objective assessment. The northerner, Grindal, assured Elizabeth 'where preaching wanteth, obedience faileth' (P. S. Seaver, *The Puritan Lectureships* (Stanford, 1970), p. 55). Harrison accepted presbyterian criticisms of the failure to create such a pastoral ministry (*Description* (1587), p. 136) and defended prophesyings for this reason; see below, pp. 180–4.

[103] TCD MS 165, fos. 314v, 179r; and see Collinson, *Grindal*, pp. 110–15, who emphasises Grindal's care in selecting preachers for sensitive cures; also Collinson, *Religion of Protestants*, pp. 84, 87, 101, for ministers such as Harrison describes.

about the insufficiency of many ministers in the 1587 *Description*, from pointing out the real cause of such insufficiencies, the worldly interests of the laity. For behind their carnal reasoning lurked Satan and Antichrist. Lay patrons perverted benefices designed to maintain preachers, either by using them to pay their personal servants in the scandalous fashion of the papacy, or by impoverishing the true preachers through simoniacal arrangements. The presbyterians had merely highlighted what Harrison had always known, but he still refused to accept that experience according to its own valuation. He did not seek realistic practical reforms from the laity, but nurtured the unrealistic conviction that lay patrons would also be transformed by the Word. For when the cooks and cobblers 'shall be removed and weeded out of the ministry, I doubt not but our patrons will prove better men and be reformed whether they will or not'. Only by indulging in such fantasies could Harrison avoid the self-destructive consequences of his ideology, for he knew full well that before the Church would again enjoy true discipline, 'I fere me that I shuld then live too long, and so long, that I should either be wearie of the world, or the world of me'. Consequently he also tried to persuade both himself and his readers that the world and its powers would be transformed by 'the single-minded bishops', who would see the livings better bestowed. Only by this benevolent interpretation could Harrison make the present ecclesiastical polity appear tolerable, and allow himself to ignore its true nature.[104]

Harrison regarded the provision of an educated preaching clergy as the key to the complete reformation of the Church, for he believed that it would transform the commonwealth so profoundly as eventually to restore something approaching apostolic harmony. Therefore he sought to provide such a ministry by a series of practical reforms, as clerically centred as any presbyterian scheme, because like the presbyterians he modelled his reforms on the institutions of the True Church. Indeed, paradoxically Harrison believed that his reforms would achieve their designated end because they excluded from any dominant role in the Church the very laity whose spiritual failings and worldly self-interest vitiated the claims of apostolic presbyterianism. Just as importantly, this desire to recreate those institutions used by the True Church to create a godly ministry, which had been subverted by Antichrist, found an outlet in Harrison's involvement in the prophesyings. He saw no place for the laity in this godly work and naturally assumed that Elizabeth's ill-advised suppression of the prophesyings represented a temporary success for Satan in his conflict with the True Church.

Like many others dissatisfied with the state of the ministry, Harrison

---

[104] *Description* (1587), p. 213; (1577), fo. 91v, which rather despairingly asserts that these reforms 'may easilie be brought to passe'.

found there practical expression for his idealism when university graduates directed their less learned colleagues in Scriptural exegesis. In some places prophesyings disguised classes integrated into a quasi-presbyterian system which made them practically independent from normal ecclesiastical control.[105] The evidence suggests that Harrison attended a more innocuous prophesying moderated by George Withers, Archdeacon of Colchester, and also including Edmund Sherbrooke, like Harrison a onetime official of Withers's Archidiaconal Court. This appears therefore to be one of the prophesyings begun in Essex early in Elizabeth's reign, encouraged and controlled by Grindal through his archdeacons. Harrison indeed describes all these conferences generally as begun 'in many of our archdeaconries', and 'erected only for the examination or trial of the diligence of the clergy in their study of Holy Scriptures'. His bishop in succession to Grindal, Edwin Sandys, also regarded the prophesyings as a force for good order which had 'the good likyng not only of suche as have chardge of government in the churche, but so manie as tender the successe of religion'.[106] Generally the bishops had been careful to restrain over-enthusiastic lay participation in the prophesyings by all social classes. Yet conservatives had launched such a successful counter-attack that when Harrison described the prophesyings in the 1577 *Description* he had to confess the embarrassing fact that contrary to his apocalyptic complaints about declining zeal, 'such is the thirsty desire of the people in these days to hear the Word', that the laity had 'with zealous violence intruded themselves among them' and he had to emphasise that they remained 'hearers only'.[107]

However, Harrison's objection to lay participation in the prophesyings differed importantly from conservative suspicions, because he saw the exercises within the context of the historical True Church. Dismayed at the political show of strength by progressives which the conferences allowed, conservatives played on the threat of social subversion to alarm a government already disturbed by the more radical prophesyings suppressed by the bishops themselves. The tenor of government fears can be gauged from the replies of Grindal and his bishops to some pointed regal questions. They consistently

[105] Collinson, *Grindal*, pp. 233–65, examines the background and events of the 'prophesyings' episode. V. J. K. Brook, *A Life of Archbishop Parker* (Oxford, 1962), pp. 278–80, gives a tendentious account of the Northampton prophesying. On the independence of Southam, see the replies of the bishops to Grindal's enquiries about the prophesyings in 1576, reprinted (with some omissions) in S. E. Lehmberg, 'Archbishop Grindal and the Prophesyings', in *The Historical Magazine of the Protestant Episcopal Church*, 34 (1965), pp. 87–145, at p. 114.

[106] Collinson, 'Episcopacy and reform', p. 113; Lehmberg, 'Prophesyings', pp. 99–109, reprinting the positive reports of Sandys' archdeacons; *Description* (1577), fo. 76r.

[107] Ibid., fo. 76r; cf. Lehmberg, 'Prophesyings', p. 110. The bishops placed more confidence in their ability to control the extremists than did Elizabeth, and their frank admissions about discovering and suppressing extremism would have been damning evidence to a suspicious conservative eye (cf. ibid., p. 113).

denied that 'artificers' had spoken at or even attended the prophesyings, and insisted that the unfortunately suggestive title did not mean that the lower orders had their heads filled with messianic hopes. As Harrison put it, by 'stumbling (I cannot tell how) at words and terms', the enemies of all religion had 'either by their own practice, their sinister information or suggestions made upon surmises unto other' secured the suppression of the prophesyings. Yet his own fears surfaced in an admission added to the 1587 *Description*, that despite the best efforts of the moderators 'some vain and busy head will now and then intrude themselves with offense'.[108]

Elizabeth and her conservative advisers took their stand on the Settlement established by statute in 1559, which provided neither precedent, authority nor necessity for an institution which enticed subjects even of 'good calling' from their ordinary parishes 'to be hearers of their disputations and new divised opinions upon points of divinity, far unmeet for vulgar people'. Only those rites and ceremonies established by Act of Parliament could be used in the Church.[109] Harrison, in contrast, objected to lay involvement in the prophesyings not because he feared that they would produce mechanic tub preachers fulminating against the established order, but because the Scriptural order gave no place to the laity. Grindal defended that same order against Elizabeth because like Harrison he believed that the Bible's account of the covenant line described all necessary institutions in the True Church; the law of God and the example of the True Church allowed bishops to revive prophesyings as necessary to increase the Scriptural learning of the inferior clergy. Because they did not depend upon the miraculous revelation of the future given only by God's grace, prophesyings should be perpetual ecclesiastical institutions. Indeed, argued Grindal, 'The ground of this or like exercise is of great and ancient authoritie' within the covenant line, 'for Samuell did practice such like exercises in his tyme, both at Naioth in Ramath and at Bethell', as did Elisha at Jericho, where *filii prophetarum* were trained 'in the studie and knowledge of the Scriptures' to serve in God's Church. As part of the teaching of the covenant line independent of the ceremonial law, Paul revived the prophesyings in the reformed primitive Church, and in I Cor. 14.3 'giveth rules for the order of the same'. This order gave no active role to the laity, insisted Grindal.[110]

---

[108] Several bishops denied that 'artificers' or 'unlearned and base persons' had participated (Lehmberg, 'Prophesyings', pp. 110,113; *Description* (1587), p. 136). John Scory, conservative bishop of Hereford, assumed that prediction was involved (Lehmberg, 'Prophesyings', pp. 115–16).

[109] The prophesyings 'contemne our lawes established' (ibid., pp. 142–3; *cf.* Collinson, *Grindal*, pp. 248–9).

[110] Grindal to Elizabeth, December 1576, in Lehmberg, 'Prophesyings', p. 136; *cf.* Collinson, *Grindal*, pp. 238, 262–3. John Walker, Archdeacon of Essex, also saw God's commandments in the New Testament 'to preach the Gospel' fulfilled at Naioth and Jericho and by Paul (Lehmberg, 'Prophesyings', p. 107).

The fact that Harrison derived a slightly different contemporary lesson from Samuel's example merely reminds us that we have to allow for individual variation within this type of thinking. The important point remains that, like Grindal, Harrison found distorted and corrupted remnants of the institutions of the True Church within the Elizabethan Church and believed that those remnants must be purified and restored to their godly function of providing a preaching ministry. Reality must be brought eventually to conform to the Word, because only the Word could defend the Church against Satan. The contrast between the Word and the world finally destroyed Grindal when he defied Elizabeth over the suppression of the prophesyings. Harrison, as we have seen, always managed to avoid facing up to this central contradiction, and in that discretion he was more typical of many moderate Puritans than was Grindal. Yet Harrison realised that the suppression of the prophesyings signified not simply a political reverse for Elizabethan progressives but a victory for Antichrist in Satan's cause against the True Church, since their supporters believed that the prophesyings had contributed to 'the diminishing of the kyngdome of Satan'.[111] Indeed Harrison boldly stated in the 1587 *Description* that the whole issue involved more than the prestige of the reforming party, for 'Satan, the author of all mischief…hath stirred up adversaries of late unto this most profitable exercise' and gained a great victory. Perhaps because he put this interpretation upon Elizabeth's actions, we find in the 'Chronology' that Harrison continued to participate in some form of learned conference with George Withers and Edmund Sherbrooke after 1576. Only one fragment of their discussions remains, but perhaps we can gauge something about their tone from the fact that Withers stressed the same approach to the Scriptures in his *ABC for layemen* as Harrison did in his 'Chronology'. Like Alexander Nowell and other devout Protestants, Withers singled out Rom. 15.4, which showed that in the Scriptures, 'whatsoever is written, is written for our learning, and therefore we should be stirred up diligently to learne those thinges which God would have taught', primarily, in Withers' view, that God's recorded judgements also applied to Elizabethan Englishmen, 'uppon whome the endes of the worlde are come, that we might be afrayed to provoke God as our Fathers did'.[112] This approach to the Scriptures both justified the prophesyings and perhaps directed the exegesis towards the further elucidation of the original institutions of the True Church.

Therefore while Grindal complained that the official suppression of the prophesyings left him 'without hope to reduce the [Church] to the original

---

[111] John Walker's opinion (ibid., p. 109).
[112] Withers, *An ABC*, sig. B2v. Harrison referred to Sherbrooke as 'Dr' (DD, 1579), in a late and cursive interlineation of his and Withers's names, perhaps written *c.* 1580 in TCD MS 165, fo. 30r.

institution',[113] Harrison continued to obey what he considered to be Scriptural commands for the Elect to take specific godly actions against Satan and Antichrist. Contemplation of the godly examples given by the covenant line might only emphasise the distance between ideal and reality, but that distance itself registered Satan's implacable commitment to subverting the True Church, and showed the regenerate the need for incessant efforts to surmount his wiles. Contemporary indifference both to these contrasts and his proposals to eliminate them did not discourage Harrison, for the truth inherited from the covenant line also entailed persecution and opposition from the weak, unregenerate reasoning through which Satan worked. Therefore when Harrison added reform proposals to the 1587 *Description* he ignored such worldly self-interest, a fact which belies the apparent conservatism of his reaction against presbyterianism at about the same time.

Analysing the inherited institutions of the Elizabethan Church according to strict Scriptural criteria, Harrison proposed that the entire process of clerical education and provision to livings should revert to the Old Testament model. He urged that the patron of a vacant living, through his bishop, should in future ask a university vice-chancellor to choose a sufficiently learned minister. By reducing the patron to a cipher good pastors would be provided, simony abolished 'and the people better trained to live in obedience toward God and the prince'. These platitudes fail to disguise a radical and unrealistic Puritan 'policy' which rejected the laity's social and economic self-interest. It contrasts fundamentally with the proposal by Walsingham and Mildmay in the Parliament of 1581 to limit ordination to those holding a nomination to a specific benefice with cure of souls in the diocese of the officiating bishop. Their proposal merely sanctified the existing patronage system, and Whitgift therefore belatedly accepted it in 1583. Harrison, however, ignored contemporary social assumptions and committed himself to following the example of Samuel, a member of the covenant line who erected the first university in Israel at Naioth, 'where he himselfe instructed the Levites in true theology' before they were called to teach amongst the people. Grindal had cited Samuel's revelatory actions in support of the prophesyings, but Harrison preferred to derive a different part of the True Church's infrastructure from the same text, and argued that if contemporary universities could be brought into alignment with Samuel's example then they would provide enough learned preachers. These two individual variations upon the same theme are less important than the shared imaginative interpretation of the Scriptures, which accepted that the history of the True Church placed specific responsibilities upon the heirs of the covenant line in their contemporary behaviour. Thus Harrison ignored not only the wider economic problems of the Church and the intrusion of the

[113] Lehmberg, 'Prophesyings', p. 134.

gently born into the universities, which threatened the provision for poor scholars and vitiated his proposals, but also his own experience of corrupt fellowship elections. For in his scheme college fellowships would be temporary training places for pastors, fellows would not simply enjoy college stipends while 'withholding better wits from...their places and yet doing little good' in their ostensible callings as teachers and preachers.[114]

Harrison's 1587 *Description* discussed another aspect of the pedagogical and pastoral True Church which survived in an attenuated and distorted form in the Elizabethan Church. That discussion underlines Harrison's desire to measure his actions according to the example of Israel, an obedience which overcame his self-interest and fostered his commitment to 'Puritan politics' rather than conventional allegiances. In February 1586 Burghley's coup against Leicester brought Whitgift, Lord Buckhurst and Harrison's patron Lord Cobham into the Privy Council. This conservative triumph probably explains Harrison's promotion to a prebend in St George's Chapel, Windsor, in the following April, and seems finally to ally him with the Hatton–Whitgift faction whose policy of aggressive uniformity influenced Harrison's criticism of subsequent 'presbyterian' parliamentary manœuvres against Church wealth. Yet Harrison's defence of cathedral and collegiate church income in the 1590s was not a self-interested apology for the status quo. He required that that wealth should be redirected to return prebends to their prophetic function. In 1577 Harrison had accepted that prebendaries 'Lernedly set forth the glory of God and further the overthrow of Antichrist' by parochial preaching outside cathedral and collegiate churches. While it encapsulates Harrison's confidence that preaching alone would overthrow Antichrist, this description also generously interpreted the contemporary institution of the prebend through a godly model, for in the primitive church, bishops and elders in every 'jurisdiction' had placed scholars in cathedral churches, to be instructed in the Word and their ministerial duties, examined and sent to vacant cures. Contemporary prebendaries by their preaching seemed to continue some of this pattern, with its emphasis on simultaneously building up the True Church and diminishing the Church of Cain through the ministry of the Word.[115]

However, in 1586 Harrison found the Royal Chapel at Windsor infected by Gentilism. Antichrist working through the familiar human weaknesses of avarice and negligence had corrupted the godly model by medieval

---

[114] *Description* (1587), pp. 149–50; Collinson, *Puritan Movement*, p. 162; V. J. K. Brook, *Whitgift and the English Church* (London, 1957), pp. 81–2; TCD MS 165, fo. 65r; *Description* (1587), p. 150.

[115] *A Collection of State Papers...from the yeare 1571 to 1596...at Hatfield House*, ed. W. Murdin (London, 1759), p. 489. Harrison also shared Cobham's antagonism towards Leicester (*Harrison's Description*, ed. Furnivall, Appendix I, p. lix); *cf.* Bancroft, *Sermon*, sigs. C4r–v; *Description* (1577), fo. 75v; (1587), pp. 139–40.

regulations that now demanded almost continuous statutory residence, forcing the prebendaries to neglect their congregations. Therefore shortly after taking up his prebend Harrison proposed in the 1587 *Description* not only the removal of these antichristian regulations but also the return of prebends to their original function within the godly system of clerical education, as with the universities reviving the functions which contemporary institutions had previously served when controlled by the covenant line, before Antichrist corrupted them. This attempt to make contemporary social institutions conform to the godly pattern ingenuously ignored the revolutionary effects of such a change upon the existing social fabric, 'sith the schooles are alreadie builded in everie diocese, the universities [are] places of their preferment unto further knowledge, and the cathedrall churches great enough to receive so manie as shall come from thence to be instructed unto doctrine'. As the culmination of this integrated system of godly education, temporary prebendaries would be 'preferred to some ecclesiastical function'.[116]

Thus Harrison believed that his regenerate reason, obedient to revelation, had been brought to understand that the continuing conflict of the Two Churches demanded general obedience to the Scriptural revelation by the whole Elizabethan Church, in order to rid it of Antichrist's influence. For ultimately the model for this desperately needed reform could be found in Samuel at Naioth, and Harrison urged his readers to 'see the Chronology following' for the successful emulation of this model in the historical struggle of the True Church against Gentilism.[117] Just as Harrison believed that the Scriptures described this single conflict from many different aspects, and that a perfect reformation could be achieved by combining the anti-papal criticisms of many medieval members of the covenant line, so he found in Elizabethan England the shattered and distorted fragments of the True Church which could be reassembled and revivified as the living Temple, by restoring them to their proper purposes. The eventual long-term consequences of his suggestions are hinted at in Harrison's comment that 'happy was that congregation, that might have an elder' out of the seminaries maintained by the covenant line in the early Christian Church. For the restoration of the True Church's godly preaching ministry would go far towards removing Harrison's practical, pastoral objections to the reinstatement of apostolic presbyterianism. Harrison's vision also circumvents the traditional patronage apparatus, which would disappear with the distorted and corrupted society

---

[116] *Description* (1587), pp. 139–40.
[117] Referring to the monasteries established by Martin of Tours to produce 'zealous ministers in the church of Christ', and intimating that the congregation rather than a lay patron might call one of these godly pastors (TCD MS 165, fo. 168v); also the example of Clemens Alexandrinus, who opposed Gentilism with his school at Alexandria, instructing Catechists 'in the principles of true religion', not 'any humaine knowledg' (ibid., fo. 152r).

which produced it as the True Church rose again. However, that contemporary system remained all too real, and Harrison's devotion to his godly ideal implied some criticism of Lord Cobham's patronage, and ultimately of the Queen whose Chapel Royal Harrison adorned. Yet he saw no benefit for the cause in resigning his prebend or refusing its income. Something could be gained by a practical reorientation of the office. To defuse presbyterian criticism of the Windsor prebendaries' scandalous absence from their cures, Whitgift with Hatton made a minor amendment to the Chapel Statutes in 1590, allowing more absence from Windsor. Harrison with the entire Chapter then signed a Chapter Act giving this permission the broadest possible interpretation. We can probably supply Harrison's motive, that if Samuel's seminary could not be resurrected at least there would be more time to preach against Antichrist outside the Royal Chapel.[118]

Despite such inevitable compromises, detailed examination of Harrison's thought has shown that his Puritanism represented the thorough-going application of continental Protestant ideas to the 'semi-reformed' condition of England. This subjective interpretation of his contemporary experience, dependent on Harrison's equally subjective interpretation of the Scriptures, dominated his understanding of time and history. Therefore he relied not upon external, human authority, but the whole of his contemporary experience, subjectively interpreted by *a priori* Scriptural criteria, to confirm the veracity of the Bible. We have seen those Scriptural criteria, derived from the contrast between the Two Churches, applied by Harrison to his contemporary experiences, in common with continental and some English Reformers. In the special circumstances of Elizabethan England this worldview united Harrison with the presbyterian Thomas Cartwright in a shared Protestant perception of popery as the inheritor of the Church of Cain. Like other European Protestants, they both held that in the destabilising conflict with Antichrist the godly models of Israel, as clarified in Christ's perfect reformation, provided the only sure defence, for Christ had defeated Satan and would defeat his minion, Antichrist.[119]

Cartwright came to the same conclusion as Harrison about the authoritative source of godly knowledge and behaviour. For Cartwright's fruitless argument with Whitgift over the details of Church government both

---

[118] Harrison recognised that prebends could be 'superfluous additaments unto former excesses' (*Description* (1587), p. 140). *Visitation Articles and Injunctions of the Period of the Reformation*, ed. W. H. Frere (London, 1910), iii, pp. 248–50; S. Bond, *The Chapter Acts of the Dean and Canons of Windsor* (Windsor, 1966), pp. 22–3. B. L. O. Bodley MS 613, fo. 53v, contains Harrison's scrupulous calculation of his 185 days of enforced residence at Windsor, which the records show that he kept (Windsor, St George's Chapel Aerary, MSS XV. 59. 13, 14, 15, 16, 17).

[119] Beza contended that men must abandon their wills and follow Christ, for they were given free will only to obey God, if they did not then their wills were in fact in bondage to Satan (McPhee, 'Beza', pp. 152–4).

originated in and foundered upon two fundamentally different conceptions
of the shape of history and its meaning for the present. Like Harrison,
Cartwright accepted that Gentilism continued in popery, so that there could
be no compromise with the ungodly. The Elizabethan Church had to be
completely purified of popery, since emulation of the revealed godly models
of the True Church remained the only defence against Satan. Whitgift
refused to accept this total contrast between Israel and Gentilism. So where
Cartwright believed that Christian liberty bound the Elizabethan Church to
the model of Israel, Whitgift argued that the true use of Christian liberty
lay in the judicious selection of good knowledge from all sources, so long
as it did not contradict Scriptural precepts.[120]

The disagreement between Cartwright and Whitgift over ecclesiastical
hierarchy was only one manifestation of this underlying difference. Cartwright insisted that popery was insidiously rotting the Church, continuing the
distortion of truth begun by the Gentiles. The Church had to be purged of
this infection, for 'whatsoever commeth from the Pope, which is Antichrist,
commeth first from the Devil'.[121] Satan's persistence and the attractiveness
of Gentilism to the appetites of natural man meant that even if popish
ceremonies 'conteined nothing whiche is not agreeable to the worde of God'
we should not share any ceremonies with them. Neither the Word, reason,
nor 'the examples of the eldest Churches, both Jewish and Christian'
permitted contemporary men to commit this folly. The history of the True
Church in both Testaments showed that God had preserved his Elect 'from
the infection of idolatrie and superstition...by outwarde ceremonies',
forbidding them even 'to doe things which are in themselves verie lawful',
if to do so would blur the distinction between the covenant line and their
opponents. Popery must be expunged by obedience to Scriptural models
which revealed the divine will.

Cartwright drew the connection between Gentilism and popery in words
which parallel Harrison's. Just as in the Old Testament crafty Satan seduced
Israel – 'by their fond desire they had to conform themselves to the fashions
of the Gentiles' – so in the New Testament to fulfil prophecies of Antichrist
God allowed the Christians 'to corrupt their ways by the same sleight of
the Divell'.[122] Popery offered only a 'bundel of corruptions...picked out
of sundry times and places', confounding truth and Gentilism. The 'constant
and perpetual wisdome' of the covenant line therefore taught that the
substance and form of God's religion should be different from idolatry, and
especially from popery.[123] Having characterised popery in this way,

---

[120] Whitgift, *Defense*, p. 746.
[121] Ibid., p. 746.   [122] Ibid., p. 474.
[123] *The Rest of the second replie of Thomas Cartwright agaynst Master Doctor Whitgiftes second answer
        touching the Churche Discipline* ([Zurich?], 1577), p. 125; *Defense*, p. 475.

Cartwright could show that the True Church presented presbyterianism as the only remedy. The heirs of the covenant line must follow 'the customes and orders of the Apostels and of the primative churches', insisted Cartwright, because 'they were our forefathers', and the conscience instructed in the fear of God 'seeketh for the light of the word of God in the smallest actions'. For those who refused to follow the Word, there remained only the 'light of reason', and the Scriptures themselves showed that this led only to the errors which the covenant line had condemned.[124] To neutralise Satan's power, 'the only examples' of the True Church should determine contemporary ecclesiastical organisation, for safety we must follow in the footsteps of the Apostles 'and of all the Churches'. Cartwright argued that the Old Testament as well as the New prescribed presbyterianism against the wiles of Satan. The eldership, for example, continued the perpetual government of the Elect 'before and under the law'. The Old Testament described elders 'so sone as there is made mention, of any fixed form of church'.[125] For both Cartwright and Harrison the earliest examples of the True Church gave external form to the true doctrines transmitted by the covenant line, and those examples therefore remained vital defences against Antichrist, though, as in the previous comparison between Grindal and Harrison, individuals could choose slightly different examples to make a similar point.

The similarities in Harrison's and Cartwright's thinking emerge in Cartwright's condemnation of ecclesiastical hierarchy because of its Gentile origins. The archbishopric, for example, 'commeth of very infamous parentage', originating in 'the idolatrous nations'. The popish hierarchy epitomised the infection of this Gentilism in the True Church; the degeneration from episcopacy to papacy also displayed the mark of Cain, and formed the steps by which 'Sathan lifted the child of perdition unto that proud title of universal Bishop'. In reply to Whitgift's retort that hierarchy suppressed heretical corruptions which aided Antichrist, Cartwright insisted that from the moment when 'this devise was established, the corruption in the Church was not diminished, but grew', a more forceful statement of the kind of view expressed by Harrison.[126] Like Harrison, Cartwright believed that truth flowed from the Elect to the Gentiles, and that Gentile criteria

---

124 *The second replie of Thomas Cartwright agaynst Maister Doctor Whitgiftes second answer touching the Church discipline* ([Zurich?], 1575), pp. 82, 94, 56.

125 *Defense*, p. 638; *Rest of the second replie*, p. 40; *cf.* Exod. 4.29. We must 'have the worde of God go before us in all our actions...for that we cannot otherwise be assured that they please God' (*Second replie*, p. 61). God had decided 'to set before our eyes a perfecte forme of his Churche' (*Defense*, p. 77).

126 *Defense*, pp. 319–20; *cf.* Harrison, above p. 174. Whitgift considered 'These steppes' the best kind of government since the Apostles (ibid., pp. 349, 445). Cartwright's thesis also condemned the papist lesser hierarchy which Harrison rejected (ibid., p. 344; *Second replie*, p. 569).

could not be applied to Israel's unique history. So when Whitgift countered that Israel had degrees of priests like the Gentiles, Cartwright quickly pointed out that 'the lordes preistes and Sacrafices were before the preistes and sacrafices of the gentiles', where without regenerate understanding a degenerate hierarchy flourished. The New Testament merely portrayed more clearly that presbyterian system delineated by the life of the True Church in the Old Testament, for God 'woulde rather have taken of his owne, than borrowed of others'.[127]

Harrison also identified the crucial issue for this view of popery, in a way which decisively separated him from Whitgift. Discussing the seemingly endless proliferation of idolatry at the end of the sixth century AD, as men cast off Scriptural restraints upon their imaginations, he pointed out that 'nedes must thei be Idolatrous that worship that [true] god after an untrue or false maner, so well as thei that ascribe godly honour to the false god which is only due unto the true'. Popery and pagan idolatry appeared indistinguishable to Harrison by comparison with the True Church. Whitgift's contrasting historical interpretation met this idea head on and offered a different view of popery and Antichrist from that of Harrison and Cartwright, one which seems decisively to separate Whitgift from the common Protestant outlook which we have been discussing. To establish that the existing hierarchy was allowable if purged of popish abuses, he had to argue that popery had no connection with Gentilism. In his view it was 'one thing wholly to worship false Gods', and quite another 'to worship the true God falsly and superstitiously'. By defining different types of idolatry, Whitgift showed that Israel had often been worse than the papists, who were only 'the same with the Israelites under Jeroboam, joining idolatry and the false worshipping of God to godly ceremonies'.[128] Whitgift did not fear the infection of Gentilism transmitted through things shared with popery, because popery did not continue the Church of Cain. He could not easily reject the central Protestant anti-Roman argument: 'I know the Papistes through foolish imitation of the Gentiles, have brought in sundrie superstitions of the Gentiles', but so qualified it as to make it almost irrelevant to the Elizabethan Church. For example, it did not apply to 'inequalities of degrees and authoritie among the ministers'. Indeed, Whitgift questioned whether popery could so 'infect the word of God, godlie prayers, and profitable ceremonies' that they could not be used when purged of errors and impieties. We should not communicate with the papists, he acknowledged, but 'use those good things well, which the Papists

---

[127] Ibid., p. 470; *Defense*, p. 321. God 'translated diverse things out of the Lawe unto the Gospell' – elders, deacons, excommunication (*Second replie*, p. 410).

[128] TCD MS 165, fos. 189v–190r; *Defense*, pp. 149, 625. To Cartwright this equalled comparing Israel with the Gentile Idumeans or Ishmaelites (*Rest of the second replie*, pp. 142–3).

have abused', including the Scriptures, sacraments, prayers and hierarchy. For these had been appointed before Antichrist appeared; only parts of popery were antichristian.[129]

Whitgift clearly assumed that there existed a way of determining good which was accessible to reason and independent of the example of Israel. His less fearful attitude to Gentilism and popery necessarily meant that in his historical vision Israel did not provide the only source of truth. Israel had had ceremonies in common with the Gentiles, he maintained, so 'the matter is not great, nor worthie of deciding' whether Israel provided the model for all good actions; the Gentiles did good things which are 'not to be rejected for the Authors sakes, though they were members of Satan'. Here Whitgift's outlook appears diametrically opposed to that which we have been examining. His evident lack of respect for the unique claims of the covenant line, and his willingness to base his assessments upon criteria drawn from outside the True Church, clearly distinguish him from the Protestant mainstream. The impetus of his argument against Cartwright brought him into areas where few of the Protestants discussed above would have cared to follow. Whitgift's refusal to equate doctrine and action polarised the two positions, for he asserted that reason, not the actions of the Elect covenant line, would determine what path the contemporary Church followed. His denial that the Church of Cain perpetually confronted the True Church as a distorted mirror-image allowed him to argue that Peter may have wisely modelled the Christian ecclesiastical hierarchy on the pagan, for order's sake.[130] The contemporary Church enjoyed similar freedom, so long as it did not contravene Scriptural precepts.

Whitgift's refusal to concede that Gentilism represented the mystical negation of truth can also be seen in his novel picture of Antichrist. He avoided the common Protestant concentration on the 'mystery of iniquity', seen in both Harrison and Cartwright. The idea that Antichrist rose with the bishops of Rome to the acquisition of supreme spiritual and temporal power threw an embarrassing amount of light upon the possibly satanic origins of other ecclesiastical hierarchies.[131] Whitgift chose to emphasise a subsidiary theme in the Protestant tradition, connecting presbyterian arguments with early heresies which had prepared the way for Antichrist, even as Antichrist worked now through presbyterian 'stirres and contentions'. To suppress schism the apostles created a hierarchy, the best counter to

---

[129] *Defense*, p. 451. The papists had some true doctrine, government and prayers (ibid., p. 476); ibid., p. 474.

[130] Ibid., pp. 323, 746. Whitgift believed that Israel also shared much with the papists (ibid., pp. 480, 320–3).

[131] Cartwright stigmatised the Elizabethan hierarchy in the apocalyptic imagery popularised by such as John Bale, e.g., 'these smokie titles of honor' (*Second replie*, p. 581; cf. Rev. 9 and Bale, *Image of Both Churches*, ed. Christmas, p. 352).

Antichrist, 'if in all places they had remained in their full force and authoritie', and we must follow this example to preserve unity. Yet Whitgift had to gloss over the commonly accepted fulfilment of prophecy, that the hierarchy only promoted concord as a defence against Antichrist 'until such time as it was turned into tyrannie'.[132] Like Harrison, Cartwright could make a more compelling appeal to apostolic 'moderate rule', which meshed with Protestant assumptions about 'the discovery of the sonne of perdition' when oppressive Gentilism triumphed over the polity of the True Church.[133]

The continuity between Harrison's and Cartwright's statements on the meaning of history brought the corollary that Cartwright also believed that the present Church could only defend itself against Antichrist by reviving the institutions of the True Church. Thus despite their individual preference for slightly different examples from the True Church as the working models for Elizabethan ecclesiastical polity, there is a remarkable similarity in their proposals for returning the debased structures of the Elizabethan Church to their evangelical purpose. Like Harrison, Cartwright believed that Oxford and Cambridge should be remodelled to conform to Samuel's university, and that because collegiate churches had been a perpetual institution in the True Church prebends should again be used to produce preachers.[134] This prophetic reorganisation represented too great a challenge to accepted social values for Whitgift, who defended university fellowships and prebends as rewards for learning and bulwarks against confusion.[135]

In different degrees other English Protestants who accepted the reality of the conflict between the Two Churches were conscious of a similar tension between the demands of prophetic history and contemporary ecclesiastical and social structures. Their individual differences of personality and circumstance helped to determine their reaction to that confrontation. For Edwin Sandys this disquieting contrast was almost non-existent. Sandys had supported the reformist group in the Convocation of 1563, and as Harrison's ordinary in 1576 had defended the prophesyings as necessary for the advancement of

---

[132] *Defense*, p. 349. This clear perception of antichristian forces explains some of Whitgift's actions. Contrast P. Lake, 'The Significance of the Elizabethan identification of the pope as Antichrist', in *Journal of Ecclesiastical History*, xxxi (1980), pp. 161–78; and see P. Christianson, 'Reformers and the Church of England under Elizabeth I and the early Stuarts', in ibid., xxxi (1980), pp. 463–82, which over-emphasises Whitgift's respect for continental Reformed opinions on Antichrist. Whitgift argued that Nicaea, 'the godlyest, and the most perfect Councell' since the Apostles, allowed archbishops and patriarchs (*Defense*, pp. 445, 349). Harrison quoted Bale on Nicaea, 'wherein Jezebelles Bedde was made' (TCD MS 165, fo. 153v). (*Defense*, p. 378.)

[133] Ibid., pp. 394–6, esp. p. 395. Whitgift's argument here appeared indistinguishable from popery to Knollys (W. D. J. Cargill Thompson, 'Sir Francis Knollys' campaign against the *Jure Divino* theory of episcopacy', in *The Dissenting Tradition*, ed. C. R. Cole and M. E. Moody (Ohio, 1975), pp. 39–77, at pp. 61, 42).

[134] *Defense*, pp. 426, 744–7.   [135] Ibid., pp. 432, 744–7.

religion. Yet he also shared Whitgift's conviction that the presbyterians were 'raised up by our spirituall and ghostly enemy', Antichrist, as part of his ceaseless attacks on the Church. Sandys defended the establishment against debilitating schism, for like the stoutest conformist he argued that 'There is no idolatry, no impiety maintained by the lawes and orders of this church'. The 'clamorous troblers of the church of God' had no just cause for provoking the 'inevitable ruine' of 'a few sillie weake ones' by dividing the Church, already under antichristian attack. Besides, Sandys insisted somewhat disingenuously, 'there is authority, we have courts, there are lawfull assemblies to heare to discusse and to determine' the justice of presbyterian demands. Yet he simultaneously bracketed the precisians with the papists as an 'irreligious crew' who could not glory in their sufferings since they 'fight for Antichrist, for heresie, for popery, for superstition, sedition, selfe will and singularity'.[136] Such uncompromising language appears irrevocably to distance Sandys from those who sought further reform within the Elizabethan Church.

Sandys differed from Whitgift however, and especially from the obdurate arguments which Whitgift deployed against Cartwright, in his ability to justify the Elizabethan Church according to the prevailing Protestant conception of the Two Churches. Sandys defended the Elizabethan Church by diminishing the contrast between it and the True Church, and by emphasising the Satanic roots of popery, which demanded solidarity within the established Church. In a sermon preached from the authoritative pulpit at St Paul's Cross, Sandys did not emphasise the virtues of the Elizabethan Church by contrasting it to popery as Whitgift did against Cartwright. Rather he dilated on the figure of the Church as Christ's boat in Matt. 8.23–4 to insist that 'Christ hath alwaies had a Church here on earth, it was begun in Paradise, sitherns it hath remained and continewed even unto this daie. And as Christ hath his boate, so hath Antichrist also his. Wherefore it behoveth us to knowe and discerne the one from the other'. The True Church and the persecuting Church of Cain represented opposite poles on the eternal measurements of Word, sacraments and discipline, and Sandys did not doubt that the Elizabethan Church stood on the right side of this perpetual division. Like other Elizabethan bishops Sandys managed to square the uneasy inheritance of the Church under the Cross with an exaggerated respect for the magistrate and a sanguine picture of contemporary England by emphasising that the 'Chief members' of the Church had always been the first to suffer persecution. Like Parker he felt that the Oxford Martyrs had

---

[136] Lehmberg, 'Prophesyings', pp. 99–100; *Sermons made by the most reverende Father in God, Edwin, Archbishop of Yorke, Primate of England and Metropolitane* (Henrie Middleton for Thomas Charde: London, 1585), pp. 339–40, 337.

somehow justified and purified contemporary episcopacy, but he also emphasised the sufferings of the covenant line, for the Prophets and Apostles had also been 'overseers' in the True Church.[137]

Indeed Sandys focussed on the covenant line since Adam as the means of showing that there could never be a compromise with popery. The Church of Cain had persecuted the True Church from the beginning, ever since 'Abel the image of the church was unnaturally murdered by the bloudy hand of his owne brother', 'This was the lot of Gods church, the portion of his elect and chosen people'. Yet 'that Romaine strumpet' was the cruellest persecutor of all. Therefore, like Harrison, Sandys emphasised that God deliberately distinguished His Church from the Gentile ceremonies: 'It is not for nothing that God was so curious in platting forth the Tabernacle, and so precise in commaunding that all thinges without exception should be doone according to that patterne'. This fact spiritually taught that all religion should precisely obey God's written will in the Scriptures, although Sandys placed less emphasis on discipline in this context than did Harrison and the presbyterians. Sandys also insisted that Scriptural criteria had to be used to reject Gentilism, for in the early Church 'the verie first thing' which the Fathers did 'in their conversion from Gentilitie to the truth was openly to proclaime defiance to the impietie wherein they had bene nuzled and trayned up', and to destroy such illegitimate knowledge.[138] Other aspects of his thought apart from his caution about human knowledge distinguished Sandys from Whitgift and united him to the common Protestant tradition. For his sense that such issues were contemporaneously appropriate to the present last hours of the world illuminates an area of potential consensus within the Elizabethan Church. Together with the most fervent presbyterian, Sandys believed that in the time of Isaiah, 'The diversitie of religion professed in these our times is...most plainely and lively depainted'. The very examples of the covenant line emphasised the gulf 'betweene Christ and Antichriste, the doctrine of God and the learning of men', a distinction which Sandys insisted must be maintained, for 'The covenant made with David is made with us, his mercies are our mercies', if we perform what God demanded of David.[139]

Like Harrison and Cartwright, but in contrast to Whitgift, Sandys argued that there were no gradations to idolatry. Once the Israelites, seduced by the worldly attractions of Gentilism, had produced a mixed religion of 'their own defiled woorkes' they separated themselves from the tiny remnant of God's Church. Popery reflected the same weakness of fallen human nature,

---

[137] Ibid., pp. 331, 190–1, 337–9. Also on the most crucial test 'England hath at no time heretofore beene blessed with so many and so faithful preachers of God's word' (ibid., pp. 9, 191).

[138] Ibid., pp. 337, 193–5, 332–3. Harrison pointed out that Orpheus had failed to do this; see above, pp. 24–5.   [139] Ibid., pp. 5, 24.

which preferred 'the meere invention of man or of Satan' to true religion. Referring to the degenerate Israelites, Sandys insisted that 'As these were then, so nowe these are', and he went on to argue that popery attracted contemporary believers in the same way that Gentilism seduced the Israelites, for 'Have wee not a longing as they had unto that from which the Lorde hath delivered us in great mercie?'. In a remarkable conflation of images Sandys illustrated his conviction that, 'by like meanes' as the guilty Israelites, the papists perpetuated the Church of Cain and disobeyed Christ in their Mass, 'sacrificing him afresh as they thought upon their hillaltars'. Consequently the True Church could be built up only by following the written corpus of doctrine and by emulating the godly models of the covenant line recorded in the Scriptures.[140] Thus not only a real difference in temperament, but also this completely different approach to the problems of contemporary reform, enabled Sandys to share more common ground with the precisians than could Whitgift. Yet Sandys' ecclesiastical career flourished because he accepted that there remained no significant discordance between the Elizabethan Church and the model of the True Church, and that the established Church therefore provided an effective defence against Antichrist.

Other important figures within the Elizabethan Church followed a similar line of thought, but their conclusions depended very much on their individual ability to resolve the tension between ideal and reality in the face of threatening Antichrist. Like William Harrison, Matthew Hutton had experienced both the Marian persecution and the evangelical fervour of Cambridge in the 1560s, and believed that the world witnessed a confrontation between the godly and the papists. Like Sandys, he rose within the hierarchy to become Archbishop of York, a promotion which to some extent reflects his ability to sublimate the more extremist consequences of his views. Yet where Sandys made both precisians and papists members of Antichrist, Hutton continued to fear the Roman Antichrist, who subverted England through ingrained traditionalism, more than the precisians, who broke ranks against Antichrist by their disobedience to lawful authority. Potentially his opposition to what human tradition 'supposed good to be done' on the basis of 'what Christ did', threatened radicalism as unrealistic as Harrison's commitment to the godly commonwealth. Yet while Hutton's fear of Antichrist sharpened his zeal, the solidarity of the Protestant establishment in the north in combatting popery helped to blunt it. For Hutton the Royal Supremacy and the Protestant social hierarchy constituted the best safeguard against Antichrist and remained far closer to the ideal commonwealth than Harrison could believe. Both Hutton and Harrison perceived presbyterian proposals in the 1590s as a cover for lay encroachment

[140] Ibid., pp. 182, 190–2, 5–7.

on the Church's wealth. But in contrast to Harrison's unrealistic proposals for restructuring the universities, Hutton defended the existing system of clerical education, which had amply rewarded his own learning and which was finally meeting the needs of the Church, against precisian proposals comparable to Harrison's. Nor could Hutton afford to be idealistic about the status of episcopacy in the face of lay arrogance. The Epistle to Titus supported the episcopate's claims to apostolic status, not the presbyterian system which Harrison had acknowledged. Access to power such as Hutton enjoyed, and the compromises which he found necessary to preserve a united front against Antichrist, might well have tested Harrison's commitment to the godly commonwealth.[141]

William Perkins reflected more deeply on continental Reformed learning than did Harrison, but he also stressed the contrast between unchanging Scriptural doctrine within the covenant line, and the perpetuation and proliferation of error in Satan's parody of the True Church. For Perkins 'the apostles agree with the prophets, the prophets with Moses and all with the first revelation made at the creation'.[142] Opposed to the Elect's priority of inspired truth stood carnal reason, which had corrupted the Jews, could be seen in patristic errors, and now threatened England, insisted Perkins, when ministers trimmed Scriptural doctrine 'to the common disposition and behaviour of the people'. Natural man's religion culminated in popery, the Church of the reprobate wallowing in carnal reason and Gentilism. Perkins assessed contemporary behaviour by these dual criteria, so that a mere 'civil conversation' was insufficient; there existed only obedience to Scripture or decline, and Perkins believed that he perpetuated Elect doctrine. For not reason but the Scriptural picture of the Elect community determined ethical norms, all human knowledge had to be integrated with and interpreted by revelation. Ministers especially had to subject their reason to Scripture, and labour for 'the experience of grace which the scriptures set before their readers', to follow Scriptural godly models and avoid the satanic errors of carnal reason.[143]

Yet Harrison and Perkins displayed contrasting temperaments, as we have seen in their different definitions of the canon of true prophecy. Perkins accepted only a narrow corpus of true prophecy, which would not 'make disquietnesse in the Church and Commonwealth'. Harrison shared more of the Old Testament prophets' alienation from contemporary norms, and was more subservient to the Scriptures in allowing categories of prophecy

---

141 P. Lake, 'Matthew Hutton, a puritan bishop?', in *History*, lxiv (1979), pp. 182–204, esp. pp. 183–96.

142 Perkins, *Workes*, i, p. 483, quoted in I. Breward, *The Work of William Perkins* (Appleford, 1970), p. 39. Professor Breward points out that this is not congruent with Perkins's Christology, but Harrison, like other Protestants, resolved this problem by seeing Christ as the perfect Reformer.   143 Ibid., pp. 32–60, 88–9.

rejected by Perkins.[144] Thus where Harrison applied Scriptural insights directly to the pastoral reorganisation of the Church, Perkins was more cautious, fearing to disrupt the social cohesion which protected the truth against the carnal reason of the common people. This created important differences in their attitudes, both to the magistrate and more generally, because they both knew that the status of the ministry constituted the most damaging contrast between existing structures and Scriptural ideals. For they both rejected the external human device of presbyterianism, and totally depended upon the inner working of the Word as the means of transforming contemporary society into Christ's Church. However, Perkins accepted the Elizabethan Settlement with fewer reservations than Harrison, and envisaged reforms within the existing social framework. The commandment of obedience to the lawful magistrate prevented Perkins from questioning Elizabeth's stolid rejection of reform, while Harrison's attempt to ensure preferment for zealous ministers would have seemed to Perkins like unregenerate impatience with Providence. Thus, to bring about his social transformation Perkins was restricted to making the most of the inherited university system, until God inspired the magistrate to remedy its deficiencies.[145] The way ahead was by small local gains, as Harrison found at Windsor.

We can place Harrison within a common Protestant tradition, a consensus within which the light of the Gospel was refracted through the lens of contemporary circumstances, and particularly the struggle against Antichrist, into a spectrum of reforming ideas, in which Harrison stood somewhere between Cartwright and Perkins or Hutton, but still shared substantial tracts of common ground with Sandys. This tradition, in which we have already put other men like Alexander Nowell and Grindal, recognised that the Scriptures depicted the True Church as the single, prior source of truth, and that its doctrines could perfect all human reason. Harrison was uniquely preoccupied with the historical evidence of that Church, and there were individual differences of emphasis within the tradition. Yet these Protestants were united by their perception of popery as the contemporary manifestation of the Church of Cain, the Satanic parody and antithesis of truth. This chapter has argued that Whitgift did not share this perception, but it should not be inferred that he was entirely isolated within the Elizabethan Church, for Richard Hooker developed similar arguments. Whitgift refused to over-react to Gentilism, and thus to popery. He differed from Hooker on some essential points, but they agreed that Israel was not the uniquely privileged single source of truth, nor that the Gentiles and Rome were its continual and complete opponents. When Hooker declared that 'the general

144 Perkins, *Workes* (1631), iii, 2nd pagination, p. 468; and see above, pp. 122–5.
145 Breward, *Perkins*, pp. 55, 40, 56, 26–8.

and perpetual voyce of men is as the sentence of God him selfe', he was making a point about the interpretation of history as the evidence of God's will, and refusing to measure his actions by the godly models of Israel, for 'the naturall measure wherby to judge our doings, is the sentence of reason determining and setting downe what is good to be done'. The presbyterians quickly reiterated the subservience of reason to revelation.[146] Hooker's view won out eventually, not because he was unanswerable in the prevailing intellectual environment but because later seventeenth-century chronological and historical scholarship established the priority of the Gentiles and removed Israel from her primacy and centrality in history. Yet for as long as Harrison could sustain the myth of the Two Churches he could also use it to determine his response to contemporary political questions, as we shall see in the following chapters.

---

[146] TCD MS 165, fo. 168r. R. J. Bauckham, 'Hooker, Travers and the Church of Rome in the 1580s', in *Journal of Ecclesiastical History*, xxix (1978), pp. 37–50, contrasts Whitgift and Hooker. Hooker, *Lawes*, I. 8. 3 (facs. Amsterdam, 1971), i, pp. 63, 66; and I. 8. 8, i, p. 68; and above, pp. 24–5. [T. Cartwright?], *A Christian Letter...unto...Hooker* ([Middelburg?], 1599), sigs. C1r–C2v, A4r–B2r, reasserts the distinction between the covenant line and Gentilism, and the self-evident truth of Scripture.

5

A reformed Prince

The preceding chapter concluded by drawing an important contrast between the assumptions which Harrison shared with other Elizabethan Protestants, and Richard Hooker's statements about the source of saving knowledge. Hooker's argument rested on scholastic notions about the law of nature, those fundamental principles of God's law imprinted in all human hearts, and which human reason might perceive at all times. Natural law theories also underpinned both Protestant and Catholic political debate in this period, but although we now turn to consider Harrison's political outlook and what it reflects about Protestant political theories in general, this chapter will suggest that Harrison largely disregarded the law of nature in seeking inspiration and justification for his interpretation of contemporary political institutions.

It further argues that for other Protestants, at least as far as they addressed themselves to other members of the True Church, the Scriptural account of the fortunes of the Elect under God's providential direction provided a source of truth superior to the law of nature. The law of nature appears subordinate to revelation when put into the general context of sixteenth-century Protestant thought, and particularly in the context of radical Calvinist thought about the covenant and its implications for contemporary political obligations. Modern historians have quite rightly stressed the indebtedness of Calvinist political theorists such as John Ponet, Christopher Goodman and Theodore Beza to scholastic, conciliarist and Roman Law political theories, which all seemed ultimately to deduce their principles from the law of nature. Yet we should recognise that for devout Protestants like Harrison and those Calvinist theorists already named, the Scriptures offered a much higher level of knowledge about God's will, and particularly about the obedience which he demanded of the Elect, than did the law of nature.

Harrison wrote a history in the form of a chronology, not an articulated political theory, and therefore we must infer his political outlook from the way in which he interpreted the past. In addition, the English situation under Elizabeth precluded the development of reasoned arguments for resistance to the established powers. Nevertheless, Harrison's historical interpretation shared many important features with the most radical Protestant political theorists, both in his general picture of the True Church and his interpretation of certain key episodes in its earthly sojourn. For Ponet and Goodman a very similar historical interpretation provided conclusive proof, at least to a regenerate understanding, that in certain specific circumstances the Elect could not tolerate the triumph of Antichrist through the oppressions of a deluded secular magistrate. While circumstances did not require Harrison to draw these ultimate conclusions from the historical experiences of the True Church, his membership of that spiritual body did make him uneasily aware of the distance between ideal and reality in the behaviour of both superior and inferior contemporary magistrates.

Like Ponet and Goodman he believed that God required the magistrate to fulfil a specific role, but as with his acceptance of presbyterianism, this belief in turn required Harrison to maintain a difficult balance between that Scriptural model and the objective political realities of Elizabethan England. In fact he went further than the radical Calvinists on certain decisive issues of historical interpretation, particularly the kind of magistracy sanctioned by the example of the True Church, and the relationship between imperial rule and true religion epitomised in the behaviour of Constantine. On these issues Harrison adopted positions which implicitly questioned the possibility of any harmonious relationship between continuous worldly monarchy and those who sought to foster true religion. Indeed his historical interpretation only provided a positive justification for contemporary magistracy when the magistrate conformed to the model delineated in the Scriptures. Worldly princes exercised only a limited and temporary power over the godly, since they served merely to restrain the erroneous doctrines and actions of the unregenerate majority. This negative justification for worldly rule reflects the essentially Augustinian character of Harrison's thinking about the origins of political authority and its consequent contemporary role.

Harrison's 'Chronology' did not defer to the unregenerate understanding in its discussion of the covenant line and worldly powers, and therefore he made no use of those arguments drawn from the law of nature which contemporary Protestant political theorists used to convince an audience which included both the Elect and their opponents. Harrison felt no need to use natural law arguments, since to the Elect the providential history of the covenant line appeared to be self-justifying. Once accepted through faithful understanding as the devout presented it, the history and contemporary status of the True Church could not be analysed according to rational criteria. Indeed, by placing Harrison's historical interpretation against the general background of Protestant political theories, we can see more clearly how those theories gave priority to political norms drawn from the covenant line and the covenant itself, over those drawn from the law of nature.

This distinction rested on the Protestant assumption that the law of nature, by comparison with the Scriptures, provided a distorted and misleading picture of true religion. Harrison recognised that 'impossible is it for man to be without anie god at all', but human reason so misunderstood God's nature that 'false relligion is never certeine'; thus educated Romans transferred their devotions from the celestial gods to the Emperor.[1] Melanchthon and Calvin had emphasised the limitations of intuitive human thinking about true religion, as we saw in the first chapter, while in England Thomas Cooper, Bishop of Lincoln, set out this common Protestant outlook in 1573, when Harrison was presenting a similar if more condensed argument in his 'Chronology'. Cooper's *Chronicle*, a redaction of Thomas Lanquet's earlier Chronicle, reinterpreted Lanquet's material according to Melanchthon's historical interpretation and republished Melanchthon's important preface to Carion's *Chronicle*. Cooper's *Exposition of...the olde testament* (1573), went on to demonstrate the conflict of the Two Churches through 'sundrye examples left for our instruction in the holye Scriptures'. He emphasised the sufferings of the True Church 'least we fall into the iudgement of carnal men, and thinke them Happie and blessed, which in deede are cursed and unhappie'. Cooper urged the regenerate to interpret their own struggles against the malice of the world as continuing the experiences of the covenant line, for 'Thus was it in the time of Hieremie and of the Prophetes. Thus was it in the Primitive Church. Thus it is now in these Latter dayes'. Cooper insisted that those who accepted God's covenant must not depart 'from the obedience of Gods holy word' to worship Him 'by their owne devises', 'because the true Saintes of God never used the like'. Cooper used the same tools as the Hebrew prophets to attack that popery which reflected the weakness of man's carnal reason, and urged his readers 'to consider hys great workes and benefites done for his defence and deliverance out of thraledome and miserye'. Most importantly, Cooper regarded the fulfilment of God's promises in the miraculous Exodus as sufficient proof of the covenant not only to 'a godly person', 'but anye man of common sense and reason'.[2]

Cooper thus believed that the Scriptural record of God's care for his Elect could overcome the erroneous intuitions of human reason from the law of nature. For in the Decalogue men might 'fully and perfectly learne those things whereof by the law of Nature we have but a single and bare taste

[1] TCD MS 165, fo. 137r.
[2] Cooper, *A briefe exposition of the olde testament*, fos. 104v (alluding to Rom. 15.4), 111v, 206r, 179v, 207v, 208r.

onlie'. While the scholastics accepted that human reason always had access to God's moral law written in our hearts, Cooper argued that this understanding could only be achieved through grace, as when at Epiphany 'The holye Ghoste was sente downe' to 'wryte the eternall lawe of God in oure heartes'. In fact, far from being freely available without revelation, Cooper insisted that 'to imprinte his holy will in oure heartes...will best be doone by the diligent reading, hearing and meditating of the holie Scriptures, by which the wil of God is learned'. This returned the argument to the history of the True Church, which showed that 'not onley the Israelites but all mankinde thorough naturall corruption are verie prone to Idolatrie and superstition' when 'destitute of the grace of God'. Therefore in both the Testaments, God distinguished His people from the ungodly by a simple ceremonial to which none of the devices of men could be added 'seemed they never so godly'. Like Harrison, Cooper argued that this revelation condemned the whole of popery, for 'This lesson is so given to the Israelites, that it may bee also an instruction to all the faithfull in the Church of God at all times, and especially in these latter dayes', while the Holy Ghost had warned (Matt. 24.4) 'that Antichrist and his ministers should use the same meanes' to seduce the Elect as Satan had in the Old Testament. What endured was a kind of obedience in which many things 'might seeme very harde or unpossible to humaine reason', for the Saints 'leave to the wisedome and providence of God, to the understandinge wherof they are not hable to attaine', whatever in His commandments 'seemeth difficulte, straunge, or absurde'.[3]

Thus Cooper applied Scriptural criteria to the natural law accessible to human reason, he did not attempt to explain the faithful obedience of the Elect in terms amenable to human reason. Indeed reliance on the intuitions of nature led men into the errors of popery and attempts to justify themselves by their works. The Church of Cain thrived when men deduced faith from the law of nature, whereas in contrast in the covenant line 'we see, that God him selfe in thys place to Abraham [Gen. 12.5] is the First preacher of our Free Justification and blessednesse by Fayth in the Seede of Abraham Christ Jesus'. Adam presumably enjoyed a similar revelation of God's eternal will. In matters of faith, therefore, the covenant line transmitted a type of knowledge far above what could be achieved by reasoning from the laws of nature, a distance measured by the contrasts between the true worship of God and its satanic parody – popery. Yet how far did this Protestant sense of an overpowering obligation to follow the Word precisely in accordance with God's unfathomable will, and thus to maintain the distinction between the Two Churches, impinge upon Harrison's political thought, and indeed upon other Protestant discussions of the secular polity?[4]

---

[3] Ibid., fos. 210v, 242r, 214r, 217v, 227r, 234v–236v, 112v, 123r.   [4] Ibid., fos. 112r–v.

Luther's perception of the invisible True Church as the 'people of God living from the word of God' allowed him to place the visible Church under the control of the godly prince. For like Augustine he argued that God had created the temporal kingdom only to preserve a civil peace amongst sinful men. Melanchthon especially regarded the temporal commonwealth as 'adiaphora'; its precise configuration remained irrelevant to saving knowledge. Accordingly both men accepted the law of nature as the positive source of justice over a wide area of civil life. Yet while man's conscience could be trusted thus far in moral knowledge, in the context of faith human reasoning powers seemed 'absurd'. God required the prince to enforce His laws in a precisely defined way, but originally Luther and Melanchthon argued that even the tyrant who refused to be bound by God's laws must be respected as forming part of God's providential design. When they sought justification for resistance in the 1530s, their secular conception of the commonwealth enabled them to rely upon the human reasoning enshrined in the feudal law and Roman private law, and ultimately to refer to the instinct of self-preservation, a part of the natural knowledge instilled by God which could be rationally perceived. Even so, while civil righteousness deserved credit within its limited sphere, the godly prince should be trained not in the political principles of 'the blind heathen teacher Aristotle', but in the Scriptures, which provided the best education in the principles underlying the civil law, and which showed the godly what they must endure rather than obey the ungodly commands of the temporal magistrate. For Luther the providential ordering of the world required the faithful to base their actions on the Word, not scholastic delusions derived from the law of nature.[5]

Harrison's conception of the commonwealth shared more in common with those Calvinists who confronted the central dilemma which the Lutherans evaded in developing their justifications for resistance by inferior magistrates. Like Luther, Calvin adopted an anti-Aristotelian explanation of the origins of political society, arguing that all magistrates had been appointed by divine providence. With their greater stress on God's immanence in every event in creation, the Calvinists consequently experienced greater difficulty in applying Lutheran resistance theories, partly because of the political situation in south Germany, Switzerland and France, but partly because their conception of political power undermined such theories. In order to oppose tyranny they had to argue that it was always evil, but in order to avoid the blasphemous suggestion that God was sometimes the author of evil they had to find another explanation for the appearance of tyranny. Radical Lutherans like Martin Bucer and Peter Martyr found that

[5] Q. Skinner, *The Foundations of Modern Political Thought* (2 vols. Cambridge, 1979), ii, pp. 9, 14–15, 5, 66–9, 199–203, 16–17, 19.

the Augustinian contention that God sometimes ordained tyrants to punish
our sins vitiated their attempts to justify resistance to tyranny, but the most
radical Calvinists such as John Ponet and Christopher Goodman evaded this
problem by making the revolutionary assertion that God did not ordain all
princes.

They based their argument on the positive picture of a godly prince in
the Old Testament, which remained normative for all times, and which
showed that idolatrous or tyrannical rule only occurred when a people
disobeyed God and sought a ruler who fitted something other than Scriptural
criteria. Essentially this reflects that interpretation of the Law and Gospel
which distinguished Calvin from Luther. Luther regarded the Old Testament
Law simply as the means to make men despair of their ability to do good,
for Christ in the New Testament had released those graced with a faithful
understanding from the bondage of the Law. Calvin found the Gospel to
be a perfect rendering of the Law which retained its contemporary moral
relevance when spiritually interpreted in the manner of the covenant line.[6]
Consequently Ponet and Goodman, and with them Beza, used the historical
examples of magistracy in the Old Testament as binding arguments, since
as repeated demonstrations of the covenant between God and His elect
people they provided the criteria of godly rule for the sixteenth century.
Although Ponet and Goodman might cite conciliarist arguments to underline
the distinction between a godly office and its ungodly holder, or like Beza
appeal to scholastic and Roman Law notions of radical constitutionalism,
they used such ideas only to convince unregenerate human reason, and
assured their godly audience that the revealed models of godly rule remained
on a higher level of knowledge. The history of the True Church took
precedence over the law of nature as a source of political wisdom for many
devout Protestants.

Harrison also insisted that ungodly rule reflected Satan's success in
seducing weak human reason into breaking the covenant. The decline in
political behaviour from the standards which God had set for the Elect
paralleled the process by which the Church of Cain gained ascendancy over
the True Church and destroyed godly religion. Harrison's 'Chronology'
recorded the historical 'proof' that Israel had enjoyed a revelation not only
temporally prior to, but also autonomous from, any criteria that might be
rationally derived from the law of nature. John Harvey represented the other
side of this perennial debate, insisting that Moses and the prophets 'reaped
exceeding great fruit even to their very best and godliest uses' from the
profound knowledge of Egypt, and that this fact added authority to their
pronouncements.[7] Yet for radical Protestants like Harrison the idea that the

---

[6] Ibid., pp. 225–7, 236, 222–38.
[7] Harvey, *A discoursive probleme*, p. 77. Polydore Vergil's widely read *De inventoribus rerum* gave
    an impressive exposition of pagan claims.

Scriptures merely exemplified the universal truths found in Gentile precepts detracted from the unique significance of the Bible as the record of the doctrines and experiences of the True Church, and diminished the contemporary relevance of the covenant line's historical relationship with God. However, François Baudoin complained that most students knew only Graeco-Roman history, to the detriment of Jewish history, while Jean Bodin frequently castigated the 'wicked' who rejected the orthodox reckoning of time and Israel's primacy.[8] Loud claims for the originality of pagan philosophy persistently counterpointed the godly stress upon the dependence and degeneracy of all aspects of that culture, upon the study of which many livelihoods depended.

The Calvinist insistence upon the perpetual relevance of Old Testament politics should be seen against this wider contemporary debate, for that wider context shows that Harrison came to support the most radical interpretation not through a dogmatic short-cut but through a careful, critical examination of the evidence. For example, his opposition to heterodox opinions on the relationship between Scriptural revelation and the law of nature did not go as far as Mattheus Beroaldus's narrow fervour, which deeply influenced Hugh Broughton's rigid Scripturalism. Beroaldus insisted that the Scriptures must be accepted without reference to pagan sources, and consistently diminished the span of pagan history, but Harrison wondered how this 'carper of all antiquities' could 'indevour safely to discredite the authority of the old prophane writers in their observations of the time to shote farder wide in most of his new conclusions than thei have done in theirs'.[9] Yet even a more careful consideration of Gentile knowledge showed Harrison that God 'created all things in their fulnesse of strength and beautie', and first of all in Israel, where direct illumination complemented the Elect's true faith with the perfect knowledge of all necessary arts and sciences, including proper political behaviour.[10] True faith and true knowledge enjoyed a symbiotic relationship within the covenant line, but without the faithful insights conferred by divine grace, the later recipients of Israel's knowledge distorted it through their fallen carnal reason into what Harrison described as Gentilism. Harrison's profoundly Augustinian outlook underpinned his radical desire to resurrect that primitive purity in faith and learning, a desire which he shared with Melanchthon, who ultimately identified 'the primary with the true'. Therefore Harrison applauded 'the famous clerke Phillipp Melanchthon, who for the elucidation of antiquities and recovery of Lerning now almost extinguished deserveth to be counted the paragon of his time'.[11]

[8] Brown, *The Methodus*, pp. 39–41, 76.
[9] TCD MS 165, fo. 95r. Beroaldus's *Chronologia* (Basle, 1577), survives at Derry (shelf-mark E.h.8), with some critical marginalia by Harrison, as do his *Chronicum* (1575) and *Chronographia ecclesiae Christi* (1564), both shelf-mark D.i.b.1.   [10] TCD MS 165, fo. 45r.
[11] Fraenkel, *Testimonia Patrum*, p. 361; TCD MS 165, fo. 121v.

Harrison considered that since this knowledge had been imparted to the covenant line in order to complement the corpus of true doctrine, its configuration echoed the shape of God's original covenant with Adam, not the framework provided by a rational interpretation of creation. Therefore he specifically rejected the current notion that God gave the Patriarchs longevity 'only therin to study Philosophi as some would have it'. Like Augustine he insisted that they received 'divine inspirations' together with the gift of faith, while that faith delimited all their knowledge.[12] Even in the most highly developed human arts and sciences 'the glory of the Greciens is not a little obscured' for the Hebrews had previously acquired all that was godly in this knowledge, 'neither by ther owne industry nor instruction of any mortall man but only and immediately from god for the furtherauns sake of his work'.[13] This interpretation of the Scriptures clearly involved some effort of the regenerate imagination, for from Solomon (*c.* 1015 BC) not only 'the rote of all knowledge of natural philosophi is most rightly said to be derived' but also 'the like may be inferred touching moral philosophy'. Harrison considered that not until 679 BC did such studies begin 'to crepe into estimation and knowledge among the Greciens'.[14] Even the unregenerate could not ignore the historical evidence which proved that Israel had enjoyed the first, pristine revelation of godly knowledge, 'for to saie oughtes of the wisdome of the Hebrews I should but speake of that whose antiquity is not unknowen nor farre to be sought of any'.[15] In Harrison's view history and chronology therefore objectively reinforced the correlation between faith and godly knowledge, and Gentile historical errors, as much as any aspect of their knowledge, manifested their infidelity. For when the Gentiles approached the knowledge which they derived from Israel outside the context of faith, they inevitably distorted it to conform to the lineaments of fallen human reason. Thus they perverted the religious meaning of the historical covenant line and its doctrines when they 'honored for their goddes' the Noachidae or turned the history of Israel into myth 'as a percell of their theology'.[16]

This radical epistemology emerges in Harrison's superficially conventional assertion that God never ceased 'to increase their mindes in wisdome that have already by his grace lerned the first point of wisdome that is to fere the Lorde'.[17] For from the evangelical viewpoint that fact really implied that the rational analyses of Greek philosophy could never enable men to construct a godly society. Indeed Harrison consigned this corrupt Gentile

---

[12] *De civitate Dei*, xviii. 39; TCD MS 165, fo. 5r.   [13] Ibid., fo. 44v.
[14] Ibid., fos. 70v, 88v.   [15] Ibid., fo. 88v.
[16] Ibid., fos. 95, 55v. E.g., the history of Elijah (I Kings. 18.41–6) became that of Agelaus, King of Corinth (TCD MS 165, fo. 75r).
[17] Ibid., fo. 44av.

knowledge to the Church of Cain, where Satan incessantly worked to diminish the authority of the Scriptures and their model of the truly godly society. No such edifying knowledge could be derived from the pagan poets and orators, 'for I find that very few of them have delt with any sounde knowledg, but onely curious pointes of Gramer, Rethorike, Logike and Vaine fables of the false goddes, Tragidies and comedies of sondry sortes where by the comon welth hath little benefite, and god lesse honor'. This deficiency reflected Gentile ignorance about God's immanence in history, since of those pagan historians who transmitted some dim awareness of God's providence 'I saie [nothing], for ther labours were best bestowed'.[18]

Even so, the limitations of Gentile historiography appear more clearly in Harrison's comment on those contemporaries who betrayed their spiritual membership of the Church of Cain when they perpetuated Gentile delusions and 'geve more credite to dead vaine poetes and historiographers for thinges long past then unto the scriptures of the living and true god, which thei accompt to be but barren and bokes not fraught with eloquens'. In their preference for 'Rethoricall invention', contemporary enthusiasts for the *studia humanitatis* 'resembled the old greciens', notwithstanding 'that at the first all knowledge was brought to them from soche indede as thei in scorne did repute as rude and barbarous'.[19] Harrison could detect throughout history the sinister members of Satan who put Scriptural teachings and reason on the same level, and who by applying rational criteria to them 'most fraudulently corrupt the simplicity of the scriptures'. Thus after the rise of Antichrist the clergy 'were to moche geven to Logike and human knowledge, and very little or nothing at all to the study of the scriptures'.[20] This uncompromising antithesis between divine revelation and deluded human reason denied reason any autonomy in determining either saving knowledge or that complementary corpus of pristine truth which Harrison believed had been uniquely revealed to the covenant line. In seeking to resurrect this Elect learning, the regenerate had to learn to restrain their reason in deference to God's prior revelation to the covenant line, and reject whatever kind of knowledge did not conform to that eternal truth.

The recovery of this pristine knowledge through biblical exegesis and doctrinal exposition preoccupied Calvin and Beza in much the same way. In pursuit of this goal Calvin selectively employed those scholastic dialectical and philosophical techniques which had been substantially transformed by

---

[18] Ibid., fo. 147r. This anti-humanist stance should not be read out of its intensely evangelical context. All these studies could be legitimately used so long as their proponents did not deceive themselves into thinking that they had any bearing on saving knowledge or on building up the True Church.

[19] Ibid., fos. 41r–v.

[20] Pagans and 'cold christians' in the early Church only allowed the Scriptures validity when they conformed to the rules of logic (ibid., fo. 151r).

humanist innovations, but neither Calvin, nor Beza in clarifying Calvin's ideas, sacrificed the biblical centre of their theology through over-confident use of such reasoning. Ian McPhee has shown that to argue that Beza sought to harmonise the principles drawn from reason and theology ignores the fact that Beza placed natural and supernatural knowledge on different levels of knowing. For while reason could be legitimately used within its own sphere when judged by and subordinate to the Word, it could not be *a priori* a source of true theological knowledge, but only reflect that knowledge by conforming itself to the Word, *a posteriori*. The way to the restoration of true wisdom lay not through rational dialectic but this kind of regenerate reasoning, which could be found only in the covenant line, where grace overcame man's sinful errors through the gift of faith. Thus for Harrison's radical Protestant contemporaries true political wisdom, together with the proper use of all other arts and sciences, could be discovered only through that grace which had instructed the covenant line in the application of the same knowledge. This knowledge could never bring men to salvation, but it complemented true faith, and even in isolation from grace amongst the pagans could contribute to social stability. Yet because they lacked the insight into the doctrines and examples of the covenant line provided by a faithful interpretation of the Scriptures, the pagan philosophers perpetrated myriads of religious errors, for 'the succession of events that we have not only seen, but that which we know to have been happening since the beginning of the world' gave the clearest knowledge of God, argued Beza. Gentile philosophical knowledge, confounded with the Gospel by the scholastics, produced a false religion together with a complementary corpus of tainted knowledge.[21]

This excursion into Protestant epistemology helps us to appreciate those nuances of Beza's political thought which modern historians have tended to overlook. For example, Michael Walzer has claimed that Beza, like all the Huguenot theorists, depended almost entirely upon the citation of historical examples to justify his political arguments. Yet Dr Walzer distorts the evidence in order to minimise the importance of the Scriptures in Beza's thought and to prove that Beza used history indiscriminately as a source of godly precedents for contemporary Calvinists. Beza claimed that the godly should accept the duty of inferior magistrates to resist tyranny because the Scriptures depicted this part of the inferior magistrate's office in David's armed resistance to Saul and the rebellion of the priestly city Libnah against Jehoram. 'These two examples,' he proclaimed, 'quite apart from the arguments above,' drawn from Roman Law, 'are, in my opinion, so clear and authentic as to give sufficient assurance to the consciences of lesser magistrates,' that in the last resort the use of arms was a legitimate defence of

---

[21] McPhee, 'Beza' (dissertation), pp. 157–60, 160, 185, 176.

their inferiors against tyranny. For David and the men of Libnah had acted in obedience to God's commands under the covenant, and the contemporary members of the covenant line had in their turn to obey this important revelation of God's will. By omitting a few decisive words at this point, Walzer makes Beza bind the consciences of his godly readers to the examples of profane as well as sacred history. Beza, however, made the vital distinction that only Elect examples should bind godly consciences, for 'I use these [pagan] examples not as rules for Christian consciences, but because they are widely known and celebrated, and also because even the affairs of pagans are not so distant from the rules of equity' that right and wrong could not be distinguished through them. Yet the fact remained that only in the Scriptures could the regenerate find an untainted revelation of God's will and a perfect demonstration of that godly obedience which they must follow.[22]

Quentin Skinner has offered a much more penetrating analysis of Calvinist political thought, including Beza's. Professor Skinner has convincingly demonstrated that the Calvinists drew upon an arsenal of radical civil and canon law precepts, and upon the tradition of radical conciliarist thought begun by d'Ailly and Gerson in the early fifteenth century, to justify the right of resistance by inferior magistrates. He has also shown that the Calvinists' determinedly anti-Thomist and anti-Aristotelian discussions of the origins and development of political society merely retraced the steps of those theologians who followed Ockham, such as Gerson, Almain and Mair. Professor Skinner therefore concludes that in stressing the godly necessity of revolution in this period the Calvinists did not make use 'of specifically Calvinist arguments', although he does discuss the claims made by Goodman and Knox that the members of the True Church promised to resist ungodly rule as part of the covenant. Thus he suggests that Beza's main problem was how to advance 'arguments from reason' to justify resistance, and that he solved it, as did other Huguenots, by turning to the natural law theorists already mentioned.[23]

While this accurately reflects Beza's assessment of his largely unregenerate audience, this proposition requires several qualifications. First, Professor Skinner's discussion infers that Beza placed rational arguments on the same level as Scriptural models, whereas we have already noticed Beza's statement that the examples of David and Libnah required no verification from the Roman Law, and that pagan history and philosophy could not bind Christian

---

[22] M. Walzer, *The Revolution of the Saints* (London, 1976), pp. 75, 78. *De iure magistratuum*, tr. and ed. J. H. Franklin, in *Constitutionalism and Resistance in the Sixteenth Century* (New York, 1969), pp. 113, 106; cf. Walzer, *Revolution of the Saints*, pp. 75–6. Dr Walzer used Franklin's edition.

[23] Skinner, *Foundations*, ii, pp. 323, 238, 326.

consciences to a certain course of action, a position which reflects his general epistemology as described by Ian McPhee. Secondly, Beza was less opportunistic in his use of natural law arguments than might at first appear, for his epistemology demanded that weak and corrupt human reason should conform to the Word *a posteriori*. He sincerely believed that he subordinated his reason to the Scriptural description of the True Church when he set out the criteria of godly political action. For he emphasised that he used civil law precepts and Roman Law maxims 'not to suggest that civil law or the opinion of this or that philosopher should be taken as *a rule of conscience*, but only to show the manifest unreason of that opinion which allows no lawful way to halt flagrant tyrrany'.[24]

Beza sought in the Scriptures those *a priori*, revealed rules of conscience whose criteria would enable him to select from both natural law arguments and the Roman Law those rational principles which conformed to the Word and made it more amenable to fallen human reason, without compromising the Word's essential message. Therefore the framework already given in the Scriptures determined the relevance to his argument of civil law precepts and Roman Law maxims.[25] Inevitably Beza underestimated the extent to which his own reason guided his Scriptural interpretation, yet we should not underestimate the sincerity of his search for models of political behaviour within the covenant line. For he believed that the original covenant with Adam and the succeeding reaffirmations of those doctrines in the historical experiences of the True Church provided the general context which constrained the regenerate understanding in its interaction with every Scriptural text, as we have seen in Harrison's reflections on 'men of like condition'. Therefore Beza sought to persuade his audience to conform to the godly models of political behaviour given in the Scriptures, directly in the case of the godly and via the mediation of the law of nature and the civil law in the case of the unregenerate.

Viewed from the perspective of Elizabethan England, such arguments posed a problem for a sincere Protestant like Edwin Sandys, who emphasised that man's natural addiction to evil precluded the natural law from being a source of saving knowledge, but could not go on to condemn whatever in the Tudor constitution did not conform to the Scriptural model of godly

---

[24] Beza, *De iure magistratuum*, ed. Franklin, p. 126 (my italics). Professor Skinner cited this edition. This interpretation of Beza's thought possibly helps to explain the conservative aspects of Calvinist political theories discussed by E. H. Kossmann in his criticism of Skinner's argument ('Popular sovereignty at the beginning of the Dutch Ancien Regime', in *Low Countries History Year Book* (1981), pp. 1–28, esp. pp. 18–23).

[25] R. E. Giesey claimed that the Huguenots used 'stylized and generalized' historical examples merely to illustrate political theories first argued on rational grounds. He does not explain how this accounts for their selective use of Roman Law to justify godly liberty. R. E. Giesey, 'The Monarchomach Triumvirs: Hotman, Beza and Mornay' in *Bibliothèque D'Humanisme et Renaissance*, xxxii (Geneva, 1970), pp. 41–56, at pp. 54, 52–3.

rule. Therefore like Luther and Melanchthon he distinguished between what the Scriptures revealed as essential for salvation, and political behaviour where, 'the will of man being free unto naturall and civill actions', the law of nature prevailed, although Sandys regarded it as inferior to God's revelation in every other area of life.[26] In contrast Harrison's 'Chronology' displays more affinities with Beza's political thought. Like Beza he emphasised Greek ignorance about the model of godly rule revealed in the Old Testament, which vitiated all their rationalising about politics from the law of nature. Israel had had no dealings with the Greeks or Latins, 'Neither were the times of the Jewish commonwealth so late as that the grecians or latin writers could get any certene notion of thestate of ther country'. Therefore the Greeks had little to say about 'the regiments of their princes'.[27] This put their political thought on a par with all their other knowledge, none of which should carry any weight with the godly independently of the Scriptures, since it established Satan's criteria of behaviour. Consequently Harrison echoed Beza's attack on 'the greatest part of Scholastic idle discourse, which confounds the Gospel with the platitudes of Aristotle' and other pagan philosophers. He drew an equally sharp distinction between Scriptural and rational standards of truth, and condemned those under Antichrist who became so far 'assotted upon Aristotle ther god that thei presumed...to affirme how he was a sound Catholicke', a confusion of truth and error also discernible amongst earlier 'cold christians' who put religion on a level with other studies where 'Euclide is the lanterne, Aristotle and Theophrast are with them in great estimation and Galene is their god'.[28]

Harrison's conception of the origins and development of the godly political society underwrote his anti-Aristotelian outlook. Apart from his statement that Enoch preached against the kingdom of Antichrist at the very moment when Cain founded the first city, we have already noticed his determined refutation of Melanchthon's defence of imperial rule, and his insistence that Cain's posterity had usurped the powers of imperial government. The Flood punished such corruptions, and Harrison emphasised the political importance of God's renewal of the covenant with Noah immediately the latter left the Ark. Rather than repeating Melanchthon's orthodox Augustinian justification of temporal power as a restraint on sin, Harrison emphasised that the covenant which had preserved and governed the godly from Adam to Noah included fundamental political principles, together with all the other rules necessary for a godly society. Preserved by the covenant line along with true faith, this revelation provided the framework for Harrison's 'commonwealth' ideals in the same way that it conditioned his view of the pastoral institutions of the Elizabethan Church.

---

[26] Sandys, *Sermons*, pp. 16, 6, 177.
[27] TCD MS 165, fos. 100r, 103r. [28] McPhee, 'Beza', p. 176; TCD MS 165, fo. 151r.

Thus the moment that Noah left the Ark, he restored religion by a sacrifice to God, who blessed Noah and his seed, 'and in thinstitution of pollitike regiment' gave him laws for diet, matrimony and justice which renewed and continued the knowledge revealed to Adam.[29] This revelation enabled Noah to give to all the people with which the Noachidae replenished the world 'sounde instructions', both for true religion and civil governance, notably the principle of 'the direct administration of justice', an element of the perpetual covenant delineating the office of the godly magistrate which we shall repeatedly encounter in Harrison's account of the godly commonwealth. Italy especially honoured Noah, for 'he caused them to abounde in worldly felicite', and left volumes of 'most excellent knowledge whereby ther Preestes became very skilfull and ther civile Magistrates no lesse provident in governauns of ther Dominions'.[30] Harrison's radical epistemology, by making political instruction part of the covenant, therefore led him to assess contemporary political actions by the standards of that covenant, and not by reference to the law of nature.

Indeed he could find no other secure basis of judgement apart from the covenant, for the law of nature could only be derived from those corrupt nations outside the covenant, where infidelity corrupted the pristine godly polity as the Church of Cain encroached upon the True Church. Idolatrous Ham destroyed the godly Italian commonwealth when he corrupted the people 'with his pestiferous doctrine and vicious conversation'. Indeed as the posterity of Ham spread over the earth they brought not only ignorance of God, but 'the bondage and servitude of mankinde', as part of the curse laid upon Ham by Noah. Despite Noah's attempts at restoration, true religion and godly polity succumbed to 'the practize of Sathan nothing else but error and infidelities grounded upon the traditions of man, whereby the true knowledge of god was abolished and mere infidelitie received over all'.[31] Yet Harrison made 'small account' of these innovations in themselves and instead emphasised that religious decline went hand in hand with political decline into tyranny, as rulers broke the limitations which God had laid upon them in the covenant. He therefore took care to emphasise the relevance of these limitations for contemporary rulers. For the 'knitting up of the whole discourse' constituted 'the cheef point of all religion', namely that 'I lerne to crave of the Lorde that he wold put ones not only into the hertes of princes but of all men without differens that thei shold attempt nothing in whatsoever dealing before thei first did consult how it might safely stand

---

[29] Ibid., fo. 9v; and see above, p. 69.
[30] Ibid., fos. 5v, 23r.
[31] Ibid., fos. 18r, 10r, 21r, 22v. Thus Ham revived the Church of Cain after the Flood, which itself reflected the depravity of human reason, for 'god had no soner in a maner framed and made a perfitt man but he fell likewise to worke to make false goddes' (ibid., fo. 27v).

with the will and pleasure of god'.[32] Again, the familiarity of the sentiment should not be allowed to detract from the radical implications of the underlying reasoning, for the contemporary continuation of the conflict between the Two Churches provided Harrison with a powerful motive rigorously to apply the revealed criteria of godly rule to contemporary rulers, lest Satan overwhelm the True Church through the temporal power. In different circumstances Ponet and Goodman had used the same argument to prove that the godly must obey God and resist tyranny, but under Elizabeth, Harrison had to fall back upon the pious hope that divine grace would enlighten the Prince about her own shortcomings by comparison with the godly model.

To a mind already conditioned to finding portentous historical and chronological patterns and parallels in providentially ordered history, abundant historical evidence appeared to underline this contrast between higher and lower levels of knowledge, godly and ungodly political behaviour. One particular parallel struck Harrison as embodying a deep religious meaning. Following the destruction of the corrupt Gentile polities in the Flood, the Greeks, argued Harrison, remained ignorant for over seven hundred years of the necessary arts of government imparted to the covenant line, until Cecrops in 1556 BC 'framed a kind of curteous behaviour amongst them'.[33] Yet the historical context of the foundation of the kingdom of Athens vitiated any claim that it or the later Athenian *polis* might have to provide a valid constitutional model, for Harrison placed Athens firmly on the wrong side in the struggle of the Two Churches. He described the faithless Cecrops as an agent of Satan, 'who seketh to deface and discredit the Authority of the Scriptures, for whereas Moses receaved his Lawes from the infallible mouth of the Lord the wily serpent now animateth the paganes to report the like of theirs', so that the foundation of an Athenian political society could be explained neither in Aristotelian natural law terms, nor in the Augustinian sense as a bridle for sin, but as sin itself. For it represented, like the Church of Cain throughout history, a satanic parody of the True Church and its godly polity. Thus Cecrops quickly devised idolatry, 'as an instrument of the devell to daunt the glory of god in one place whilest the lord by his servant Moses was as diligent in therection of true relligion in the wildernesse of Sinai in another'. Moreover, just as those who afterwards remained faithful to Israel's ancient constitution, reaffirmed by the covenant line at Sinai, formed part of that same regenerate covenant line, so in the first moments of the Athenian *polis* 'the people were as it were not onely

---

[32] Like popery, Ham's ceremonies were 'so beautifull and full of variety to the eie that the simple people were wonderfully delighted with them' because they appealed to carnal appetites (ibid., fo. 28r). D. C. Allen, *The Legend of Noah*, pp. 116–17, drains these events of any polemical significance.   [33] TCD MS 165, fo. 42r.

infected but also utterly poisoned with the bane of their destruction'.[34] Those graced with a faithful understanding of history could find in these events the spiritual contrast between the political manifestations of the Two Churches, between human readiness to decline into idolatry and tyranny, and Israel's return to the pristine godly commonwealth through one of the series of reformations which punctuated the history of the True Church.

Events at Sinai revealed the limitations of human reason both in setting up a godly polity and also in trying to analyse it according to rational criteria. At Sinai a divinely appointed system for the direct administration of justice remedied the failure of a rationally devised constitution to maintain equity. The hierarchical system of judges advised by Jethro collapsed under the weight of business as the cases referred to Moses increased faster than he could resolve them. God therefore established seventy more judges 'of the most ancient' to hear these difficult cases. This example demonstrated the limitations of a judicial monarchy and the need for a broadly based system of justice within the congregation. Moreover, these men who constituted 'the highe Senate or counsell of the Jewes' did not come from the nobility more typical of a settled state, but had 'borne office among them sometime in Egypt' and had dispensed direct justice under persecution.[35] This distinction, emphasising their doctrinal purity and their practice of the type of government given in the covenant to Noah, received dramatic confirmation in the gift of prophecy which 'fel upon Eldad and Medad also', and which put their judgements on a different level from those of other magistrates. The renewal of the covenant at Sinai therefore involved a restatement of the duties of the godly magistrate, which committed Israel's magistracy to the preservation of true religion above secular ends. Generally, Israel's history revealed the intimate connection between godly rule according to the Scriptural criteria taught by the covenant line, and true religion, for her magistrates became tyrannical as she became more idolatrous. Indeed, more than anything else the final triumph of idolatry under Antiochus marked 'thend of the Jewish regiment heretofore used and hensfurth insueth another kind of pollicie in governaunce altogether in confusion, whereby we maie see how worldly men do wrestle by humaine wisdome' when God abandoned the Jews after their final breach of the covenant.[36]

---

[34] Ibid., fos. 49v–50r, 44r, and *cf.* Numa 'for wanting faith what could his doing be other then very sinne' (ibid., fos. 86v–87r). Harrison's providential historical interpretation would obviously suggest that the historical contrast between Athens and Sinai was a deliberate revelation to the godly.

[35] 'As Cornelius Bartram doth also coniecture in his politia Judaica published of late.' Harrison's copy of Cornelius Bertramus, *De politia judaica, tam civili quam Ecclesiastica, iam inde a suis primordiis, hoc est, ab Orbe condito, repetita* (Geneva, 1574), is now Derry shelf-mark H.ii.a.54, but contains no marginalia. See Exodus 18.17–27, Numbers 11.10–30.

[36] TCD MS 165, fo. 44v. Beza however emphasised that Jethro's hierarchy survived the change from aristocracy to monarchy. Solomon organised it 'with more precision', so that it

Harrison's discussion of Israel's godly constitution puts his use of Aristotelian political categories into its proper context. For Harrison's devotion to Elect knowledge showed him that because of its basis in rational criteria the familiar Aristotelian analysis of the three types of government and their debased forms could not begin to comprehend Israel's status under God's immediate care.[37] For a conformist thinker, Aristotle's discussion provided the boundaries of the argument, and his encomium of monarchy could then be applied to Israel's history to produce further examples of the natural law of political development towards monarchy.[38] Harrison refused to concede that rational, natural law criteria would provide the framework to interpret godly rule in Israel, for that first and purest source of divine truth should guide the interpretation of Gentile affairs. Indeed he cited Aristotle's confession that Greek philosophy, including political thought, derived from the Samotheans in Gaul, for they were descendants of righteous Japhet whose followers, the Druids, retained some genuine religious knowledge as well as being 'notable Magistrates'.[39] This deprived reason of any autonomy in assessing proper political behaviour, for it allowed Harrison to believe that Aristotle had derived indirectly from the Elect whatever in his political doctrines conformed to Scriptural criteria. Otherwise, like all Gentile philosophers, Aristotle remained ignorant of Israel, and particularly of the type of magistracy conferred upon the covenant line, and his reliance on the evidence of idolatrous Gentile monarchy vitiated his analysis.

This did not prevent Harrison from using Aristotle's terms, for his rational criteria could be legitimately used within a limited sphere. Yet he never applied those terms as confidently as Calvin, who at times in the *Institutes* found it necessary to prove from Israel's ancient constitution that 'aristocracy, or a system compounded of aristocracy and democracy, far excels all others' because 'the Lord confirmed it by his authority when he ordained among the Israelites an aristocracy bordering on democracy, since he willed to keep them in best condition'. Calvin submitted Israel to worldly, Aristotelian categories in his anxiety to restrain those extremists 'who deny that a commonwealth is duly framed which neglects the political system of Moses, and is ruled by the common laws of nations', but Harrison had more

---

remained a permanent restraint on rulers (*De iure magistratuum*, ed. Franklin, p.110). The Geneva Bible also commended Jethro's godly advice (marginal note to Exodus 18.24).

[37] Harrison, *Description* (1587), p. 28, criticises Aristotle's mistaking 'by humane reason' of secondary causes for the primary cause of political change.

[38] See the royalist Bishop Henry King, trying to counteract radical interpretations of Israel's monarchy similar to Harrison's (*A Sermon Preached at St Paul's March 27 1640* (London, 1640), p. 15), and Raleigh, *History*, II.xvi.1, rehearsing further arguments that monarchy 'is framed from the Pattern of his sole rule, who is Lord of the Universal'.

[39] TCD MS 165, fo. 23r. Through a similar process of diffusion Aesop, Hesiod and even Plato owed their heightened awareness of the pretensions of the mighty to their contact with the Elect during the Babylonian diaspora, contact which revitalised the vestigial knowledge of God and His laws in these fallen men (ibid., fo. 95r).

sympathy with those who argued that Israel did not merely obey the law of nature.[40] Consequently he remained unimpressed by the claims of Jean Bodin and Peter Martyr that the *aristocratia* of the Jews began just after the death of Joshua, for, as we have seen, Harrison regarded this as a period when Israel forgot the marvellous works of the Lord in the Delivery, and therefore fell into idolatry.[41] Thus when Harrison acknowledged that 'monarchiall regiment is the first, of longest continuauns and therefore the most excellent', this did not represent a complete capitulation to those arguments which would justify contemporary monarchy on its own terms, according to the laws of nature, no more than did his concession that aristocracy and democracy 'necessarily' develop towards monarchy. For these statements were occasioned by a discussion of the corrupt monarchy of Nimrod. Outside these rational criteria stood the Scriptural model, which set another standard of rule for the covenant line, and one which, as partakers in the covenant, God commanded the godly of Elizabethan England to struggle to attain. This imposed a greater obligation than simply repeating the standard Calvinist complaint that monarchy often declined into tyranny 'without any gret troble'.[42] In fact it committed Harrison to seeking evidence for the survival of Israel's godly constitution in Elizabethan England. His eventual success in finding such evidence, which allowed him subjectively to bring ideal and reality closer together, diminished the radical implications of his historical account of godly rule, which in important details went beyond even the outspoken analyses presented by Ponet, Goodman and Beza.

Like these radical Calvinists, Harrison stressed the crucial distinction between the office of ruler, which God had ordained, and the person of the ruler, for the prince was 'goddes officer to minister his lawes and the sincere ordinaunces ordained for the benefite of his people', and in fulfilling that clearly defined function, magistrates 'either are or ought to be the exacte ministers of the same'. The significant equivocation of this last statement epitomises Harrison's difficulty in fully confronting the problem of a ruler who refused to be God's minister, and although he counselled obedience to 'whosoever doth truly administer the law', the particular circumstances of the English Reformation prevented him from articulating justifications for disobedience. He had no compunctions about recognising that in his day the three types of government defined by Aristotle were inextricably intermingled with their debased forms through 'iniury of time and corruption of

---

[40] Calvin, *Institutes*, IV.xx.8; IV.xx.14. Yet many extremists did not adhere to a rigidly literal biblicism, stressing instead that in reborn Christians the spirit transcended the limits of the written Word (G. H. Williams, *The Radical Reformation* (London 1962), p. 828).

[41] TCD MS 165, fo. 47r; and see above, p. 22.

[42] Ibid., fos. 12v–13r. Calvin thought that it very rarely happened that a monarch's will 'never disagrees with what is just and right' (*Institutes*, IV.xx.8), while Beza believed that even the best monarch inevitably abused his powers (*De iure magistratuum*, ed. Franklin, p. 116).

manners', since monarchs aped the tyrant for whom 'nothing is well done wherein…his gaine is not provided for'.[43] Yet like many moderate Puritans, Harrison found himself so indebted to the existing ruling elite for the limited amount of reformation that had been achieved that he had no alternative to pious exhortation, even when that elite proved largely indifferent to the commands of the Word. Therefore like other zealous Protestants, but in contrast to a figure such as Edwin Sandys, he lived in unhappy coexistence with the political structure which supported his preaching, but which he knew had become debased from God's purposes.[44]

The Old Testament clearly revealed that purpose, for the written doctrines and experiences of the covenant line revealed the essential ordinances for a godly commonwealth. Just as the godly models of the True Church in Israel highlighted the imperfections of the Elizabethan Church for Harrison, so Israel's political structures gave him a deeper understanding of the earthly character of contemporary rule, which retained only vestiges of its original function of leading men to faith. Many godly functions had been distorted through the influence of the Church of Cain, which Harrison considered had placed its mark on worldly dominion when it usurped the first empire from the race of Sem. Harrison encountered other examples of magistracy in the Old Testament which further enhanced his suspicions about worldly 'policy' by comparison with the True Church. For example, his interpretation of the election of Saul in I Sam. 8–12, when contrasted with other contemporary views, reveals the implications of his particular historical vision, and helps to place Harrison more precisely in the contemporary spectrum of political opinion than any discussion of his use of Aristotle's eventually limited categories.[45] In their use of these categories, conformists examined contemporary monarchical rule in the light of universal natural law which also had jurisdiction in the Scriptures, while Harrison felt that the present must obey the unique revelation in the Scriptures. Popular chronicles repeated Melanchthon's interpretation of Saul's election which developed the Augustinian justification for worldly rule. Calvinists used the same episode to place careful limits on the magistrate's use of his powers and to evolve means of redress against tyranny. Harrison believed that Israel committed a grave sin in demanding a king, an argument which put him alongside the most radical Calvinists, John Ponet and Christopher Goodman, who argued that tyranny arose when men disobeyed God.

[43] TCD MS 165, fos. 12v–13r.
[44] John Foxe knew that much was amiss, but like Harrison felt unable to rock the boat 'because God so placed us Englishmen here in one common wealth, also in one Church as in one shippe together' (quoted in Olsen, *Foxe*, p. 178).
[45] TCD MS 165, fos. 4r–v, also stresses the factual limitations of Aristotle's knowledge.

Harrison was fully aware that many of his contemporaries regarded the events surrounding Saul's elevation as crucially relevant to sixteenth-century political obligations. He realised especially that some interpreters argued for unrestrained monarchical authority by reference to the apparent divine sanction for Saul's kingship, 'for soche is the nature of Adames heires that thei will rather seke to take and gather liberty by the infirmities of the godly then indevour to follow ther good insample in seeking how to serve and please god from the bottomes of ther hartes'.[46] This contrast between the misconceptions of carnal reason, which further compounded the relative errors sometimes committed by Israel, and godly obedience to righteous examples, can be found in Christopher Goodman, who insisted that 'we are bonde to seke the wil of God manifested to us in his Scriptures'.[47] John Ponet also repeatedly emphasised that Scriptural history did not simply confirm precepts derived from human reason, but taught a higher form of truth in God's commands. Therefore the true Christian 'must seke what God will have him to doo', and 'whatsoever God commaundeth man to doo he ought not to considre the matter, but straight to obeie the commaunder'.[48] Ponet sought to convince the godly of their duty to resist and even kill tyrants through the same kind of Scriptural interpretation by which Harrison sought to reform the faith of his readers and hearers. Ponet contended that 'ther be certain examples and paternes in the holy Bible', which he referred 'to the further debating and judgement of thine owne conscience, through the holy goost, by whose providence they are enrolled for our learning', not only to justify resistance but to act as a blueprint for the godly common-wealth, for which latter purpose at least Harrison examined the contrasting examples of Samuel and Saul.[49]

This contrast between the minatory prophet who enjoyed an intimate relationship with his God and the distinctly worldly politician exemplifies Harrison's basic lack of interest in what we would consider practical politics. He primarily concerned himself with the covenant line, which ensured that Israel enjoyed prosperity 'so long as thei served the Lord', who 'guided them...by his Prophets', not by kings or inferior magistrates. This bias also appears in his statement that the Book of Kings should be renamed the book of 'the greater prophets' since the narrative mainly concerned those to

---

[46] Ibid., fos. 28r–v.

[47] Thus the Apostles approved 'no obedience but that which is lawful, that is to say, according to God's appoyntment and ordinance' (C. Goodman, *How superior powers ought to be obeyed* (John Crispin: Geneva, 1558), pp. 7, 112). All men had to follow Daniel, Peter and John, and disobey idolatrous commands (ibid., pp. 71–2).

[48] Ponet, *A short treatise of politike power*, sigs. D1v, D2r.

[49] Ibid., sigs. B4r–B5v, H5r. Note that Ponet paraphrases Rom. 15.4. Those who failed to resist Mary lacked this prophetic insight into the present and 'neither remembre that which is past, nor forsee that which is to come, but onely (as unreasonable creatures) loke upon those thinges that be present' (ibid., sig. L2r).

whom God had chosen to reveal His will.[50] For when idolatry infected Israel it inevitably brought tyranny with it, so that, as Harrison sourly commented on the fall of Samaria, there had been 'many kings in Jerusalem and Israel and some more are yet to come in Juda, but as here and ther one fered the lord so the greater part were wicked and ungodly'.[51] To this extent his world-weariness exceeded that of Calvin or Beza, who chose to emphasise the godliness of Israel's inferior magistrates as well as her princes. Consequently Harrison remained indifferent to the secular mechanisms by which princes achieved power, whereas Beza was anxious to stress the elective rights enjoyed by the Israelites and their subsequent power to advise and correct the prince whom they had created.

Beza cited the example of David, who though designated by God, still had to be elected by the people, 'who dutifully obeyed the will of God in choosing him', but Harrison paid more attention to the religious functions of the office and cold-bloodedly ignored questions of political right. He regarded Saul's son, Isboseth, as being as much a legitimate King as David, for he exercised the office of a prince, although God set up David. Harrison added that the Israelites recognised this divine nomination 'and made a League' with David, but he was less impressed by this than by David's personal godliness, which fitted him for his office. The contrast between these two interpretations reflects the fact that Beza sought to restrain rulers who vigorously supported false religion, and rather naively believed that in England proper restraints on royal power had produced happy results for true religion.[52] Having actually experienced the Elizabethan regime, Harrison had learned to be sceptical about its willingness and ability to achieve full reformation, whether through the prince or the inferior magistrates. At the same time, Harrison maintained the delicate balance between ideal and reality by refusing to recognise publicly the indifference of the ruling elite to his exhortations.

Harrison's belief that the formal structures through which power was exercised mattered less than the ends to which that exercise of power was directed also helped him to diminish the difficult contrast between England's monarchy and Israel's polity, although he still cherished the Old Testament example as an ideal kind of rule for the godly. Indeed he could not forget that monarchy had accompanied the idolatry which Israel had sinfully borrowed from the Church of Cain. Thus under the Judgeship of Abimelech, Israel not only forsook God and served Baal, but as part of this abandonment of the historical covenant in favour of idolatry, Abimelech 'doth affectate

---

[50] TCD MS 165, fo. 130v, and see above, pp. 85–6.
[51] Ibid., fos. 88r, 89v; and *cf.* Calvin: 'the holy kings are greatly praised in Scripture because they restored the worship of God when it was corrupted or destroyed' (*Institutes*, IV.xx.9).
[52] Beza, *De iure magistratuum*, ed. Franklin, pp. 117–18; TCD MS 165, fos. 67r–v.

a kingdome also over the Lordes people'. The godly rejected his tyranny. The motives behind Israel's desire for idolatry – their envy of the supposed wealth, power and 'carnall liberty' of the Gentile nations, substantially resembled their reasons for demanding a king. In godly contrast to the degenerate religion and justice produced by carnal reason, Harrison looked to the example of Samuel, who by preaching God's mercy to the Israelites persuaded them to destroy their idols, but just as importantly discharged his religious duty as a godly magistrate, putting down idolatry with one hand and dispensing justice with the other. Therefore he both 'visited the churches of god every yeare with great zeale and diligens' and reproved the people 'for desiring a king most grievously'.[53]

Harrison's views on Samuel and Saul therefore contrasted with the more conventional interpretation, put forward by Melanchthon in Carion's *Chronicle*. Like other Lutherans, Melanchthon stressed the magistrate's role as the guarantor of order, and therefore emphasised the insecurity inherent in the intermittent rule of the Judges. Thomas Cooper repeated this in his popular *Chronicle*, while Richard Grafton's *Chronicle* introduced a different emphasis, claiming that the Judges ruled continuously, 'created partly by the aucthori of wise men, partly set up by the speciall calling of God'.[54] Grafton also glossed over the decisive change from judges to kings, into which Harrison read sinister significance. While trying to express the uniqueness of Israel's polity, Grafton diminished the significance of the Judgeship by transmuting it into contemporary monarchical terms, speaking of 'a speciall kingdome' given with the Decalogue, so that 'the Church, the Kingdome and the true worde of God' always persisted in Israel.[55] This traditional view persisted even after Calvinist political theorists introduced the powerful argument that Deuteronomy 17.14–20 limited the powers of princes. Raleigh cited conservative views to the effect that Moses in Deut. 17 supported Jacob's prophecy in Gen. 49.10 and God's promise to Abraham in Gen. 17.6 that Israel should have a kingdom, texts which not only proved monarchy intrinsically excellent but in Henry King's opinion reserved the choice to God 'by a law never to be reversed', setting up an authority 'which God intended as Absolute, as it is lawful'.[56]

Varying interpretations arose over other details of the history. Harrison identified a close correlation between Israel's faith or apostasy and its secular condition before Saul, but those who approved of Saul's election pointed to those deficiencies in the Judgeship which required the continuous remedy

---

[53] Ibid., fos. 57v, 66r, 59r, 67r.
[54] Melanchthon, *Carion's Chronicle*, fos. 13r–v; *Cooper's Chronicle* (1565), sig. D4v; and *Grafton's Chronicle*, ed. H. Ellis (London, 1809), i, p.20.
[55] Ibid., p.20, paraphrasing *Carion's Chronicle*, fo. 13r: 'These princes by an Hebrue custome were called Judges'.
[56] Raleigh, *History*, II. xvi.1; King, *A Sermon*, pp. 35–6.

of a strong king. Raleigh rehearsed opinions that before Saul 'when it fared best with them, they did but defend their own Territories' or recover parts lost. This removed the question from obedience to God to the rationalisation that under the Judges 'every man hath observed what civil war Israel had' and how they lived many years in servitude.[57] The royalist, Henry King, recalled that there was 'No law then but lust and will the Rule of each ones Action', justifying the creation of a strong, centralised monarchy. Even Calvin noted that in contrast to those holy kings who reformed religion, Scripture 'places anarchies among things evil because there was no king in Israel, each man did as he pleased' (Judges 21.25).[58]

Those Protestants determined to apply the standards of the Old Testament to contemporary rule were not dissuaded by the evidence of anarchy under the Judges. Beza stated that when God 'governed through the judges whom he had chosen...Israel's government was truly monarchy', 'incomparably the best that ever was' because 'at its beginning the Eternal Himself was its monarch'. Beza's claim that the Judges conducted a 'happy government' and that the Israelites failed to appreciate their good fortune, paralleled Harrison's rejoicing in the fact that the Judges achieved office 'neither by election nor succession' but 'by speciall assignation' from God. Where Melanchthon dwelt upon the deficiencies of this system, Harrison regarded any danger as illusory, for when Israel sought a king she forgot 'in the meane season that god was their defender'. His assurance that God would fulfil the promises in the covenant enabled Harrison to believe that Israel's obedience to God's commands secured for her at crucial moments divine aid through the Judges, and he maintained that ideally this type of rule could ensure prosperity in the present. Therefore 'let not any of us...fere as though we should suffer want if we gave over our minds to serve him...sins he will not suffer one here of the godly to fall unto the grounde'.[59] In his concern to establish the divine origins and universal relevance of the Judgeship, Harrison, like Beza and Goodman, ignored or minimised the evidence of anarchy under the Judges emphasised by apologists for Saul's election. Thus he avoided the evidence of Judges 17–21 by following Gilbert Genebrard's suggestion that 'the five last chapters of the Boke of Judges are wrong set and shold immediately follow the second chapter of the same'.[60] This rearrangement introduced several hundred years between the evidence of anarchy and the

[57] Raleigh, *History*, II.xvi.1.

[58] King, *A sermon*, p. 39; Calvin, *Institutes*, IV.xx.9.

[59] Beza claimed that only the refusal of contemporary kingdoms to emulate this obedience necessitated his treatise (*De iure magistratuum*, ed. Franklin, p.116); TCD MS 165, fo. 67r.

[60] Ibid., fos. 48v–49r. Nor did God appoint the Judges to punish transgressions, for Israel repented before God 'raised up Judges for them' (ibid., fo. 47v). The annotators of the Geneva Bible found it impossible to resolve these two conflicting traditions, because they were embedded in the text itself. See the marginal note to Judges 17.6. See above, p. 80 on Genebrard.

time of Saul and Samuel, and made the anarchy a brief interlude between two Judges. Similarly, Harrison barely mentioned the iniquities perpetrated by Samuel's sons, upon which Raleigh and Henry King elaborated as the immediate reason for Israel's demand for a king.[61]

Therefore Harrison found the humanly devised institution of continuous monarchy basically antipathetic to the aspirations of the godly. For although on the election of Saul 'some comend the Jewes as beginning now only to wexe worldly wise and be like unto other well governed comon welths...in mine opinion ther doing was mere folishnesse, what nede he to leane to man that hath the living god to be his buckler and sheelde'. By thus making his reason conform to revelation even in the sphere of politics, Harrison distanced himself from those who shaped revelation to accord with reason in political matters. Melanchthon, for instance, argued that 'God is not displeased' with Israel's demand for a prince 'because he doth mysprayse the governaunce of a kyng...but hee is displeased with the peoples desyre of newfanglinesse'. In contrast Harrison accepted the institution directly given by God as the starting point of his political thought and refused to assess it according to the rational criteria of the natural law which in the judgement of many contemporaries exalted monarchy. Instead he emphasised Israel's 'double offens' not only in abandoning the godly Judges and thus mistrusting God's providence, which 'alwaies defendeth his [churche] chosen in most convenient maner', but also in presuming 'by ther worldly wisdome' to alter the divine form of government. By asserting that Israel fell into Gentile errors in demanding a king like the infidel nations, Harrison demonstrated that a people could elect a prince not ordained by God when they partook of the errors of human reason which characterised the Church of Cain. This put him alongside Ponet and Goodman, who resolved the Protestant dilemma about resisting magistrates, who the Scriptures taught had all been ordained by God, by insisting that God did not ordain tyrants, but that a populace deluded by their own fallen reason could elect a governor who would ignore the principles of godly rule and act tyranically.[62]

Yet Harrison's discussion of the implications of Israel's new monarchy appears more radical than the analyses of Ponet and Goodman, both in what it says and what it omits to say. Goodman, while he also condemned undue reliance on corrupt human reason as disobedience to God, acknowledged that

---

[61] Raleigh, *History*, II.xvi.1; King, *A Sermon*, pp. 39–40.
[62] TCD MS 165, fos. 66v–67r, and note Harrison's alteration of 'churche'. *Carion's Chronicle*, fo. 145, substantially repeated by Beza, *De iure magistratuum*, ed. Franklin, p. 116, and paraphrased in *Cooper's Chronicle* (1565), sigs. D4v–D5r. But the Geneva Bible, like Harrison, emphasised God's displeasure because Israel 'wolde be governed as were the Gentiles' (marginal note to I Sam. 8.6). The influence of the Church of Cain caused Israel to err in seeking monarchy, an element in Calvinist political theory not fully explained by Skinner, *Foundations*, ii, pp. 229–30.

kings had a role allotted to them in the divine scheme. Ponet acknowledged that 'without politike power' oppression and destruction would prevail.[63] Harrison apparently regarded all continuous human rule as fundamentally a product of corrupt human reason, and in his most profound detachment from contemporary reality seemed to regard the True Church, ruled by the Word and Spirit, as the only worthwhile institution. The covenant line provided the only certain rule of life, for all human institutions inevitably deteriorated. In the True Church, God had created a spiritual kingdom which depended not upon coerced obedience to human law but upon faithful obedience to the Word, 'thereby to mainteine ther freedome as a chosen people whom not men but god himselfe' governed. That ghostly polity required inspired leadership from the Judges only at times of crisis precipitated by the oppressive instincts and seductive idolatry of the surrounding kingdoms. While it might constitute a bleak comment upon Harrison's feelings about contemporary England, and emphasises the wholly negative justifications for worldly rule, this is also a much starker interpretation than that put forward by Beza. Beza found in pre-monarchical Israel the inferior magistrates who he believed must always defend the godly against tyranny. In his moments of most profound alienation Harrison appeared to regard all human political behaviour as corrupt, in so far as it followed rational criteria, for just as 'wicked men by policie do seke by all possible meanes to settle themselves in such tenures as thei have obteined or comen by through their ungodly dealings', so a man who 'runneth to man and maketh flesh his defens' thereby enters 'more depely into the curse which saith cursed is the man that in his heart goeth from the Lorde and taketh man for his defens'. Any political system which defended itself according to the law of nature and not according to the law of God must for that very reason be suspected by the godly, and it may be that Harrison's comments about ungodly 'policie' defending ill-gotten 'tenures' indirectly reflect his suspicions about the self-regarding elite of Elizabethan England.[64]

Harrison's refusal to accept worldly power at its own valuation also reflects his pessimism about the ability of any human magistrate to defend true religion in the struggle between the Two Churches. Indeed, his pessimism surpassed even that of the most radical Calvinists, for in order to maintain that attitude he had to overlook Deuteronomy 17.14–20, in which God prophesied that Israel would ask for a king after the settlement of Canaan, and set out the conditions by which a king should be selected and rule under the covenant. Harrison's determination to deny that Saul provided an example of lawful rule, and to show that in electing him Israel rejected the best possible constitution, forced him to ignore this text. This silence put

[63] Goodman, *Superior Powers*, pp. 11–12, 47, 50; Ponet, *Of politike power*, sigs. A5r–v.
[64] TCD MS 165, fos. 66v–67r; Beza, *De iure magistratuum*, ed. Franklin, p. 106.

him outside a broad spectrum of Protestant opinion which used that text to establish the proper relationship of ruler and subject. Calvin believed that Deut. 17.14–20 instructed subjects rather than magistrates, but the influential notes to the Geneva Bible spread the notion that as part of the covenant these rules bound kings to foster true religion and submit their wills to God's will. Ponet emphasised that these verses delimited 'The true right and prerogative of a king', and therefore bound all princes to obey them. Goodman applied these rules given to Israel directly to the situation of England under Mary, for if we obeyed God's will revealed in his Word 'we nede no more to doute, then if God shulde now speake unto us out of the heavens, as then he did to the Israelites'. Thus the covenant allowed him to disallow the 'election' of princes who supported 'papistrie and idolatrie', and the rule of women and foreigners, whatever title they might claim 'by civil policie'. Goodman further applied this test to Saul's election to show that despite 'God himselfe appoynting his people to have a kinge' in Deut. 17.14–20, they 'yet came not to suche pride to desire an Emperour' such as Saul proved to be. For 'thoghe he was appointed and anoynted in Goddes furie, yet was he not of the Lordes chosing after this meaning of Moyses', that is, according to the Scriptural criteria given in Deut. 17. Saul provided a salutory lesson in the delusions of worldly policy and the dangers of using rational criteria to formulate political norms.[65]

Seen in the general context of his thought, Harrison's silence on Deuteronomy 17 suggests not that he refused to restrain contemporary princes by its rules, but that he declined to use it to justify the sort of godly rule envisaged by Beza, Ponet and Goodman. Indeed, Harrison's experience of Elizabeth's government seems only to have taught him that in its present form monarchy was irrelevant to human society's true purpose, 'because our hope is not fixed in thinges transitorie, but is laid up above with god in heaven from whens ech godly man doth loke to reape deliverans'.[66] In the particular context of this conclusion, Harrison's silence on Deuteronomy 17 appears to be no accident. Not only did he avoid the Calvinist attempt to use it to portray an ideal human ruler, but also, whereas Melanchthon saw the historical rediscovery of Deuteronomy as the catalyst for the periodic reformations led by the kings of Israel, Harrison minimised the importance of that book in the reformation under Josiah. The accounts in II Kings 22 and II Chronicles 34 agreed that the accidental discovery of Deuteronomy spurred Josiah to renew the covenant, but Harrison made that fact incidental

---

[65] *Geneva Bible*, marginal notes to Deut. 17.14–20; Calvin, *Institutes*, IV.xx.9., but see ibid., IV.xx.4 on the ruler's duties. Ponet, *Of politike power*, sigs. F5r–F6r; Goodman, *Superior powers*, pp. 49–53, 50. Here Withers and Harrison differed; the former paraphrased Scriptural texts on kingship to describe godly rule, especially citing Deut. 17, 'and therin for his continuall direction he must read all the dayes of his life' (*An ABC*, sigs. G2v–G3v).
[66] TCD MS 165, fos. 32r–v.

to Josiah's great Passover, and instead emphasised his earlier destruction of idolatry. That iconoclastic reformation reflected Josiah's obedience to the prophets, rather than his knowledge of a book which legitimised monarchy as central to the proper ordering of the commonwealth.[67] Thus while those who cited Deuteronomy 17 could still believe in monarchy as a means of godly rule, Harrison's experiences had taught him not to hope for complete reformation within human structures, but only to expect reformation and a new kind of political behaviour when all members of the commonwealth finally received grace to obey the Word.

The depth of Harrison's alienation from contemporary princely rule, which all too frequently betrayed its Gentile origins by its failure to provide true religion and combat idolatry, is most apparent in his interpretation of Samuel's warning to Israel in I Samuel 8.11–18. Samuel described the heavy demands which a king would make on Israel, and the particular circumstances of Elizabethan England seem to have coloured Harrison's explanation of this prophecy, for those circumstances had made him intensely conscious of the sharp contrast between Israel's condition under the Judges and the situation of the godly in England. Therefore, just as he minimised the evidence of anarchy before Saul, so he emphasised the fulfilment of Samuel's vision, which conformists preferred to ignore. Protestants offered two broadly differing interpretations of Samuel's words, and the proponents of each side distorted the arguments of the other. Beza maintained that Samuel set out 'the principle of tyranny, not of royal government', and insisted that 'they are much mistaken who take these words of Samuel as authorising anything a king may please to do'.[68] Raleigh offered a more traditional view, concluding that much of what Samuel foreshadowed 'was not intolerable' but was always borne 'by free consent of...Subjects'. Richard Grafton also applied rational criteria to Samuel's revelation, legitimising such a wide royal authority for an English audience by rephrasing Samuel's words in the customary terms of the rights of kings over their vassals. His emphasis on consent represents one strand of contemporary English political thought, while on the other side James I, according to Raleigh, saw in Samuel's words 'what Subjects ought with patience to bear at their Soveraign's hand'. Although reality did not match this high-flying view, Raleigh also perceived that traditional thinking did not seek to limit the will of kings according to the divine ordinance in Deuteronomy 17, whereas those who 'would be ruled by their own discretion' used Deuteronomy to reject all that Samuel foresaw, as tyranny.[69]

[67] Ibid., fos. 89v–90v.   [68] Beza, *De iure magistratuum*, ed. Franklin, p.117.
[69] *Grafton's Chronicle* (1809), i, p.22; Raleigh, *History*, II.xvi.1, considered these impositions 'not only not grievous, but by the vassals of all Kings according to their birth and condition desired'. Melanchthon glossed over the prophecy because it contradicted his attempt to minimise the importance of the change of rule (*Carion's Chronicle*, fo. 13v).

Goodman and Ponet could afford to be more outspoken than Calvin and Beza in contrasting contemporary rule with the divine model in Deuteronomy, but even they agreed that I Samuel 8.11–18 described a ruler given in God's wrath as a punishment for sin. Goodman urged perpetual vigilance against similar encroachments upon the rights of subjects, while Ponet argued that Israel unwisely demanded 'a galaunt and pompous king', such as 'the Gentiles hade, who were in dede tyrannes'.[70] Neither of them went as far as Harrison did in stating that tyranny not only derived from the essential character of the Church of Cain, but also that tyranny inevitably developed in any continual monarchy. Harrison was apparently unique in regarding Samuel's prophecy as not merely a description of degenerate monarchy but a reflection on all monarchy as viewed from the perspective of the covenant line, and a justification of the Judgeship. For God announced through Samuel that 'the perpetuall Magistrate shold prove an yrkesome and hevie burden unto them by dealing hardly with them and exacting of soch impositions as other Magistrates [daily] did daily thrust upon ther subiects'. This Scriptural example helped to crystallise Harrison's unease about secular power over the True Church, but the two preoccupations upon which his concern focussed owed much to the contemporary predicament of zealous English Protestants. For he argued that with Israel's monarchy 'ere long ensued breach of the law division in governaunces and impurity of doctrine', not as a result of disobedience to the rules of Deut. 17, but because of the fact repeatedly demonstrated by the Scriptures, that 'kings and princes love nothing lesse then to be bound unto lawes'. Consequently 'it happeneth often times that thei applie relligion to ther owne comodities as may appere by the doings of Jeroboam and kings of Samaria'.[71] As the political manifestation of the covenant, the Judgeship had zealously furthered true religion and its complementary requirement of obedience to the law, but Harrison remained keenly aware that the ruling elite in England neglected both these duties, despite the urgings of godly preachers.

Such a pessimistic outlook might have driven Harrison into impotent extremism and complete alienation from the status quo, if he had not been able to detect remnants of Israel's ancient constitution in Elizabethan England, in the same way that he discovered institutions of the True Church hidden under corrupted forms in the Elizabethan Church. Protestant critics of the previous generation had established this prophetic interpretation of objective reality, basing their arguments on the examples of the Scriptural covenant line. Hugh Latimer, for instance, claimed that the rights and duties of Edward VI could be found in the example of Solomon, while the Scriptures equally bound godly preachers to correct erring princes in

[70] Goodman, *Superior Powers*, pp. 149–50; Ponet, *Of politike power*, sig. F4r.
[71] TCD MS 165, fos. 66v–67r, and note the change of tense from 'daily' to 'did daily'.

the way that Micah had corrected Ahab, for 'How like are we Englishmen to the Jews, ever stubborn, stiff-necked and walking in by-ways'.[72] Yet the Edwardine 'commonwealth' preachers skirted the contradiction which preoccupied Harrison, and they more willingly accepted the need to overlook the blemishes in Tudor monarchy, in order to reduce it to the Scriptural model by their preaching. Twenty years on, Harrison might remember 'an excellent prince, and one that after his death was greatly missed among his people', but even in this context he still felt it necessary to ask 'what is courage without piety, what is manhode without vertue, what profiteth it for a man to conquer or be lorde of the whole world with the losse of his oune soule'.[73] For his extensive experience of Elizabeth's court had only increased his desire to assess worldly rule by Scriptural criteria, because a prince 'indevouring to procure amitie with man' could stumble 'upon the displeasure of god' if his actions were 'grounded only upon civile and worldly pollicie, without advise taken at the mouthe of the lorde'.[74]

Harrison's appreciation of the antipathy between 'worldly pollicie' and the interests of the True Church therefore led him to assess tyranny not by the rational criteria of conventional political discourse, but by the individual ruler's relationship to true religion. This could produce some disturbingly unworldly interpretations. Contemporaries believed that Louis XI had effectively established absolutism in France by trampling upon traditional privileges, but Harrison found all this irrelevant to the main question, for he linked Louis' legal and administrative reforms with a minor but relatively pure reformation of the Church, because Louis ordered 'that the churche shall be served and frequented with more reverens, which later I would wishe also were better loked to in my time here in England'.[75] Setting aside those broad-based social and political mechanisms which underpinned the Elizabethan regime and which procured 'amitie with man', Harrison seized upon the one aspect of worldly rule which really interested him. Within this unworldly scale of values Harrison assessed the relative merits of Louis XI and Elizabeth in a way which would have disconcerted most Elizabethan Englishmen, for he judged the characters and abilities of princes in terms of obedience to God's commandments rather than according to worldly criteria.[76] This absolute scale of values could also be used to reassess parts of the Protestant historical tradition already generally accepted in England.

[72] *The Works of Hugh Latimer*, ed. Rev. G. E. Corrie (Parker Society: Cambridge, 1845), i, pp. 117–18. William Turner also felt that he was not bound to obey the magistrate in accepting ceremonies unknown to the Scriptures (W. K. Jordan, *Edward VI. The Threshold of Power* (London, 1970), p. 370).

[73] TCD MS 165, fo. 229v.

[74] Ibid., fo. 74r, the example of Jehosaphat's alliance with Ahab.

[75] Ibid., fo. 314v. See Smith, *De Republica Anglorum*, ed. Dewar, p. 54, on Louis' absolutism.

[76] Harold Harefoot allowed in popish ceremonies 'but soche as he was soche doctrine he did admitte' (TCD MS 165, fo. 254v).

Bale had identified King John as a proto-Protestant, but Harrison considered that although 'he was often glad to annoie the prelates' his hatred of error did not lead him to become a godly ruler: 'wold to god his knowledge had bene soche in true relligion as his zeale was to remove the errors of the false'.[77]

Harrison's acceptance of this rigorous standard of judgement made it correspondingly more necessary to find evidence of some form of godly rule in Elizabethan England, for the Scriptures showed the certain fate awaiting that ruler who ignored godly 'policy'. Harrison could evolve no practical way of enforcing true religion other than appeal to the prince, while such a predicament merely intensified his awareness that 'among princes a thing once done is well done and to be done oftentimes, though no warrant be found therefor'.[78] His only recourse against these evil actions based on spurious human reason was to reiterate the previous experience of the covenant line, which demonstrated that only godly zeal in the prince could maintain the commonwealth. Like the prophets of the Old Testament covenant line, he sought to make rulers aware of God's unchanging justice, which would judge their actions according to their contribution to the fate of the True Church and their obedience to the Word rather than worldly policy. Amaziah, for example, prospered initially through his godliness, 'but afterward giving ere to flatterers, and the persuasion of soch worldings as in all their dealings had an eie to ther own welth and comodities', he first became negligent in zeal towards God, and then an idolater. Finally he acted entirely in accordance with worldly policy, and 'enterprising unnecessary warres contrary to the admonitions of the prophetes' he was defeated and the Temple spoiled. God provided 'a iust punishment for his carelesse behaviour and dealing toward the Lord' in his eventual murder by his rebellious nobility, 'for how can a prince assure himself to have his subiects loiall and faithfull unto him, when he himself is untrue and disloyall unto god?'.[79]

Objectively speaking this pattern of retribution seems irrelevant to the realities of Tudor politics, but we should remember that Harrison's Protestant faith rested only upon the security of God's promises, and that therefore he had to trust implicitly in the contemporary relevance of eternal, unchanging divine justice. For 'albeit that it hath not pleased the most highe god to execute the sentens of judgement upon all princes that have bene disobedient unto him', yet certainly 'soche as are touched this way are left for examples to their successors to beware of the like calamitie'. Therefore Harrison

[77] TCD MS 165, fo. 301r; and contrast Georges Edelen in *Description*, ed. Edelen, pp. xxii, 21. On Bale see Blatt, *Plays of John Bale*, pp. 120–8, 105; M. McCusker, *John Bale, Dramatist and Antiquary* (Bryn Mawr, 1942), pp. 90–2.

[78] *Description*, ed. Edelen, pp. 24–5, significantly a comment on royal interference in the Church.

[79] TCD MS 165, fo. 78v; John Jewel also drew this connection (Booty, *Jewel*, p. 201).

confidently expected that idolatrous tyrants would be swept aside by the fulfilment of God's will.[80]

This profoundly unrealistic and deliberately unworldly standpoint explains why Harrison could give no very convincing answer to the central question 'whether the subiect ought to prescribe unto the prince what he ought to do or the prince unto his subiects'. He could only reiterate that both had a duty to 'beleive in god according to his word and likewise so incident to the prince to defend and promote the cause of the gospell as to the subject to obeie the same'. Therefore while in general he seems irredeemably pessimistic about Elizabeth's ability to fulfil the criteria of godly rule, for the same reasons he could become wildly over-enthusiastic when she gave some sign of fulfilling, if not actually recognising, her godly calling. The very reliance on Old Testament models which made him sound like a minatory prophet also forced Harrison to change his tone completely when confronted by what he took to be the Scriptural model in action. His fears about the implications of worldly rule for true religion did not prevent him from envisaging a place for the secular magistrate within his ideal commonwealth, a place strictly limited by the Old Testament example of godly rule and therefore absurdly narrow in the contemporary context, but which theoretically could secure reformation. Because Harrison saw the present as one of the respites of reformation frequently given by God to the True Church, he attempted to bring contemporary magistracy closer to the ideal by applauding those remnants of godly rule which he discerned in Elizabethan England. In doing this his impotent position further released his imagination from practical constraints.[81]

Essentially he developed into a godly model the traditional belief that the prince had a duty to protect the poor against the oppressions of inferior magistrates, concluding that the covenant had originally enjoined this duty and that Elect magistrates had obeyed this divine injunction. Harrison therefore built his flimsy structure upon the unshakeable conviction that Israel had maintained along with true religion 'the direct administration of justice', originally revealed to Adam and revived with Noah who taught it to his posterity as a complement to their true faith.[82] The concept had two different but complementary aspects. First, this Scriptural godly model required superior magistrates to perambulate throughout their territories as

---

[80] TCD MS 165, fo. 78v. Though kings and princes act against Christ, the Church and the Gospel 'yet we are assured that all they can do nothing', agreed George Withers (*An ABC*, sig. G3r). Even Raleigh at his bitterest gave these examples of God's eternal justice a safer, more general application (*History*, II.xix.3).

[81] TCD MS 165, fo. 168r; *Description*, ed. Edelen, p. 41. Pessimism prevailed, however, for 'it is the course of the world rather to change superstition for superstition then to leave of superstition at ones for altogether' (TCD MS 165, fo. 196r).

[82] Ibid., fo. 5v, and see above, p. 212.

the peripatetic Noah had done, and like the Patriarch they had to correct the errors and arrest the decline into tyranny of their inferior magistrates. Second, justice had to be dispensed in the first instance and in the localities to the same standard as at the centre, so that only the most difficult cases could be appealed to the superior magistrate, who had both to keep a close watch on inferior magistrates and reserve his energies for the most complicated cases, while making himself accessible to his aggrieved subjects in the localities. This differed from previous attempts by humanist political advisers and 'commonwealth' reformers to make royal justice at the centre more accessible to the poor.[83] Under Edward VI, Latimer, Lever, Bradford and Knox had to contend with a breakdown in the traditional system, and Ridley lambasted 'ungodly loathsomeness to hear poor men's causes', but Harrison felt that the poor too often resorted to the central courts in the name of contention rather than justice.[84]

Harrison rejected these conventional assumptions because his vision derived directly from the Old Testament, rather than from the common stock of Christian humanism and radical Protestantism. The Scriptures enabled him to envisage a system of justice in England which was only really practical within a gathered congregation, all of whose members faithfully recognised the supremacy and finality of divine law and accepted the supervision of a tireless godly magistrate who obeyed the Word. For that system was directed towards the preservation of religion as well as justice. This ideal state of affairs had existed under Moses at Sinai, where Moses judged the gathered congregation of Israel. Harrison detected a fundamental contrast between this godly polity and the Gentile parody which Satan set up through Cecrops at Athens, as we have seen. The Scriptural account of events at Sinai also demonstrated the difference between the rational, human organisation of justice and the truly equitable divine system, which preserved both true religion and justice. In Harrison's view this simple system persisted in the settled nation under the Judges, for under God's law and within this absolute scale of values, even capital punishment could be applied by the simplest form of justice, being meted out by the nearest relative or the whole

---

83 This had been peddled as a political panacea for generations. See J. Guy, *The Cardinal's Court* (London, 1977), pp. 41–9; B. Bradshaw, 'The Tudor Commonwealth', in *The Historical Journal*, xxii (1979), pp. 455–76, at pp. 458–9; and C. Ross, *Richard III* (London, 1981), pp. 173–4. Steven Vaughan urged Cromwell to adopt a system of direct local justice (Elton, *Reform and Renewal*, pp. 45–6). Sir Thomas Smith rejected these unrealistic and insular notions; his wider experience of European affairs showed that the English jury system was the quickest and most just possible (*De Republica Anglorum*, ed. Dewar, p. 96).

84 'If there were smaller rooms and fouler ways unto them, they would enforce many to make pauses before they did rashly enter into plea' (*Description*, ed. Edelen, p. 176). Ridley quoted by W. R. D. Jones, *The Tudor Commonwealth* (London, 1970), p. 67. Latimer's fourth Lent Sermon of 1549 expanded on the pattern in Luke 18.1–8 to excoriate bribery and the law's delays (*Works*, ed. Corrie, pp. 150–70, citing Rom. 15.4).

populace, without requiring any judicial enforcement. However, by the time of Eli, only the minority who feared God kept 'the true execution of justice and exact performauns of the rites and ceremonies of relligion', two linked expressions of the same faith, and therefore God abandoned Israel to her fate.[85] Once again the true servant of God, Samuel, provided both the link with the ancient traditions of the True Church and a contrast with the new style of government in Israel. Not only did Samuel's impartial justice provide the model for many pious hopes, but Harrison emphasised that he 'visited the churches of god every yeare with great zeale and diligens', reforming religion corrupted by Satan and supervising those congregations ruled by God's law.[86]

Samuel not only continued the covenant line but mediated between God and all Israel, so that Harrison regarded his style of magistracy as a universal model, traces of which he was eager to detect amongst the better Gentile princes. For example Artaxerxes not only judged the suits of the poor in person, but arranged that they should have freer access to his queen 'and be the better herd in her progresses'. Yet while a sober sense of duty animated the best princes, too often the deficiencies of inferior magistrates frustrated their good intentions. Harrison found several historical examples which paralleled the contemporary English failure to enforce the law of hue and cry, under which in theory inferior magistrates and local communities had to assume collective responsibility for stolen goods.[87] The failure to enforce this law further underlined how far England had degenerated from the original style of justice, and how carefully the godly superior had to supervise venal inferior magistrates in order to restore the kind of sober responsibility which Harrison presumed had prevailed under Samuel.[88] Not only the slackness but also the unjust rigour of lesser magistrates had to be remedied, for history providentially interpreted showed that to avoid rebellion rulers had to disregard the acquisition of loot and control their officers 'who polled rich and poore and bought and sold the romes at their pleasures making merchaundise of the lawes'.[89] The fact that 'there is nothing wherewith I am less acquainted than with our temporall regiment'

---

[85] See above, pp. 213–14 and TCD MS 165, fos. 57v, 64v.

[86] Harrison marvelled 'that being a judge he did never wrong to any man, nether toke any bribe to hinder the right or hurt his commonwealth', which may say something about Harrison's assessment of Tudor justice (ibid., fo. 67r).

[87] Ibid., fos. 106v, 333v.

[88] Harrison recounted 'mine own experience' that 'covetous and greedy parishioners' refused to apprehend and imprison thieves for fear of the cost, and constables flatly declined to pursue the hue and cry. Sir Thomas Smith, from whom Harrison took his account of the hue and cry, was far more sanguine about the system (*Description*, ed. Edelen, p. 194; *cf. De Republica Anglorum*, ed. Dewar, pp. 107–8).

[89] TCD MS 165, fo. 186v. Even the flinty Canute justified his worldly success by his belated attention to the impartial administration of justice (ibid., fo. 253r).

enabled Harrison to parrot these familiar sentiments, but he could also add some shrewd criticisms from his own experience of the manipulation of the jury system by 'the craftier or stronger side'.[90] Indeed, the familiarity of some of Harrison's pronouncements on the commonwealth should not obscure the fact that in the interplay between myth and reality in his thought, generally represented by the contrast between his 'Chronology' and his *Description*, Scriptural models had a decisive influence on his interpretation of everyday reality. He sincerely believed that Elizabethan England had to be seen in the light of the enduring covenant, however impractical Scriptural solutions for contemporary problems might appear to human reason. This context enabled him to take over and transform the commonplaces of humanist social thought, to make them conform to his conception of the godly commonwealth. Thus he did more than merely repeat humanist complaints about self-interest as the barrier to honest counsel, for he chose to focus on the sufferings of the poor, not the frustrations of humanist pedagogues. Turning from local justice, Harrison complained that those around the prince prevented the appeals of the poor from being heard, 'especially if their redresse do touche the increase of the comon welthe and restrainct of private lucre in soche men as are of power and great gainers by those enormities'.[91]

Harrison's deference towards what he considered to be the Scriptural depiction of the ideal commonwealth explains the naivety of his social vision. Having simplified the problems of Tudor society in order to make them conform to the pre-existing Scriptural framework, in which a disordered society merely reflected Satan's pernicious influence as transmitted through the seductive errors of the Church of Cain, Harrison could propose an equally simple solution in the restoration of true religion and justice. Godly rule could slay this hoary old dragon of self-interested magistrates and misinformed princes. The fact that Harrison's vision of godly rule appears hopelessly limited in the Tudor context further reveals how narrowly Harrison drew the boundaries of the legitimate exercise of political power in deference to Scriptural models, and how little he felt it necessary to ponder on the subject when there existed a Scriptural precedent.[92] The godly examples of Noah and Samuel therefore encouraged him to regard even dubious princes in a better light when they went on a Progress. He held no brief for the tyrannous Empress Eirene, but considered that in her Progress through Thrace she had done well in repairing the defences of the Empire, and especially in that she devoted herself to 'the hering of the complaints

---

[90] *Description*, ed. Edelen, pp. 93, 173, 91, 89. Harrison's criticisms are of course absent from his source, Sir Thomas Smith's *De Republica Anglorum* (ed. Dewar, pp. 99–100).

[91] TCD MS 165, fo. 279r.

[92] Beza appears quite sensible in contrast, expecting the subject wronged by an inferior magistrate to get redress from his sovereign (*De iure magistratuum*, ed. Franklin, p. 103).

of the poore oppressed with the iniurious dealinges of the riche and soche as are set in authority over them'.[93] Thus against his consistent expectation of oppression by inferior magistrates Harrison could set the hope of relief by superior magistrates, who at the moment of personally dispensing justice in his view most nearly justified their conventional descriptions as 'gods', for they emulated God's punishment of the oppressors of the Elect when they descended upon the oppressors of the poor. King Edgar provided an English example of this *deus ex machina*, not only uniting England but in his progresses executing thieves and examining 'how justice was ministered and whether gentlemen still behaved themselves amise in oppressing of his poore subiects or not of whose inurious dealinges he was often times advertised'.[94]

Harrison's misgivings about Elizabeth's attitude towards true religion reflect his perception of the disparity between the model of godly rule which he believed that she should follow, and her actual behaviour. Therefore his doubts could be transformed into the most extravagant praise at those intoxicating moments when he experienced at first hand those aspects of her traditional political activities which he believed fitted the godly model. Harrison regarded Elizabeth's regime in a totally different light 'when it pleaseth her in the summer season to recreate herself abroad and view the estate of the country and hear the complaints of her poor commons injured by her unjust officers or their substitutes', as he interpreted her progresses in his *Description*.[95] For although Harrison discovered in the Scriptures a view of the world that highlighted the ambiguous nature of worldly rule, he could adopt the most subservient attitudes towards a magistrate who he believed fulfilled God's calling when she dispensed justice in the manner of the Old Testament Judges. His eagerness to find some evidence of godliness in Elizabeth's actions also reflects his reluctance to face the logical consequences of his general assumptions about the problematical relationship between worldly princes and true religion. His dilemma epitomised the conflict between texts such as Romans 13, with their command to obey all magistrates without distinction, and the general requirement of the Scriptures that magistrates must help to build up the True Church. Finding evidence of Elizabeth's contribution to this task made it easier for Harrison to accept the duty of obedience without harm to his delicate conscience. Just as his generous interpretation of the Elizabethan episcopate and the educational institutions of the Church allowed him to see ways in which both could easily be restored to their evangelical function, and enabled him to evade

---

93 TCD MS 165, fo. 219r.
94 Ibid., fo. 238v.
95 *Description*, ed. Edelen, p. 227. Whitgift claimed to detect an ecclesiastical variation on this in Cartwright's defence of presbyterianism; he trusted that Cartwright did not mean 'to have the prince hear all matters herself: you will give her leave to appoint under-officers' (*Works*, ed. Ayre, II, p. 367).

the extremist consequences of his acceptance of presbyterian historical arguments, so the fortunate survival of evidence about Harrison's reaction to one of Elizabeth's progresses helps to balance his other comments upon her worldly rule.

Elizabeth visited Audley End on 26 July 1578, during her Progress towards Norfolk. Perhaps for the occasion of her passage through Saffron Walden, Harrison drafted a loyal address of excruciating servility which survives, very appropriately, on the flyleaf of his copy of the sixth volume of the *Magdeburg Centuries*, which collected many examples of godly princes. No evidence survives to show that Harrison actually presented his address, but the heavily amended draft, while it superficially follows the conventional line about the 'most myghtye renowned prince and most highe lord blessed of god', also raises the point about what exactly Elizabeth was doing on her Progress. Harrison naturally confessed that he was 'overwhelmed, amased in the maiesty of your royall highness estate' and unable adequately to express 'our thankfull myndes to your soverayne maiestie and our harty joye for this your happy journey unto us'. Yet he really plumbed the depths of self-abasement when he remembered that God had preferred Elizabeth 'unto so glorious dignitye to exequute his owne office not among infidels and papistes, but even where the kingdome of his owne soune is established'; therefore 'who are these of lowe callinge basse condition small wealthe and smaller auctoritye that they shuld have any place to come in your presence'.[96] Harrison's assumption that Elizabeth had come to give justice to her 'poore vassalles' and reform religion not only caused him to change his tone about princely rule to a greater degree than the situation might seem to have warranted, but also made him reassess the Church. In other contexts he accounted it only 'semireformed', but here he felt able to describe it as Christ's kingdom, established in contrast to popery and infidelity. Subsequent events in fact helped to enhance this prophetic interpretation of Elizabeth's actions in the light of Samuel's example. Within a few days, Privy Council enquiries about prominent local recusants led to Harrison being appointed to attempt to convert a local gentleman, Rooke Grene, from his popery. Although Harrison apparently failed 'to bring him to conformitie in Religion', Elizabeth's seemingly godly intervention on this occasion may have temporarily exempted her from Harrison's criticism of 'princes of our time of whom some canne dispense with ther subjects either for frendship or gaine to use their [popery] idolatry still'.[97]

---

[96] Written on the first blank leaf of the *Sexta Centuriae Ecclesiasticae Historiae* (Basle, 1562), Derry shelf-mark D.i.d.4.

[97] *Acts of the Privy Council of England*, ed. J. R. Dasent, new series, X, 1577–8 (London, 1895), pp. 313, 323–4, 327; XI, 1578–80 (London, 1895), p. 174. TCD MS 165, fo. 73r. Harrison may possibly have known that during this Progress the Privy Council acted to establish the ascendancy of a group of 'hot Protestant' magistrates in Norfolk and Suffolk. On this action see Collinson, *Religion of Protestants*, pp. 156–7.

When confronted by a prince who he believed to be fulfilling her allotted role within the True Church, Harrison could momentarily ignore the tension between ideal and reality which more consistently dominates his work, a tension which could force him to draw disquieting conclusions about the inherent antipathy between worldly power and true religion. This profound suspicion appears most obviously in his assessment of Constantine's place within the history of the True Church. In the long run only preaching could transform the existing society into a godly commonwealth, and no great hopes could be placed in the self-seeking magistrate. Therefore Harrison came to the surprising and apparently unique conclusion that Constantine's personal interference had disastrously distorted the Church and weakened it against Antichrist, that his reign offered a clear example of the pernicious consequences when men sought to advance God's cause by worldly means. In part this conclusion reflected Harrison's fundamental disagreement with Melanchthon's view of the Four Empires. Where Melanchthon claimed that the godly posterity of Sem had ejected Ham's descendants from the first Empire and thus vindicated the contemporary exercise of sweeping magisterial powers, Harrison emphasised that not only did the Church of Cain seize power from the godly, but also Satan used the ungodly usurper, Nimrod, to create a distorted parody of the True Church, by spiriting him away in emulation of God's translation of Enoch into heaven.[98] These facts cast a long shadow over all succeeding empires, including the Roman Empire, and Harrison made no exception of Constantine's reign.

Comparison of Harrison's views with the contemporary estimation of Constantine thus shows the depth of his suspicions about the magistrate. Constantine became a national apocalyptic hero in Elizabethan England, personally immune from criticism even by those who condemned as the source of all later evils the security and wealth which he had introduced into the Church. Bale set the tone for the English radical Protestant view of Constantine, whose 'devocion and zeale' bred wealth, 'but the doughter choaked the mother, and engendred the monster ambition, who also...did in the ende devoure her grandmother Religion'. Yet even when Bale most sharply criticised the worldliness which entered the Church during his reign, Constantine himself remained above reproach. Edwin Sandys, less worried by the fact that under Constantine the bishops and 'chiefe professours' obtained 'lawfull possessions', rejoiced that Constantine 'gave so many and so great tokens of a minde detesting all impietie and burning with the love of Christ Iesus'.[99] A recent study has shown that Constantine's usefulness as a potent mythical figure in both religious and political propaganda protected him from serious humanist historical criticism, and that his British

---

[98] TCD MS 165, fos. 5v, 15r–v; *cf. Carion's Chronicle*, fo. 6r, and see above, pp. 102–6.
[99] Bale, *The Pageant of Popes* (1574), fo. 24v; Sandys, *Sermons*, p. 333.

ancestry and religious zeal formed popular polemical themes.[100] This common view united establishment figures like John Aylmer with those like John Studeley who had come to doubt the establishment, and with John Jewel, who displayed more realism about the limitations of Elizabeth's government.[101] Above all, John Foxe made Constantine a commanding figure in the English historical consciousness, at first by identifying Elizabeth as the 'second Constantine', and then by making him the linchpin of his apocalyptic chronology when Elizabeth failed to live up to the godly comparison.[102] Even the outspoken radical Thomas Brightman, who, in reaction to James I's failure to deliver the Church from Antichrist's power, began Antichrist's reign with this first Christian prince, regarded Constantine as the Church's 'manlike and stout champion', the child of Rev. 12.5.[103]

Harrison rejected this accepted picture of Constantine and saw him instead as an archetypically cynical manipulator of religious sentiment, who distorted the True Church from its proper nature as a mystical body of the Elect and by subordinating it to worldly 'policy' transformed it into merely an expression of the imperial civil polity. His reasons for attacking Constantine ultimately reflect his antipathy towards all earthy pretensions to supremacy over God's creation which failed to refer continually to the divine will. This reaction formed part of the consistent historical interpretation underpinning his world-view. Harrison's reading of the Old Testament shows his distaste for that type of absolute power which coupled tyranny with idolatry and which epitomised the deluded fantasies of human reason, while there is an obvious disparity between Constantine's imperial dignity and the kind of magistrate which the Old Testament sanctioned. However, Harrison's profound disenchantment with human polity can also be explained by reference to the particular authors whom he chose to cite in support of that analysis. A number of Greek authors figure prominently amongst those he cited in his discussion of Constantine, written into the 'Chronology' during the 1570s. They included some whom, it has been claimed, J. J. Scaliger first introduced to Western readers in his *De emendatione temporum*, published in 1583. These authorities attracted Harrison because their historical interpretation of the growth of monarchical government implicitly denied contem-

---

[100] W. J. Mulligan, 'The British Constantine: an English historical myth', in *Journal of Medieval and Renaissance Studies*, 8 (1978), pp. 257–79, shows the various uses of the myth from the twelfth to the eighteenth centuries, but overlooks its apocalyptic role in the sixteenth century.

[101] J. Aylmer, *An harborowe for faithfull and trewe subiectes* (Strasbourg, 1559), sig. A4r; J. Studeley, Ded. to Thomas, Earl of Sussex, in trans. of *The Pageant of Popes*, sigs. *a2r, *a4v, *br–v; Jewel, *Defence of the Apology*, in *Works*, ed. J. Ayre (Parker Society: Cambridge, 1850), pp. 986–8. See also Christianson, *Reformers and Babylon*, pp. 29–33.

[102] Olsen, *Foxe*, pp. 42–5, 71, 75, and see p.66.

[103] W. M. Lamont, *Godly Rule, Politics and Religion 1603–60* (London, 1969), pp. 35–52. Professor Lamont over-estimated the extent to which Brightman abandoned the Constantine myth. See Brightman's *Revelation of the Revelation* (1615), pp. 404–10, and Olsen, *Foxe*, pp. 77–9.

porary claims of divine authority for absolute monarchy regardless of its relationship to religion. Like Harrison they placed the origins of monarchy in the period of Gentile corruptions after the Flood, and stressed that ungodly rulers like Nimrod had risen to power through the manipulation of a populace which had lost the conception of godly rule taught by Noah.[104] Some of those authors in both Latin and Greek versions survive from Harrison's library.[105]

This probably accounts for the considerable space devoted to the Byzantine Empire in the 'Chronology', where Harrison dwells upon the examples of providential judgement in Byzantium. He deliberately used the Greeks to give his readers a clearer insight into the divine punishment reserved for tyrants. Manasses' description of the unnatural cruelty of the Empress Eirene provided a salutary contrast to the eulogies of the Latin historians, for although the Greeks rivalled the Latins in idolatry, 'yet you see how they condeme this empresse, whereas the latine writers dwelling farre of and not understanding the bottom of her dealing do yet commend her as godly princess and very zealous gentlewoman'.[106] He also approved of those Greek historians who openly commended the deposition of tyrants like the homicidal Emperor Aurelius Carinius: 'It was time saith Suidas to make awaie with soch a monster for in his daies people went to pot as pultry to the table'.[107] Yet because Harrison did not distinguish between Greek and Latin, nor emperor and oppressed, but between godly and ungodly actions, he could use his Byzantine sources critically. For example, the Emperor Leo abolished images in AD 723, and 'a man maie esily see of what relligion Zonaras was by his malitious report of the history of this emperour, for he concealeth althings that maie sound unto his honour and hideth nothing that maie set furth the contrary'.[108]

[104] J. W. Johnson, 'Chronological writing: its concepts and development', in *History and Theory*, ii (1962), pp. 125–43, esp. pp. 143, 135.

[105] Besides numerous other Greek historians, Harrison used seven of the eleven listed by Johnson: Cedrenus, Zonaras, Suidas, Michael Glycas, Macrobius, Solinus and Xiphilinus. He also owned Constantinus Manasses, *Annales* (Basle, 1573) in Latin, now bound with Michael Glycas, *Annales* (Basle, 1572) as Derry shelf-mark E.h.24. His copy of Julius Solinus, *Rerum Orbis memorabilium Collectanea* (Lyons, 1541) is now Derry shelf-mark E.f.11. Xiphilinus, *Vitae Pompeii Magni et Caesarum usque ad Alexandrium Mammaene filium* (M. Stephanus: Geneva, n.d.), now Derry shelf-mark E.h.30, came from Harrison's library, while his *Epitome historiae Romanae* (n.p., n.d) in Greek, is E.h.29. Harrison's marginalia in these works are exclusively chronological, reflecting the differences between Greek and Latin chronology. The 'Chronology' frequently cites Cedrenus, Zonaras, Suidas and Macrobius, but their works are not extant from Harrison's library.

[106] Typically of the papists, 'thei make her a sainct rather for her cruelty then her piety '(TCD MS 165, fo. 222r).

[107] Ibid., fo. 159r. He used 'Sosinius a greeke writer' to debunk English 'vaine opinions' of Constantine the Briton, usurper in the Western Empire *c*. 407–10. (ibid., fos. 172v–173r).

[108] Ibid., fo. 210r. Yet he used Zonaras on the extortions of the Emperor Claudius Nicephorus (ibid., fo. 222r).

Harrison used the Byzantine historians to criticise Constantine because they presented him in terms which fitted Harrison's previous suspicions about the malevolent influence of princes upon religion. This did not mean that the poorest enjoyed a monopoly of faith, but merely that Harrison identified with Christ's experience, which showed 'how according to the word of truth, the wise, the riche and mighty of the world trusting in themselves are either unwilling or els refuse to come when thei be called'. The security of worldly plenty blinded men to the historical significance of their present actions. Therefore Christ's 'most comfortable newes could not be receaved of the preestes and rulers but most cruellie...thei inveighed against him, and therto in most despite full and execrable maner not only reviled but also...finally excommunicated' Him.[109] Those who followed the dictates of human reason inevitably ended up in the Church of Cain, and Constantine provided the most striking example of what happened when princes felt themselves to be insulated from the prophetic consequences of their actions; his reign showed the dangers which threatened when the True Church relied too heavily upon the worldly prince, who pursued his own interests according to the criteria of natural reason.

Harrison's conclusion is more striking because he did not deny patriotic claims that Constantine was the legitimate son of Constantinus Chlorus and Helena 'the daughter of Coelus a noble man of Brytteine'. Indeed he went out of his way to counter those foreign authorities who made Helena an ostler and Constantine a bastard.[110] He also associated the British with Constantine's triumph in Italy. Yet while he admitted that 'his behaviour in the first ten yeares was like unto that of an excellent Magistrate', he also asserted that in the following decade 'he found the waie to filtche his subiectes like a theef, but in the last decade of all he lived like a begger by reason of his immoderate liberality as all the histories do report'. This contrasts strongly with Richard Hakluyt's more commonplace assertion that Constantine preferred godliness before riches.[111] However, Raphael Holinshed provides the most significant contrast, for the distance between their respective historical interpretations, which prevented Holinshed from using more of Harrison's 'Chronology' in his *Chronicles*, appears most dramatically in their treatment of Constantine. Holinshed consciously reacted against Harrison's heterodoxy on this vital part of the national myth.

109 Ibid., fos. 163r, 138v. The wealthiest were the 'grettest murmurers against the heavenly providens' (ibid., fo. 185v).
110 Harrison shrewdly picked out the 'historical' reason for this error, tracing it to those 'flatterers' who monopolised princely courts and tried to disinherit Constantine after the second marriage of his father (ibid., fo. 158r).
111 Presumably Harrison meant all the Greek histories (ibid., fo. 161r); R. Hakluyt, *The Principall Navigations* (George Bishop and Ralph Newberie, deputies to Christopher Barker: London, 1589), pp. 2–3.

He insisted that Coel, 'the grandfather of Constantine', was not merely a nobleman, as Harrison stated, but a king, for although 'of the regiment of this prince, Harrison maketh no mention in his chronologie', yet 'verily if I shall speake what I thinke, I will not denie but assuredly such a prince there was'. Holinshed went on to refute alien claims to Constantine, which Harrison possibly brought to his notice, but he refrained from printing in his *Chronicles* Harrison's criticisms of Constantine in the 'Chronology'.[112] Holinshed perpetuated the myth that Constantine 'made his native countrey partaker of his hygh glorie and renoune which...he purchased and got through the circuit of the whole earth'. Nothing could be allowed to detract from the reputation of the national hero, so Holinshed's factual and uninspired account included a sober commendation of Constantine's secular policy, presenting him in his traditional role as the paradigm of a Christian prince.[113]

Holinshed continued this theme in his assessment of Constantine's religious policy, for 'Many workes of great zeale and vertue are remembred by writers to have bin done by thys Constantine and his mother Helene', said Holinshed, 'to the setting forth of God's glorie and the advancing of the faith of Christe'.[114] At this point Holinshed and Harrison decisively parted company, for Harrison followed Michael Glycas in believing that Constantine 'was never constant or zealous unto religion but rather geven like a good husband to gather riches and provide for thinhaunsment of his children'.[115] These differences arose because Harrison and Holinshed started from fundamentally different assumptions. For those who accepted rational political arguments drawn from the law of nature, and therefore accepted that the historical actions of princes themselves determined the criteria of princely behaviour, Constantine remained a godly model. Harrison rejected this traditional pattern, and argued that princely actions had to be directed by God's law given to all believers, and not by princely will. God required princes to help build up the True Church and punish all who disobeyed God's law. Measured by this uncompromising standard, Constantine accord-

---

[112] Holinshed, *Historie of England*, in *Chronicles* (1577), pp. 88–9. Mulligan, 'British Constantine', pp. 272–3, cited this as the first printed doubt about Constantine, unaware of how much it owed to TCD MS 165.

[113] 'A manne in whome many excellent vertues and good qualities bothe of mynde and bodie manifestly appeared...a prince of great knowledge and experience in ware, and therewith verie fortunate, an ernest lover of iustice, and to conclude born to all honour' (*Historie of England*, in *Chronicles* (1577), pp. 90, 92).

[114] Ibid., p. 92. Abraham Fleming, editor of the 1587 edition of the *Chronicles*, also revered 'that most godly and religious Emperor Constantine': *A treatise of blazing starres* (London, 1618), sig. D2r. See also Walter Travers's opinion, as translated by Thomas Cartwright, of 'Constantine the great that godly Emperor', in whose time 'the churche was poisoned with riches' (*A full and plaine declaration of Ecclesiasticall discipline* ([M. Schirat: Heidelberg], 1574), p. 119).

[115] TCD MS 165, fo. 161r. Harrison's copy of Glycas's *Annales* contains no marginalia.

ing to Harrison 'was enemy to no relligion' and therefore his acceptance of Christianity was superficial and misleading.[116] He made an 'outward pretens' of religion, but although he did much for the worldly condition of Christians, his baptism was merely an insincere public relations exercise, since 'he wold nedes be reputed for a religious Christien'. Further, because he accepted baptism only shortly before his death, 'divers did judge of him that he smelled of the Novatien heresy', an opinion that Harrison maintained against the contrasting interpretation given by Eusebius and followed by Foxe in his *Actes and Monuments*, that Constantine deferred his baptism 'with a pretensed purpose to be baptised in Jordane', as Harrison put it.[117]

The central reason why Harrison considered that Constantine had proved especially dangerous to the Church was that although he was 'but a feble Christien', he had interfered in matters of doctrine.[118] Since Constantine had never achieved a faithful insight into the apocalyptic struggle between the Two Churches which was going on all around him, he had been responsible for introducing a dangerous 'mixed' religion into the True Church. This decisive intrusion into doctrinal matters by the secular power alarmed Harrison as much as similar contemporary claims disturbed John Jewel. Like other Protestants wishing to pursue reformation to its proper conclusion under Elizabeth, Jewel and Harrison were extremely sensitive to the dilution of truth that occurred when magistrates, accustomed to making judgements according to worldly criteria, interfered in the definition of saving knowledge.[119] Thus in Harrison's account, Constantine recalled the Arians without reference to the Catholic clergy 'but trusted to his owne judgment which was not great in the knowledg of the scriptures'. For Harrison this admission of heresy both demonstrated the boundaries of godly rule and had immediate relevance as a warning against the toleration of Elizabethan recusants, for 'Hereby we may see what sute of frindes doth eftsones in matters of equity and relligion, also what it is for a civile magistrat to leane unto his owne wisdome in cases of doctrine', for princes inevitably confounded all religion if they ignored the advice of the godly interpreters of the Word.[120]

[116] Ibid., fo. 164v.
[117] Ibid., fo. 161r. Following Eusebius, Foxe claimed 'Baptisme he deferred even unto his old age, because hee had determined a iourney into Persia, and thought in Jordan to have been baptised' (*Actes and Monuments* (1583), p. 101). Harrison stated that a troublesome Arian belatedly baptised Constantine after he had recalled the heretic from exile (TCD MS 165, fo. 162v).
[118] Ibid., fo. 161r.
[119] Jewel, *Defence of the Apology*, in *Works*, ed. Ayre, pp. 986–8. On the other hand to demonstrate the secular obedience that pastors owed to the prince, Harrison like Jewel used the example of Solomon and Abiathar, although he remained uncertain whether 'thei be or should be' protectors of the Church (ibid., pp. 987–8; TCD MS 165, fo. 62v).
[120] Because 'it is impossible for one man to be exquisite in all thinges', it was hard 'for a prince to be an exquisite divine and able to iudge of sincerity of relligion without especiall grace which wanted force in Constantine' (TCD MS 165, fo. 163v). Constantine even presumed to pronounce on the Donatian heresy (ibid., fo. 161v).

Constantine, the stout defender against Antichrist, thus in Harrison's account becomes personally responsible for the decline in the Church. Even worse, he may have deliberately embarked upon an antichristian course, subjecting the Word to worldly policy. Harrison compared Constantine's dissimulation to that of the Old Testament King Asa, for both allowed themselves to be influenced more by atheistic courtiers than godly preachers, a fact which showed how little the godly could trust both the prince and the inferior magistrate. Harrison conceded that Constantine began well, 'but alas he continued not to thend in like perfection of zeale for as cold christiens and worldlings be no christiens so for all his faire face he proved at the last not onely a parricide but also an Arrian if not a Novatian', and 'a cruell persequutor of the christian Orthodoxes'. Constantine's infidelity sprang from the area where godly reform inevitably gave way to baser consider-ations, for Constantine was 'led therto by certeine of his court that liked those errors and had corrupted certaine great Ladies and gentlewomen (whom he favoured) to keep him in that state'. Harrison presents an inverted image of Constantine, not as the princely ideal to be emulated, but as a perpetual warning about the problems facing the True Church under worldly monarchical rule, and as an insight into contemporary failings. Just as the continuity of the True Church gave the experiences of the covenant line contemporary relevance, so on the other side this example showed,

What harme gentlemen that are flatterers, Heretikes, Atheists and worldlings do in princes cortes [for they] alwaies pleasing the prince (but for their owne turnes) and thinking a litle religion to be ynough for a gret many of ther calling are often occasion that god is gretlie dishonored, the prince abused, and the commonwelth defrauded not onely of the gospell but of her due prosperity to satisfie ther Ambition and botomlesse bagges of Avarice that never will be filled.

Although patently a religious reinterpretation of the familiar humanist 'problem of counsel', the fact that Harrison directed this attack against Constantine is more important. Indeed he found such contemporary relevance in this model of ungodly courtly behaviour that his pen ran on to the conclusion that Constantine's Christian zeal 'was full of inward infirmitie and soche indede as most gentlemen of our daies do usually professe as supposing a little relligion to be yeat ynoghe and ynough for a great many of ther calling', a reflection which he later prudently crossed out.[121]

Above all, Constantine's major contribution to the decline of the Church proved to be his mixing of 'policy' and the Word, for although in his time 'both peace and poison entered into the churche', Rome had been

---

[121] Ibid., fo. 161v. Aylmer (*An Harborowe*, sig. A4r) called Elizabeth 'our English Helena', but Harrison recalled Helena's flirtation with Judaism and her idolatry, and argued that she 'proved a superstitious Christian' (ibid., fos. 162r, 163v).

contending long before his reign for that supremacy which denoted Antichrist.[122] Not simply the prospect of worldly promotions but the willingness of influential men to advance them seduced the clergy. Heresies, for example, now seriously split the Church 'which in time of persequution could do nothing so much harme because the pagan magistrates wold geve no ere unto them nor mainteine the Authors, and soch as did set them furth'.[123] Indeed Harrison's real objection to the nature of Constantine's conversion to Christianity, and the reason why it appeared to him to have such contemporary relevance, was that it raised the problem that also confronted the Elizabethan Puritans – how to deal with a state–inspired reformation which by its very nature had to be broad enough to be politically enforceable, but fell far short of that pure community of the gathered saints which constituted the eternal True Church. Thus after Constantine's intervention, political debts handicapped the Church in its pursuit of the reorientation of society along the lines of the Gospel community. Harrison consequently underlined that although Christianity spread over the Roman world, it succeeded 'in sondry wise, for some renounced their Idolatry onely because they saw it fall so fast into contempt, and of this sort many became mere Atheistes in minde thoughe outwardly thei semed to give countenauns to the word'. Others pretended conversion 'onlie upon persuasion that eche man is bounde to follow the behaviour and ordinaunces of the prince', which Harrison considered to be 'in the same degre of Atheisme'. Some served both Christ and the idols, 'hoping to hit upon the right one', while many dissembled, becoming 'professors of the word outwardly', and yet inwardly waiting for the prince to change again, 'utterly hating our relligion as wicked and most detestable'; the rest simply followed the crowd. This analysis strikingly parallels contemporary Puritan analyses of religious beliefs in Elizabethan England, and like the contemporary predicament ensured 'that the smallest company became followers of Christ of mere zeale unto truth and hatred of Idolatry', especially since Constantine manifestly appeared to 'be none of the most ernest sort'.[124]

Harrison's treatment of this apparently irreconcilable contradiction between the spiritual nature of the True Church and the worldly structures with which it had become enmeshed not only contradicted the accepted historical interpretation which for many Elizabethans provided part of the justification for the Royal Supremacy, but also in its revelations about the courtly influences upon the duplicitous Constantine contravened the accepted limitations

---

[122] Ibid., fos. 162r, 161r. The reference to poison echoes Bale, *Works*, ed. Christmas, p. 35.
[123] TCD MS 165, fo. 163r.
[124] Ibid., fo. 163v. In England also 'zeale to devotion wexeth cold' (ibid., fo. 314v), another feature common to the Church under both Constantine and Elizabeth. *Cf.* Collinson, *Religion of Protestants*, pp. 200–1.

of historical enquiry into 'the hidden meanings of princes'. For while Harrison's search for historical precedents seems to be so commonplace as to hardly warrant being called a methodology, and his concern with the 'problem of counsel' obviously reiterates previous humanist fears, the fact that he considered those notions within the unique context of the True Church gave an unusually radical tone to his historical interpretation. The particular circumstances of the Reformation in Elizabethan England served to exaggerate that radicalism, however much some of Harrison's complaints seem merely to voice the perennial clerical outlook. Therefore Holinshed omitted from his *Chronicles* Harrison's outspokenly revisionist arguments on issues such as Constantine's historical role. For Harrison's interpretation effectively implied that every supervisory magistrate would, in the course of pursuing his worldly prosperity, have a deleterious effect on the Church by establishing it without sufficient regard for God's law, and inevitably exacerbating the tensions thus set up. The secular magistrate therefore appeared to Harrison to provide only a flimsy defence against Antichrist's incessant attacks. The following chapter will discuss whether Harrison found any other human political structures in the commonwealth which might help the True Church to defend itself against Antichrist.

6

A reformed commonwealth

The history of the True Church showed William Harrison that the human institution of perpetual monarchy was inherently unable to overcome worldly considerations in order to achieve a full reformation. Yet this bitter lesson contradicted his careful acknowledgement that the presbyterians, whose historical vision of the True Church he shared, threatened dangerous social upheaval in their attempts to reconstruct the godly society without tarrying for the magistrate. Despite his low opinion of princes in general, Harrison had dutifully to suspend his disbelief about Elizabeth's commitment to further reformation. This tension can be partly resolved by an examination of Harrison's views about England's relationship to the ideal godly commonwealth, but an element of incoherence must always be allowed for in his thought, since he belonged to that historical majority of individuals whose less than rigorous thinking allowed them to accept simultaneously a number of logically contradictory propositions. Harrison's very situation encouraged such a lack of rigour, and his subjective interpretation of his contemporary political, social and economic environment also partly explains why this tension never became a destructive element in his thought, why he never developed his views to their logical, extreme conclusion.[1] In this connection we have seen how on different occasions the actions of the political elite both dispelled Harrison's doubts and revived them. The tension between these states of mind was resolved by considering those actions in the light of God's commandments to defend and build up the True Church, and now we can expand that assessment to include both the inferior magistrates and the commons, and their social and economic activities, for Harrison believed that all contemporary actions remained subject to the godly criteria given to the covenant line in the beginning, and consistently reaffirmed ever since.

Harrison's diagnosis of the ills of the commonwealth, and some of the remedies which he proposed, clearly owed much to the tradition of

---

[1] For instance he regarded tyranny as both a divine punishment for sin and the result of disobedience by a deluded people when they elected a prince who refused to obey God's calling for a ruler. See below, pp. 254–5.

Protestant social comment established by the Edwardine 'commonwealth' preachers, and beyond them to the humanist social critics of the early sixteenth century. Like them he identified the acquisitive instincts of self-interested individuals as the chief enemies of the good of the whole community, whether those individuals happened to be princes, courtiers, or enclosing landlords. Like the humanists he solemnly warned that neglecting the common weal brought about the decay of the commonwealth and the eventual overthrow of the prince. His solution, the encouragement of godliness in rulers and ruled, echoes the more self-consciously Christian emphasis which the northern humanists gave to the Italian humanist requirement that wise princes should seek the classical virtues. Yet Harrison, like some of the Edwardine 'commonwealth' preachers, saw the whole issue in a different context from the humanists, and his definition of godly behaviour differed accordingly. Thomas Becon, a Cambridge disciple of Hugh Latimer, shows how these Protestants put the social abuses defined by their humanist predecessors into a new, apocalyptic context, and how that more clearly defined struggle against Satan made human self-interest appear to be Antichrist's means to subvert not only the commonwealth but also the True Church which had recently been liberated from Satan's power. Becon traced the antichristian Church: 'even from the beginning of the world they have lacked in no age. Neither lacke we examples in thys our tyme', and asked 'who knoweth not that the church of the papistes is the ryghte Synagoge of Sathan, and the verye churche malignaunt, of whome David speaketh' in Psalm 26.[2]

In this context, which gave Satan a new prominence, the social evils which the humanists bemoaned as the evidence of an unvirtuous commonwealth became more overtly acts of disobedience towards God, meriting punishment as sin. Conversely, true obedience to God's commandments would re-create the godly commonwealth, so that Becon wished that 'all kings, princes, dukes and rulers' would follow David's example and 'straitly look unto the observance and true keeping of the most holy commandments of God'. Such obedience, while obligatory for 'so many as hope to be saved' would also ensure that rulers and subjects fulfilled their respective callings, and thus establish the godly commonwealth. True religion therefore underpinned the righteous commonwealth, for 'as the scriptures testify', the prince who obeyed God enjoyed a peaceful reign, while the idolatrous inventions of the tyrant contributed to the social and political decline which ensured his overthrow.[3]

Like Becon, Harrison presumed that only the prince who obeyed God

---

[2] T. Becon, *The Actes of Christ and of Antichrist, concerning both their life and doctrine*, in *Worckes* (3 vols. John Day: London, 1564), iii, fo. 396r.

[3] Ibid., i, fos. 157v, 167r–v.

could expect obedience from his subjects, for the protection of divine law extended only to those powers that fulfilled their ordained calling. One Northumbrian king, for example, foisted popish vestments on his clergy, but 'as he presumed to bring in soche trinkettes without Authority so contrary to Law was he himself ere long expelled out of his kingdome, a iust plague and ponishment for his former dealinges'.[4] By tying the fate of the commonwealth very closely to the fate of the True Church, the 'commonwealth' preachers and their Puritan successors, including Harrison, established a standard of godliness far more precisely moulded to the details of Israel's covenant with God than that put forward by the northern humanists. Both Ponet and Goodman insisted that the Scriptures not only described the true calling of a godly prince, but also in listing his functions gave the outlines of the godly commonwealth. To Ponet the failure to overthrow Mary reflected the general failure to build up that godly commonwealth. Erasmus and More had also prescribed godliness as the sovereign remedy for a sick commonwealth, but had used that term as a synonym for the ability to distinguish rationally between good and evil, and to follow the good precepts of God's law written in the hearts of all men.[5] Working within a different scale of values, Harrison subordinated human reason to the Scriptural depiction of the social norms observed by the faithful covenant line, in contrast to which the unrestricted use of fallen human reason by the Church of Cain had produced an uncaring, self-interested society.

This transformation in contemporary social thought reflected the Protestants' distrust of unaided human reason, and their consequent emphasis on the perpetual criteria of the covenant, rather than the natural law, as the basis for a godly society. Harrison's interpretation of the Scriptures as an account of the Two Churches thus allowed him to remodel familiar humanist topics, such as 'the problem of counsel', according to the framework established by the covenant line. Thus he defined his predicament as an evangelical Protestant preacher under Elizabeth according to the consistent pattern of persecution endured by the True Church, for 'when many wise men have found out the best for the maintenauns of their commonwelth and country, their divise is often made frustrate either by one prince and the close practizes of soche as whisper to him the ere to the contrary for ther owne lucre or satisfaction of desire or els by the brainelesse multitude which never dealeth with any forecast or deliberation'.[6] This obviously echoes earlier humanist complaints, but where the humanists had ignored the common people and

---

[4] TCD MS 165, fo. 220v.
[5] Skinner, *Foundations of Modern Political Thought*, i, pp. 221–33, esp. p. 232, although Professor Skinner underestimates the extent to which Protestant 'commonwealth' critics differed from the humanists, as at p. 225. Ponet, *Treatise of politike power*, sigs. B4r–B5v, and esp. sigs. L5v–L6v.   [6] TCD MS 165, fos. 95v–96r.

directed their advice to the policy makers, Harrison saw his social remedies in the wider context of the struggle against Antichrist and the Church of Cain. Therefore, while the humanists bemoaned the self-interested opposition of courtiers, Harrison also expected the commons to join the self-seeking opposition, for popery appealed to their carnal reason just as it appealed to that of princes and courtiers. Thus along with the outlook and tone of the Old Testament prophets Harrison also acquired their belief that the majority usually opposed the truth, a belief which his parochial experiences only served to confirm.[7] In Harrison's view, every section of society seemed ranged against the godly preacher in its refusal to obey the Word, but because in contemporary circumstances only the prince possessed sufficient power to achieve social reform without social upheaval, the obduracy of the chief magistrate caused him greatest dismay.

Protestants perceived princes from a variety of standpoints. In a zealous moment Bale pitied them, 'being but wormes, dust and ashes', while Raleigh's greater experience of princely temperaments persuaded him to restrict to the Old Testament the right of zealots to address the prince 'in terms unfitting his estate'. Only the Scriptural prophets enjoyed divine sanction fearlessly to reprehend 'the errors of their kings'.[8] Harrison advocated reform in the style established by the members of the covenant line, such as Elisha, for fifty-seven years 'a faithfull counsellor' to the kings of Israel and Judah.[9] Thus, at least in his 'Chronology', the deference demanded by a hierarchical society took second place to the Scriptural criteria which determined the preacher's relationship to the prince. Motivated by the historical interpretation which he believed he shared with the prophets, Harrison considered that when zealous ministers faithfully expounded God's plan for the commonwealth out of the Word, then rulers had a duty to listen. In this belief he followed the 'commonwealth' preachers, and especially Hugh Latimer, whom he claimed to have heard 'occulte sed feliciter' under Mary.[10] Latimer had followed the Pauline teaching of Romans 15.4, demanding that the Bible should become the pattern of all human activities, and therefore he not only reinterpreted contemporary evils by fitting them into the Scriptural framework, but also sought to solve them by Scriptural remedies. The Word provided a clear insight into the real meaning of the contemporary world. 'Let the preacher therefore never fear to declare the messages of God unto all men', urged Latimer, for the preacher must expound every man's calling; 'If he preach before a king, let his matter be concerning the office of a king'. He therefore applied the details

---

[7] Ibid., fo. 74r.
[8] Bale, *Pageant of Popes* (1574), sig. e. 3v; Raleigh, *History* (1687), II. xvi. 2 and 4.
[9] TCD MS 165, fo. 78v.
[10] Parry, 'Puritanism and history', pp. 21–2; and see above, pp. 226–7.

of Deuteronomy directly to Edward VI's actions, despite the resultant anachronisms.[11]

Harrison also considered that the prophets had 'to reprove all estates and denounce goddes heavie wrath against them for ther wickednesse and sinne', but while this put princely 'solemnities and ceremonies in our times' into their proper context, as devices invented by the Gentiles to dazzle the lowly, Harrison did not allow the godly critic to harangue the prince irreverently. Moreover, only the prior claims of the Word and the True Church enabled the preacher temporarily to abandon his proper subjection, for an ungodly irreverence distinguished the antichristian Church, such as an early heretic who attacked an Emperor 'with more vehemence and bitternesse then becometh a subject to use unto his prince the quarrel being his owne and not goddes'.[12] This proper precaution once noted, Harrison's perception of his own role as adviser to princes drew a great deal of its perhaps bumptious self-confidence from the earlier history of the covenant line. While he remained very sensitive about the princely inclination to oppose the truth and to allow self-interest to distort the Church, he found impressive evidence in the Scriptures to support the notion that preaching could accomplish God's will. Asa's early lukewarmness and ignorance of God's ordinances for religion had succumbed to Azariah's preaching: 'his hart changed within him...now dothe he waxe very hote'. Yet this success only highlighted the same contemporary problem in the endless struggle against Satan, for when Asa erased idolatry 'he left a president unto all other princes of our time', who tolerated idolatrous popery for money or out of friendship. This precedent, and the subsequent fate of the True Church, therefore forbade the toleration of recusancy through fines or considerations of social position, and showed 'that neither kinred nor authoritie shold be regarded toward soche as by ther behaviour do blaspheme god and dispise his worde, but justice be executed upon them even to the very uttermost'. Harrison's comment reveals the central contradiction of his position – he exalted the secular magistrate as the guardian of true doctrine, but demanded that that magistrate should ignore all worldly political considerations in fulfilling that divinely appointed role.[13]

Harrison's delimitation of the princely office thus appears eccentric to the contemporary reality, and unlike the humanists, who mostly compromised their principles in seeking practical resolution of 'the problem of counsel', he required princes to vacate their thrones and reverently listen to the preachers of the Word. This particularly applied to the central question of

---

[11] A. G. Chester, *Hugh Latimer* (London, 1954), pp. 187–8. See also the discussion of Latimer and other 'commonwealth' preachers in D. M. Loades, *The Oxford Martyrs* (London, 1970), pp. 92–100, for many parallels to Harrison's thought.

[12] TCD MS 165, fos. 80r, 66r, 178v.　　　　　　　　[13] Ibid., fos. 72v, 73r.

the determination of doctrine, which all Protestants jealously guarded against secular interference. Harrison gave shape to this cosy clerical pipe-dream in the history of one Leontius, Bishop of Tripoli, who opposed the fourth-century Emperor Constantius even though the latter 'willed alwaies to honor the preachers of the word sithe thei were gods labourers and worthy doble reverens', for Constantius presumed to determine doctrine himself. Harrison found Leontius's burning zeal for the truth more commendable than the politic wisdom with which other bishops accepted the godly Emperor's doctrinal pronouncements, but he still managed to believe that Constantius humbly accepted the restrictions which Leontius placed on 'humane authority'.[14] Yet more often the Word required preachers to criticise the worldly ambitions of princes, and in this area Harrison found less hope for Elizabethan evangelicals. Although preaching of the Word had reformed Asa's faith, his reaction to prophetic criticism of his worldly policy against Baasa of Israel showed the fundamental and irreconcilable conflict of interest between princes and preachers. By imprisoning Hanani the seer and killing 'sondry of his best subiectes', Asa reminded Harrison that 'soche are many princes that so long as thei maie do what thei list thei seme good men', but the acid test came 'when thei are required to measure their deeds by the law of god', for 'then wexe thei angry and seke matter against the dutifull preacher, as if his reprehensions and exhortations to the fere of the lord were a diminuation and hindrauns of their prerogatives'. Perhaps with an eye to publication Harrison crossed out this tendentious conclusion, leaving the safer analysis of Asa's specific offences in trusting man rather than God.[15]

Harrison perceived a dangerous tension between 'policy' and religion in his own times because that had been the perpetual predicament of the True Church. The 'Chronology' repeatedly describes the preacher of truth receiving abuse and persecution from a worldly Court, and this obsession reflected and conditioned that perception of his times which Harrison shared with other radical Protestants. Indeed for such men the experience of worldly indifference or persecution merely confirmed their membership of the True Church alongside Ezekiel and Micah, 'sithe princes and peres', said Harrison, 'will not comonly be touched by their goodwilles but live as lawlesse without law of god or man farder then thei do like of'. However, the examples of the covenant line did not allow preachers to humour princes

---

[14] Leontius also required the Empress to rise at his entrance and kneel to receive his blessing, 'and that I sitting downe she stand with reverens to here my wordes out of goddes word till I geve her a token to return unto her throne' (ibid., fo. 166r). The implications of these views would not have been lost on contemporary magistrates, if Harrison had been foolish enough to reiterate them publicly.

[15] Ibid., fo. 72v. Harrison's friend and ecclesiastical patron Alexander Nowell received a spectacular public rebuke from Elizabeth when he dared to attack her use of the cross in her private chapel (Collinson, *Religion of Protestants*, pp. 34–5).

and 'avoide the madnesse of soche as were in authority'.[16] On the contrary, and like Latimer before him, Harrison took his cue from Micah's lone battle against the arrogant pomp of Ahab's court, for 'therin also he left a noble admonition to his successors' in the covenant line, amongst whom Harrison counted himself, 'that truth is not alwaies to be found among the greatest nombers nor continually with soch as be of most authority'.[17]

The historical example which most clearly shows how Harrison diminished the conflict between policy and religion at the heart of the problem of counsel also reveals his outspokenness in the context of the Elizabethan Church. Contemporary churchmen of a wide variety of opinions looked to the example of Ambrose, Bishop of Milan, for guidance in defending the integrity of the Church and restraining the behaviour of princes by speaking out in God's cause. Yet while Romanists made much of the fact that Ambrose excommunicated Theodosius after the Emperor had deliberately massacred thousands of citizens at Thessalonica, Elizabethan clerics chose to interpret this excommunication as a successful example of zealous exhortation rather than a punishment. Edwin Sandys believed that Ambrose had 'brought the Emperor Theodosius himself to unfeigned humility and hearty repentance'. By the end of Elizabeth's reign there was a growing tendency to interpret Ambrose's action as merely a withholding of the sacrament, not full excommunication.[18] In 1576 Grindal had consciously chosen to follow the Ambrosian model very closely in passively resisting Elizabeth's demands that he suppress the prophesyings, and had paid for his anachronistic attachment to the standards of the primitive Church with suspension from office.[19] Grindal's fate may explain the growing reticence of Elizabeth's bishops in advancing their claims to Ambrosian authority over doctrine and ceremonies, but, writing at about the time of Grindal's disgrace, Harrison had far fewer reservations about the responsibility of ministers to ensure that princes submitted their consciences to the correction of the Word. He quite baldly stated that Ambrose 'excommunicateth Theodosius and doth not suffer him to enter into his church' after the massacre at Thessalonica. Harrison emphasised that Ambrose rebuked and excommunicated the Emperor 'after a zealous and humble maner', but he made no bones about the fact that this 'censure wrought so in the minde of the mighty Emperor that he submitted himself within a few monethes' and received 'absolution'.[20] Clearly Harrison's remoteness from the more spectacular

---

[16] TCD MS 165, fos. 165r, 219r, and note the murder of Ezekiel (ibid., fo. 90v).
[17] 'Hatred of the prince, number of adversaries, stoutnesse of talke and violent deling...cold not prevaile with him' (ibid., fo. 74r; cf. Chester, *Latimer*, p. 173).
[18] Collinson, *Religion of Protestants*, pp. 24–8, quoting at p. 25 *The Sermons of Edwin Sandys*, ed. J. Ayre (Parker Society: Cambridge, 1841), p. 72.
[19] Collinson, *Archbishop Grindal*, pp. 242–6, and *Religion of Protestants*, pp. 29–31.
[20] TCD MS 165, fo. 170v, following the Greek historians Glyca and Sozomenus, who also helped him to see through Constantine's pretensions, an insight not shared by many Elizabethan clerics (see Collinson, *Religion of Protestants*, p. 26).

explosions of Elizabeth's imperious temper enabled him to be this blunt, but his tone also reflects his conviction that the very nature of royal courts required the godly preacher to be an alert watchman for the True Church.

Harrison realised that ministers had to avoid being both too severe and too lax in fulfilling this duty. In their zeal to protect the Church, the godly had to avoid the antichristian course taken by the papacy. God had given the prince all temporal authority, and the papacy's disobedient usurpation of that power had marked the rise of Antichrist, 'whereas Christ himself refused not to paie tribute in token that touching his manhode he was subject to the temporall power according also to the saieng of Peter…Againe Christ said that his kingdome was not of this worlde'.[21] Yet Harrison only used the classical texts on obedience, Romans 13 and I Peter 2, to defend this conventional Protestant distinction, which condemned 'the papists' who 'contemned the temporall magistrate who god commaundeth eche christien to obeie'.[22] Outside this support for the secular magistrate against Antichrist, Harrison clearly felt little desire to inculcate implicit obedience to a society which he considered in many ways disobedient to the Word. The godly did not need to be reminded of their duty to obey the secular magistrate, but Elizabethan society needed to be recalled to its proper obedience to the Word. Others demanded obedience even to idolatrous tyrants, 'for it pleaseth God sometimes to punish his People by a tyrannous hand: and the Commandment of Obedience is without distinction'. Harrison similarly asked 'what is a greater token of the wrath of god then to have an insolent and negligent prince', but he did not couple this with the commandments on passive obedience.[23] Moreover, not only did his preoccupation with the True Church make him indifferent to princely claims upon the subservience of their subjects, but his concentration on the duties that God demanded of princes made him conceive of a ruler sent in God's wrath not simply as an absolute tyrant but also as a 'negligent' prince. In Harrison's historical interpretation God punished sin by sending a ruler who would be deaf to the appeals of the oppressed, and who would ignore 'commonwealth' ideals.

Such a punishment exactly matched the sins of ungrateful and disordered commonwealths. For example, 'the divine appointed order' had set the Normans over the Saxons, and left the latter powerless to resist until the time appointed, because the English had refused God's grace 'and woulde not heare when God by his preachers did call us so favourably unto him'.[24] Even though the degenerate Saxon commonwealth had fully merited God's wrath through its disobedience, the Scriptures showed that like Israel, England could be absolved from this punishment by accepting the preaching which

---

[21] TCD MS 165, fo. 275r.
[22] Ibid., fo. 294r. In this context, Henry II became 'supreme hed' and Becket's 'iust desertes', execution (ibid., fos. 207r, 294r).
[23] Ibid., fo. 330v.   [24] *Description* (1587), p. 7.

would reconstruct the godly commonwealth. For tyranny reflected the pretensions of Gentile princes, and could be positively resisted not by rebellion but by a reformation of religion and society which would please God and lead to the lifting of the punishment. That reformation must be continued in passive defiance of the ungodly commands of tyrants. This was as far as Harrison could go under Elizabeth, although his argument parallels Goodman's belief that God's plagues could be removed by reverent receiving of the Gospel 'and framing our lives therunto'. Goodman and Ponet had interpreted Romans 13 as a command to obey only that power which defended good and punished evil, and by defining the ruler's calling according to Scriptural models they had presented an insufficient ruler as a hindrance to the godly commonwealth, just as 'dumb dogs' were to the preaching ministry of the True Church. Harrison remained uneasily vague about what would happen if Elizabeth and indeed all constituted authority became an obstacle to the achievement of the godly commonwealth.[25]

Indeed this alarming prospect made it all the more vital that preachers did not err on the side of laxity in their relationship with rulers, for while Harrison never drew together his thoughts on disobedience he perceived that God's constant justice had with an encouraging regularity brought down ungodly rulers by rebellion. The humanists had previously threatened that rulers who followed their own interests and neglected the public weal would find themselves facing sedition and discord, and the destruction of the commonwealth.[26] The early Protestants had taken over this equation and underlined the providential connection between rebellion and the failure of princes to fulfil their calling. 'If yea fear your commons, so testify yea against yourselves that yea are tyrants', concluded Tyndale, while Cranmer also emphasised the inevitable consequences when the prince refused to perform his divinely given office: 'when kings and chief rulers suffer their under officers to mis-use their subjects, and will not heare nor remedy their people's wrongs when they complain, then suffreth God the Rebel to rage'. Nevertheless, like other 'commonwealth' preachers, Cranmer insisted that subjects should obey all rulers, including the tyrant, and drew back from explaining precisely how God's justice might punish contemporary princes.[27] Christopher Goodman felt no such qualms; starting from Calvin's definition of ruling as a legitimate calling, he subjected the ruler to God's laws, so that the people should not become 'brute beastes, without judgemente and reason, thinking all things lawfull which their Rulers do', for ungodly rulers 'oght no more to be taken for magistrates but punished as private trans-

---

25 Goodman, *Superior Powers*, pp. 38, 111, 83; Ponet, *Of politike power*, sigs. D3v–D4r.
26 Skinner, *Foundations of Modern Political Thought*, i, p. 223.
27 W. Tyndale, *The Practice of Prelates* (1530), in *Works*, ed. H. Walter (2 vols. Parker Society: Cambridge, 1848), i, pp. 388–9; *Miscellaneous Writings and Letters of Thomas Cranmer*, ed. J. E. Cox (Parker Society: Cambridge, 1846), ii, p. 188.

gressors', an argument which used Roman private law theories in strict subordination to the Scriptural criteria of the covenant.[28]

Harrison also adopted this stricter test of the prince's actions, adding to the humanist concern for the common weal the Protestant fixation on the prosperity of the True Church as the critical measure of any ruler. History showed that under God's justice only princes who followed advice derived from the Scriptures could expect divine blessing on their endeavours; therefore they had 'to take order that the Lord might be daily honored' and the people 'holden within the limits of his obedience', an obedience directing the behaviour of all members of the commonwealth towards the type of human society commanded by God.[29] This 'commonwealth' definition of the princely office demanded that the ruler should curb damaging private interest groups, that he should advance education and above all foster that preaching ministry which alone could accomplish a genuine reformation, and at the same time discipline the ungodly clergy while opposing the papacy. Judging princes according to these criteria, Harrison therefore concluded that tyrants or incompetents who failed to match up to these standards deserved their fate. Thus in words which parallel those of Goodman he claimed that Henry III 'declared himself...to be no king' by his failure to oppose the antichristian papacy. Only once in the 'Chronology' did Harrison argue that rebels were 'men void of all obediens and contemptuous of god and the law of nature', and the context makes it clear that his description derives less from the law of nature than from the fact that the ungodly clergy inspired this rebellion against a relatively godly prince.[30] Consequently the delicate balance in his thought between his desire to do his utmost to encourage godly rule, and his acknowledgement that devastation was 'the comon rewarde of all civil discorde' found some sort of resolution in his attempt to assess all rebellions according to whether they had been directed against an ungodly or godly ruler.

By this means he adapted the prevailing Protestant charge that the antichristian clergy had stimulated baronial rebellions in medieval England, to enable him to describe those princely qualities against which Antichrist had directed his fury.[31] Even William the Conqueror, otherwise a hateful figure for Harrison, earned grudging respect because the clergy who had backed his conquest stirred up an ungodly rebellion when they discovered that 'he would rule rather by the good advise and counsell of soche as were

---

[28] Not only inferior magistrates but the common people must make their princes obey God's laws (Goodman, *Superior Powers*, pp. 148, 118–19).

[29] The princes of Israel suffered punishment because they allowed the people 'to transgresse the commaundement whose guidauns was committed by god unto them' (TCD MS 165, fo. 210v).   [30] Ibid., fos. 308v, 223v.

[31] 'None in those days once hissed against them but suffered death for it' (Bale, *The Image of Both Churches*, ed. Christmas, p. 350).

skilfull then be led by the practizes of those that fished alwaies for their owne lucre and commoditie'.[32] In the context of providential history this humanist commonplace became transformed into an important prophetic theme. In the more complex circumstances of John's reign, Harrison sided with the King as the lesser of two evils, for although he recognised the role played by the antichristian popish clergy in creating baronial unrest, and acknowledged that John required 'dutifull obediens' from those lowly clergy 'not proude and of more highe stomache then stode with their calling', he refused to justify all John's actions simply because he had withstood Antichrist. He argued that John had not met the traditional requirements of a 'good lord', and that he had been equally happy 'by faire means to reduce his nobility from ther errors, or to requite malice with malice'. Indeed John seemed 'not so covetous as he was crafty', while among his first acts as King he had imposed a heavy tax 'for the whiche he had many a curse and little good will of his comons after the same so long as he lived'. Harrison could afford therefore to see the failings of both sides, for in that degenerate commonwealth worldly ambitions had obscured the true end of government in the reformation of the Church, and he lamented 'the gret negligens now used in the care of the pastorall charge by the princes and peres of the worlde'. He personally identified with the godly of that period who 'right wel understode thei might finde fault at will, but not redresse the error', for he found himself in the same predicament.[33]

By applying these Scriptural criteria, which he identified with 'commonwealth' principles, Harrison managed to some extent to circumvent the theoretical objection that to resist tyranny was to resist God's just punishment for sin. Circumstances never required him to make the distinction between God's will and oppression as unequivocally as some Calvinist political theorists, but his analysis of Saul's election already discussed shows that he accepted that the deluded members of the Church of Cain might set up a tyrannical magistrate as part of their disobedient flouting of God's will. Furthermore, he did not equate even successful rebellion with God's will. Thus he came down on the side of Richard II against Henry IV because Richard's legislation met many of the demands of 'commonwealth' idealists. Harrison gave education a central role in the maintenance of the commonwealth, and therefore applauded the fact that Richard 'favoured his universities merveillously and made mo lawes for their maintenauns then any prince' before or since. Given these indications of the character of Richard's rule, Harrison remained undecided about whether 'the heavy yoke of king Henry' had represented 'the wrath of god due for our sinnes' or merely

---

[32] TCD MS 165, fo. 270r.

[33] Ibid., fos. 304v, 303r, 301v, 302v, a far harsher view of John than Bale's *King John*.

resulted from the people's 'inconstancie and king Henries tyranny'.[34] In the years of exile from Marian England, or in the circumstances of the French Wars or the Dutch revolt, Calvinists felt it necessary to stress the crucial distinction between tyranny and God's will, but under Elizabeth Harrison had little need to resolve his own uncertainty about the right of resistance to tyranny, and concentrated much more on the fact that God's unchanging justice required princes to obey the Word in their care for the commonwealth, or they would face the consequences.

Accordingly he readily believed that the subjects of a tyrannous prince would rebel when that prince disobeyed his calling and gave ear to worldly advice. Convinced that 'there is no counsell that can prosper against the lord', Harrison confidently assumed that wicked counsellors received just punishment from that God 'against whom they do resist'.[35] The Old Testament history of King Rehoboam showed the inevitable consequences when princes and courtiers followed the rational criteria of degenerate human reasoning in formulating policy, forsaking the limitations of the covenant and adopting the strategies of Gentile absolutist rule. For Rehoboam 'supposed it ynough for a king to be placed in regall seate and to be a good husband for his kingdome', an echo perhaps of Calvin's definition of Cain's ungodly behaviour, 'and that even for that onely cause all men wold have him in reverens and honor'. Disobeying the covenant and its restrictions on his behaviour, Rehoboam surrounded himself with rash young courtiers who assured him 'that the best waie to governe was cruell dealing and holding of his subiectes in most extreme servitude', but his disobedience towards God lost him the goodwill of the commonwealth upon which all princes depended, for the Ten Tribes eventually 'forsoke Rehoboam outrightes', killing his representative and almost killing the King himself before they seceded.[36] Wiser princes recognised the conditional nature of obedience and therefore sought to profit the whole body politic rather than self-seeking courtiers, for the people, said one, 'may live without us but how can I defend my possession without them', another version of the dictum frequently cited by resistance theorists that a people may exist without a magistrate, but not a magistrate without a people.[37] Harrison's desire to define tyranny not as a divine punishment but as the magistrate's failure to fulfil his calling as defined by the covenant therefore led him to reject Xenophon's attempt to whitewash the reign of Cyrus 'making him finally to die in his bedde which

---

[34] TCD MS 165, fo. 351r. Richard protected English industry, prohibited unlawful games, encouraged archery, restricted retaining and punished vagabonds (ibid., fo. 341v). Harrison sympathised with critics of Henry's 'unlawfull aspiring to the crowne and deposition of his sovereine' (ibid., fo. 350v). Ponet's discussion of Henry's rebellion is less decisive (*Of politike power*, sig. G3r).   [35] TCD MS 165, fos. 46r, 71r–v.

[36] Ibid., fos. 71r–v.   [37] Ibid., fo. 78r.

is not comon with tyrants'. Constantly aware of God's unchanging justice, Harrison preferred to believe that Cyrus had been slain by his rebellious subjects.[38]

Harrison's teleological scheme of the True Church and the demands which it imposed upon the magistrate gives point to his strictures, for the inexorable logic of that teleology threatened princes and rulers who refused to contribute to the building up of the Church. He concerned himself not with a rational moral code, but with the history of the True Church and what its demonstration of God's providence meant for the present. Therefore, if we compare his historical interpretation with the more conventional view of history in the contemporary *Mirror for Magistrates*, we can more fully appreciate the strength of Harrison's conviction that God had covenanted with the Elect to protect from tyranny those who obeyed Him, to preserve the godly ruler and cast down the ungodly. The often unsophisticated historical explanation given in the *Mirror* relied very heavily on the humanist concept of Fortuna, whether as the classical blind goddess of destiny, or in the form of Fortune's wheel, which raised to worldly eminence and then cast down a succession of her victims. Some contributors to the *Mirror* even gave Fortune autonomous control of history, to the apparent exclusion of Providence, but the most remarkable feature of this process is its impartiality. The blind goddess and her remorseless wheel first favour and then destroy not only the wicked but also those who fulfilled Tudor 'commonwealth' ideals and sought the common weal before their own.[39] Logically, of course, this vitiated the *Mirror*'s pretensions to teach magistrates how to rule properly, but Harrison enforced the lesson much more strictly.

He drew a much closer connection between princely actions and the rewards promised by the Scriptures. For example, where Pausanias stressed the role of destiny in the deposition of a cruel king of the Argives, he chose to underline instead 'the wicked demeanor and ungodly behaviour of the lewd and cruell tyraunt', which had received due punishment. He also criticised authors who tried to suppress evidence connecting the tyrannous actions of princes with their inevitable fate, for 'it is great marvell to me' how Orosius and Sebastian Foxe had missed clear evidence of oppression and consequent rebellion in Spain, but 'Peradventure ther lieth somewhat in ther definition of tyraunt more then I conceave'.[40] In contrast to the kind of

[38] Ibid., fo. 32r.

[39] W. Baldwin et al., *A Myrrour for Magistrates. Wherein maye be seen by example of other, with howe grevous plages vices are punished; and howe frayle and unstable worldly prosperity is founde, even of those whome Fortune seemeth most highly to favour* (Thomas Marshe: London, 1563), sig. C3v: 'Thus was the warden of the common weale / The Duke of Glocester gyltes made away'; and sig. I2v: Richard Neville, Earl of Warwick: 'The common weale was styll my chiefest care'.

[40] TCD MS 165, fos. 46r, 34av. He drew attention to the frequency with which the Spaniards resorted 'to the slaughter and expulsion of ther kinges' until one prince decimated the inferior

reasoning found in the *Mirror*, however, the most striking feature of Harrison's ideas about rebellion is his reluctance to believe that any prince who met 'commonwealth' criteria could have encountered rebellion and deposition. For to accept such suggestions would be to doubt Providence and the certainty of God's promises. Therefore there remained only one avenue of escape from such unsettling thoughts. After concluding that Ganges, the mythical settler of India, had satisfactorily shown that 'manhode lieth not so moche in spoiling of enemies as the preservation of subiectes and soche as are inferiors', Harrison had to confront evidence of 'his slaughter procured by his rebellious subiectes'. The fact that Ganges had promoted peace and justice persuaded Harrison to ignore this apparent affront to divine justice, 'sith I gesse that there is some confusion in the part of his history with other princes of his name'.[41] Clearly Harrison attached more importance to the Scriptural criteria of godly rule and their attendant assurances than to what he otherwise regarded as sound historical evidence.

If the circumstances of Elizabethan England did not require Harrison to develop justifications for resistance, then they certainly required him to develop this rigorous conclusion, that under God's law tyrants 'are comonly dispatched by hatred and rebellion'. For 'soch are many princes oftentimes that thei thinke to serve god and to rule are sondry mens callinges, and that to be godly concerneth not them, but their subiectes, and soche as make their living by preaching of the gospell'.[42] Princes who preferred to justify their actions according to the rational criteria of the law of nature, rather than conform to the course of action required by God's law, needed to be reminded of God's eternal justice, especially because the prince 'is but a man and to be ledde by affection and flattery as other men commonly are'. Humanists would have agreed, but Harrison concerned himself much more than they did with princely disobedience to the precise commandments of God's law, 'for asmoche as thorow his aboundauns of welth he is more esily seduced and trained to sinne' by parasitic courtiers. Thus, when the Emperor Justinian II followed this course he 'founde his iust rewarde that is to saie the losse of his estate'.[43]

This emphasis on the detailed responsibilities of the princely office, and the strict enforcement of divine retribution on those rulers who failed to

---

magistracy (ibid., fo. 201v; and see fos. 188v, 189v, 197r and 199v, for examples of Spanish rebellions).

[41] Ibid., fo. 14r. One could argue that here Harrison tried to make human reason defer to revelation.

[42] A pointed reflection on the 'good magistrate' Jehoram, who was 'wicked but not so wicked as his predecessors' and as the prince during a partial reformation perhaps a relevant parallel with Elizabethan England (ibid., fo. 75v).

[43] Harrison here relied on the Byzantine historian, Manasses (ibid., fo. 204av). *Cf.* the palace coup against Amaziah 'whome god no doubt wolde have kept out of their violens if he had walked in his preceptes with a faithful and upright hart' (ibid., fo. 76v).

observe them shows how Protestants adapted the commonplaces of humanist political thought in order to advocate godly rule. Thus Harrison could not bring himself to condemn all rebellion because he saw the justice of dissent when a prince indulged his self-interest 'or the motions of any who often pretended his honor but more often his owne profite and advauntage and for private gain to themselves and soch as bribe them do many times worke mischeef unto the commonwealth whereby infinite sorts of people do suffer extreme peniury'.[44] While this statement encapsulates several familiar elements of humanist social and political thought, its more uncompromising tone derives from Harrison's concern with the building up of the True Church and the kind of orderly social behaviour which manifested its doctrinal purity. His refusal to give a respectful camouflage to his convictions about the punishments which Providence had reserved for princes who disobeyed God made it impossible for Holinshed to print much of the 'Chronology' in his *Chronicles*, for Holinshed deliberately refrained from enquiring into 'the hidden meanings of princes' and gave less prominence to the providential meaning of history.[45]

Harrison firmly believed that princes prospered or suffered according to the zeal with which they obeyed God, just as the True Church waxed and waned in accordance with its doctrinal purity, and so he considered that by distorting the stable equilibrium of the godly society tyranny produced rebellion. This general conviction did not lead him to see inferior magistrates as the guarantors of the godly society, for they might share all the human weaknesses of the prince. Harrison could only justify resistance by inferior magistrates when it was directed against ungodly rule, and towards the proper end of setting up that godly commonwealth wherein every individual would strive to use the abilities given him by divine grace to fulfil his calling.[46] As long as he could discern some remnants of this static ideal in Elizabethan England he did not have to draw from providential history the drastic conclusions which to the godly would justify resistance. Yet his perception that in general the English ruling elite could not be relied upon to bring about the godly commonwealth also made it difficult for him to envisage any practical political alternative to pious exhortation. This perception followed from Harrison's acceptance of certain radical humanist notions

---

[44] An early lesson for the same Artaxerxes who used the Royal Progress for its correct purpose (ibid., fo. 102r). See above, p. 231.

[45] Benbow, 'The Providential Theory of Historical Causation in Holinshed's *Chronicles*', pp. 264–76; and see above on the contrasts between Harrison's and Holinshed's accounts of Constantine.

[46] Thus Harrison made Providence the guiding hand turning Fortune's Wheel, for he commented on a noble rebel who died in beggarly exile that 'the nerer a man is to the toppe of his felicity the nerer he is unto his fall and overthrow', but made this 'a marveilous iudgement of god' upon an ungodly rebellion.

about what constituted nobility, but it primarily stemmed from his realisation that the True Church had usually suffered at the hands of the ruling elite in its struggle against the unregenerate, and that contemporary England provided plenty of evidence to support the conclusion that the aristocracy were playing their usual nefarious role by making religion subordinate to worldly policy.

In exile from Mary, Ponet followed the radical humanist course and identified nobility not with inheritance but with the practice of virtue; he therefore called upon the true nobility of England to deliver the oppressed people from tyranny and remove the traitorous nobles who had betrayed their country into popery.[47] Later, Beza applied Calvin's justifications for resistance by inferior magistrates to the situation of the Huguenots, and bitterly complained that the ancient constitutional right of godly courtiers to restrain royal power by the Word, which he believed still flourished in England, had been subverted in France by ungodly flatterers. He therefore found it expedient in 1562 to use 'policy' as a legitimate method of propagating the gospel, and helped to draft the Edict of Toleration.[48] While it did not dictate the ceremonial of a national church, this Edict went some way towards creating a 'mixed' religion. Harrison's experiences of the English Court and of the local magistracy in Essex made him far less hopeful about the prospects of achieving further reformation in collaboration with the nobility. He knew enough about Elizabeth's Court, to which he had access through Lord Cobham, to be able to distinguish the good behaviour of Elizabeth's ladies-in-waiting from the 'common courtiers' whose great learning was only matched by their licentious living. He believed that the edifying influence of the numerous Bibles, copies of Foxe's *Actes and Monuments* and 'some histories and chronicles' about the Court limited the worst depravities, which, however, went unchecked in English noble households.[49]

Harrison appears to have found little evidence amongst the Essex magistrates of the kind of godly justice dispensed in this period at nearby Bury St Edmunds, where a group of Protestant preachers found practical confirmation for the notion that without the support of the magistracy religion would decline into idolatry and superstition. He acknowledged the natural inclination of the people towards idolatry, but unlike the ministers at Bury St Edmunds he never seems to have achieved a complementary working relationship with the local justices whereby the magistracy enforced the moral 'discipline' required by the ministry while the ministry exhorted the commons to humble submission to the commands and punishments of

---

47 Ponet, *Of politike power*, sig. G7r.
48 Beza, *De iure magistratuum*, ed. Franklin, pp. 118–19, 38–9.
49 *Description*, ed. Edelen, pp. 227–31. Note the lack of any reference to edifying Court sermons.

the magistracy.[50] This partly reflects the failure of the hot Protestants of north-west Essex to dominate the local Commission of the Peace in the way that they did at Bury St Edmunds. Saffron Walden never became a New Jerusalem. Even worse from Harrison's point of view, many inferior magistrates had been compromised by their active participation in the Marian persecution, Sir Anthony Browne being one prominent local example. Browne attended the Essex Quarter Sessions in 1563 and 1564, and Harrison's account of his offensive behaviour there may explain why the government had singled him out from the many other Justices who had supervised the burning of Protestants and demoted him from the Queen's Bench. Harrison felt that Browne's unpleasant personality offended against common assumptions about the sobriety required of a magistrate, and recalled his 'jesting and taunting of soche as came before him as having a great felicity in that kind of mockery'.[51]

Browne did not survive long on the Commission, and some strong Protestants achieved social prominence in Harrison's locality, bringing with them deep convictions about the necessity for God's law to determine the content of human law, and demanding a severe moral discipline similar to that instituted at Bury St Edmunds. Yet cooler heads dominated the Commission, a fact which perhaps explains Harrison's complaints about the general failure to punish immorality with sufficient severity. The civilian and dispassionate scholar Sir Thomas Smith was active on the local bench during the long intervals of a Court career whose failure cannot be attributed to any excess of religious zeal. Smith's *De Republica Anglorum* shows that he found English legal institutions perfectly suited to contemporary needs, and he calmly ignored attempts such as Harrison's in the *Description* to assess those institutions by eternal prophetic standards.[52] From the 1570s the Justices of the Peace in Essex took their cue from Sir Thomas Mildmay and Sir John Petre, two men not only amongst the most socially prestigious but also the most active members of the Commission. Mildmay never wavered from mainstream Protestantism, but Petre, like his father Sir William, remained a discreet but firm papist, whose formal conformity to the established Church enabled him to retain his local power-base, but who never compromised his Catholic beliefs and connections in order to pursue the fruits of office at Court. Indeed, far from promoting further reformation, Sir John Petre used his influence as a county magnate to lessen the persecution

50 Collinson, *Religion of Protestants*, pp. 141–88, esp. pp. 153–70.
51 TCD MS 165, fos. 124ar, 235v. J. Samaha, *Law and Order in Historical Perspective. The Case of Elizabethan Essex* (London, 1974), p. 75.
52 Ibid., pp. 68–70, 74; M. Dewar, *Sir Thomas Smith* (London, 1964), pp. 121–3; *De Republica Anglorum*, ed. Dewar, pp. 99–116; and see above, pp. 230–2.

of Catholics in Essex.[53] Thus despite the intermittent presence on the bench of figures like Thomas Meade, a local landowner in north-west Essex and a Justice of the Common Pleas whose will provided for two learned and discreet Cambridge divines to preach at his funeral, Harrison did not envisage a godly partnership between the local ministry and magistracy which would enforce severe discipline.[54] Indeed, social leadership in the immediate area of Radwinter had devolved upon the Wiseman family, who remained convinced recusants to the extent of exclusion from the Commission of the Peace until nearly the end of Harrison's lifetime, despite his temporary success in bringing them to outward conformity during his ministry at Wimbish in the 1570s. His 'Chronology' dates from that same period and reveals his doubts about the religious commitment of English inferior magistrates, at all levels from the local squirarchy to the greatest courtiers.[55]

Other Elizabethan Protestants who nursed hopes of further reformation shared these misgivings, giving a new emphasis to the religious aspect of earlier humanist fears about the destructive consequences which courtly self-interest would have for the commonwealth. When Bale had introduced the theme of the self-seeking flatterer to his Protestant audience he had emphasised malevolent clerical influence over the prince, but later Protestants, including Harrison, felt that some lay magistrates now represented the greatest obstacle to godly reformation. The Protestants continued to stress the conflict between the commands of the Word and 'politic wisdom, or rather fleshly foolishness', which Bale had warned must be resolved in favour of the Scriptures.[56] Thomas Becon admonished Edward VI to depend on the Scriptures for divine guidance, not 'the doting fancies of those pestilent flatterers', while Bucer complained that courtiers tried to 'reduce the whole of the sacred ministry into a narrow compass...altogether unconcerned about the restoration of church discipline'.[57] Bucer's disciple, Edmund Grindal, felt that the threat of worldly self-interest which overshadowed religion at Edward's Court might soon be fulfilled under Elizabeth, when parasites would use their influence to create a 'mixed uncertain and doubtful'

---

[53] A. C. Edwards, *John Petre. Essays on the life and background of John, 1st Lord Petre, 1549–1613* (London, 1974), pp. 9–10, 21–2; Samaha, *Law and Order*, pp. 69–72. The hot Protestants, Robert, Lord Riche and Sir Thomas Wroth were less prominent on the Commission of the Peace (ibid., pp. 69–70).

[54] F. G. Emmison, *Elizabethan Life: Wills of Essex Gentry and Merchants* (Chelmsford, 1978), pp. 105–6; Samaha, *Law and Order*, p. 153.

[55] Ibid., p. 155; and see above, pp. 160–1.

[56] Bale, *Image of Both Churches*, ed. Christmas, pp. 485, 555; and ibid., p. 362, on the numerous examples of this conflict 'in the chronicles and histories'.

[57] Becon, *David's Harpe*, in *Works*, ed. Ayre, p. 300. Bucer quoted in Collinson, *Archbishop Grindal*, p. 55.

compound of popery and the gospel.[58] Harrison therefore subscribed to a persistent tradition in Protestant thought, and his 'Chronology' shows that he perceived both the rejection of the Word by the laity and their interference in the Church as manifestations of the Church of Cain, where corrupted human reason subordinated the Scriptures and God's commandments to rational criteria and the traditional behaviour of contemporary society. The pernicious consequences could be seen throughout the Elizabethan Church. Harrison refused to accept that the ministry of the Word should conform itself to accepted social norms, and announced in the *Description* that he had rejected Sir Thomas Rugband's offer of a simoniacal contract for the living of South Runcton, Norfolk.[59]

Like other radical Protestants who wished to free the teaching and preaching institutions of the Church from the influence of 'policy', of civil wisdom, Harrison emphasised that the Scriptures not only determined true doctrine but also provided the criteria by which to assess 'policy'. He did not agree that relations between the ruling elite and the visible Church could be governed by the law of nature, but argued that the Scriptures also showed what the True Church required from the inferior magistrate. Thus despite his failure to draw much comfort from the religious behaviour of Elizabethan noblemen and gentlemen, he could conceive of a role for the courtier within the True Church. For the Scriptures showed through the example of Joseph that as 'ther is none that comonly do more mischeefe then the godlesse, parasitical and covetous servitor', so 'ther is none that maie do more good in a realme then a good courtier', for 'the godly do alwaies encrease the good dispositions of the prince unto pyety...daily redy instrumentes to benefit the Church of god, and zealous to procure his true service'. This argument represents more than just an extrapolation from one aspect of humanist exhortations, for it forms part of the general framework of Harrison's thought which contrasted the covenant line of the True Church with their opposites in the Church of Cain. The True Church included those learned and godly courtiers who had 'merveilously aided' the early growth of Christianity, while under triumphant Antichrist a few of the better clerics had allied with the more judicious courtiers to attack the wealthy popish clergy. Indeed the word 'parasites' had originally denoted 'soche wise men as had a tolleration to saie truthe in presens of the king...but because these of counsellors became flatterers' the word acquired its contemporary meaning.[60]

Joseph represented the ideal godly courtier, who benefited the True

---

[58] Ibid., p. 60. Calvin complained that princes tried to organise religion 'according to their will and fancy' (ibid., pp. 89–90).

[59] *Description* (1587), p. 104.   [60] TCD MS 165, fos. 34v, 161v, 309v, 115v.

Church by increasing princely piety and zealously furthering godly ceremonies. His actions reflected his faithful obedience, and Harrison found at
least one contemporary courtier who matched the standard of godly
behaviour set by Joseph. Without Scriptural warrant Harrison described
Joseph as Keeper of the Privy Seal and vicegerent to Pharaoh, an anachronistic
description which reveals his intriguing identification of Joseph with Thomas
Cromwell. They shared similar humble origins but met contrasting ends, for
Joseph 'was not envied nor hated of the nobility and soche as had aspiring
mindes', an uncommon experience, especially for 'a straunger or man of
mean estate advanced unto honor as maie be seen in Cromwell'. Harrison
assimilated Cromwell to the True Church partly because Cromwell encountered the same self-interested opposition to the reform of religion which
the covenant line had suffered in every generation. In this context Harrison's
account of Joseph's 'godlinesse, foreknowledge of thinges to come, obediens,
chastity and notable faith', which enabled him with God's blessing to plant
'the churche and knowledge of god aboundauntly in Egypt' has obvious
implications for his opinion of Cromwell's reforming activities. The Scripturally centred assumptions of Harrison's thinking about Cromwell can
be seen in contrast with the opinion of his scholarly friend Gabriel Harvey,
who cited Cromwell as one of the several examples of the public abilities
required from a successful courtier, not as an individual who fulfilled the
calling of a godly courtier.[61]

Few subsequent Tudor courtiers had lived up to the example of Joseph
and Cromwell, however. Indeed neither contemporary circumstances nor
the history of the True Church led Harrison to expect that courtiers would
advance true religion, although for the same reasons he could not ignore the
Court, nor its influence over the Church.[62] Yet his thought shows an
important shift from the confidence of the Edwardine preachers and their
Elizabethan successors that by preaching the Word where the greatest evils
existed the greatest good might be done.[63] He preferred the godly example
of Samuel, who after the misguided election of Saul 'chose rather to leade
a private life farre from the court than to be nere the king and plaie the
flattering hypocrite'.[64] For when confronted by the obdurate worldliness of

---

[61] Ibid., fo. 34v. Cromwell, 'one of the noblest counsellors that ever England bredde' (ibid.,
fos. 70v–71r), thus figured in Harrison's mythical covenant line, though Bale gave him a more
aggressive role against Antichrist; *A mysterye of Iniquyte* (1545), sig. E5r. See G. R. Elton,
Reform and Renewal (London, 1973), pp. 11–12, on Harvey's discussion of Cromwell.

[62] Harrison's visit to the Court at Greenwich in May 1584 is unlikely to have been his only one,
given his comments above, p. 259 (*Description* (1587), p. 38).

[63] The 'Chronology' cites only one pagan philosopher in favour of this, and mentions very few
Court sermons (TCD MS 165, fos. 107v, 312r).

[64] Not sulking, merely retaining his principles, one assumes (ibid., fo. 67r).

the Court, Harrison had to acknowledge that 'neither preaching of the word, nor civile honesty' could restrain the licentious behaviour of all estates.[65] Where godly preachers had enjoyed some influence over Edward VI, Harrison felt that Elizabeth's Court ignored zealous preachers, and glumly concluded that 'in the halles of kinges...god is sildome zealously honoured' because flatterers controlled princes by pandering to their basest instincts, advancing themselves by doing down the godly. This gave the experiences of Moses at Pharaoh's Court immense contemporary relevance, for Moses had encountered the same kind of satanically inspired opposition that prevailed at Elizabeth's Court. Indeed, even 'in the most clere light of the Gospel', Satan 'will not cease to captivate our mindes and the senses of our rulers' who are 'willingly...ledde even into palpable darknesse without knowledg of their estate', admitting great errors into religion and thus promoting ungodly living.[66]

Thus, like every other part of society, 'carnal courtiers' followed their sensual, earthly instincts, but with the greater scandal that their self-interest ran counter to the full enactment of godly laws.[67] The Scriptures abundantly demonstrated this negative influence, for the commonwealth of Israel declined as true religion became increasingly mixed with worldly elements, and tyrannical government entered. The Old Testament recorded the whole predicament of the True Church under worldly rule, for those self-seeking worldlings who persuaded Amaziah into war against the warnings of the prophets also created a 'mixed' religion by the introduction of idolatry.[68] Their fatal lack of insight into the role of true religion, which under godly rulers provided the firmest support for the magistrate, led them to embrace worldly policies which always brought 'gret trobles and calamityes...as by the manifest histories is esie to be perceived', said Harrison. Another prince of Jewry also provoked God's anger by confusing temporal and ecclesiastical rule 'at the instigation of some of his fetching hedded courtiers' who fed 'his desirous humour' to serve their own turns. Yet these courtiers received due punishment for their disobedient disregard of God's delimitation of the princely office, in the disobedience of their inferiors, and 'if our christian princes could onely lerne to find out soche flatering chapmen' then they would avoid God's wrath and 'assure themselves of the hartes of all their

---

[65] Harrison wanted the Cross in Cheapside converted into a pasquine (after the classical model) and a quarter day set aside 'for soch as wold with a Visor on ther face, note ther soch thinges as thei shold know worthy reformation'. No doubt Harrison would have elbowed his way to the front to inform 'the higher powers', 'because the best of all thinges is onely reported to them' (ibid., fos. 146r–v).

[66] Ibid., fos. 41r–v, 160v, 119r, ibid., fo. 137r.

[67] For example on adultery (ibid., fo. 154r).

[68] Ibid., fo. 78v. Similarly 'wicked and atheisticall courtiers which made none or very small accompt of true relligion in respect of worldly pompe and vanitie' persuaded Ahab to stop the ceremonies of true religion (ibid., fo. 83v).

subiectes'.[69] Until princes and courtiers obeyed God's law and established pure religion undefiled by the traditional preoccupations of contemporary society, they could not enjoy the security which those traditional relationships were supposed to achieve. For like other Protestants Harrison conceived social order as a reflection of the perfect divine order which worldly rulers failed to observe, thus laying themselves open to the threat of divine retribution for their disobedience.

This well-meaning piety can be too easily dismissed as irrelevant to the more realistic preoccupations of sixteenth-century political thought. Such a reaction would overlook Harrison's preoccupation with the True Church, and the fact that his fear of 'policy' broadly reflected the assumptions of other evangelical Protestants. More importantly, we should recognise that their outlook owed much to their reactions to Scriptural history, and most importantly that they applied that framework to the present because contemporary politics seemed to rehearse the perpetual experiences of the True Church. Israel thus defined the ungodly courtier as sensual, indifferent to any religion and lacking those divinely given talents required for his godly office.[70] Such were the men responsible for the introduction of idolatry into the Temple, marking the advent of confused government in Israel. Such were the men who refused to believe Christ when the True Church stood in complete contrast to the Church of Cain, respectively represented by Christ's disciples and the secular state. Thus while Christ preached and reformed the Church, the Roman authorities, like their sixteenth-century counterparts, bought and sold ecclesiastical offices, 'so that now not gods law but mens avarice was universally regarded'. The imperial, Gentile authority which had destroyed the godly commonwealth also totally depraved the religion of the visible Church, so that Israel in the time of Christ exemplified an antichristian society. For 'when the Lordes portion came ones into these courtiers handes (who supposed heaven and yerth to be now in their arbitrement and disposition)', said Harrison, 'it was not long after ere thei and all ther gaines with the state of the commonwealth fell likewise into ruine...a due reward for these their unrighteous dealings'.[71]

The providential pattern which established the contemporary relevance of these conclusions continued to work itself out after Christ. Constantine had brought the previously persecuted Church into the orbit of the Court, so

---

[69] Ibid., fo. 126v, of course a Protestant commonplace.

[70] Jason obtained the High Priesthood by simony although unfit for the office, and led the priests away from the holy sacrifices 'to sense plaie' and Hellenism, so that they 'became Idolatrous ruffians, sword plaiers and ribaldes', completing Satan's subversion of the visible Church (ibid., fo. 124r).

[71] Ibid., fo. 139v. For contemporary courtiers 'Divinitie is policye, their zeale is Atheisme and their God is the devill', announced the radical, John Dove (*A Confutation of Atheisme* (Edward Allde for Henry Rockett: London, 1605), pp. 4–5).

that courtly influence accelerated the prophetic decline of the True Church into a 'mixed' religion. For Harrison the major figure of Chrysostom symbolised the perennial enmity between the godly and those around the prince, a contrast which resulted from Chrysostom's conscious emulation of Old and New Testament prophets. Putting the Word above his friendship with the Empress, Chrysostom preached a Court sermon against those who lived without fear of God and who 'confounded...religion and Atheisme vertue and vice and heaven and hell as if thei were Lordes of all'. Chrysostom's preaching dramatised the perpetual, stark contrast between 'policy' and the Word, for worldly courtiers always 'dispose thestate of the churche and minister after their owne mindes, as thoughe god and his word were to be ordered by them'. Political actions should be guided by Scriptural criteria, not worldly human reason. Chrysostom suffered exile for his attack, and Harrison read the entire episode in terms of the prophetic model established in the Old Testament.[72] Heresies flourished once the nobility took an interest in the Church, for they 'never regard the conditions but the person of soche as are about them', as Harrison shrewdly pointed out.[73] The way in which the Arians exploited this fatal weakness paralleled the process by which private profit prevailed over the common weal, for they bribed 'the nobility and their reteiners' to petition the prince to further their 'mallicious causes', and they succeeded because the nobility concerned themselves more with the profits of clientage than with 'whether any relligion went forward or not'.[74] Pagan idolatry, heresy and popery all epitomised for Harrison the satanic nature of the Church of Cain, which appeared also in that courtly interference whereby the demands of the present for worldly order and social cohesion placed restrictions upon obedience to God's absolute commands.

Where the Word demanded a lively faith, political considerations imposed the dead and mixed order which betrayed Satan's influence. Some kings of England had attempted to oppose papal usurpations, but the barons, seduced by their confessors, undermined their resistance and hastened the rise of Antichrist.[75] The final satanic parody of the godly commonwealth appeared

---

[72] Arguing that Chrysostom, as a member of the covenant line, compared his exile with the fate of Isaiah, Daniel, Stephen and John the Baptist, and was therefore 'a man armed and redy to the feld', 'and so shold all christiens that are christiens unfeignedly' follow the repeated examples of the covenant line and let no punishment deter them from denouncing evil (TCD MS 165, fos. 171v–172r).

[73] Ibid., fo. 170r. Note the implication for Lord Cobham and his crypto-papist chaplain (above, p. 144).

[74] Ibid., fo. 160v; the advancement of the Eutychian heresy by similar means reminded Harrison that 'often times the higher powers being bribed become servaunts unto the bribours without regard of the goodnesse of their cause and princes againe seduced by nobility do not alwaies regard so moch wherin as how thei maie do them pleasure that sue unto them' (ibid., fo. 174v). Later, orthodox courtiers adopted heresy to flatter a heterodox prince (ibid., fo. 176v).

[75] A recurrent feature after John, e.g., under Henry III (ibid., fo. 312v).

when courtiers abandoned their proper calling to become priests, and priests became courtiers, producing an absurd mixture. Noble warrior bishops mocked Christ's humility, for 'thei comonly regard not somoche the flocke of christ as their owne honor welfare and pompous maintenauns of a temporall port and countenauns'.[76] At this point when dealing with the same theme in the *Description*, either Harrison or Holinshed realised the need for caution, for the 'Chronology' discussed the malevolent influence of the Court upon religion more forcefully than the *Description*. Although in the latter Harrison drew a well-known contrast between the sober attire of the Elizabethan clergy and 'the blind Sir Johns' who resembled 'a peacock that spreadeth his tail when he danceth before the hen', only the 'Chronology' attributes this to 'soche roysting preestes as served in the court', and who opposed all attempts at reform.[77] The 'Chronology' also appears more outspoken about other aspects of noble behaviour, for the *Description* manages to skirt around the fact that the nobility had abandoned their former temperate drinking habits, but the 'Chronology' connects it to their general disobedience towards God which had contributed to the degeneration of English society from the ideal form. For their former 'frugalitie is almost growen into contempt' and now noble hospitality 'produceth nothing more then dronkenesse whoredome and therwithall all other maintenauns of sinne, and nedless waste of the giftes of god which might be better employed if more respect were had from whens thei came and to which end thei were bestowed upon us'.[78] Contemporary noble behaviour represented a waste of those abilities which God had provided for the inferior magistrates to build up the godly commonwealth.

Harrison therefore perceived the contemporary nobility within the context of their often troubled relationship with the True Church, and his limitation of noble status to those inferior magistrates who obeyed God's calling and used their authority to further true religion shows how, like other Protestants, he developed the ideas of the most outspoken humanists in a new direction. Like those humanists who criticised the conventional confusion of nobility with inheritance and wealth, he protested that 'it is only vertu which shold be mother to that estate', but Harrison's definition of virtue owed much less to the classical criteria reiterated by the humanists than to his conception of the role which God had called the nobles to play in the ideal, but essentially static, godly commonwealth. The northern humanists especially stressed that all rulers should strive to achieve godliness, but their

---

[76] Ibid., fo. 208v.
[77] *Description*, ed. Edelen, pp. 36–7, where Harrison asks the reader to 'peruse well my Chronology ensuing'; cf. TCD MS 165, fo. 277r, and see Parry, 'Harrison and Holinshed's Chronicles', pp. 794–805, on this connection, made after 1576.
[78] TCD MS 165, fo. 62r. George Withers also implied that courtly 'voluptuousnesse' incurred the curse of Eccles. 10.16–17 (*An ABC*, sigs. G2v–G3v); TCD MS 165, fos. 70v–71r.

definition of that attribute gave far greater room to free will and human reason than Harrison could allow.[79] He tied nobility far more closely to actions which helped to build up the True Church and commonwealth as the Scriptures portrayed them, and required obedience to those revealed criteria. This definition produced a much more critical tone in the 'Chronology', where Harrison discussed the historical encounters between the True Church and the nobility, than in the *Description*, which treated them in more conventional, contemporary terms. Thus, discussing the sale of coats of arms in the *Description*, he concluded that 'No man hath hurt by it but himself who peradventure will...bear a bigger sail than his boat is able to sustain'. Dealing with the same corruption in the 'Chronology', he held more fiercely to 'the honor of the calling', condemning the fact that for the heralds 'lucre of the fee' outweighed any service to the commonwealth.[80] Leaving aside the interesting question of Harrison's self-censorship in the *Description*, we can see how in the 'Chronology' he found great contemporary significance in the degeneration of nobility from its original role in the commonwealth. For although 'the first originall of true gentilitie' had been military service which qualified a man to be councillor to a beneficent ruler, 'afterward it did degenerate in many to plaine tyranny, eche noble man seeking to be without compasse of law', as Harrison believed they did still.[81] This degeneration in aristocratic behaviour from its original ideal not only reflected on contemporary ills and involved a change from virtue to inheritance as the definition of nobility, but also epitomised the contrast between the contemporary commonwealth and its ideal godly model.

Indeed, where contemporary political moralists used edifying classical examples to remind all rulers of their subjection to the law, Harrison cited a similar story, about the creator of a penal statute becoming its first victim, to show that noblemen in particular, despite their high social position, remained subject to the law. Harrison feared that if the 'peres of a kingdome' broke the law, 'the inferior sort will follow', and therefore although he proposed 'to write a Chronology and no exhortatory treatize', he felt it necessary to emphasise the significance of this moral example, for 'surely whatsoever myne indevoure it is souche a glasse for my countrymen of all estates to behold and loke upon as the like againe can not be found amonge all the Pagane writers in the world'. Because it conformed to the Scriptural criteria of noble behaviour this example became a godly admonition to contemporary peers, although Harrison knew that he was entering deep waters, and a similar example 'I might exemplifie in mine owne time, but

---

79 Ibid., fos. 11v–12r. The Utopians, for example, lived a Christian life without Christian revelation (*Utopia*, ed. E. Surtz (New Haven and London, 1964), pp. 53, 130–2, 141–3).

80 *Description*, ed. Edelen, p. 114; cf. TCD MS 165, fos. 11v–12r, 23r. Harrison's contrast between the true knights and 'carpet knightes' of the Hundred Years War gave a chivalric tone to the humanist argument (ibid, fos. 346r, 347r).   81 Ibid., fo. 19r.

I dare not, wherfore I must let other gesse, whereat I shote herein'. His self-censorship testifies to the seriousness with which he expected these views to be taken. Thus where Calvinist resistance theorists worked hard to prove that the prince had to obey the positive laws of his country because they reflected divine law, the arrogance of the English nobility caused Harrison to emphasise that the inferior magistrate on whom those theorists relied for redress also had to obey the law.[82] Where the nobility led in ignoring the rule of law, their retainers followed, 'thinking it sufficient buckler for them against all men (whatsoever their dedes be) to get a livery on their backes and badge on their sleeves'. The more cautious *Description* did not dwell upon the lawlessness of the inferior magistrates and their followers.[83]

Harrison also underlined the providential historical dimensions of another current humanist argument about the role of the nobility. Northern humanists had criticised the nobility for forsaking their martial calling and soiling their hands with agriculture and trade. Harrison reiterated this fixed picture of society in his *Description*, which lamented that those who 'degenerate from true nobility' in this way 'must nedes prove in time the confusion of that country wherein such enormities are exercised'. Yet he also believed that this contemporary complaint fitted into a threatening historical pattern, in the same way that the neglect of education and the decline of preaching formed part of a process leading to the destruction of a commonwealth. In disobeying God's commandments and forsaking their proper calling, a degenerate nobility had repeatedly proved symptomatic of a decaying commonwealth. For example under a timorous queen the Babylonian aristocracy 'betoke themselves to husbandry, pilling their tenauntes by extreme avarice', until her successor 'busied the heddes of his subiectes again' by war. In the most degenerate society, under Antichrist, the clergy had forsaken their proper pastoral calling and revealed their fallen nature by their invasion of agriculture and trade.[84] Thus when some English noblemen reacted to the price inflation by seeking to augment their incomes through direct personal involvement in agriculture and trade, they not only offended against conventional notions of proper aristocratic behaviour. From Harrison's point of view they threatened to bring down upon Elizabethan England the same divine retribution which had been suffered by other commonwealths that had become distorted from God's plan through the pursuit of individual self-interest, as determined by rational criteria. Harrison's intense respect for God's commandments, and his trust in the unchanging nature of divine justice, therefore made integral to his personal

---

[82] Ibid., fos. 42r, 70v–71r; and see Ponet, *Of politike power*, sigs. C6r, C7r.
[83] Retainers received pardons even for hanging offences (TCD MS 165, fo. 349r); cf. *Description*, ed. Edelen, p. 231, which deliberately avoids discussing retainers.
[84] *Description* (1587), pp. 204–6; TCD MS 165, fos. 48v, 349r.

vision of the godly commonwealth the achievement of an ideal but essentially fixed society, within which every estate obeyed God's calling. The contemporary English nobility appeared unable to contribute to the achievement of that vision and therefore laid themselves open to punishment.

The particular political weaknesses upon which Harrison focussed clearly derived more from rational precepts than he wished to acknowledge, but he concentrated upon specific historical examples of commonwealths which he understood to adumbrate the experience of the godly commonwealth in the Old Testament. The experiences of Israel, not rational political theories, established the criteria by which to judge all commonwealths. Thus Harrison gave a detailed explanation for the defeat of the Huns in the seventh century, discovering the same weaknesses which had brought down other nations and which threatened to leave England open to invasion by the forces of Antichrist. This 'commonwealth' interpretation reflects the unworldly reasoning of the Puritan prophet, not objective political explanation, yet its obvious casuistry nevertheless throws important light on Harrison's view of the Elizabethan nobility and his strong conviction that they invited God's wrath because they usually acted in their own interests rather than for the common good. Factions amongst the Hunnish nobility had caused the destruction of the wise and the promotion of fools who 'regarded nothing more than their own welth and authoritie'. The nobility not only sold justice but also entered husbandry which 'made them covetous oppressors of the commonaltie wherby thei were hated'; indeed they 'left of all orderlie keeping of the people in obediens and geving themselves to other trades thei supposed themselves never to have fleced their tenauntes ynoughe' so that their subjects deserted them in the national crisis.[85] This analysis differed from what we would consider historical reality to the same extent that Harrison's vision of contemporary England differed from the objective reality. At least in the 'Chronology', Harrison's Scripturally informed vision forced that reality into a providential, historical dimension where facts took on larger significance and actions received severer judgements, as we have already seen in the contrasting interpretations of noble behaviour in the 'Chronology' and the *Description*.

At least one contemporary example encouraged him not to lose hope, however, and it perhaps reflects Harrison's cautious self-censorship that the one occasion in the *Description* where he did apply stricter criteria to noble behaviour led him to contribute to the myth of the 'good Duke' of Somerset. This underlines how much his viewpoint owed to the tradition developed by the Edwardine preachers, yet he also extended that tradition

---

[85] The suggested remedies echo the humanists: flatterers should be removed, the nobility prevented from entering husbandry and forced into martial pursuits, and encouraged to practise politically vital 'liberality' (ibid., fo. 203v).

by applying it to Robert Dudley as fitting the role of the self-centred courtier who threatened calamity for the commonwealth. In both cases Harrison's perception of a prophetic pattern, rather than the objective facts, dictated his thinking. Harrison's liking for the 'learned and godly Duke of Somerset' whose untimely death he possessively claimed 'took him...from us all', owed much to the belief that the commonwealth always flourished where good learning supported that preaching which, by instilling the duty of godly obedience in all estates, beat off attempted subversion by Satan and Antichrist.[86] Political decline paralleled the growth of ignorance. According to Harrison this lesson, hard learnt in Israel and reiterated in the Byzantine Empire, had been repeated by Somerset in defending University lands against 'greedy gripers'.[87] Somerset thus opposed those self-interested courtiers who would bereave the commonwealth of its chief asset, and aligned himself with that prophetic interpretation of history which commonly asked 'If learning decay...what shall we look for else but barbarism and tumult?'. This consequently justified Somerset's popularity as 'the good Duke', and in Harrison's opinion such evidence of regenerate understanding, intimating membership of the True Church, outweighed evidence of Somerset's wilfulness, self-aggrandisement and arbitrariness, such as his pillaging of St Paul's to build Somerset House. Harrison believed that Somerset House 'should have been well finished and brought to a sumptuous end' if Somerset had lived, and overlooked evidence of the incompetence which brought about his downfall, evidence which Harrison probably encountered.[88] Applying Scriptural rather than worldly criteria, Harrison excused Somerset's pretensions to absolute power because of the godly ends to which Somerset apparently directed that power. On the other hand, Leicester's entirely conventional methods appeared odious because of Harrison's suspicions about his motives.

Harrison's patron, Lord Cobham, had conducted a political vendetta against Leicester for some years before Harrison wrote in the lost Derry 'Chronology' his comments on Leicester's death. Whether or not Cobham had any influence over Harrison's opinion, those comments show that

---

[86] Compare Harrison's reference with that of Somerset's devoted servant, Thomas Norton (*Original Letters Relative to the English Reformation*, ed. H. Robinson (Parker Society: Cambridge, 1846), p. 340).

[87] In an otherwise unrecorded speech which Harrison may have invented to serve this cherished myth (*Description*, ed. Edelen, pp. 226, 80–1).

[88] Ibid., pp. 80–1, 226. One possible source was Sir Thomas Smith, who came to regret his complicity in Somerset's circumvention of the Privy Council, and use of proclamations without reference to statute (Dewar, *Smith*, pp. 59–60, 63, 67). On Somerset's failings see G. R. Elton, 'The Good Duke', in *Studies in Tudor and Stuart Politics and Government* (3 vols. Cambridge, 1974–83), i, pp. 231–7; and D. Hoak, 'Rehabilitating the Duke of Northumberland: Politics and Political Control, 1549–53', in *The Mid Tudor Polity c. 1540–1560*, ed. J. Loach and R. Tittler (London, 1980), pp. 29–51, at pp. 29–35.

Harrison was one Puritan who disliked 'the Puritan Earl'. Indeed his views came perilously close to those of *Leicester's Commonwealth*, a polemic attributed to Robert Parsons, only leaving implicit Parson's explicit charge that her favourites dominated Elizabeth. Harrison claimed in his contemporary note that 'all men, so farre as they durst, reioysed no lesse outwardlie' at the death of Leicester in 1588 than for the victory over the Armada. However, Harrison's portrait concerned itself less with the real details of Leicester's career than with how Leicester fitted an archetypical role. Like the author of *Leicester's Commonwealth*, Harrison emphasised the Earl's similarity to those other pernicious royal favourites, 'Peers Gavestone and Robert Veer, some time Duke of Ireland'.[89] According to this Derry 'Chronology', Leicester fitted the general pattern of the self-interested tyrant, for 'Nothing almost was done, wherein he had not, either a stroke or a commoditie', but TCD MS 165 further shows that Harrison recognised more direct parallels with Gaveston and de Vere in Leicester's 'scraping from the churche and comons, spoile of her maiesties thresure, and sodeine death of his first wife', which 'procured him soche inwarde envie and hatred'.[90]

Although Gaveston and de Vere eventually fared worse than Leicester, this fact did not diminish the force of the historical parallel, which in Harrison's interpretation of providential history gave Leicester's career particularly ominous overtones. Clearly Harrison's definition of tyranny derived more from abstract political reasoning about history than from the Scriptures, but in the first instance the Earl's apparently negative attitude towards the True Church dictated Harrison's interpretation of his actions. Indeed, like other evangelicals Harrison theoretically devalued the importance of reason and insisted that the history of Israel should lead the interpretation of English history, just as the Word generally guided and restrained reason. This explains why he so eagerly seized upon those elements of Somerset's policies which conformed to the standards set in the Old Testament commonwealth, just as he read so much into Elizabeth's actions during her Progress. On the other hand, when he interpreted contemporary England in the light of the continuing struggle between the regenerate and unregenerate, it became correspondingly more important to show how Leicester took the part of the quintessential evil courtier, who set out to seduce the prince and at whose touch true religion would wither and die. Such an

---

[89] McKeen, 'A Memory of Honour', pp. 248–53; Clark, *Kent*, pp. 128–9; *Harrison's Description*, ed. Furnivall, Appendix I, p. lviii–lix. *Leicester's Commonwealth* compared Leicester with Gaveston, de Vere, Spenser and Mowbray, citing similar parallels to the incidents Harrison mentioned (Campbell, 'Historical Patterns', pp. 145–6).

[90] Gaveston sold royal treasure for his own use (TCD MS 165, fo. 329r), and dissipated Edward II's revenues (fo. 328r), while de Vere divorced his first wife to marry a baseborn woman (fo. 347r), gave bad counsel for his own profit (fo. 347v) and favoured the papist clergy over the laity (fo. 348r).

insight enabled Harrison to ignore Leicester's known sympathy for the godly, and his diligence in fulfilling even minor sinecures.[91]

Had it been published, the 'Chronology' in TCD MS 165 might have raised a few eyebrows because of its unequivocal attacks upon the religious standing of the nobility. However, the Derry 'Chronology' especially would have fallen foul of the Privy Council's sensitivity to attacks on royal favourites, revealed in their punitive measures against Holinshed's *Chronicles* in 1587 and particularly Leicester's *Commonwealth*.[92] Harrison was on safer ground in his discussion of Parliament, which he subjected to the same examination as other institutions and individuals in the commonwealth. Adopting the perspective of the True Church and its social corollary, the godly commonwealth, made Harrison extremely sensitive to the evidence consequently revealed which suggested that England possessed not only a 'semi-reformed' Church but also a semi-reformed society. He therefore examined Parliament to see whether it contributed to the reform of those deficiencies which in other commonwealths had grown into enormities sufficient to bring down divine punishment. Thus although Harrison's account of Parliament completely depended upon Sir Thomas Smith's *De Republica Anglorum*, his interpretation of its powers shows his greater concern with its role in furthering reformation and resurrecting the godly commonwealth.[93] Like Smith, Harrison asserted Parliament's legislative supremacy and the notion that in theory it represented all men, although as a cleric he felt it necessary to point out that the clergy made up one of the three estates with the nobility and laity, whereas Smith did not mention Convocation.[94] Smith did give a long list of Parliament's areas of competence, amongst which he simply mentioned that it 'establisheth formes of religion', and 'giveth formes of succession to the crowne'. Harrison's description differs in several important respects. Perhaps more influenced by vague constitutionalist notions than Tudor reality, he announced first and more stridently than Smith that 'This house hath the most highe and absolute power of the realm, for therby kings and mighty princes have from time to time been deposed from their thrones'. Then

---

91 W. J. Jones 'The Exchequer of Chester in the last years of Elizabeth I', in *Tudor Men and Institutions*, ed. Slavin, pp. 123–70, at pp. 129–31, shows how Leicester used a minor office to provide the genuine equity sought by Harrison.

92 A. T. Castanien, 'Censorship and historiography in Elizabethan England: the Expurgation of Holinshed's Chronicles' (unpublished Ph.D. dissertation, University of California, Davis, 1970), pp. 261–72, and Campbell, 'Historical Patterns', p. 149, for the Council's measures against *Leicester's Commonwealth*.

93 Book II, Chapter 7, 'Of the High Court of Parliament and Authority of the Same', added to the 1587 edition (*Description*, (1587), pp. 173–6; ed. Edelen, pp. 149–62); cf. *De Republica Anglorum*, ed. Dewar, pp. 78–85, although Harrison briefly discussed Parliamentary law-making in 1577 – *Description* (1577), fo. 99v.

94 *Description* (1587), p. 173; ed. Edelen, pp. 149–150; cf. ibid., p. 170.

summarising Smith's other details, he went straight on to claim that Parliament 'either disannulled or reformed corrupted religion'.[95] These two godly functions of correcting princes and supporting true religion are thus made to appear to be the objectives of those legislative procedures which Harrison then copied verbatim from Smith, a significant distortion of Smith's original intention.

The 'Chronology' belies Harrison's apparent confidence about Parliament's godly role in the *Description*. In the former, Harrison showed that while at times Parliament could be used for godly ends, it could also be manipulated against true religion, partly because the Scriptures gave it no definite role in the godly commonwealth so far as Harrison could see. Like many contemporaries, he traced the powers of the Elizabethan Parliament in unaltered form through the medieval period, and found its membership under Canute little different from that under Elizabeth.[96] Under princes determined to achieve some measure of Church reform, Parliament could reduce or abolish papal exactions. Under Richard II it attained something equivalent to the sixteenth-century Reformation by enacting that papal power 'shall no more extend over the Ocean', abolishing appeals to Rome and banning papal bulls.[97] Under the same enlightened prince it passed a series of measures for the benefit of the commonwealth.[98] When a prince trod on too many clerical toes, however, the clergy used their influence over 'some of the superstitious and unstable hedded Barons' to take up Parliamentary time with debate about 'the great charter, thinking that waie to bridle the king'.[99] Magna Carta merely reflected the unceasing attempts of Antichrist to subvert all movement towards the godly ideal, and so, although Harrison wrote in the 1587 *Description* with apparent confidence about Parliament's role, a few years later the Derry 'Chronology' recorded his apprehension that extremists were manipulating the most carnal of Commons members, the outlaws, against the best interests of the Church. Although wiser heads prevailed both in 1589 and 1593, and Parliament fulfilled its traditional function and passed the usual number of 'good profitable lawes', history showed that here, as among princes and inferior magistrates, carnal reason posed the greatest threat to the True Church.[100]

---

[95] *De Republica Anglorum*, ed. Dewar, p. 78; *cf. Description* (1587), p. 173; ed. Edelen, p. 149.

[96] Canute's Parliament comprised 'his papes or Byshops and Erles, vice lordes, vicares, hundreders, Aldermen, prefectes, prepositi Barons, Valvasors and towne greves' (TCD MS 165, fo. 235r). The 'old estate of the Israelites' involved consultation with 'the congregation or company of citizens' sitting 'as it were in common counsell', but this type of government, despite its reminder of Harrison's London origins, represented something less than the ideal under the Judges (ibid., fo. 102r).

[97] Richard II's Parliament legislated against monastic impropriation of benefices and subjected bishops to the King, touching their temporalities (ibid., fo. 348r). See ibid., fo. 328r, for similar actions under Edward I.

[98] Ibid., fo. 347v; Harrison clearly associated the two ideas.   [99] Ibid., fo. 336v.

[100] *Harrison's Description*, ed. Furnivall, Appendix I, pp. lix–lx.

Harrison's concentration on the sufferings endured by the True Church in this world, and the fixed parameters for the godly commonwealth which emerged from that experience, left him profoundly disenchanted with existing social and political structures which failed to conform to that ideal. Yet that disenchantment turned to fervent praise when he felt able to discern in some part of those structures actions which appeared to obey God's commandments in the same manner that the Elect covenant line had obeyed them. These moments of recognition rescued Harrison from an impotent limbo from which he could not otherwise escape by obedience to conventional worldly powers. For within this minimal political vision, the carnal reason which determined the nature of worldly powers seemed antithetical to the interests of true religion. By this same criterion, Harrison consequently concluded that the common people also menaced the survival of the True Church. Indeed, they posed a potentially greater threat not only because of their greater numbers but also because of the stubbornness with which they held fast to their delusions. Therefore, although he did not trust the inferior magistrates and sided with the oppressed in appealing to the prince for redress, Harrison did not expect the oppressed to bring about godly reformation when the prince failed in his duty. He did not lose faith in existing institutions to the extent of sharing John Field's despairing conclusion that 'the multitude and people…must bring the discipline to pass which we desire'.[101]

Like the Edwardine preachers, Harrison's fear of the malevolent influence of worldly magnates on the *societas christiana* was only surpassed by his real horror of the social upheaval which a too forceful demand for godly rule would produce. To that extent he shared Matthew Parker's concern that a reign of terror would result if subjects discussed 'what is tyranny', and tried 'to discern whether his prince, his landlord, his master is a tyrant', but his standard of judgement appears more closely tied to Scriptural models than was Parker's. Harrison also followed Scriptural teachings in his commonplace, selective approach to the poor, an approach which has been crudely described as class hatred.[102] As with other Protestants, Harrison's sympathy with the growing numbers of the innocent impoverished did not extend to 'idle beggars through their own default', who deserved severe punishment because 'they are all thieves and caterpillars in the commonwealth, and by the Word of God not permitted to eat, sith they do but lick the sweat from the true laborers' brows' and bereave the deserving poor of their due.[103]

---

[101] Quoted in Collinson, *Religion of Protestants*, pp. 189–90.
[102] *Correspondence of Matthew Parker*, ed. J. Bruce and T. T. Perowne (Parker Society: Cambridge, 1853), p. 61; cf. p. 437. See C. Hill, *Society and Puritanism in Pre-Revolutionary England* (London, 1969), pp. 265, 268–87, which ignores the Puritan deference to Scriptural attitudes towards the poor, preferring to see their remedies as merely fearful repression.
[103] *Description*, ed. Edelen, pp. 182–3.

Like other 'commonwealth' writers, Harrison took a leaf out of Thomas More's *Utopia* when he similarly condemned the nobility for their 'superfluous heaps' of serving men who 'give themselves to idleness that otherwise would be brought to labor and live in order like subjects'.[104] Yet one should hardly expect Harrison, the author of an account 'Of degrees of people' conventional enough to be plagiarised by Sir Thomas Smith, to go further with More and argue not only that virtue defined the truest nobility but also that the poorest were the most virtuous. In fact, Harrison apparently identified in social terms with the 'honest gentlemen, citizens, wealthy yeomen' who he believed had most to fear from redundant retainers, not the destitute with whom those retainers competed for the limited generosity of the better-off.[105] Only the day labourers and poor husbandmen amongst his own parishioners seemed to Harrison to offer any prospect that this 'fourth and last sort of people' might be made godly against all historical evidence. For Harrison's recognition that self-seeking superiors unjustly oppressed the commons, like his nostalgic admiration for the yeomen of England, perhaps derived from an archetype which he applied to his parishioners. But when he considered English society as a whole, that archetype gave way to a more powerful model derived from the history of the True Church.[106] For the covenant line had always struggled against popular idolatry, natural man had always been in the majority, and Elizabethan Protestant preachers seemed to relive this experience in their exhausting attempts to re-establish the True Church despite popular conservatism. Harrison believed that Satan had always been able to delude the carnal reason of most human beings, and this belief dictated his assessment of the Elizabethan masses. He identified with the oppressed godly members of the True Church, not simply with the oppressed.

For although Harrison found individuals amongst the 'last sort of people' who appeared to be true members of Christ's Church, he could not escape the conventional Protestant wisdom that as a body the people were bewitched by idolatry, and that preachers could never hope to overcome either traditional popery or the 'subculture of irreligion' which modern historians have identified as the general reaction to Protestant attacks on folk Catholicism. To a great extent Harrison's belief that the great majority 'incline already towards Atheisme' followed the current rhetorical convention amongst Protestant preachers which identified external, ceremonial belief with the lack of any real religion.[107] His distinction of various qualities

---

[104] Ibid., p. 119; *cf.* More, *Utopia*, ed. Surtz, pp. 21–2.
[105] *Description*, ed. Edelen, p. 119; More, *Utopia*, ed. Surtz, pp. 53–4. Smith, *De Republica Anglorum*, ed. Dewar, pp. 65–77; and see the discussion of this borrowing in Parry, 'Harrison and Holinshed's Chronicles', pp. 802–4.
[106] *Description*, ed. Edelen, pp. 117–20, on the yeomen.
[107] TCD MS 165, fo. 314v; Collinson, *Religion of Protestants*, pp. 190–9, esp. p. 199.

of religious belief following Constantine's corrupting interference in the Church echoed those Puritan analyses which stressed the dangerously neutral religion of the fickle majority who merely followed the prince's religion.[108] Harrison's ministry at Radwinter and Wimbish, in its failure to eradicate the belief in magical practices and to evangelise more than a few individuals, epitomises the narrow appeal of Protestantism's dauntingly intellectual religion, whose moral rigour appeared unattractive beside an easygoing popular religion which defined good behaviour according to commendably human criteria, which nevertheless to Harrison would have encapsulated all the flaws of unregenerate human reason.[109] Even the most rhetorically sentimental Protestant statements about the commons included a caveat against the religious limitations of their reasoning powers. Bale fervently believed that in the last days under sincere preachers the disregarded 'shall utter the hidden wisdom of God to the confusion of the great wise men and sage seniors of this world', but also acknowledged that without instruction in the Word 'the wavering-witted multitude, the slippery and unstedfast number' rushed to obey the Whore of Babylon 'of fear and not of love, so throwing themselves into a most confused chaos or vaut of doubtful dotage'.[110] Harrison continued this tradition of self-conscious populism by defending against the contempt of the 'galliauntes' around the prince those toiling masses 'by whom their estate is mainteined', citing the humanist image of the tree of the commonwealth. Yet he also knew that preachers had to keep a close rein on 'the brainelesse multitude'.[111]

Harrison's own identification with the commons remained within the boundaries set by what he conceived to be the godly commonwealth depicted in the Scriptures. Thus on the one hand while he echoed the peasantry's traditional appeal to the prince against local oppression, he condemned the revolt of 1381 which sought such redress, because that uprising had threatened to destroy the learning vital for the preservation of the godly commonwealth. In itself this reflects the gulf between the Protestant intellectual and the concerns of his audience, but on the other hand the high ideals to which Harrison wished to direct that learning also conflicted with conventional religious assumptions. Godly learning would direct the poor into more dutiful paths, but it would also end what Harrison considered their uncertainty and inconstancy about religion. For the people not only undermined the commonwealth through their disobedience, but also, and more importantly, weakened the cause of true religion because they

[108] TCD MS 165, fo. 163v; Collinson, *Religion of Protestants*, p. 200.
[109] See above, pp. 157–63, Collinson, *Religion of Protestants*, pp. 201–2; and see Calvin on Cain's outward good fellowship – *Commentarie...upon... genesis*, sigs. H8r, I2v.
[110] Bale, *Image of Both Churches*, ed. Christmas, pp. 400–1, 494. Christianson, *Reformers and Babylon*, pp. 18–19, appears to overlook Bale's doubts about the lower orders.
[111] TCD MS 165, fo. 114v.

'ronne hedlong where thei se the prince to begin to leane', a tendentious interpretation of what most Englishmen would have regarded as a dutiful obedience to the Prayer Book.[112] Harrison sought to defend not the status quo but his ideal of a fully reformed Church and commonwealth, which was threatened both by princely self-interest and popular willingness to follow the prince to destruction. Godly, learned preaching would teach both prince and people to pursue the proper ends of human society – chiefly the nourishment of the True Church. Under the rule of the Word both sedition and sycophancy would be replaced by an equilibrium between prince and people which would exclude divisive oppression.[113]

Harrison's historical interpretation therefore justified the Puritan assertion that not so much the turbulence of the people as their weakness for idolatry and ignorance of the Word presented the greatest obstacle to the achievement of the reformed ideal. Since the time of Noah, when the inventors of idolatrous ceremonies 'made them so beautifull and full of variety to the eie that the simple people were wonderfully delighted with them', those who wished to control the masses had pandered to their sensuality.[114] After Christ, a godly Emperor who followed Old Testament models in opposing idolatry encountered resistance from 'the brainelesse people…in ther headstrong rage for the quarrell of the Idolles'.[115] Popular religion in Harrison's view revolved around idolatry, for where the people did not follow the prince's will they both clung to traditional pagan ceremonies and 'gredily imbraced' innovations when 'Sathan practized to reduce a christian gentilisme into the churche of christ'. Harrison's eradication of rogation processions and other traditional religious observances in Radwinter can thus be placed in the context of the contrasting tradition which he was conscious of inheriting from the Edwardine preachers, and hence from the covenant line. He attempted to eradicate the remnants of the fleshly Church of Cain and to bring Christian liberty to the poor 'whom anie man may lead whither he will by the bellie, or as Latimer said with beefe, bread and beere'.[116] Harrison's strictures against church-ales, as with so many Puritan complaints, are not borne out by the records of the Church Courts, perhaps because of their well-known administrative weaknesses, but his other views are perhaps more important in that they straddle the divide which it has been suggested

---

[112] Ibid., fo. 226v.

[113] Whitgift discounted the seductiveness of idolatry and flatly blamed 'the people' who 'are commonly bent to novelties and to factions, and most ready to receive that doctrine that seemeth to be contrary to the present state, and that inclineth to liberty' (*Works*, ed. Ayre, i, p. 466).

[114] TCD MS 165, fo. 28r; for example, the Romans (ibid., fo. 96r).

[115] Logically this contradicts the idea that the people always followed the prince's religion (ibid., fo. 211r).

[116] Ibid., fos. 127v, 253v; *Description* (1587), p. 57, referring to the papists using such devices 'to linke in the commons unto them'.

existed between the metropolitan concerns of much Elizabethan 'complaint-literature' and the more old-fashioned Protestant obsession with abolishing traditional communal pastimes. Harrison condemned both rural entertainments and London theatre-going, a range of targets which reflects both his attempts to Protestantise his Essex parishioners and his acquaintance with evangelical and Court circles in the capital.[117]

Both types of activity revealed the common people's dangerous susceptibility towards satisfying their carnal desires rather than living in obedience to the Word, which vitiated any claims they might have to maintain that sober balance between all estates which distinguished the godly commonwealth. Writing perhaps the earliest reference to purpose-built theatres in London, Harrison added to the growing body of evangelical Protestant complaints about players who 'presume to deale even with the holy scriptures' on the stage. The early Reformers had found drama a useful medium for conveying their anti-papal message, but Harrison could not believe that 'plaiers and parasites, minstrelles, and maskers were sent by Christ to preach unto the people'. Some Protestants could still defend this particular use of visual images as a useful supplement to the growing evangelical emphasis on the Word, and Harrison knew that his attack on those who 'make those Poperipe and ungracious toies equall unto good sermons' would 'offend some who wold seme to be wise and zealous with the truth'. Yet he asked them to consider that not only had the Word been 'brought from a pulpet to a stage but also that ther are certeine theatres, or odde houses as thei call them builded for the same' which bred theft and adultery. The whole development only emphasised how carnal reason and human sensuality provided Satan with the means to distort the commonwealth from its godly purposes and thus weaken the True Church. For 'soche is Sathan that in the most clere light of the Gospell [he] will not cease to captivate our mindes and the senses of our rulers', causing them to admit 'most grosse errors and willingly to be ledde even into palpable darknesse with out knowledge of their estate'. Returning to the same subject much later in the Derry 'Chronology', Harrison harped upon the theme of the theatres as 'semenaries of impiety' and 'houses of baudrie'.[118] Yet he also regarded them as symptomatic of a disobedient commonwealth, since 'It is an evident token of a wicked time when plaiers wexe so riche that they can build suche houses', and their toleration only emphasised the distance between what God commanded and what Englishmen did.[119]

Harrison also found contemporary society distorted from its ideal form

---

[117] Emmison, *Elizabethan Life: Morals*, p. 275.

[118] TCD MS 165, fo. 137v; Collinson, *Religion of Protestants*, p. 234; *Harrison's Description*, ed. Furnivall, Appendix I, p. liv.

[119] Ibid., p. liv; 'our plaiers have soch frendship of erth and ashes to uphold them that god and his gospell hath no power to pull them downe' (TCD MS 165, fo. 104r).

in many of its economic relationships. Like the earlier humanists and many other Puritans, he attributed this degeneration to the individual pursuit of self-interest at the expense of the common good, and accordingly demanded that the general welfare should take precedence. He therefore concentrated on those economic activities which reflected the selfish and heedless pursuit of personal gain. Yet he also saw self-interest in a different context from the humanists, for he regarded it as an aspect of human reason and free will which Satan had manipulated in order to destroy that static godly society in which the interests of the True Church predominated. Satan sought to replace this with a corrupt society within which men could be more easily seduced into pursuing those worldly ends which coincided with their destructive self-interest. Therefore, although we are no longer burdened with a 'commonwealth' party, we should notice Harrison's belief that some of the many individuals who contributed to the 'commonwealth' tradition belonged to the covenant line, and that they had propounded a vision of society entirely antipathetic to that of the satanic Church of Cain.[120] We have seen that he regarded Thomas Cromwell and the Duke of Somerset as godly rulers, and praised the preaching of Latimer, Cranmer and Ridley, and he also had a high regard for other Edwardine martyrs such as John Hooper.[121] Harrison's relationships with Edwardine stalwarts who had survived those heady years, men such as Robert Recorde and Sir Thomas Wroth, perhaps had some foundation in a shared outlook on society. Recorde wrote on 'the image of a perfect commonwealth', a work which Harrison could have seen.[122] Wroth had been a Marian exile at Strasbourg, where he befriended Grindal, and Harrison's *Description* made special mention of Wroth, who provided another personal link between the Edwardine 'commonwealth-men' and Elizabethan Puritanism by his patronage of the godly.[123]

While the spirit of their arguments clearly owed much to earlier humanists, the Edwardine preachers and the Elizabethan Puritans also shared an intense awareness of the contemporary relevance of the historical experiences of the covenant line, and stressed the responsiblity which that

[120] G. R. Elton demolished the concept of a 'commonwealth party' in 'Reform and the "Commonwealth-Men" of Edward VI's reign', in *Studies*, iii, pp. 234–53.

[121] Harrison misunderstood Cromwell, who sought to channel enlightened self-interest rather than to construct a godly commonwealth by zealous discipline (Elton, 'Commonwealth-Men', p. 237). He called Hooper 'that worthy father and constant martyr of Christ', and referred to Hooper's *An oversight, and deliberacion upon the holy Prophete Jonas* (J. Daye and Wylliam Seres: London, 1550), another example of the Protestant exhortation of princes to obey God's commandments in their calling (TCD MS 165, fo. 86v).

[122] *D. N. B.* s.v. Recorde, Robert; on Harrison's connection with Recorde see Parry 'Puritanism and History', pp. 99–101, and below, p. 306.

[123] C. H. Garrett, *The Marian Exiles* (London, 1966), pp. 344–6; *Description*, ed. Edelen, pp. 279, 426; Collinson, *Puritan Movement*, pp. 264, 340.

history placed on the regenerate individual to act in accordance with the Word. Some historians have tried to limit 'commonwealth' ideas to a specific historical context. Whitney Jones has related them to the emergence of problems reflecting the profound changes occurring within the contemporary economy. In contrast Arthur Ferguson has characterised them as an endearing but dotty obsession, contrasting them with the more practical conclusions of more realistic observers. Neither approach puts 'commonwealth' ideas in their true context, for both ignore the historical assumptions about the True Church which conditioned much Protestant social thinking. If one can make the dubious assumption that an idea has a history, then the history of 'commonwealth' ideas must also deal with current Protestant beliefs about the True Church and its social manifestation, which we have already examined. Perhaps more importantly, we should notice that the obsession of certain evangelical Protestants with the fate of the commonwealth formed part of their wider concern that the Church should be brought to its fully reformed state. From the viewpoint of Protestant 'commonwealth' propagandists, the economic and social evils which they deprecated showed how Antichrist furthered Satan's purposes by ceaselessly working through natural man's appetites to subvert the commonwealth and Church. Thus despite Ferguson's condescending remarks, the 'commonwealth' preachers, who often emerged later as Elizabethan Puritans, approached contemporary evils in complete seriousness from the viewpoint of the Scriptures, for the teachings transmitted by the covenant line offered effective remedies for those evils.[124]

Placing 'commonwealth' ideas in the wider context of enduring Protestant anxieties about the fate of the True Church, threatened by the activities of self-interested individuals in social and economic as well as ecclesiastical matters, gives a fresh insight into their nature. For although Whitney Jones acknowledged the arbitrariness of using 1559 as the terminal date for his discussion of 'commonwealth' arguments, he also claimed that this date marked the end of the 'crisis period' which had given particular urgency to the discussion. He argued that the aftermath of Ket's rebellion, the fall of Somerset and the martyrdom of several outstanding Protestant social reformers had blunted the edge of idealism.[125] This attributes too much to merely contingent historical circumstances, for the Protestant historical interpretation which detected Satan behind selfish behaviour continued to encourage the sense of crisis in which 'commonwealth' ideas flourished.

---

[124] For example, 'Much of what [Robert] Crowley says should not, of course, be taken quite literally. Like many of his fellow preachers and pamphleteers, he speaks habitually in the accents of the prophets, comparing himself to Jonah, Daniel and Christ' (A. B. Ferguson, *The Articulate Citizen and the English Renaissance* (Durham, North Carolina, 1965), p. 265). This misses the whole thrust of the Puritan argument.

[125] W. R. D. Jones, *The Tudor Commonwealth 1529–59* (London, 1970), p. 42.

Harrison, for example, mixed 'Puritan' and 'commonwealth' ideals in one programme: 'I would wish that I might live no longer than to see four things in this land reformed, that is the want of discipline in the church, the covetous dealing of most of our merchants in the preferment of the commodities of other countries and the hindrance of their own', the abolition of Sunday markets and the restoration of woodland. Like other Elizabethan Puritans he related economic problems and the resultant distress to an apocalyptic scheme, and did not abandon that scheme in better times.[126]

This connection can best be seen if we concentrate on one aspect of Harrison's 'commonwealth' ideas, for although Harrison described marketing methods in more detail than Latimer, his understanding of market forces seems no greater. Only once in this large area of discussion did Harrison make the conceptual link between human actions and impersonal market forces that would enable him to understand the emerging new economy. Otherwise Harrison's comments only differed from previous complaints about the neglect of Christian values in his greater experience of the market place, itself liable to produce a more zealous condemnation, and his new appreciation of wealth as a necessity for the magistrate to defend the Reformation.[127] At least, this is so if we consider his *Description* in isolation from the 'Chronology'. When we follow Harrison's original intention and read the two works side by side, we restore the prophetic, historical dimension of the *Description*. Now we can see that Harrison discussed English society in the light of an historical process which had revealed many different facets of the godly society at different times.

The boundaries of the static hierarchical society of devout and industrious harmony envisaged by Harrison and other 'commonwealth' writers can be conveniently summarised in Thomas Becon's prayer that God would 'only grant me a necessary living'.[128] While this ideal of abstemious frugality accurately reflected the restrictions upon consumption imposed by a delicately balanced economy, it also reflected the assumption repeated by Harrison 'that God hath bestowed sufficient commodities upon every country for her own necessity', and that outside certain recognisable limits the pursuit of conspicuous consumption represented disobedience to God and threatened to disrupt society.[129] The proper distribution of the natural resources

---

[126] *Description*, ed. Edelen, pp. 281–2.
[127] Elton, 'Commonwealth-Men', pp. 238–42, on Latimer's emotional condemnation of the evils of an increasingly specialised market; *cf. Description*, ed. Edelen, pp. 247–53, on Harrison's 'own experience', but 'more peradventure than I shall be well thanked for'. See ibid., p. 356, on how raising rents would improve the production of saffron.
[128] Quoted in Jones, *Tudor Commonwealth*, p. 96.
[129] Thus God 'showeth Himself a loving and merciful father unto us, which contrarywise return unto him, in lieu of humility and obedience, nothing but wickedness, avarice, mere contempt

provided by divine grace would therefore lead to the same self-sufficient and just equilibrium in the economy which the proper use of the gifts of grace would produce in civil government and the Church. This ideal drew its force from the contrast which Harrison detected between the society of godly Israel and that encountered amongst the Gentiles, which paralleled the contrast between the True church and the Church of Cain. The covenant line had obediently used the divine gifts of all socially necessary arts and sciences in a manner circumscribed by faith. Later the Hebrews transmitted these skills to the Greeks, so that 'soche as thei name to be authors of these thinges were the first that brought them into ther country' from Israel. Yet immediately that the Greeks approached this knowledge outside the restraints of true faith they distorted it and used it in an increasingly divergent manner, because only faith ensured the proper use of this knowledge, God 'never ceasing to increase ther mindes in wisdome that have alredy by his grace lerned the first point of wisdome, that is to fere the Lorde'. Without this faithful understanding the Gentiles quickly developed frivolous arts 'for the maintenauns of vaine pompe and curiositie and porte', while in contrast the Elect, enlightened by their true faith, 'sought after no such voluptuous trades, neither gave themselves to serche for anymore than was necessary for the competent maintenauns of themselves'.[130] Harrison considered the social behaviour of the covenant line to be normative for his own times, as an important defence against the kind of behaviour which Satan had encouraged amongst the Gentiles and now sought to make general in England. Thus, Harrison discovered within the history of the True Church many lessons about current economic ills, such as enclosures. For that contemporary phenomenon represented the unfettered, unregenerate use of divinely given resources, ignoring the boundaries which true faith had set upon their exploitation.[131]

Harrison's discussion of enclosures also clearly shows how rational criteria influenced his Scriptural interpretation, for he applied the reasoning of earlier humanist 'commonwealth' arguments to the text. Yet while Harrison's approach to the Scriptures paralleled the humanist approach to classical texts, Harrison assumed that the Scriptures provided a kind of knowledge inaccessible to unregenerate human reason, and that in fact unaided human reason only produced those contemporary evils which he condemned by reference to the covenant line. Generally insensitive to the effect of historical context on human nature, humanists read their contemporary circumstances

---

of His will, pride, excess, atheism, and no less than Jewish ingratitude' (*Description*, ed. Edelen, pp. 364–5).

[130] TCD MS 165, fo. 44av; 'if any arte or skill nedefull for mans necessite do flourish in our times I doubt not but it did the like in these daies' (ibid., fo. 4r).

[131] Ibid., fo. 5v, on the carnal abuse of divine gifts.

back into the past which they imagined had created their sources, and returned from those sources anxious to recreate those idealised historical circumstances in their own society. For Protestants such as Harrison their deep sense of responsibility to recreate the ideal society of the covenant line described by the Scriptures overcame any awareness of objective differences between past and present; indeed, it dominated their interpretation of their sense impressions and made them suspect any reality which did not conform to Scriptural criteria. Harrison's discussion of enclosures therefore shows how he subjected his rational interpretation of objective contemporary facts to the prior dictates of revelation. Here also the Protestant insistence that the Spirit could reveal itself through the Word directly to the believer, without human interference, becomes a matter of interpreting the Scriptures without adapting them to justify present circumstances. Richard Hooker later exposed the self-deceptions of this approach, but for Harrison the present merely continued the history of the covenant line, so that he believed that he had not made the Scriptures conform to contemporary rational criteria.

Yet although Harrison's condemnation of enclosures shows that his reason did impinge upon revelation, perhaps a more important influence on his reasoning was the general historical context unearthed by his lengthy and painstaking reading of the Scriptures. For he had to choose between two interpretations of contemporary behaviour, to decide whether enclosure provided a welcome check to accelerating population growth in an already overcrowded country, or whether it caused an absolute fall in the population. His answer conformed to the lesson taught by the covenant line in their ceaseless struggle with the Church of Cain, that fertility provided the means by which the number of the Elect would be furnished and the True Church built up by their godly lives. Therefore enclosures aided Satan and Antichrist in their attempts to subvert the True Church, for by working through debased human appetites Satan sought to inhibit fertility and diminish the number of the Elect. We have already seen in discussing Harrison's attitude to Merlin's prophecies that observing the actual process of enclosure during his ministry at Radwinter probably heightened Harrison's awareness of its evil consequences, especially since as a right-thinking 'commonwealth' man and official of the Archdeacon's Court Harrison already knew the degenerate state of Elizabethan Essex.[132] Enclosures also acquired sinister significance through Harrison's associating them with the 1588 prophecy, a sombre nexus discussed above. That prophecy encouraged anxieties about rural

---

[132] Smith, *A Discourse of the Common Weal of this Realm of England*, ed. M. Dewar (Charlottesville, 1969), p. 50; *Description* (1587), p. 112. The manor roll of Bendish Hall, Radwinter, records fines for hedgebreaking in 1564 (E.R.O., D/DK M37), In 1610 the 21 acres of 'Walden laye', part of the Radwinter glebe land, were 'now devided into three partes and sett with quicke sett by the Parsons successively' (E.R.O., D/DVv 21) – could Harrison himself have been an encloser?

unemployment and fears about the effect of depopulation upon national defence, and this sense of crisis further justified fears about the immediate future.[133]

Enclosers therefore tempted the divine wrath, for they caused that depopulation which 'is the destruction of a kingdom'. The 'great plenty of corn and cattle...beside a more copious procreation of human issue' had been diminished by the encroachment of enclosing graziers on common land and the creation of game parks, great causes 'of the ruin of a commonwealth'.[134] Courtiers who promoted overseas colonisation, including Harrison's Essex neighbour Sir Thomas Smith, frequently claimed that England had never been more densely populated than under Elizabeth. Harrison in contrast preferred local evidence of depopulation to the arguments put forward by enclosers 'that we have already too great store of people in England', for despite the increasing number of beggars 'I know what I say by mine own experience'. In order to sustain this Scriptural interpretation against inescapable evidence of population increase, he had to discount the fact that 'some one cottage be here and there erected of late which is to little purpose'.[135] To support this view Harrison added material to the 1587 *Description* which emphasised the increasingly depressed condition of the Essex peasantry, and claimed that antiquarian research would prove statistically that 'England was never less furnished with people than at this present'.[136] Once more Harrison came into head-on conflict with contemporary reality, for by reading the present in the light of the Scriptural account of antichristian manoeuvres, by finding in the sufferings of the displaced peasantry the perpetual experience of the True Church, Harrison could conclude in line with his historical interpretation that 'this misfortune hath not only happened unto our isle and nation but unto most of the famous countries of the world heretofore, and all by the greedy desire of such as would live alone and only to themselves'.[137]

[133] Even the clear-headed Smith had become alarmed by the pace of enclosure between 1530 and 1550, and feared the dissolution of the state in the *Discourse* of 1548, although he later recovered his composure (*Discourse*, ed. Dewar, pp. 49–52, 118–20, and see above, pp. 128–30, on Harrison's fears).

[134] Converting the country 'from the furniture of mankind into walks and shrouds of wild beasts' was a 'curse of the Lord' (*Description*, ed. Edelen, pp. 256, 257).

[135] A. L. Rowse, *The Expansion of Elizabethan England*, pp. 136, 138–9; D. B. Quinn, 'Sir Thomas Smith (1513–77) and the Beginnings of English Colonial Theory', p. 552; *Description*, ed. Edelen, p. 258, refusing to believe those who argued 'that youth by marrying too soon do nothing profit the country but fill it full of beggers, to the hurt and utter undoing (they say) of the commonwealth' (ibid., p. 256).

[136] Ibid., pp. 257–8. This owed something to similar remarks in Higden's *Polychronicon* and Harrison's research in a manuscript 'sometime written as it seemeth by an undersherriff of Nottingham' under Edward IV. Note his statistical argument about the declining numbers of towns and villages (*Description*, ed. Edelen, pp. 215–16), and his wish to pursue the study in manorial records (ibid., p. 257), for the Domesday survey was now outdated (TCD MS 165, fo. 260v).   [137] *Description*, ed. Edelen, p. 216.

Harrison's refusal to believe the abundant evidence of an increasing population reveals the dangers involved in making a too simplistic connection between his contemporary experiences and his reading of the Scriptures, as well as between current economic problems and 'commonwealth' complaints. His complex vision of the lineaments of the Scriptural commonwealth enabled him to avoid what he considered to be the inherent imperfections of human reasoning about contemporary occurrences, revealed in arguments like Sir Thomas Smith's. Harrison selected from the deceptive sense-impressions of a multifarious contemporary phenomenon that which most consistently conformed to Scriptural teachings. Thus his thought displays a constant interaction between his use of the Scriptures and his interpretation of the present. Once he had achieved this insight into the present, however, Harrison's retrospective temperament led him to regard it as a divine revelation and made it impossible for the present to support a contradictory view.

Harrison therefore cut through the considerable arguments in favour of enclosure by finding in the story of Naboth's vineyard (I Kings 21) a single Scriptural incident which established an invincible historical pattern.[138] Harrison found in the actions described there an impressive demonstration of the distortions which the ungodly, represented here by the idolatrous Jezebel, habitually introduced into the balanced godly economy, typified by Naboth's ancestral vineyard which had other resonances in the Scriptural context. For 'When I reade the historie of Ahab and how Jezabel killed Naboth for his lande and possessions,' said Harrison, 'me thinke that I see a godly admonition therin unto all soch as practize nothing more than to ioyne house to house and land to land and often times after soch a sort as Jezabell did with Naboth'. By countenancing worldly courtiers who seduced him into ungodly beliefs and satanically inspired actions, Ahab not only hindered the increase of the Elect but threatened that stable, fixed and delimited godly commonwealth which the prophet Micah had summarised in the picture of every man under his own vine. The repetition of Jezebel's ungodly selfishness in Elizabethan England would bring the same consequences and invite a similar visitation of God's unchanging justice as had befallen Ahab.[139]

---

[138] Of course enclosures had to be uppermost in Harrison's mind for him to make the connection, for Raleigh interpreted the story as a general warning about 'power severed from piety' (*History* (1687), II.xvi.1). Melanchthon cited it to defend the subject's right to preserve his property from the prince, as did the Geneva Bible (Skinner, *Foundations of Modern Political Thought*, ii, pp. 69, 320*n*. 1).

[139] TCD MS 165, fos. 74r–v: 'by laying house to house and land to land', Henry VIII's nobility created the shortage of soldiers of which he often complained (*Description*, ed. Edelen, p. 257). See Micah 2.1–2 and 4.4 against enclosures, quoted with other prophets by Arthur Dent to show that oppressing the poor by enclosures was one of the many 'signs of condemnation' in the English commonwealth (*The Plaine Mans Path-way to Heaven* (For Robert Dexter: London, 1601), pp. 200–3).

This pattern could be discerned in other nations throughout history, for while in Israel Satan worked through the unregenerate, in Rome he advanced his cause through those who put their private profit before the good of the whole. There the nobility 'by enclosing and eating up of the cominaltie and their comons' created an imbalance in the previously frugal but equitable Roman commonwealth, which eventually led to the fantastic dissipation, the inflation and depopulation that undermined both the Republic and the Empire. Harrison refused to accept excuses for aristocratic avoidance of the *lex agraria*, for 'the truthe is that the noble gentlemen and rich sort of the citizens incroched upon the feldes, pastures and fedings of the comon people' by unlawful usury 'and crafty conveighauns'.[140] Harrison's emphasis on the contrast between aboriginal Italian frugality and later Roman gluttony was not merely the typical complaint of the sour Puritan critic, for it involved the basic economic issue of the distribution of wealth and resources within a society.[141] Harrison essentially believed that the further any society departed from an equitable distribution of resources, the more it came under Satan's influence as that increasing inequality fed upon itself to completely destabilise social relationships. To supply their conspicuous consumption, in Harrison's opinion the most 'pernicious plage that can happen to a kingdome', the Romans created game parks which dispossessed the self-sufficient peasantry and 'in my time ther are more of that kind of inclosures in England than in all Europe'. Once more Harrison found himself isolated by his own regenerate reasoning in an interpretation of contemporary England which was not shared by the great majority of Englishmen still sunk in carnal reason, for 'although it be true yet am I sure that fewe men will beleve me'.[142] By reading Roman history with the eyes of faith, Harrison reorientated it to illuminate contemporary problems, and to emphasise that if England followed Rome towards greater economic inequalities then she would share Rome's fate.

Harrison still felt it possible for England to return to the equitable godly 'competence' which had distinguished Israel during her days of faithful obedience, both because the owners of many parks 'begin now to smell out that such parcels might be employed to their more gain, and therefore some of them do grow to be disparked', and because he could look to the prophetic example of King John.[143] Merlin had prophesied John's godly destruction of enclosures, and Harrison accepted that part of Merlin's

[140] TCD MS 165, fos. 101r–v, 102r.
[141] For example, the Romans made a law against gluttony, and 'I wold the like were made in England' (ibid., fos. 124r–v).
[142] Ibid., fo. 129v, citing Andrew Boorde, *Dietary of Health*, ed. F. J. Furnivall, EETS, extra ser. X (London, 1870), p. 274.
[143] *Description*, ed. Edelen, p. 259; and see *Studies of Field Systems in the British Isles*, ed. A. R. H. Baker and R. A. Butlin (Cambridge, 1973), p. 364, on this reversal of enclosure to satisfy the increasing demands of the London market.

prophecies because they agreed with the criteria which he found in Scriptural prophecy. This 'commonwealth' message particularly applied to John's destruction of enclosures, for John had fulfilled the office of a godly prince both in rescuing the poor from the oppressions of 'the welthier sorte' and in swearing 'that he would not suffer wild beasts to feed upon the fat of his soil and see the people perish, for want of ability to procure and buy them food, that should defend the realm'. In this passage in the *Description* Harrison combines several features of the 'commonwealth' programme for returning the realm to its ideal state, and by comparing the *Description* with the 'Chronology' at this point we can also discern how Harrison associated these historical patterns of behaviour with the problems of Elizabethan England, for the reference to Andrew Boorde's opinion on English parks, which followed the description of Roman parks in the 'Chronology', followed the reference to John in the *Description*.[144]

Harrison therefore envisaged a godly society which would follow in the path taken by Israel in those periods when the renewal of the covenant had restored her to obedience to God's law and thus re-established that social, economic and political equilibrium which remained the ideal for all 'commonwealth' writers and preachers. This vision proved unrealistic and unobtainable in the face of economic self-interest. Yet it is inadequate to call it a 'very Christian' conception of the state, and to describe it merely as an imaginary past.[145] Such a description fails to account for the subtlety with which 'commonwealth' idealists used the Scriptures to criticise their own society, and it ignores their fixation on the experiences of the covenant line, which instilled in them the obsessive fear that unless England returned to godly behaviour, Antichrist would break in. As an account of Christ's perfect reformation, the New Testament thus provided a blueprint for the new society, for it represented the most complete renewal of the covenant in the history of Israel and the clearest differentiation between truth and error. The Gospel not only restored the spiritual understanding of God's commandments which had been lost by the followers of the Jewish ceremonial laws, but transformed the teachings which had been repeatedly given to the covenant line since Adam and remained summarised in the Decalogue. Now that doctrinal foundation-stone of the commonwealth in Israel became a universal rule for Christian society, so that if men, said Harrison, 'did fulfill all that which christ ther required of them ther shold be no nede of any new traditions or canons to be ordeined whereby as by a short waie thei shold

---

[144] See above, pp. 136–7, on Merlin; TCD MS 165, fo. 129v; *cf. Description*, ed. Edelen, p. 259, John's anti-enclosure drive complemented his confrontation with Antichrist, for most of the enclosure belonged 'to the abbots and prelates of the clergy' who accordingly distorted his motives in their chronicles (ibid., pp. 258–9).

[145] As did W. K. Jordan, *Edward VI: The Young King* (London, 1968), p. 417.

obteine everlasting life'.[146] History showed that to disobey these commandments led only to further degeneration and eventual retribution, so that in applying this pattern to Elizabethan England Harrison gave eloquent testimony to his fears about the future of that commonwealth.

[146] TCD MS 165, fo. 162v.

7

A reformed natural philosophy

Harrison's strictures against the pursuit of individual self-interest at the expense of the community, discussed in the previous chapter, clearly have some bearing on the long-established controversy about the relationship between Protestantism and the acceptance of a capitalist scale of economic values. Other aspects of his thought, however, are also very relevant to the currently more fashionable debate about the possible connections between the more uncompromising strands of Protestantism, the capitalist outlook, and the emergence of recognisably 'modern' approaches to scientific investigation. This chapter will not discuss those debates at greater length than is necessary to put William Harrison's thought into its historiographical context. Instead it will suggest that the general framework of Harrison's thought already discussed offers a better context in which to assess his views about economic endeavour and the investigation of nature, and that this individual context gives important insights into Protestant thinking about social and economic relationships, as well as Protestant attitudes towards scientific enquiry and its implications for the contemporary economy.

In both these areas Harrison's thought follows a pattern of reasoning familiar to us from previous chapters, recalling the strict limitations which he placed on the use of human reason in the interpretation of prophecy, history and chronology, in the organisation and direction of the Church, and in the determination of proper political and economic actions. Harrison believed that in all these spheres of human activity the Scriptural revelation of God's commandments should act as an *a priori* restraint, both compensating for the inherent weaknessess of fallen human reason, and enabling regenerate reason to discern the legitimate boundaries of those spheres of activity, by following Scriptural criteria rather than the rational criteria proffered and preferred by deluded human reason. This dogmatic distinction between legitimate and illegitimate behaviour Harrison carried into the spheres of economic activity and natural philosophy. The previous chapter discussed the means by which Harrison detected ungodly behaviour in the market, and especially in the selfish contrivance of enclosures, and it now remains to relate those ideas to the current debate about Protestantism and capitalism, a debate which also concerns itself with Protestant attitudes towards the investigation of Nature. Most of this chapter deals with Harrison's reactions to some contemporary methods of interpreting Nature, and argues that his approach to natural philosophy was consistent with the rest of his thought. It suggests that Protestant theories about natural philosophy cannot be divorced from their theological premises, and particularly from their Scripturally determined epistemology.

The continuing discussion about the importance of Protestant theological ideas in eroding traditional Christian values and enabling the development of a capitalist scale of values still broadly follows the framework set out by Max Weber in his pioneering study of *The Protestant Ethic and the Spirit of Capitalism*. R. H. Tawney slightly redefined those limits to include a more concrete definition of capitalist endeavour than Weber had proposed, and Christopher Hill further streamlined and popularised the argument in several well-known studies. The first point to be made about Weber's thesis, and one which has tended to become obscured in subsequent discussion, is that the 'Protestant ethic' as he defined it was not a deliberate attempt to justify emerging capitalist practices; rather it sanctified certain kinds of behaviour which had the unforeseen consequence of preparing the way for capitalism. Weber regarded Calvinism in particular as the type of Protestantism whose theology was most conducive to later capitalist practices, but he never argued that Calvinists intentionally sought to justify those practices, claiming instead that they helped to create a climate of opinion in which those practices became religiously acceptable. This raises our first problem, however, because Weber acknowledged that Calvin, the Calvinists, 'and other Puritan sects' not only did not promote 'the spirit of capitalism', but that capitalist practices were 'unforeseen and even unwished-for results of the labours of the reformers'. They were 'even in contradiction to all that they themselves thought to attain'. Weber also admitted that he was concerned to draw out those later consequences of Reformation thought which might seem 'incidental and even superficial' beside the main emphasis of the teaching of the Reformers. Therefore only if one accepts Weber's sociological methodology can one accept his thesis. For a historian the idea of reading back from later examples of Protestant capitalist thought to the original sources of Protestantism is fraught with difficulties. For to emphasise only those elements of Protestant thought which contributed to later capitalist values is to give a very selective and distorted picture of Protestantism. The very essence of Protestant thought is that it taught the believer to select from other sets of ideas according to Scriptural criteria, but to select ideas from Protestant thought according to criteria drawn from other sets of ideas is to discard the Scriptural centre of Protestantism and to substitute something else in its place. Thus one can hardly call this a case of Protestant 'influence' upon later ideas.[1]

Tawney made two important qualifications to Weber's argument. The first appeared necessary because Weber's *Protestant Ethic* had neglected the impact of changing economic practices upon the development of Calvinist theology, and had apparently assumed that Protestantism remained essentially unchanged from the sixteenth century onwards. Tawney correctly pointed out that all Weber's evidence about English Protestant attitudes in favour of capitalist economic behaviour dated from after the Restoration. He went on to argue in his *Religion and the Rise of Capitalism* that the most interesting feature of Protestant economic thought was its transformation between the sixteenth century, when it fiercely defended traditional moral values in the market place, and the later Stuart period in England, when changing economic circumstances gave a new importance to its latent individualism and altered traditional Protestant teachings against the pursuit of worldly gain as an end in itself.[2] Tawney made a second qualification by accepting criticisms which showed that the 'capitalist spirit' had existed in earlier centuries and in Catholic regions, and that the concept of the calling, on which Weber placed great stress as the motivating force behind the rational conduct of their affairs by the pious bourgeoisie, had not been Luther's invention.[3] Consequently we may claim the support of both Tawney and Weber for the assertion that William Harrison's wish to curtail economic behaviour, in accordance with what he considered to be a divinely sanctioned scale of moral values, was entirely typical of zealous Protestants in the sixteenth century.

Weber's definition of the 'Protestant ethic' leaves us with several problems, however, apart from the obvious but important point that this definition did not allow for historical change in the content of Protestant thought. The central problem concerns his key concept of 'rationality', the ability to foresee and plan for the steady accumulation of relatively small profits by careful business methods within a capitalist market economy. He distinguished this from the traditional but irrational pursuit of profit by

---

[1] M. Weber, *The Protestant Ethic and the Spirit of Capitalism*, tr. T. Parsons (London, 1950), pp. 89–90, 157; R. H. Tawney, *Religion and the Rise of Capitalism* (London, 1948); C. Hill, *Society and Puritanism in Pre-Revolutionary England* (London, 1969), esp. Chapter IV, pp. 121–40, 'The Industrious Sort of People'; and 'Protestantism and the Rise of Capitalism', in *Essays in the Economic and Social History of Tudor and Stuart England*, ed. F. J. Fisher (Cambridge, 1961), pp. 15–39. See also the survey of the subject in M. J. Kitch, *Capitalism and the Reformation* (London, 1967). This bibliography is intended to be indicative rather than definitive.

[2] R. H. Tawney, Foreword to Weber, *Protestant Ethic* (1950), p. 9; *Religion and the Rise of Capitalism*, pp. 211–26, 'A Godly Discipline versus the Religion of Trade'; and pp. 227–51, 'The Triumph of the Economic Virtues'.

[3] Tawney, Foreword to Weber, *Protestant Ethic* (1950), p. 7, and Preface to the 1937 edition of *Religion and the Rise of Capitalism*, pp. xi–xii in the 1948 edition.

adventurous speculation, and argued that the new outlook reflected the Calvinist obsessive fear of God's wrath and consequent anxiety to placate that anger by the minutest obedience to God's commandments in his calling. Once one of the Elect had received divine grace to achieve an effective faith and had been reborn in Christ, his whole life subsequently became a work of sanctification by which to achieve assurance of salvation and sublimate fears of damnation. Weber's conclusion that 'In practice this means that God helps those who help themselves' is a rather crude gloss on the social impli-cations of Calvinist salvation theology and one which has gained unfortunately wide currency.[4] In fact it reflects Weber's mistaken emphasis on reason as the guiding principle behind Calvinist theology, and his failure to recognise the deep suspicions which Calvinists entertained about human free will. This latter omission explains his confusion of eighteenth-century Methodists, founded by a theological Arminian, with the seventeenth-century Precisians, theological double predestinarians who developed Beza's restrictive theology of grace. In particular they denied that humans could seek salvation of their own free will, and undercut any presumptions to certainty of salvation by a kind of spiritual book-keeping. Instead they emphasised the 'false' faith of the reprobate, indistinguishable to human perceptions from the true faith of the regenerate.[5]

Weber's misplaced emphasis on Calvinism's systematic and rational determination of moral conduct therefore fails to stress sufficiently those Scriptural restrictions with which Calvinists, and indeed all zealous Protestant theologians, hedged round their own reason in deducing their ethical systems. This finally led him to the curious conclusion that the Calvinists' 'whole attitude toward life' displayed a 'rational suppression of the mystical, in fact the whole emotional side of religion'.[6] This may accurately describe some later type of Protestant businessman, but in fact not only Calvin but other major Protestant theologians reacted sharply against the typically humanist attempt to subordinate religion to rational criteria, fearing that that would open the way for the entry of free will. They therefore gave full weight to the mystical aspects of faith, not only regarding such central matters as God's nature, but also His presence in time and history and the spiritual nature of the Elect congregation. This mystical aspect of Protestant thought appears in Harrison's emphasis on the mysterious revelation of God's will in historical and chronological patterns, for a purpose beyond the compre-hension of human reason. Like other zealous Protestants, Harrison carefully

---

[4] Kitch, *Capitalism and the Reformation*, p. xvii, discussing Weber's *General Economic Theory* (New York, 1961). Weber's use of 'Calvinist' is accepted for the convenience of the argument. It cannot be considered an accurate description of the theology even of many of Calvin's avowed followers, let alone the majority of Protestants in the century after his death.

[5] Weber, *Protestant Ethic*, p. 117; and *cf.* McPhee, 'Beza', pp. 150–2, 213–19.

[6] Weber, *Protestant Ethic*, pp. 117, 123.

measured his own spiritual state not according to the standards of worldly success which Weber appears to attribute to his rational Calvinists, but by the standards of the suffering, oppressed covenant line, adopting that faithful understanding of the visible world which made him intensely suspicious of its opportunities.[7]

Weber related his interpretation of rationalist Protestant psychology to the 'Protestant ethic', which he defined as an emphasis on working hard in one's calling, on carefully organising one's time in order to avoid dissipating it, and on self-discipline, together with a preoccupation with thrift, with limiting personal consumption to avoid enslavement to worldly possessions. As well as having obvious advantages for a capitalist economic system, in Weber's view the 'Protestant ethic' helped to undercut the traditional perception of labour as a short-term means to an immediate subsistence end, and to sanctify work as an end in itself, eventually creating a plentiful supply of capital to promote further economic advance. Tawney's valuable observations that the 'Protestant ethic' was not uniquely 'Protestant', and that Protestant theologians did not come to terms with capitalist forms of economic activity until the later seventeenth century, for reasons remote from the concerns of sixteenth-century Protestants, need to be reiterated at this point.[8] Not least because in essentially restating Weber's thesis Christopher Hill has made it more difficult to place William Harrison's thinking about economic activity in its proper context. On the one hand, in a short essay on 'Protestantism and the Rise of Capitalism', Dr Hill accepted that 'there is nothing in Protestantism which leads automatically to capitalism', and also summarised Weber's original, subtle argument that 'In a society already becoming capitalist, Protestantism facilitated the triumph of the new values'.[9] Yet on the other hand his more influential *Society and Puritanism in Pre-Revolutionary England* has sweepingly restated Weber's dictum that 'Protestantism is suited to a competitive society in which God helps those who help themselves', while drawing a stark contrast between the popery 'suited to' static agricultural societies and the Protestantism 'suited to' emergent capitalist states. This difference of emphasis may perhaps reflect two distinct facets of the same general thesis, but there are more difficult problems raised in *Society and Puritanism* which have to be resolved before we can place a man of Harrison's generation and opinions in a context recognisable to a wide range of readers.[10]

The first problem concerns the lack of any evidence of Protestants

---

[7] See Chapter 2, pp. 59–64, and see below, pp. 296–8.
[8] Tawney, Foreword to Weber, *Protestant Ethic* (1950), pp. 8–9.
[9] Hill, 'Protestantism and the Rise of Capitalism', p. 36.
[10] Hill, *Society and Puritanism*, p. 129, which does not specify how these societies are 'suited' to different religions. Are we to understand that any 'static agricultural society' *must* be popish?

ascribing positive religious value to capitalist economic and social values before the Civil War. Tawney long ago discovered this weakness in Weber's thesis, and indeed the whole thrust of Harrison's thought supports Tawney's contention that Protestant thought had to undergo profound alteration under the pressure of external forces before it could be brought to countenance capitalist practices, which in Harrison's day had been roundly condemned as the anti-social activities of self-interested individuals. Dr Hill gets round this problem of evidence, and in the process revives Weber's undifferentiated Protestantism while blurring Tawney's distinction. Dr Hill's most eloquent exposition of the industrious and laborious 'Protestant ethic' draws heavily upon a pamphlet of 1689, itself a tendentious, Whig interpretation of religious history which attempted to show 'how religion has in all ages been promoted by the Industrious Mechanick'. In a nimble piece of footwork worthy of the Whig pamphleteer, Dr Hill side-steps the absence of Protestant sentiments favouring capitalism before the later seventeenth century, by insisting that 'there are few elements in the author's case which cannot be found in very early Protestant writings, or which cannot be deduced from the logic of those writings'. Unfortunately he can only find support in the Catholic writings of Nicholas Sanders for his assertion that 'The protestant religion was in fact promoted most of all by the industrious Mechanick' in the sixteenth century.[11] This is a long way from Dr Hill's more considered reiteration in his essay, of Weber's original argument that Protestants unintentionally secured the triumph of capitalist values. The more simplified argument in *Society and Puritanism* also overlooks Tawney's distinction between sixteenth and early seventeenth-century Protestantism and its later forms. That distinction needs to be reaffirmed, for it focuses attention, as Dr Hill does not, on the intentions with which sixteenth-century Protestant divines like William Harrison propounded their social and economic teachings. For they criticised not only the under-use but also the mis-application of God-given resources, and their inequitable distribution throughout society.

This brings us to our second problem, that the paucity of evidence in support of the thesis put forward by Weber and Hill reflects the real limitations of the English economy in the sixteenth century. For Harrison's strictures against idleness highlight the practical problems of a subsistence economy where voluntary underemployment resulted from the absence of consumer goods sufficient to create a classical cycle of supply and demand, beyond the most basic necessities of life. This partly explains the general pessimism amongst Protestant preachers about the effectiveness of their exhortations; even if Englishmen had felt inclined to follow their commands,

---

[11] Ibid., pp. 132–3. Contrast Hill's industrious mechanic Reformer with Harrison's covenant line of ascetic and spiritually inspired preachers of reform.

the manifest failure of a century of Protestant preaching to modify working practices testifies to the absolute restraints imposed by the contemporary economy, which according to individual social station and outlook promoted either dissipation or idleness. Not until influences other than religious exhortation transformed the economy did circumstances occur which enabled many Englishmen to accept their preachers' well-worn arguments for strenuous labour and temperate behaviour, and which allowed them to put that particular vision of the Christian life into practice. Dr Hill insists that 'Puritanism' helped to bring about this change, by advocating 'regular systematic work' which 'was required if the country was to break through this vicious circle' of underemployment and establish an economy within which the availability of cheap consumer goods would encourage the population to work continuously and in a disciplined manner. He does not explain why Protestant preaching failed to produce this transformation in behaviour at any time in the century before the later Stuarts, nor why the 'Protestant ethic' was suddenly enabled to overcome the difficulty which had thwarted its practical application since the reign of Elizabeth.[12]

In fact Protestant preachers like William Harrison did not direct their exhortations against patterns of behaviour which restricted the growth of the economy, for like all their contemporaries they conceived of it as a 'zero sum', as a fixed amount of wealth and resources. When powerful and greedy individuals secured a disproportionate share of those resources, most obviously by enclosing common land or manipulating the local market, others suffered. On the other side many angered God by refusing to utilise fully those precisely limited opportunities which He had given them. This imbalance reflected the distortions which fallen human reason had introduced into the godly and fearful use of resources bestowed by God to ensure the competent maintenance of mankind. Such an ideal of self-sufficiency corresponded to the real under-utilisation of resources in the contemporary subsistence economy, but it precluded the concept of growth in that economy, and especially militated against the consumerism which Dr Hill identified as vital to the triumph of the capitalist ethos. Indeed the ascetic element in Protestantism identified by Weber, Tawney and Hill appears more relevant to a relatively rigid, subsistence economy than to a capitalist economy dependent upon the mass consumption of goods beyond those required for what Harrison considered a 'competent living'.[13]

Harrison's notions of godly social and economic conduct reflect this

[12] Ibid., pp. 121–3. For the reasons given above, this selective belief in Protestant preaching cannot be considered a straightforward 'influence'.

[13] P. Anderson, *Lineages of the Absolutist State* (London, 1974), pp. 34–6, which together with E. F. Heckscher, 'Mercantilism', in *Revisions in Mercantilism*, ed. D. C. Coleman (London, 1969), points out that the 'zero-sum' conception was so universally accepted as to be the justification for mercantilist policies.

tension between his ideal, the proper utilisation of the resources bestowed by divine grace, and the objective restrictions and distortions of the contemporary economy. Indeed, Elizabethan England provided a particularly clear example of a distorted commonwealth which neglected the opportunities offered by God, for 'there is no nation under the sun that can say so much as ours, sith we do want' nothing that is 'convenient for us'. While God 'showeth Himself a loving and merciful father unto us' in bestowing His gifts so plentifully, the English 'contrarywise return unto him in lieu of humility and obedience, nothing but wickedness, avarice, mere contempt of His will, pride, excess, atheism, and no less than Jewish ingratitude'.[14] This damning catalogue of contemporary evils, by singling out 'avarice' and 'excess', reminds us that the habits of capital accumulation and consumption did not fit into the Protestant vision of the godly commonwealth. By connecting England's miserable status with the degenerate commonwealth of the apostate Jews it also emphasises Harrison's presumption that social and economic behaviour could not go beyond the boundaries set by the antithesis to the faithless Jews, the godly covenant line. This restrictive and conservative Scriptural model required a return to patterns of behaviour which Harrison believed that the Scriptures described, and which in fact constitute the truly distinctive 'Protestant ethic'. Yet here the objective of purposeful disciplined labour was to thank God for his bounty and to build up the faithful godly commonwealth in the form which the Scriptures required. Indeed, like other sixteenth-century Protestants, Harrison seems to have considered that contemporary instances of capitalist enterprise exemplified the society of natural man, the satanic Gentile parody of godly Israel, where infidelity led to excesses which mocked Elect frugality.

Harrison's reiteration of those Christian commonplaces which historians have subsequently rationalised into a distinctive 'Protestant ethic' should be read within this dualistic context. He complained that 'in England...what with eating, plaieing and sleping we spende three quarters of our time unprofitably', but he made this remark in the context of an attack upon conspicious consumption by the Roman nobility and a defence of frugality which was preoccupied with the proper utilisation and distribution of fixed resources, rather than buoyed up by any prospect of future improvement.[15] Harrison certainly considered idleness the greatest threat 'to the steadfast persisting of the godly', but this emphasis on the godliness of labour did not necessarily condone the capitalist ethos, as the dogged Puritan advocacy of restrictive 'commonwealth' legislation in despite of economic reality makes clear. For like other Protestants, Harrison conceived of godly labour in the context of a static economy where the entrepreneurial instinct was a dangerous luxury. He was not unique in lambasting thrusting individuals

---

[14] *Description*, ed. Edelen, pp. 365, 364. [15] TCD MS 165, fos. 124 r–v.

who 'in respect of their owne lucre and advauntage...contempne wholesome estatutes made by their superiors, to the behofe of the comonwelth '.[16]

As well as denigrating entrepreneurial skills, Harrison took a dim view of that capital formation which was also a vital precondition for a capitalist industrial revolution. Riches did not make a man evil, and money properly used was a cherisher of learning; despite the massive inequalities of Elizabethan England, Harrison could still entertain the scholar's cosy vision of a 'competent living'. But other forces at work in the contemporary economy reminded him that some of the earliest apostates from Christ had been 'old, cold and wealthy'. Uneasily aware of the contrast between the golden mean of the philosophers who contented themselves 'with a little', and the nascent consumerism on which capitalism would feed, Harrison feared that his vision of the godly commonwealth would be thwarted by the appetites of natural man, for 'our desire is never satisfied...if we have not the riches of Cresus and Crassus, the talentes of Pythius Mysius, the Lordshipes of Jaire the Giliadite, the flocks of Laban the Syrian and herdes of Job after he was restored, we accompt ourselves to have nothing '.[17]

In resisting economic innovations which epitomised the delusions of carnal reason, Harrison followed a consistent Protestant tradition which emphasised the limits to rational interpretation of the external world and consequently sought to restrain human exploitation of that world. Men could not pursue their own wills and acquire what their self-interest dictated, for just as the Scriptures corrected the misapprehensions of distorted human sense impressions, so did revelation determine how men should use the world, not in order to satisfy their own lusts, but to glorify God. Calvin observed that Adam fell 'by his owne faulte', 'after he was endued with the light of understanding' and that through his own reason Adam 'separated himselfe from God, whereby...he was deprived of all perfection'. This meant that mankind 'in vaine...seeke knowledge in the workemanship of the worlde, except they be such as being humbled already with the preaching of the Gospell, have learned to submitte their whole witte and understanding of minde to the foolishness of the crosse, as Paule tearmeth it'. This ecstatic vision begins at the Gospel interpretation of Nature, for only when interpreted in this way does Nature lead to God, since 'they whiche without godlinesse search out the causes and natures of thinges, and by speculation remove and separate God, and the sense of godlinesse farre from them' confounded themselves by their own errors. Faithful acceptance of the Scriptural promises of Christ remedied the limitations of human perceptions, for our eyes failed to see what 'the workmanship of heaven and earth representeth, or else that the knowledge whiche may be had thereby, may

[16] Ibid., fos. 68v, 90r; and see *The work of William Perkins*, ed. Breward, pp. 72–6.
[17] TCD MS 165, fos. 113r, 156r, 109r.

suffice to salvation', and this fundamental blindness meant that 'the Lorde calleth us unto him without any profite by his creatures'. Only by accepting from the beginning that 'his will is a rule of all wisedome' could men really understand the world, 'For by the Scripture, our guide and schoolemistresse he doth not onely shew unto us those thinges, which otherwise we shoulde not knowe, but also doth almost constrayne us to beholde the same, no lesse then dimme and thicke sighted eyes are holpen with spectacles'.[18]

From this viewpoint, the Scriptures tell us what to see, and show us how to interpret those sense impressions when we observe the world. The proper understanding of Nature reflects an individual's saving knowledge, although the knowledge of God derived from Nature follows the pattern set by the Scriptures and cannot be arrived at independently of the Word. Because as always Satan 'goeth about to intangle our mindes', 'for we please and flatter our selves, so little we perceive howe mortall the sickenesse of sinne is, and howe great wickednesse possesseth all our senses'. Nor could human reason regard the order of Nature as an autonomous area of investigation, for 'there was nothing more contrarie to the iudgement of fleshe and bloud' than that God would destroy his creation in the Flood, 'because this was to overthrow the order of nature which he had established'. Human understanding remained so puny that it required the Scriptures to determine how mankind should use God's gifts, because 'we may enioy all these riches, which are here offered unto us, even as the Lorde hath ordeined and appointed them to our use', and 'all thinges are ordeined for mans use, to the ende he, being the more bound unto God, might addict him selfe wholy unto the obedience of his lawe and will'. Both the investigation of Nature and the exploitation of natural resources through the knowledge thus gained therefore had to follow the strict limits imposed by the Scriptural revelation of God's will, since 'To be occupied in the searching out, whereby thou art kept from beholding the author, is diligence il bestowed, but to enioy Nature in eche condition and part, and not to acknowledge the author of the benefite, is too filthie ingratitude'. This meant that no aspect of intellectual, economic and social life could be religiously neutral and independent of censure by the Scriptures, 'But let us rather remember, that bycause men doe prophane, through filthie abuse, the noble and precious gift of God, he is the revenger'. The present confusion of languages testified to the godly the awesome power of this divine vengeance, for as an innovation of human free will and reason, the Tower of Babel showed that 'he must needes directly assaile God, which goeth beyonde his boundes'.[19]

---

[18] Calvin, *Commentarie…upon…Genesis*, sigs. B3r, B2v–B3r, B1v–B2r, B2v, B2r, B2v.
[19] Ibid., sigs M7v, O3r, N2v, B2v, B3r (and note the parallel to Harrison's charge of English ingratitude, above), P2v, Q4r. See Wilch's *Time and Event*, pp. 126–8, on the limits to exploitation set by the Scriptures.

Starting from much the same premisses as Calvin, Bullinger also concluded by contrasting the faithful obedience of the covenant line, who lived and believed as revelation directed them, with the disobedience of those 'takyng parte against God' with Satan. The Church of Cain manifested its distorted religion in its 'voluptuousnesse and inordinate lustes', by the addiction of its members 'to unlawful spendyng and consumyng of that they may get to advoutrye', and this identification of consumption, even consumerism, with the deceptions of human reason and the wanderings of human free will provided the perfect foil to Bullinger's Protestant asceticism. Yet Bullinger's ascetic outlook on the world also conformed itself to revelation, and he discovered in the second commandment 'a figurative precepte' against the economic crimes characteristic of the Church of Cain, particularly 'oppressyng the poore, by usury, by extorcion, by falshode and disceate', crimes which could be recognised in contemporary Europe.[20] Protestants therefore could not escape God's demands that they obey His revealed will in all their encounters with the external world, whether as investigators of Nature, or exploiters of its resources, at which point they entered into economic relationships with other men which were also strictly limited by Scriptural teachings. Disobedience would thrust them into the Church of Cain, where the gratification of will and self-interest determined behaviour in a manner much closer to the amoral operations of the capitalist economy. Neither in the economy, nor in science, nor in technology, where those circles of activity overlapped, could Protestants divorce human understanding from the prior revelation of the Scriptures.

This interpretation of the thought of two major Protestant theologians conflicts with R. K. Merton's thesis that 'Puritanism' provided an incentive for the pursuit of the new learning, for the theological assumptions of these Protestants clearly made them suspicious of such studies, and encouraged them to limit the scope of these endeavours as well as the interpretation of the data obtained. Such an approach also casts doubt on Christopher Hill's popularisation and simplification of Merton's argument into the contention that Puritanism, science and capitalism were in some way connected.[21] John

---

[20] Bullinger, *The Olde Faythe*, sigs. A6r, C8v-D1r. Compare Harrison's comments on the oppressive Roman nobility, above, p. 287.

[21] See R. K. Merton, 'Science, technology and society in seventeenth century England', in *Osiris*, iv (1938), pp. 360–632, esp. pp. 439–70, now republished as *Science, Technology and Society in Seventeenth-Century England* (New York, 1970), with a new Preface. C. Hill, 'Puritanism, Capitalism and the Scientific Revolution', in *The Intellectual Revolution of the Seventeenth Century*, ed. C. Webster (London, 1974), pp. 243–53; also C. Hill, *The Intellectual Origins of the English Revolution* (London, 1965). Recent critics of the thesis include T. K. Rabb, 'Puritanism and the rise of experimental science in England', in *Journal of World History*, vii (1962), pp. 46–67; and 'Religion and the rise of modern science', in *Intellectual Revolution*, ed. Webster, pp. 262–79; and R. L. Greaves, 'Puritanism and science: The anatomy of a controversy', in *Journal of the History of Ideas*, xxx (1969), pp. 345–68; but especially J. Morgan, 'Puritanism and science: A reinterpretation', in *The Historical Journal*, xxii (1979), pp. 535–60,

Morgan has already shown that the Protestant theologians generally shared Calvin's outlook on the study of Nature. Dr Morgan has also pointed out the errors in Merton's methodology, for the latter first grouped together seventeenth-century scientists, then proved to his own satisfaction that the great majority of them were 'Puritans' and consequently concluded that 'Puritanism' somehow helped to make science socially prestigious.[22] This approach not only illuminates the dangers of a sociological rather than historical approach to the past, but also highlights the weaknesses in Weber's analysis, for Merton consciously followed Weber's approach and consequently arrived at the Weberian conclusion 'that Puritanism inadvertently contributed to the legitimacy of science'. The key word here is 'inadvertently' for Merton was fully aware that Christian theologians, and particularly Protestant theologians, had frequently warned against the subversive influence which the investigation of the external world had upon revealed dogmas. Taking Calvin as the dominant influence 'on English life', Merton therefore attempts to argue that English Calvinism 'represents a marked development' of Calvin's thought, and that Englishmen only accepted those Calvinist doctrines 'congenial to tendencies developing in other compartments of culture', so that 'Puritanism was integrated with many [incipient] cultural trends', especially capitalism. At this point Merton proposed the nexus between 'capitalistic culture', science and technology, and 'Puritanism', and referred to Weber and his followers, but the historian is left to wonder what influence Calvin had over those who merely selected from his work that which they found congenial.[23]

Indeed this amounts to no historical proof at all that Calvinism helped to make science acceptable, because the influences which accomplished this task were all external to Calvinism, as Merton's argument implicitly admits. In a footnote (a curious place to find 'One of the basic results of this study'), Merton claims 'that the most significant influence of Puritanism upon science was largely *unintended* by the Puritan leaders'.[24] Like Weber's similar conclusion about Protestantism and capitalism, this depends upon the reader accepting a kind of intellectual 'influence' which is entirely contingent upon autonomous, external developments, so as to produce a result utterly contrary to the original intentions of the writer and the internal structure of his thought. Even the most blinkered historian of ideas would find it difficult to share Merton's enthusiasm for the paradox that although 'Calvin himself deprecated science...from him stemmed a vigorous movement

which gives an exhaustive bibliography (pp. 535–40). Dr Morgan and this writer have independently come to the conclusion that Puritan divines placed strict limits on the use of reason in the investigation of Nature.

22 Ibid., pp. 540–2.

23 Merton, *Science, Technology and Society* (1970), pp. xvi–xvii, xvi.   24 Ibid., p. 58 *n.* 6.

which furthered interest in this very field'. This asks us to accept that scientists could select ideas from Calvinism according to criteria derived not from the Scriptural centre of Calvin's teachings but from natural philosophy and other parts of intellectual life, and still remain Calvinists. Like all the Reformers, Calvin asked to be believed only so far as he conformed to the Scriptures. But it is perhaps consistent with Merton's distaste for 'esoteric theological treatises' that he asks us to accept the opposite, to still consider as Protestantism the type of reasoning which all Protestant theologians condemned, and which sought to subordinate *a priori* Scriptural criteria to the corrupt criteria suggested by human reason.

Thus while Merton has to acknowledge that Calvin's contempt for the physical sciences closely followed Patristic teachings, he contends that this consistent Christian element amongst Calvin's followers 'was submerged by the implications of his other tenets, which led to directly opposed developments', although what these implications were and how they contributed to diametrically opposed conclusions Merton does not explain. Even more puzzling, since Merton accepts Calvin's conservative attitude towards scientific discoveries, is his insistence that Calvinism 'inevitably inspired the pursuit of natural science', for given the basic tenets of Calvinist theology it seems a strange kind of inevitability which arrives at the opposite conclusion. However, Merton's thesis appears weakest when confronted by the evidence that science failed to flourish at Calvin's Geneva until the mid-eighteenth century, because Merton then found it necessary to make a subtle distinction between 'the authority resting in Calvin himself' and 'the implications of his religious system'. Given that Calvin was then two centuries dead, the first must refer to his writings, and if we leave aside the influence at Geneva of subsequent Calvinist theologians, together with the question why they had not previously turned Calvin's theology on its head, we are left with the 'implications' of his system, which apparently did not occur to the savants of Geneva until they found themselves in circumstances entirely different from those in which Calvin had written. The sensible historian must conclude that only after Geneva had rejected Calvin's restrictions upon intellectual life could the pursuit of scientific knowledge be carried on independently of religious supervision, and that this suggests that there was only a negative relationship between Calvinism and science.[25]

In order to test the validity of this general argument, that the Scriptural centre of Protestant thought necessarily militated against unrestricted enquiry into Nature, the remainder of this chapter concentrates on the specific example of William Harrison. Trained in Protestant theology, and with pronounced ideas on free enquiry in natural philosophy, the interpretation of sense data and the application of technological knowledge, Harrison offers

[25] Ibid., pp. 58, *n.* 6, 59, 73*n.* 56, 100 and *n.* 52, 101–2.

an ideal test case. Following the processes of his thought also emphasises the importance of allowing for considerable individual variation within any generalisation about Protestantism and science. Above all, the preceding chapters allow us to put Harrison's thinking on natural philosophy into its proper theological, historical and epistemological context, rather than taking it out of context by abandoning the Scriptural centre of his thought in pursuit of a sociological explanation of his views. The discussion deals particularly with Harrison's dogmatic objections to the Hermetic version of natural philosophy, and shows the wider significance of these objections for our understanding of Protestant attitudes to contemporary science, for Harrison's arguments were particularly characteristic of zealous Protestants. It also reveals the limitations of Merton's methodology, for if we were to follow his approach we would have to conclude that Harrison's selective attitude towards Hermeticism made him a Hermetist.

The Hermetic philosophy derived largely from texts attributed to Hermes Trismegistus, who was accorded the status of a *priscus theologus*, a very ancient source of divine wisdom, in the mistaken belief that he had been an Egyptian priest-king who had received divine revelation of true doctrine and insight into the powers of the cosmos, about the time of Moses. Given the contemporary respect for the most ancient sources of knowledge, large claims have been made for the influence of the Hermetic philosophy on many areas of sixteenth-century thought, not least on natural philosophy. Against this background the publication in 1614 of Isaac Casaubon's *De rebus sacris et ecclesiasticis exercitationes XVI* is commonly regarded as a watershed for the contemporary reputation of Hermes Trismegistus, and thus for all magical operations under the aegis of the Hermetic philosophy. Casaubon demonstrated that the Corpus Hermeticum was a derivative compilation of the first century AD, and this discovery is usually seen as the catalyst for a decisive change in the contemporary perspective, undermining the influence of the Hermetic philosophy.[26] This conclusion overestimates the status of the Hermetica in the sixteenth century, for Harrison's 'Chronology' shows

[26] I. Casaubon, *De rebus sacris et ecclesiasticis exercitationes XVI* (London, 1614), pp. 70–87; M. Pattison, *Isaac Casaubon* (Oxford, 1892), pp. 335–6; *Hermetica*, ed. W. Scott (4 vols. Oxford, 1924–36), i, pp. 41–3; and especially F. A. Yates, *Giordano Bruno*, pp. 1–19, 398–403. Casaubon's originality is accepted even by those who diminish the importance of Hermeticism for 'Hermetic' thinkers, e.g., R. S. Westman, 'Magical reform and astronomical reform: The Yates thesis reconsidered', in R. S. Westman and J. E. McGuire, *Hermeticism and the Scientific Revolution* (Los Angeles, 1977), p. 10; and by those who emphasise the differences between Hermeticism and scientific methodology, like J. L. Heilbron, Introductory Essay in *John Dee on Astronomy: Propaedeumata aphoristica*, ed. and trans. W. Shumaker (Berkeley and Los Angeles, 1978), pp. 40–1. General works, such as P. Burke, *The Renaissance Sense of the Past* (London, 1969), pp. 62–3, concur, but more recently F. Purnell, 'Francesco Patrizi and the critics of Hermes Trismegistus', in *The Journal of Medieval and Renaissance studies*, vi (1976), pp. 155–78, has shown that Gilbert Genebrard published arguments similar to Casaubon's in 1580. I am indebted to Dr D. P. Walker for this last reference.

that forty years before Casaubon proved that the works of Hermes Trismegistus were compiled in the early Christian era there was already a widespread scholarly opinion which rejected the traditional dating. Casaubon's textual criticism was not therefore totally original, but developed ideas which had circulated as early as the 1570s. Evidence of such earlier criticism obviously reflects upon the contemporary reputation of Hermes.

More importantly, this particular application of humanist textual techniques reflects a general dogmatic viewpoint, evident in Augustine's criticisms of Hermetic idolatry and demon-worship, which deeply influenced sixteenth-century thought. Dogma and textual criticism combined to destroy Hermes's authority as an ancient divine revelation, and to diminish the importance of the Hermetic philosophy for contemporary scholars. Studies of Hermeticism have neglected these facts, over-simplified and distorted the intellectual currents of the sixteenth century, and through the close study of the single strand of Hermetic thought perhaps inflated its importance for contemporaries. This is particularly true of the alleged connection between Hermetic magical practices and emerging scientific methods. The following discussion will attempt to show that it was possible to accept Neoplatonic natural philosophy without being indebted to Hermetic ideas, and that the Hermetic picture of man as manipulator of Nature was less important in formulating the scientist's role than has been claimed.[27] It goes on to show how Harrison's religious criticisms of Hermeticism have important implications for his attitude to contemporary science, and concludes that Harrison had profound religious reasons for applying the same limitations to contemporary science that he applied to Hermetic knowledge. Moreover, the fact that the 'Chronology' deals with many contemporary topics of scholarly concern suggests that Harrison's criticisms of the Hermetica in that work may provide a specific example of a more general viewpoint.[28]

Harrison's treatment of Hermes Trismegistus in the 'Chronology' represents his mature views, but his acquaintance with and interpretation of the Hermetic texts also reflect his education and subsequent experience of the varying currents of contemporary learning. To understand Harrison's approach to the Hermetic philosophy therefore, we have to go back to his Oxford days, and even beyond that period to his time as 'an unprofitable grammarian' at Westminster School. His early grounding in good letters left him with the familiar humanist contempt for barbarous medieval Latin, but

---

[27] J. E. McGuire also distinguishes Hermeticism from Neoplatonism in 'Neoplatonism and active principles: Newton and the *Corpus hermeticum*', in *Hermeticism and the Scientific Revolution*, ed. Westman and McGuire, pp. 95–133. Heilbron contrasts modern scientific methodology with Hermetic denigration of reason and emphasis on individual inspiration and secrecy, and on an animism which neglected regularity in Nature (*Propaedeumata aphoristica*, ed. Shumaker, pp. 37–40). This present discussion reinforces Heilbron's argument.

[28] The 'Chronology' was talked of in Gabriel Harvey's circle (Parry, 'Puritanism and history', pp. 124–30, 107).

more importantly it introduced him to the techniques of textual criticism which he later applied to the Hermetic texts.[29] Not surprisingly, the devotees of Hermes Trismegistus dismissed such a critical apparatus as grammarian pedantry. As an undergraduate at Christ Church and probationary fellow of Merton, Harrison combined this Latin grammarian tradition with the Greek philosophical strand in humanism, belying the antithesis which Frances Yates has attempted to draw between them.[30] However, Harrison's views on Hermes may have been decisively affected by his traumatic religious experiences at Oxford. He took Roman Catholic orders at Christ Church in 1556, but became a Protestant before July 1558, a change which forced him to reassess the Hermetic philosophy and his other studies in the light of Scriptural teachings. Harrison's interest in the Hermetic philosophy and its practitioners probably dates from his popish years, reflecting the Catholic syncretist approach to the Hermetic revelation as a confirmation of Christian truths.[31] He wrote anti-Lutheran marginal notes in a volume containing Thomas More's translation of the *Life of John Picus Erle of Myrandula*, a work which may have initially persuaded Harrison to accept the magical undertones of the Hermetic philosophy by placing them in the context of ascetic piety.[32] At some point he also acquired a 1532 edition of Marsilius Ficino's *De triplici vita libri tres*, whose third book, *De vita coelitus comparanda*, described talismanic magic within the Hermetic system.[33] Harrison's copy of the *Corpus hermeticum* is not extant, but he certainly used Ficino's edition, in which Ficino's *argumentum* claimed extreme antiquity for Hermes as the founder of a true theology, transmitted by a succession of *prisci theologi* to Plato.[34]

While deeply immersed in Hermetic philosophy, Harrison also followed the Oxford medieval tradition of natural philosophy, which would ultimately tend to diminish the importance of Hermeticism in his thought. His 'Chronology' suggests the style of his abortive fellowship studies, singling out the 'Merton School' of mathematicians and astronomers, whose chief legacy to Harrison seems to have been the testing of received knowledge

---

[29] Harrison praised the classical grammarians and condemned barbarous scholastic Latin which distorted the Scriptures (TCD MS 165, fos. 124ar, 221r, 350v).

[30] Yates, *Bruno*, pp. 159–68. But her argument can only apply to Erasmus, and may not even be true of him; see below, p. 323.

[31] D. P. Walker, 'The *prisca theologia* in France', in *Journal of the Warburg and Courtauld Institutes*, xvii (1954), pp. 205–59, reprinted in Walker, *The Ancient Theology* (London, 1972), pp. 63–131, on Catholic syncretism, particularly characteristic of Italian writers.

[32] *Life of John Picus Erle of Myrandula*, tr. Thomas More [1510?], now Derry Diocesan Library shelf-mark A.ii.g.8.

[33] Marsilius Ficino, *De vita coelitus comparanda*, in *De triplici vita libri tres* (Basle, 1532), Derry shelf-mark K.h. 17. On Harrison and talismans, see below, pp. 318–23.

[34] Yates, *Bruno*, pp. 14–17, on the *argumentum* and its genealogy of wisdom, referred to by Harrison in TCD MS 165, fos. 38v, 42v; for further proof that Harrison used Ficino's edition, see below, pp. 312–13.

by observation and experiment. However, humanist-inspired, rigidly Aristotelian studies were in fashion at Oxford, and Harrison's well-known complaint about fellowship elections in the *Description* reflects his failure to become a full fellow of Merton. The 'Chronology' reveals his bitterness that an elegant but superficial commentary 'upon some pece of Aristotle' was now more highly valued than a work in the older College tradition.[35]

Yet Harrison remained loyal to the Merton experimental method, perhaps because it brought him into contact with some of the leading contemporary natural philosophers. His fellowship thesis may have been based on the 'collection' of the 'profound astronomer' William Rede, fellow of Merton and Bishop of Chichester in the fourteenth century. Harrison once possessed this manuscript, and he also frequently consulted a work on planetary conjunctions by another Merton fellow, John Ashenden.[36] These treatises and others from the Merton school were at one time in the library of the polymath Robert Recorde (d. 1558). Recorde's critical re-examination of inherited abstract Aristotelianism by original thought and experimentation owed much to the Merton tradition. He popularised this approach and the practical application of theoretical concepts in a series of vernacular mathematical textbooks. Harrison shared these ideals and had access to historical manuscripts in Recorde's library, as well as intimate knowledge of some hitherto unknown aspects of Recorde's antiquarian work.[37] Apart from sharing this practical, experimental ethos, Harrison was linked by patronage with Leonard Digges (1530–63) and his son Thomas (1550–95), and perhaps also with John Dee. The Digges were clients of the Brooke family, to which Harrison also attached himself before 1559, and Harrison referred familiarly to Thomas Digges's pioneering vernacular popularisation of the Copernican cosmology. Yet while he accepted Digges's argument that Copernicus had only revived the ancient Pythagorean cosmology, Harrison reluctantly rejected the Copernican thesis because it could not account for observable changes in the cosmos as convincingly as the Ptolemaic system.[38]

[35] Parry, 'Puritanism and history', pp. 16–21.
[36] Ibid., pp. 16–21. Rede's 'collection' is now Bodleian Library MS Digby 176. On Ashenden, TCD MS 165, fo. 337v.
[37] J. Bale, *Index Britanniae scriptorum*, ed. R. L. Poole and M. Bateson (Oxford, 1902), pp. 96, 200, 223, 411; F. R. Johnson and S. V. Larkey, 'Robert Recorde's mathematical teaching and the anti-Aristotelian movement', in *Huntington Library Bulletin*, vii (1935), pp. 59–87, esp. pp. 77, 82–3; Taylor, *The Mathematical Practitioners of Tudor and Stuart England*, pp. 167, 313; and Feingold, *Mathematician's Apprenticeship*, pp. 116–18; TCD MS 165, fos. 212r, 302r, the latter a reference to Recorde's attempts to collate the manuscripts of Roger Hoveden and Simon of Durham.
[38] Leonard Digges was deeply implicated with the Brookes in Wyatt's rebellion (D. M. Loades, *Two Tudor Conspiracies* (Cambridge, 1965) pp. 50, 81); T. Digges, *A perfit description of the caelestiall orbes according to the most auncient doctrine of the Pythagoreans*, appended to *A Prognostication everlastinge...published by Leonard Digges, gentleman. Lately corrected and augmented by Thomas Digges* (London, 1576). Harrison perceived the Copernican system within a closed

Frances, Lady Cobham, was godmother to one of Dee's children, and Dee also combined antiquarian studies similar to Harrison's with an interest in the practical application of scientific knowledge. Dee republished one of Recorde's treatises on applied mathematics, and after the death of his close friend Leonard Digges, tutored his son Thomas. These intellectual and social connections may account for a reference in one of Dee's notebooks to a manuscript 'bought of Harrison', although the surname is too common to be certain that this was our William Harrison. Dee and Harrison shared friends and collaborators in Raphael Holinshed, John Stow, Gabriel Harvey and William Camden.[39] Yet although Harrison had at least looked into Dee's *Propaedeumata aphoristica* and accepted its claims for the miraculous existence of the cosmos, he did not follow Dee in his increasingly occult and magical conclusions, that the sympathies uniting the cosmos could be exploited through Hermetic ceremonies and practical Cabala or number magic.[40] For although Harrison had encountered the Hermetic philosophy in a formative period for his thought, and continued to be interested in works in that genre, his attitude towards it was decisively altered when he became a Protestant and resigned his Merton fellowship sometime before July 1558.

Harrison's change of religion manifested his conversion to a stricter, Augustinian view of pagan knowledge which was shared by many European evangelicals. It would be tedious and otiose to reiterate D. P. Walker's detailed analysis of this viewpoint in numerous European writers across a wide devotional range.[41] It is more important, especially for Protestant evangelicals, to set their criticisms of the *prisci theologi* and their attendant magic in the context of the historical interpretation delineated in Harrison's 'Chronology' and discussed in the foregoing chapters. For in that context

universe, not the infinite cosmos proposed by Thomas Digges (TCD MS 165, fo. 215v), but anyway 'the accesse and recesse of the first movable, the alterations of the severall latitudes of the planettes' and the movement of winds and tides counted against Copernicus (ibid., fos. 108v, 117r).

39 Cobham was not Dee's only patron, but see *Autobiographical tracts of Dr John Dee*, ed. J. Crosby (Manchester, 1851), pp. 10–12; *The Private Diary of John Dee, and the Catalogue of his Library of Manuscripts*, ed. J. O. Halliwell (London, 1842), pp. 33–4, 40–1; and *Calendar of State Papers Domestic 1591–4*, ccxlviii, no. 121, p. 513; P. J. French, *John Dee, the world of an Elizabethan magus* (London, 1972), pp. 56, 188–99, 163; Parry, 'Puritanism and history', pp. 99–139 and *passim*; Taylor, *Mathematical Practitioners*, p. 166; Bodleian Library, Corpus Christi College Oxford MS 191, fo. 83v. On Dee and Holinshed, Stow, Harvey and Camden, see French, *Dee*, pp. 133–7, 203–5.

40 Harrison only cited the first aphorism, and his amanuensis garbled the title (TCD MS 165, fo. 142v; cf. Shumaker, *Propaedeumata aphoristica*, pp. 35–6, and Heilbron's Introduction, *passim*). The latter shows that Dee's growing Hermeticism paralleled his declining contribution to scientific knowledge.

41 Even at his most liberal, Augustine emphasised that whatever in Platonism conformed to faith had been stolen from Israel, and that attempting to reach God through contemplating Nature led to idolatry like that of Hermes Trismegistus (*De civitate Dei*, VIII. 9–19; and Walker, *Ancient Theology*, pp. 63–131).

the familiar theme of a continuity between Gentile ideas and developing Christian dogmas took on a new and more sinister significance. As a specific application of a general theory, Harrison's historical explanation explains why Protestants so vehemently denied claims that the *prisci theologi* were divinely illuminated. There were differences of emphasis, but essentially all the evangelical critics examined by Walker assumed that the Gentiles were indebted for whatever was valid in their philosophy to God's prior revelation to the Elect. From this perspective it appeared that the Gentiles had mingled these divine verities with the bewildering variety of errors characteristic of natural reason, so that apparent 'anticipations' of Christian dogmas could appear mixed with idolatrous magic in the works of a *priscus theologus* like Hermes Trismegistus.[42] Harrison's thought reveals that this common view of the diffusion of true knowledge was an essential part of the Protestant world-view, since it was a key argument in the fight against popery.[43]

For, as we have noticed, looking back from 1565 Harrison was convinced that when he took popish orders he had become 'a shaven worshipper of Baal'. That very deliberate description reflected his recently acquired Protestant, dualistic conception of history as a perpetual conflict between the True Church and the Church of the Gentiles.[44] Harrison believed that the Elect covenant line preserved along with true faith its corollary of true knowledge. The revelation to Adam was essentially the same as that revealed by Christ, and its criteria remained normative for the present, because although the fortunes of the True Church fluctuated, in each generation a minority of true believers called to reform the Church transmitted, along with true doctrine, those insights into Nature and divine philosophy which had been granted to Adam. Only in Christ was this knowledge purified by an absolute distinction between truth and error, but the sum total of this inheritance, revealed in the Scriptures, constituted a perfect reformation of doctrine and knowledge.[45] Against this normative standard arose its satanic parody, the Church of the Gentiles. Because the Gentiles lacked that faith which perfected knowledge, Satan had been able to work through natural man's reason and appetites to distort the pristine knowledge which the Gentiles received from the Elect. A genealogy of corrupt knowledge had thus been established, resulting in religious, social, moral and intellectual decline amongst the Gentiles by comparison with Israel.[46]

---

[42] Walker, '*Prisca theologia*', pp. 210–12; and *Ancient Theology*, pp. 70–3.

[43] Intent on establishing Hermes's authority, Frances Yates devoted barely two pages to this fundamental criticism (*Bruno*, pp. 157–9) – the corollary is her unrecognisable picture of the theological climate of Elizabethan England (ibid., pp. 187–8).

[44] Harrison's autobiography written in Bale's *Scriptorum*, Derry shelf-mark D.ii.d.7. On the following, see above, pp. 13–19.

[45] Fallen man could only achieve an imperfect reformation. See Chapter 4, pp. 166–7. See above, p. 206, on the flowering of natural philosophy in Solomon.

[46] This reversed the Hermetic interpretation of the genealogy of *prisci theologi* from Hermes to Plato, as found in Ficino (Yates, *Bruno*, pp. 14–15). G. F. Pico believed that the *prisci theologi*

Even Israel was not immune to the seductions of this degenerate knowledge, and only the rediscovery of normative Scriptural truth and the rejection of Gentile errors had arrested the periodic decline in her fortunes. Harrison detected a similar process after Christ, and regarded contemporary popery as the recrudescence of satanic Gentilism in the Church, which had to be purified by a return to Elect knowledge and its normative criteria for Church and society, set out in the Scriptures. Thus like other Protestants Harrison believed that the case against Rome depended upon a critical reappraisal of Gentile philosophy, a belief which Renaissance syncretists had done nothing to discourage.[47] In the context of this universal apocalyptic struggle Harrison, like many European evangelical Protestants, had to sort through his intellectual baggage and cast out the filthy rags of popery, rejecting some of his former beliefs as the errors of corrupt Gentile reason. The Hermetic philosophy was one casualty of that process.

During the 1560s and 1570s, Harrison spent much more of his time studying theology, exploring the ramifications of the Scriptural godly commonwealth. In this more intensely evangelical context he saw that his essentially Gentile humanist training had concentrated on works which neither contributed to the building up of that godly commonwealth nor honoured God.[48] In the light of his new faith Harrison could believe that the Merton experimental philosophy was part of Elect true knowledge because John Ashenden and Philip Repingdon, two of the fellows, 'sustained no small vexation' from their popish enemies 'for the testimony of the gospell'. In contrast Harrison's conviction that Aristotle was but 'a pagan heretike' limited his acceptance of Aristotelianism. Compared to the Scriptural ethical model, Platonic virtue was only 'as the gentiles measured the same', and Harrison's allegiance to the Ptolemaic cosmology was tempered by the belief that Ptolemy detested divinity. Indeed because they ignored the first cause 'it is the nature of most profound Astronomers to

constituted a genealogy of superstition mixing truth stolen from Israel with idolatrous religion and diabolical magic, to which the Florentine Platonists were damnable heirs. The Protestant Johan Wier viewed the *prisci theologi* within an apocalyptic interpretation similar to Harrison's, and thus more vehemently criticised their degenerate Egyptian magic, which like Plato's teaching he regarded as entirely separate from Moses's true theology (D. P. Walker, *Spiritual Magic*, pp. 146–51, 152–6).

[47] E.g., 'Some wishing well to [Ptolemy] because thei reverens and honor his lerning do dreame that he was a christien', but indeed his learning itself prevented him from accepting Christianity (TCD MS 165, fo. 148v). See McPhee, 'Beza', pp. 158–68, for Beza's similar views.

[48] He proceeded B.D. in 1571 and began but did not complete the exercises for the D.D. (Parry, 'Puritanism and history', pp. 51–3). His criticism of Gentile curiosity in grammar, rhetoric, logic and mythology (TCD MS 165, fo. 147r) has been noticed above, pp. 206–7, but again the intensely evangelical context of this remark must be stressed. Elsewhere he condemned the deliberate destruction of Gentile arts and sciences, because they indirectly derived from God (ibid., fo. 180v), and Gentile learning could produce some social improvement (ibid., fo. 124av).

be cold Christians'.[49] Harrison's reaction to the Hermetic philosophy should therefore be seen in the wider historical context of evangelical reactions to Gentile knowledge, a context which suggests that his criticisms of Hermes may have been commonplace. For Hermes had to be compared to the 'line of the right wise' who constituted the Church throughout the generations. Augustine formed an important link in this chain, for he reformed the Church, which had previously accepted many Gentile errors, by a relatively complete return to Apostolic true doctrine. Harrison was more critical of Augustine's teachings than Magisterial Reformers such as Melanchthon, yet in following Augustine's argument on Hermes Trismegistus Harrison re-affirmed his membership of the True Church and his utter opposition to the seductive errors of the Gentiles. It was from the standpoint of a radical, dogmatic Protestant that Harrison approached the Hermetic texts by the 1570s.[50]

The physical evidence of his 'Chronology' reveals that Harrison expended much time and effort on the problem of dating Hermes. An early note was covered by a considerably amended and expanded version in Harrison's autograph, with still further marginal additions. However, even the earliest version was concerned to show the indebtedness of degenerate Gentile knowledge to Israel's prior divine revelation. In the treatises of Hermes, said Harrison, 'we maie perceave how farre the gentiles had already swarved from their elders', the Hebrews, 'notwithstanding that in many thinges his writinges agree and are in a maner one with those we have of Moses'. In this Protestant historical interpretation, what for Ficino had been Hermes's greatest claim to attention becomes damning evidence of degeneracy. Hermes did not anticipate or corroborate Christian dogmas, but had polluted Elect knowledge with Gentile fantasies. The second version of this note makes it clearer that Harrison condemned Hermes by a comparison with the doctrine transmitted within the covenant line and expounded by Augustine. For although Harrison did not deny that Hermes 'was a man somewhat affected unto religion', by Augustine 'his impieties are not only detected but also his time a little more made manifest'. Harrison referred to *De civitate Dei*, viii.26, which condemned the god-making passages in the Hermetic treatise *Asclepius* for their demon-worshipping idolatry, as part of a general attack on pagan reliance on demons as intermediaries between God and men. In contrast to this deceitful and diabolical tradition represented by Hermes, Augustine had reasserted the greater antiquity of Israel's pure divine knowledge.[51]

---

[49] Ibid., fos. 334r, 108r, 110v, 113r, 148v.
[50] Ibid., fo. iv, and above, pp. 29–30, on his selective approach to Augustine.
[51] TCD MS 165, fo. 42v; *cf. De civitate Dei*, viii. 19–26, xviii. 39, and *Hermetica*, ed. Scott, pp. 339–41.

In citing Augustine, Harrison was not simply appealing to a Father against whom other authorities could be brought, but appealing to the eternal doctrine of the True Church since Adam, which found particular expression through Augustine. Therefore it is hardly possible to over-estimate the weight of Augustine's argument for Harrison and his evangelical contemporaries. Protestants who recognised the distinction between the Two Churches, and they were many, could be assured of their election only by following the eternal doctrine of the True Church. Even less radical thinkers must have been impressed by Augustine's immense authority. To ignore the wide currency and acceptance of Augustine's criticism of Hermes is to distort our understanding of the Reformation and the sixteenth-century climate of opinion.[52] Indeed Casaubon's philosophical and grammatical analysis of the Hermetic texts started from this dogmatic premise, that it was contrary to Scripture for God to reveal his mysteries more clearly to the Gentiles than to His chosen people.[53]

Augustine, however, still accepted that Hermes was a very ancient source of knowledge. Ill-equipped to detect that the Hermetic texts were a relatively recent compilation, Augustine identified their author with the grandson of the elder Mercury or Hermes, the grandson of that Atlas traditionally accounted contemporary with Moses. Although this made Hermes far later than the earliest custodians of Elect knowledge, Augustine believed that he had lived long before the Greek philosophers.[54] This made it easier for those still determined to embrace the Hermetic philosophy to discount Augustine's criticisms or to condemn only the magical parts of the Hermetic texts, as later intrusions. However, Harrison supplemented Augustine's dogmatic criticisms with evidence procured by those humanist techniques in which he had been trained, evidence which showed that the Hermetica were far later and thus more degenerate than Augustine had believed. This was objective evidence of a kind which Hermeticists could not easily reject. Harrison was able to arrive at his conclusion partly because he approached the texts not just as profound philosophical statements but as pieces of evidence useful for his primary purpose of establishing an exact chronology. In pursuit of this end a critical eye had to be brought to bear on every textual detail. Yet however important Harrison's criticisms may have been to contemporaries, they are clearly more important to us if they were derivative rather than if they were original. Therefore we should note that Harrison also minutely examined the texts because contemporary scholars had already noticed anachronisms within them. The very fact that he discussed their authorship

---

[52] As in Yates, *Bruno*, p. 187, and its curious comments on John Foxe.

[53] Casaubon, *De rebus sacris*, p. 72. Ironically, even as Casaubon wrote, historical scholarship was undercutting his dogmatic position, establishing the priority of Gentile knowledge.

[54] *De civitate Dei*, xviii. 39; in Harrison's 'Chronology', Atlas is mentioned at 1640 BC (TCD MS 165, fo. 38v).

further suggests that the Hermetica were the subject of heated contemporary debate.

In the long and heavily amended second version of his note Harrison discussed six Hermes, and especially the third of that name, whom 'Ficinus the Platonist' claimed to be the author of the Hermetica and who in Harrison's 'Chronology' is shown to flourish around 1565 BC.[55] However, Harrison presented internal evidence that although the books were 'misticall and profound' they dated from long after the fall of Troy, which his 'Chronology' recorded at 1181 BC. The evidence he presents shows that he had closely read the *Corpus hermeticum* in Ficino's edition, for he was struck by the fact that the *Pimander* was not only indebted to Moses but also 'maketh mention' of the Sibyls. In fact this was a printer's misreading of Ficino's translation of the Greek for divination by trees, so that one of the ways in which God communicated directly with men was given as 'per Sibyllam'.[56] As for what Harrison calls the 'Aesculapius', the mention of Asclepius the first physician shows that 'what so ever he was that wrote the said treatizes', he lived after the fall of Troy.[57] Therefore none of the six 'historical' Hermes was author of the Corpus Hermeticum, for the last had died shortly before the Trojan war. Other references showed Harrison that the author was grandson to this last Hermes and contemporary of a grandson of Asclepius. He realised that to many this was a disagreeably novel conclusion, but he still left open the question whether the Hermetica were written by Hermes or 'some other later man that liked to entitle and father the same upon Mercurie because of the misticall and profound' philosophy they apparently expounded.[58]

Although Harrison's evidence still showed that Hermes was far older than the most ancient Greek philosophers, that was enough to devalue his authority and confirm the greater antiquity and purity of knowledge in the Elect covenant line. The Hermetic philosophy was conclusively shown to be a derivative Gentile corruption of Elect knowledge. Still more important is an argument which shows that Harrison was reflecting current opinion, and that other scholars believed the Hermetica to be even later than he had concluded. Besides the anachronisms already mentioned, the author 'doth make mention of Phidias' said Harrison. Yet he later interlined the

---

[55] Ibid., fo. 42v.

[56] On Troy, ibid., fo. 61v. Ibid., fo. 42v; *cf.* Purnell, 'The critics of Hermes Trismegistus', pp. 162–3, who shows that Gilbert Genebrard later made the same point in *Chronologia* (1580). See *Hermetica*, ed. Scott, i, 235. 19; and *Corpus hermeticum*, ed. A. D. Knock and A. J. Festugiere (4 vols. Paris, 1945–54), i, 182.19. Harrison first mentions the Sibyls at 1147 BC (TCD MS 165, fos. 63r–v), but he knew that the corpus was not so old – see above, pp. 131–41.

[57] Ibid., fo. 42v; *cf. Hermetica*, ed. Scott, i, 359, and Cicero, *De natura deorum*, iii.22. Harrison registered Asclepius at 1268 BC (TCD MS 165, fo. 56v). The *Asclepius* also mentioned the Latin language, which Harrison believed was published by Latinus in 1199 BC (ibid., fo. 60v).

[58] Ibid., fo. 42v.

qualification 'as some do note', and although he gives no sources this probably referred to the second edition of Gilbert Genebrard's *Chronologia*, published in 1580. For at the end of this discussion Harrison referred to the entry for Phidias elsewhere in the 'Chronology', at 446 BC where a marginal note originally recorded a mention of Phidias in the Asclepius. Harrison later altered this to read 'as some do write', for 'having redde bothe his bokes in my time I remember [not] in which of them he dothe appere to speake of him'. In fact Genebrard had cited an authentic part of the Corpus Hermeticum (now referred to as CH XVI-XVIII) unknown to Ficino when he made his translation, hence Harrison's confusion. Isaac Casaubon also pointed out that the Hermetica mentioned Phidias, drawing upon what we can now see was a persistent scholarly tradition dating from at least the 1570s. This evidence appeared to make Hermes almost contemporaneous with the earliest Greek philosophers, and Casaubon made much of their lack of reference to Hermes.[59]

Two conclusions can be drawn from Harrison's initial acceptance of Genebrard's argument. It suggests first, that Genebrard's criticism of the Hermetica was very quickly and broadly disseminated, for Harrison abandoned work on TCD MS 165 for a larger version of his 'Chronology' soon after 1580, and his hurried marginal insertion about Phidias may have been one of the latest entries in this manuscript. Moreover, while Harrison was clearly an intelligent and often refreshingly novel scholar, he was not in the forefront even of English scholarship. Therefore his use of the recondite Phidias reference, buried admittedly in a chronological work which he had briefly consulted in its first edition, suggests that he was remarking upon a subject of general scholarly discussion.[60] There is also the necessary corollary that Genebrard's criticism fell on well-prepared and fertile ground, for Harrison's initial willingness to accept his opinion without consulting the actual texts reflects his previous deep-seated suspicions about the Corpus Hermeticum. Genebrard's ideas may have been particularly well received in the evangelical Protestant circles in which Harrison moved, for the dogmatic belief in the priority, continuity and completeness of Elect knowledge was a striking feature of Puritan thought.[61] Indeed, perhaps more than his textual critique of the Hermetica, this dogmatic belief determined Harrison's

---

[59] Ibid., fo. 42v; cf. fo. 103v, and Purnell, 'Critics of Hermes Trismegistus', pp. 162–4, on the textual history of this passage. See also Casaubon, *De rebus sacris*, pp. 73, 86, and *Hermetica*, ed. Scott, i, 276.4.

[60] Parry, 'Puritanism and history', pp. 412–16, on the compilation of TCD MS 165. Harrison's failure to name Genebrard may mean that his information was verbal. He cited Genebrard's *Chronographia in duos libros distincta* (Paris, 1567) at TCD MS 165, fo. 34v (*Chronographia*, sig. A3r), fo. 48v (sig. A3v), fo. 126v (sig. C2r) and could hardly have missed Genebrard's initial doubts about Hermes at sig. C1r (not 'fol. C' as in Purnell, 'Critics', p. 160), but one cannot say whether this started Harrison off on his independent critical examination.

[61] Parry, 'Puritanism and history', pp. 37–45, and Chapter 4, pp. 145–53, on Harrison's radical Protestant connections.

approach to other elements of the magical, cabalistic, occult and arcane knowledge generally classed as *prisca theologia* by their devotees. For it had the additional important effect of persuading Harrison to pursue his scientific studies according to Scriptural, rather than occult, criteria, rejecting all other explanations of the workings of the cosmos.

For that reason he rejected the Orphic tradition, frequently regarded as the residue of a seminal pre-Platonic religious tradition, whose parallels with Hebrew monotheism and Christian trinitarian mysteries encouraged Renaissance syncretist attempts to reconcile Christianity and Platonism. But the Orphic hymns were also used by Neoplatonists as preparations to philosophical contemplation, and combined with magic could lead even to religious ecstacy.[62] Harrison reiterated the patristic argument that Orpheus, the 'divine poete', was indebted to the Pentateuch and other Elect treatises for his religious insights, but he 'swarveth from the truth because he was an infidell' and 'for want of perfite instruction' metamorphosed monotheism into polytheism, 'and soch corrupted doctrine as he was trained up in'. Because Orpheus lacked that faith which perfected reason, his works only interpreted Elect doctrines according to the Gentile criteria of natural reason, so that he could not use that knowledge creatively and reject his errors by reference to Scriptural criteria. The Scriptures were self-sufficient, and did not require confirmation from the distorted imitations of deluded Gentiles.[63] For the same reasons Harrison rejected the Sibylline Oracles, whose dubious numerological predictions encouraged the Hermetic fixation on Pythagorean and Cabalistic number manipulation as a lever on cosmic powers. He used Sebastian Castellio's edition of the Oracles, but rejected his attempt to present the Sibyls as witnesses to ancient religious truths which, combined with Christianity, could produce a *renovatio mundi* – a programme deeply indebted to Hermeticism. Harrison regarded the Oracles as a chaotic recension of numerous Gentile prophecies, within which truth was severely limited to fragments derived from the Elect. The rest, ignorant of Scriptural prophecy, demonstrated the flaws of natural reason in their erroneous guesswork about the shape of history and chronology.[64]

The sharp division between Harrison's outlook and the Hermetic system already emerging from this discussion also allows us to distinguish his

---

[62] D. P. Walker, 'Orpheus the theologian and Renaissance Platonists', in *Journal of the Warburg and Courtauld Institutes*, xvi (1953), pp. 100–20, esp. p. 100; Walker, *Ancient Theology*, pp. 22–4. Renaissance scholars knew that the Orphica dated from several periods (ibid., p. 29; 'Orpheus', p. 104).

[63] TCD MS 165, fos. 56r–v.

[64] Castellio, *Orthodoxographia* (Basle, 1555); Harrison's copy, Derry shelf-mark A.i.g.2, contains his identifications of the succession of Roman emperors prophesied by the Sibyls (ibid., pp. 1468–1522, esp. p. 1497), but as mentioned above, p. 133, the Sibylline understanding of Scriptural prophecy was 'even as thei that lie bounde in spelnica Platonis have the divine similion of those thinges that perteine to true felicitie' (TCD MS 165, fos. 10v–11r).

increasing fascination with chronological patterns and parallels, evident in the 'Chronology', from the aims of those who pursued Cabalistic number manipulations both within and outside the Hermetic philosophy. Although the numerical symmetries he laboriously unearthed were not always justified by canonical prophecy, Harrison understood that they were only indices to God's will and not causes in themselves. The Hermeticists believed that the fabric of Nature depended upon those numbers which permeated the hierarchy of worlds comprising their universe, and John Dee was not alone in eventually believing that the kind of occult numerical manipulations commonly attributed to Pythagoras allowed the adept to rise from the physical world to gnosis with the One in the divine sphere, where the secret universal laws would be revealed. Harrison allowed that Pythagoras's divinity and mathematics were elevated by acquaintance with Elect knowledge, but he ridiculed contemporary revivals of 'an old kind of arithmancie fathered on Pythagoras, yet never invented by him', especially, as we have seen, Jean Bodin's Cabalistic attempt to give numerology the direction of history even to the extent of limiting God's will. Essentially Bodin gave numbers an influence analogous to that which the planets were held to have, but just as Christian liberty assured us that the heavenly bodies were merely God's agents without power in themselves, so 'anie hidden mysterie' in Bodin's numbers could not impinge upon eternal Scriptural doctrines such as 'the gift of grace and free mercie unto the penitent'. There was no short-cut to regeneration and Elect understanding of the cosmos through 'Pythagorean' mathematics or Hermetic Cabalistic speculations. Only the Scriptures held the key to Nature.[65]

This same Scripturally based distinction between Elect knowledge perfected by faith and Gentile knowledge corrupted by infidelity determined Harrison's attitude to the Cabala itself. He distinguished sharply between the divine insights offered to the Hebrews while they held the true faith and the unfettered ramblings of the Jews after their apostasy. The Jewish Cabala was therefore typical of a nation 'delited with fruteless allegories and Pythagoricall suttleties gathered out of the positions and significations of nombers and letters which are for the moste parte more curiously then [wisely and] profitably invented as may appere by the common Cabala wherin thei put great confidens'.[66] This clearly separates Harrison from Pico della Mirandola, who had fused the Cabala with the Hermetic texts, claiming that both were a Christian means for magical understanding of the super-celestial world.

[65] French, *Dee*, pp. 22, 74, 105–7; Pythagoras was allegedly indebted to Hebrew mathematicians, whose true faith limited their application of mathematical knowledge (TCD MS 165, fo. 96v); Harrison, *Description* (1587), p. 28, and above, pp. 115–21, on Harrison's change of mind over Bodin's numerology.

[66] The adjective shows that he could distinguish between the Jewish and Christian versions (TCD MS 165, fos. 75v, 46v).

From Harrison's point of view Pico's intricate calculations with the Hebrew alphabet were merely elaborating the degenerate tradition of the Church of Cain, and multiplying errors which could only be corrected by reference to Elect knowledge.[67]

Harrison's 'Chronology' gives both an historical account of the *prisci theologi* and a discussion of the contemporary proliferation of their errors in cosmological and magical theories. Just as his vision of the covenant line put the *prisci theologi* in their proper light, so his allegiance to the doctrines transmitted by that covenant line prevented him from sharing the occult vision of the universe. Harrison refused to waste time, for example, on the 'great matters Michael Eitzinger doth dreame of in his Cabalisticall pentaplon', although he did warn that Eitzinger's strange interpretation of Daniel's seventy weeks would hopelessly confuse accepted chronology, while his innovative demarcation of the ages of the world merely manifested Gentile errors. Harrison remained loyal to Augustine's division of six ages, for that reflected Elect knowledge and commemorated the struggle of the Elect in this world.[68] Harrison's discussion of the enigmatic *Pentaplon* gives an unusual perspective on the Hermetic proposition that intelligences or angels (the objects of Pico's Cabalistic invocations) governed the planets influencing earthly events. For in claiming that the seven planetary angels governed the world's history for set periods, Eitzinger according to Harrison followed the corrupt genealogy of Johannes Trithemius, Abraham Ibn Ezra, John Basilius Herold, Theodorus Graminaeus and Henry Cornelius Agrippa, although they differed over the length of these periods. Harrison argued that while their chronological errors revealed their ignorance of the Scriptures, the claims of these men that the planetary angels totally controlled earthly events denied God's providence and endangered the many who from his apocalyptic viewpoint 'incline already towarde Atheisme'. Indeed Trithemius's emphasis on the wonderful effects performed by the stellar spirits was 'unspeakable impietie not comely for a christien to reade or understand of'. Here the boundaries between legitimate and illegitimate knowledge were emphatically drawn, for such doctrines challenged that Christian liberty which had always been preached by the Elect.[69]

---

[67] Yates, *Bruno*, pp. 92–110. Harrison dismissed Pico's reference to Enoch's book of dimensions in his commentary on the Cabala, 'because I have redde of it in none other author, so farre as I now remember' (TCD MS 165, fo. 4r); Yates, *Bruno*, pp. 145–6, claimed that Johannes Trithemius's *Steganographia*, ostensibly a handbook of cryptography, was used for Cabalist angel magic, but perhaps because he was alienated by Cabala, Harrison did not see this, merely condemning the book for its dubious political uses (TCD MS 165, fo. 131r).

[68] M. Eitzinger, *Pentaplus regnorum mundi* (Antwerp, 1579), pp. 35–6; TCD MS 165, fo. 8v, and see *De civitate Dei*, xxii.30.

[69] Harrison appears to have assimilated this genealogy of wicked knowledge to the Church of Cain, TCD MS 165, fo. 2v; *cf.* Johannes Trithemius, *De septum secundeis, id est, intelligentiis, sive spiritibus orbes post deum moventibus* (Frankfurt, 1545). Harrison's list of Trithemius's

Therefore there was no straightforward correlation between Harrison's wide reading in occult philosophy and his interpretation of the cosmos. He continually assessed occult teachings according to the Scriptural limits of legitimate knowledge, limits set by the historical experience of the Elect and the doctrines which they had transmitted. Sometimes these limits were sharply drawn, as around the god-making passages in the Asclepius, which described the vivifying of idols by attracting demons into them – for Harrison believed that Satan's efforts to foster idolatry amongst the Gentiles had been aided by his magical creation of moving idols.[70] Such limits were more subtly traced around the related subject of mechanical marvels, where contemporary fears of demonic magic and modern interest in applied science overlap. Harrison's reasoning was Scripturally based, but unlike many contemporaries he did not condemn the production of mechanical animals as wicked demonic magic. He accepted that they could be produced by 'mere arte and not by any superstitious or suspicious magike'. His point was that such 'vaine and curious' creations were an abuse of human intelligence, contributing nothing to the creation of that equitable commonwealth which the Scriptures demanded. The interest of Renaissance magi in mechanical marvels has been seen as a direct stimulus to 'the will to operate in genuine applied science', but given the limitations on the application of human abilities inherent in Harrison's Puritan line of thought, it is doubtful whether those seeking to better the human condition would become interested in the principle behind these toys while it was applied to such a useless purpose.[71]

Alchemy, described by Frances Yates as 'The Hermetic science par excellence', was also beyond the pale. Harrison believed that its great contemporary reputation was symptomatic of a society horribly distorted from the Scriptural model and intent on producing those unnecessary and fruitless innovations which epitomised the delusions of unaided human reason. God had provided the Elect with all the arts and sciences needed for a competent living, and crowned them with the Scriptures. But 'so moche do we make of error and so litle of the truth' that many students treated alchemical 'trifles' more reverently than the New Testament. This increasingly fashionable but 'vaine study' had spread from 'fantasticall heddes' among the clergy to ruin many gentlemen and nobles. Alchemy also undermined Harrison's rather fixed vision of society by seeking substances which threatened an already precarious economic equilibrium. As an attempt to add to God's creation, which He had considered sufficient for mankind's sustenance, this 'covetous practize' needed to be stamped out, and Harrison

planetary angels corresponds to that in his *Steganographia*, rendered inaccurately in Yates, *Bruno*, p. 145 *n*. 3. Thomas Erastus shared Harrison's horror of this doctrine (Walker, *Spiritual Magic*, p. 158).   [70] TCD MS 165, fos. 132v, 109v.

[71] Ibid., fo. 226v; *cf.* Yates, *Bruno*, pp. 147–50.

dismissed contemporary alchemical treatises as 'not worthy the perusall and reading'. He did not deny that alchemy was capable of some remarkable effects, but that was beside the point – it was a waste of time more fruitfully spent on 'better indevours'.[72]

Harrison was irritated by the superfluous innovations of unregenerate reason, but although he criticised the irreverent use of human and cosmic powers his acceptance of the providential control of all events allowed him to believe in a magical, Neoplatonist universe in which all things were sympathetically linked. Thus he believed in the possibility of magical operations, and more importantly that within very strict limits a Christian could legitimately perform them. Eventually against an authoritative body of orthodox opinion he defended a typical practice of Hermetic magi – the concentration of beneficial stellar influences through the special composition and construction of talismans. He believed, however, that his method of reasoning and the tradition which he drew upon remained distinct from the Hermetic philosophy. He knew that there was a wicked and degenerate form of this knowledge, a legacy of faithless Gentile distortions of the truth. But that wicked talisman magic itself taught 'the cheef point of all religion', that every human endeavour must be assessed by 'how it might safely stand with the will and pleasure of God'. This included both the familiar justification of astronomy as a glorification of God, and a strictly limited acceptance of judicial astrology which clearly shows how Harrison judged all knowledge according to Scriptural criteria. In all these endeavours he followed the fundamental principle that God never ceased 'to increase their mindes in wisdome that have already by his grace lerned the first point of wisdome that is to fere the Lorde'. His fearful respect for the boundaries which God had set around the rational interpretation of the cosmos particularly distinguishes Harrison's thoughts about astrology.[73]

Only so long as its predictions confirmed God's will revealed in Scriptural prophecy was astrology 'one of the good giftes of god'. The destruction promised to false prophets in Jer. 14.13–15 constituted a universal lesson against the 'impudent audacitie' of those who 'preferre the second causes' and contradicted Scriptural prophecies. Astrology was limited to 'the scope of nature and her effectes', indeed the real 'effectes of the heavens and sterres', but only as they were 'the handywork of god'.[74] Harrison's apparently orthodox Neoplatonist belief that the four sublunar elements gave the heavens 'great force' upon everything beneath the Moon was

---

[72] Ibid., pp. 150–1; *cf.* Harrison, who spoke from extensive knowledge of medieval alchemical treatises, not Renaissance Paracelsian alchemy (TCD MS 165, fos. 137v, 341r, 343v); he criticised a contemporary alchemical chaplain in the Tower, one Brocke (ibid., fos. 93r–v).

[73] Ibid., fos. 28r, 1v, 44av.

[74] Ibid., fo. 91v; typically, these false prophets promised peace and plenty where God's prophets threatened the sword and famine as punishment for sin. See above, pp. 52–5.

therefore heavily qualified by the prior determination of the Scriptures. The heavens only promoted the historical fulfilment of Scriptural prophecies, or provided special tokens of God's wrath.[75] This subtle process of selection involved more than a crude sifting of the Scriptures to find an appropriate text, as we have seen in Harrison's attitude to the 1588 prophecy. He dismissed Cyprian Leovitius's interpretation of a great conjunction in AD 293 because Christians were liberated by their faith from fear of the threatening heavens, not needing to 'seeke for thexecution of the purpose of god out of the heavens and sterres' when God's will was revealed in the Scriptures. But Harrison eventually accepted Leovitius's prediction that another great conjunction in 1583 would make 1588 a climactic year because it chimed with apocalyptic prophecies of global destruction by fire.[76] Therefore Harrison's Scripturally informed concept of providential control made the sympathetic connections within the cosmos important, and prevented him both from accepting Thomas Erastus's own thoroughgoing Scriptural argument denying any stellar influences, and from joining the irreverent who derided the admonitions of the heavens. Harrison was capable of naturalistic explanations of occurrences, and could scoff at vulgar credulity about the apparently magical operations of Nature.[77] He frequently realised that excessive diligence in recording the historical consequences of portentous natural phenomena would show him 'to be superstitious in soche matters'. Yet despite the need for caution in reporting the fabulous, even where he found events implausible he felt constrained to report them lest he suppress evidence of God's handiwork 'and therby deprive him of his glory for the same'.[78] Consequently he continued to see God's threatenings behind natural portents, for 'as I fere them not so I despise them not but make profite of them so farre as thei maie...give me an occasion to repentauns', a clear limitation on their interpretation.[79]

The boundaries of legitimate and forbidden enquiry were set by Harrison's subjective reassessment of received knowledge according to Scriptural

---

[75] Here Christian liberty exposed limitations in the godliness of the Merton School. Rede's 'collection' once owned by Harrison contained John Ashenden's treatise on conjunctions of 1357 and 1365, of which, said Harrison, 'our frantike astrologiens did prognosticate many thinges as though the lord god direct all his doinges here in erth after the courses of the planetes and sterres' (Bodleian Library MS Digby 176, fos. 34ff.; cf. TCD MS 165, fo. 339av, and R. T. Gunther, *Early science in Oxford* (15 vols. Oxford, 1920–67), ii, pp. 58–9.

[76] TCD MS 165, fo. 160r; and see above, pp. 125–8.

[77] On Erastus see Walker, *Spiritual Magic*, pp. 156–8; Harrison, *Description* (1587), pp. 128–31, preferred natural explanations of superstitious folklore, and dismissed much folk magic (ibid., p. 110).

[78] TCD MS 165, fos. 198r, 282v, and L. M. Buell, 'Elizabethan portents: Superstition or doctrine?', in *Essays Critical and Historical dedicated to L. B. Campbell* (London, 1950), pp. 27–41.

[79] Citing Joachimus Camerarius, *Norica sive de ostentis libri duo* (Wittenberg, 1532) at TCD MS 165, fos. 65v–66r; see above, pp. 112–14.

criteria, and since this process was ostensibly directed by faith, reason could not undermine knowledge sanctified by the Scriptures.[80] So through reasoning only partly visible in the extant evidence, Harrison justified the making of astral talismans by reference to God's will and the account in the Scriptures of that Elect knowledge which was delimited by the Elect's obedience to God's will. For he was especially anxious to show that his talismanic magic completely differed from idolatrous Gentile beliefs, which he believed continued in contemporary Hermetic ceremonialism. Thus he reinforced his belief in the distinction between Elect and Gentile traditions of knowledge, and his assumption that all legitimate Gentile knowledge derived from the Elect. It is important then to notice his conflation of underlying Neoplatonic doctrines and Elect knowledge, when he accepted that inferior earthly bodies received impressions from the superior heavens 'whose merveilous substauns or nature and effectes do set furth the glory of god after an incomprehensible maner', a paraphrase of Psalm 19.1 which he also used to justify astronomy. For at first sight Harrison's attitude to 'the profound mysteries' of astrology resembles Hermetic elitism; he believed that the effects of the heavens were known only to a few, but that such 'depe and secrete knowledge' was often perverted 'through the lewdnesse of the Artificers', and should therefore be kept secret for fear of injuring the user.[81] His immediate insistence that this secret knowledge was 'neither diabolicall practize nor superstition' was also echoed by Hermeticists, but he was perhaps more justified than they were in drawing a distinction between 'the sciens' he was advocating and the distorted Gentile image of it which remained 'among witches and sorcerers'. For although Ficino emphasised the differences between wicked medieval magic and his rediscovered Neoplatonic theurgy, an elaborate ceremonial of Orphic hymns and arrangements of natural substances directed at the planetary intelligences formed an essential part of his spiritual quest.

Harrison not only rejected Orpheus and condemned the belief in planetary intelligences, but also bracketed Hermetic ceremonies with dubious medieval practices and contrasted both with his own, non-ceremonial, use of talismans. Like Ficino he emphasised that 'This is natural the other is devilish', but Harrison tolerated neither the wicked counterfeits of sorcerers nor the Hermetic 'fond fumigations' and 'vaine Characters' trusted by so many. For the Hermetic rituals were those familiar corrupt rites of the Church of Cain 'which Sathan by his pollicy and for the maintenauns of Idollatry hath

---

[80] Inevitably to the modern eye reason had a larger part to play than Harrison acknowledged in the determination of legitimate knowledge.

[81] 'Artificers' was here not a social comment but referred to unlearned magicians; TCD MS 165, fos. 230r–v. Cf. Yates, *Bruno*, p. 138, for similar exclusiveness in Agrippa's *De occulta philosophia*, elaborating on elitist sentiments in the *Asclepius* and Ficino's work. Harrison criticised *De occulta philosophia* in TCD MS 165, fo. 26v.

annexed' to Elect talismanic magic. As part of the universal growth of Gentilism, a central core of revealed truth had become obscured by a bewildering and proliferating number of ceremonies through which Satan worked on the corrupt faculties of natural man. Harrison was adamant that 'It is therefore the art of collion of influences that I do commend, and not the other vaine ceremonies which superstition and error have sithens added to the same'. By simply mixing the 'sensible and insensible' beams of the heavenly bodies, whose forces were imprinted in both sensible and insensible objects, the skilful workman could create effective talismans. The Satanic innovations of convoluted ceremonial only polluted Elect knowledge, and were therefore forbidden to mankind.[82]

Harrison's lengthy argument was designed to answer critics who 'use a generall kind of reprehension of every thinge wherin thei have no skill', and who condemned the use of talismans as an invocation to demons. To counterbalance the weight of authority against this practice, Harrison cited Aquinas's acknowledgement that all human creations 'are partakers of some of the celestiall influences', and discounted his criticisms, as well as Augustine's disapproval of talismans, as directed against 'the induction of the people to Idollatry' through images, not their non-idolatrous use.[83] Far from being glib casuistry, Harrison's interpretation of Augustine, an important witness to Elect knowledge, is an indication of the firmness of his belief that he was not worshipping demons. He felt that he was reviving ancient Elect knowledge subsequently distorted by Satan, and would have nothing to do with devilish and abominable 'barbarous praiers, bondes and adiurations', 'set furth in sondry bokes with figures and praiers most beautiful and adorned with great countenauns of piety'.[84] Convinced that he had penetrated to their Satanic inspiration, Harrison could never have been taken in by

[82] Ibid., fos. 230r–v; *cf.* Symphorien Champier, *Liber de quadruplici vita* (1507), which referred to 'suffumigations' to show his disapproval of Ficino's incense-wreathed astrological magic (quoted in Walker, *Spiritual Magic*, pp. 167–8).

[83] TCD MS 165, fo. 230v, citing Aquinas, *Summa theologica*, 'Secunda Secundae quest. 97 [*sic* for 96]', Art. ii, which acknowledged occult powers in natural bodies but condemned astrological images as tacit compacts with demons, made explicit by invocations. Champier echoed this and Aquinas's conclusion that talismans were effective through demonic rather than astral influences (Walker, *Spiritual Magic*, pp. 167–8); Johan Wier also followed Aquinas in classing talismans as demonic magic (ibid., p. 153), while Erastus stigmatised all magical effects as demonic delusions (ibid., p. 158). See also *De civitate Dei*, vii. 5. Harrison's copy of Wier's *De praestigiis daemonum et incatationibus* (Basle, 1583), is Derry shelf-mark H.ii.d.5.

[84] TCD MS 165, fos. 149v–150r. For 'no man can require to see or be present at soche toies without the high offens of god and iust desert of his wrath and indignation, except it be to reprove the doers, deterre them from their lewdnesse or hange them up for their iniquities for as none but curious heddes are inquisitive after soche ungodly practizes so none hath power to practize this develish knowledg but reprobates and castawaies or at the lest wise soche as stand upon the brinkes of destruction and ruine' (ibid., fo. 232v), an extremely radical criticism of conjuring (*cf.* Thomas, *Religion and the Decline of Magic*, p. 256), which may refer to Hermetic 'magical' effects.

Hermetic ceremonies. To emphasise this to doubting contemporaries, he cited works supporting his position, which within the framework of contemporary knowledge signalled to the learned that he would have no truck with the 'wicked and detestable practize' of conjuring devils who 'counterfeict obediens'. His references also remind us that he was working within an ancient Neoplatonic tradition historically distinct from the Hermetic tradition, that one could be interested in astral magic in the sixteenth century without accepting the authority of Hermes Trismegistus.[85]

In support of his proposition that it was possible to create effective talismans without demon-worship, Harrison cited Thabit Ibn Qurra al-Harrani's *De imaginibus* and Porphyry's *Epistola ad Anebonem*.[86] These works were by no means pure witnesses to original Elect knowledge, and Harrison warned his readers 'to avoide ther errors growing up in length of time by the pollicie of Sathan' working through fallible human reason. However, historical ignorance about Thabit allowed Harrison to assume that his *De imaginibus* represented the continuation of Elect methods of performing astral magic.[87] The work also encouraged this belief because although it described ways of making statuettes, rings and seals to achieve different purposes, as its modern editor points out, it gave unusual emphasis to astrological powers at the expense of magical ceremonial. It specified neither shapes nor materials for talismans, and used real words for inscriptions rather than magical mumbo-jumbo. Harrison may have found a distant echo of the miraculous brazen serpent created by Moses at God's command in Thabit's project for a talisman to draw away snakes, although the 'Chronology' does not specifically claim that the brazen serpent was a wonder-working talisman.[88] Harrison's use of Porphyry also reflects his belief that he was dealing with traces of legitimate knowledge in otherwise questionable Gentiles, for Porphyry's letter had been lengthily examined by Augustine in *De civitate Dei*. Augustine commended Porphyry's sophisticated, ironic demolition of vulgar demon-worship, while pointing out that through faith the least

---

[85] TCD MS 165, fo. 233v. This also reveals the flaw in R. K. Merton's reasoning.

[86] *Thabit ben Corat de Tribus imaginibus magicis* (Frankfurt, 1559); cf. F. J. Carmody, *The Astronomical Works of Thabit B. Qurra* (Berkeley and Los Angeles, 1960), pp. 167–97, and *Hermetica*, ed. Scott, i, 103–5. Porphyry's *Letter to Anebon* usually accompanied Iamblichus's reply, *De mysteriis*, and was printed in *Iamblichi Chalcidensis ex Coele-Syria de mysteriis liber* (Oxford, 1678).

[87] Perhaps following a corrupt manuscript, Harrison believed that Thabit (c. AD 835–901) flourished circa AD 1208 (TCD MS 165, fo. 303v). Thabit's works were the product of a 'Hermetic' Chaldean sun cult, parallel to but not really related to the Greek Hermetica (Carmody, *Thabit*, pp. 15, 167–8).

[88] Ibid., pp. 168–9; cf. Book of Numbers 21.4–9, and TCD MS 165, fo. 46v. The Geneva Bible, Harrison's Bible, did not recognise the brazen serpent as an astral talisman, though it did have magical effects; it cross-refers to 2 Kings 18.4 and Hezekiah's destruction of the serpent after it was 'abused to idolatrie', another example of the degenerative process which Harrison tried to reverse. Cf. TCD MS 165, fo. 84v.

learned Christian could more effectively denounce their diabolical organisation. Nor would it have escaped Harrison's notice that Porphyry's emphasis
on the logical absurdities of popular demonology was echoed by Augustine
in other parts of *De civitate Dei*, including the chapters in which he
criticised the demonology of Hermes Trismegistus. Therefore in default of
any direct Scriptural or patristic support Harrison resorted to Gentile
authorities whose stress on a non-demonic astral magic he believed was
consistent with and essentially continued Elect knowledge.[89]

Harrison also cited Desiderius Erasmus, reminding us that contemporaries
saw no division between the grammarian and literary, and the philosophical
and magical traditions in humanism. Eager to bolster his case, Harrison noted
Erasmus's confession that painful kidney stones were much relieved by 'the
figure of a lion made in gold under a certeine constellation', although 'if
all thinges had concurred' in its construction it would have been more
effective. In fact Erasmus kept an open mind about the talisman's influence,
but in claiming his support Harrison was demonstrating that talismanic
magic could be compatible with an evangelical religious outlook and remain
distinct from ritualistic occult practices, redolent of satanic Gentilism. He
was emphasising a pious, uncomplicated and direct astral magic consistent
with the Protestant sense of a direct relationship with God, independent of
intercessionary powers.[90]

Harrison's magic needs to be carefully distinguished from Hermetic
occultism, but it leads to evidence about his attitude to experimental natural
philosophy, where he is clearly distinguishable from the Hermeticists. What
to us is a difficult contradiction between the defence of hidden magic and
the public, rational investigation of the regular and repeatable workings of
Nature is resolved by Harrison's single purpose in both endeavours – the
release of Elect knowledge from its Gentile servitude. The Scriptures
revealed the general limits of Elect knowledge and thus provided the means
to test the truth of any Gentile proposition. But the Scriptures were silent
on many points of detail, so that experience in its formal dress of
experimentation, constrained by the Scriptural world-view, could be a vital
adjunct to Scriptural testimony about Nature. Harrison's crucial assumption
was that as far as human reason was permitted to understand it, God ordered
Nature according to regular laws, for that allowed Harrison to believe that
observation guided by Scriptural criteria could winnow out the chaff of

---

89 Ibid., fos. 230r–v; *cf. De civitate Dei*, Books x and xi, and viii. 16–26.
90 TCD MS 165, fos. 230r–v; *cf. Opus epistolarum Des. Erasmi Roterodami*, ed. P. S. Allen (12 vols.
   Oxford, 1905–58), i, pp. 45–6, and R. H. Bainton, *Erasmus of Christendom* (London, 1969),
   pp. 109, 292. Erasmus turned against Johannes Reuchlin when his energetic promotion of
   Cabalistic studies raised the spectre of a religious revival based on Judaic ceremonialism
   (C. Zika, 'Reuchlin and Erasmus: Humanism and occult philosophy', in *Journal of Religious
   History*, ix (1977), pp. 223–46).

deluded Gentile inventions, leaving grains of revealed Elect knowledge. All these operations had to obey Scriptural revelation, which remedied the deficiencies of fallen human senses, and prevented the repetition of those delusions which characterised Gentile knowledge. It provided an absolute boundary for the interpretation of experience. Inevitably this theoretical objective ran into the same practical difficulties as the recovery of the primitive Church from its degenerate form in Elizabethan England. But as a scientific methodology it was a significant advance on the Hermetic secret spiritual quest for divine revelation of the hidden laws of the universe, since it allowed Harrison to contribute to the painstaking compilation of those scientific facts which were repeatable and objectively true to experience. The fact that his experiments were fairly trivial and unoriginal does not detract from his adoption of a recognisably modern scientific methodology, strictly limited by his obedience to Scriptural revelation.[91]

Harrison's acceptance of the legitimacy of talismanic magic involved him in the defence of Albertus Magnus and Roger Bacon, partly because evangelicals thoroughly alienated by contemporary magic accused them of diabolic practices, but also because they were both important advocates of the experimental method. G. F. Pico, for example, stigmatised Bacon as a demon-worshipping necromancer, while Johann Wier denounced Albertus Magnus as a superstitious maker of talismans whose damnable doctrines had been imbibed by Ficino.[92] From this perspective Albert and Bacon were encamped amongst the Gentiles, but Harrison took a more discriminating view and considered them the most learned philosophers of their age, rather lamely excusing Albert, to whom 'many trifles' were erroneously ascribed, while taking a more positive line about Bacon. He ignored Bacon's suspicious interest in alchemy and mechanical contrivances, and instead seized upon his lament 'that the church is ruled more by the law of man than of God'. Just as Harrison sanctified the Merton experimental tradition by recording evidence of godliness amongst the fellows, so this statement was a clue that associated Bacon with the hidden True Church and thus made his legacy of the same experimental method a means, in Harrison's eyes, of discovering Gentile delusions about Nature. Harrison's radical Protestantism thus sharpened the current emphasis on experience as a means of testing theoretical Aristotelian pronouncements, for his criticism of conventional scholastic discourse was only a means to the end of sharing the Elect vision of the universe.[93] While this superficially implies some connection between

---

[91] Harrison did not see the pursuit of natural philosophy according to Elect criteria as a means of achieving, or as a substitute for, Scripture's detailed revelation of saving faith. He merely sought to resurrect that Elect knowledge which was an adjunct of the covenant line's true faith, as part of his own godly obedience.

[92] Walker, *Spiritual Magic*, pp. 147, 153.

[93] TCD MS 165, fo. 243v; cf. D. C. Allen, *Doubt's Boundless Sea* (Baltimore, 1964), pp. 52, 76.

his Protestantism and his interest in the investigation of Nature and the application of knowledge thus acquired, it means more fundamentally that he imposed stricter limitations upon such studies than had the scholastics. His discussion of contemporary developments in herbal medicines, for example, first acknowledged that in abundance of efficacious herbs no other nation was 'more plentifully endued with these and other blessings from the most high God', and then went on to mention his own garden of rare and exotic herbs. Yet he pursued his botanical studies always conscious of the need for God to 'grant us grace withal to use the same to His honor and glory and not as instruments and provocations unto further excess and vanity, wherewith His displeasure may be kindled'. For 'God in nature hath so disposed His creatures that the most needful are the most plentiful', 'for our consolation and comfort', and only the most wilful and perverse imagination would want to go beyond this perfect dispensation and its limitations on speculation.[94]

Harrison's 'Chronology' was not a systematic scientific treatise, nor do his scattered discussions of natural philosophy always keep to his maxim that what was 'written in philosophy is not alwaies answerable to experiens'. But his general recognition of regular laws at work in Nature allowed him to castigate numerous uncritical compilers of things 'ridiculous, magicall or oft impossible by nature' on entirely rational grounds of observation and experiment. Following Giambattista della Porta's *Natural Magic*, he emphasised the futility of reiterating untested theoretical assertions, specifically claims that vessels made from ivy would not hold wine, and that garlic affected the magnet.[95]

Relying on a perhaps fallible memory, Harrison dramatised the contrast between the assertions of authority and his own observations in his discussion of Cato's aphorism that a vessel of ivy will not hold wine. In *De agri cultura* this was a 'test' of whether wine had been watered, for Cato claimed that the wine would soak through an ivy vessel and the water remain. Porta refuted this already magical claim by repeating classical demonstrations that any porous material would allow the water to soak away, leaving the wine.[96] Harrison's interpretation of Cato's aphorism reveals his stronger disposition towards perceiving magical forces, for he alleged that Cato said that an ivy vessel of wine 'will never leave swelling and boyling over', until the wine was thrown out.[97] But Harrison also related his failure to achieve this effect

---

[94] *Description*, ed. Edelen, pp. 268–71.

[95] TCD MS 165, fo. 285r, and see for example fo. 144v; ibid., fo. 145v, quotes the preface to *Natural Magic*, for which see *Natural Magick by John Baptista Porta* (London, 1658), facs. ed. D. J. Price (New York, 1958). On ivy, see ibid., bk. 18, ch. iv; on the magnet, see bk. 7, ch. xlviii. Porta's magical explanations of natural events conflict with his rational conclusions from careful experiments in this work.

[96] *Natural Magic*, 18. iv; cf. Cato, *On Agriculture* (London, 1934), Aphorism cxi.

[97] TCD MS 165, fo. 18v; cf. Cato, *On Agriculture*, cxi: 'a vessel of ivy wood will not hold wine'.

by repeated experiments 'more than 6 times with Malmesy and sacke', and although he corrected his reading of *De agri cultura* in his later *Description of Britain*, he repeated that Cato lied in claiming a magical antipathy between wine and ivy 'as some of our reading philosophers without all manner of practice' continued to believe. While Harrison had disposed of any occult quality in ivy, he was still some way short of Porta's observation that the porosity of all materials was at issue, but the quality of his scientific thinking was less important than his grasp of the fundamental principle that within the limited sphere of knowledge accessible to human reason the experimental method was the test of truth.[98] Harrison had proved by similar repeated experiments that garlic did not alter the powers of the magnet, and although his reports of his experiments make them seem rudimentary beside William Gilbert's, a common methodology distinguished them both from the subjective interpretations of the Hermetic magi.[99]

A proper appreciation of Harrison's admittedly limited scientific abilities must acknowledge that while his radical Protestantism freed him from the search for occult powers and endorsed instead the recovery of objective facts amenable to rational explanation according to regular laws, it also limited the scope, interpretation and application of that knowledge. Essentially he rejected one mystically determined interpretation of Nature, Hermeticism, for another, the Scriptural. This clearly divides his methodology from 'Baconian' empiricism, which was unrestrained by religious zeal. For Harrison fully shared the conviction of other Puritans that the perfect Scriptural revelation of God's will and the demands of a godly life could not be confirmed or augmented by reasoning from Nature. Puritans were intensely aware that while natural philosophy could inspire wonder and humility it could also bring 'sinfull imaginations of our owne unbrideled wits'. Man's senses were so easily deceived by Satan that only by accepting the prior restraints of religion could he achieve saving knowledge. Surveying the baffling conflict between the Ptolemaic and Copernican systems, which revealed the limits of human understanding, Harrison wearily concluded that, 'this we know, that we know nothing'.[100] Therefore while Harrison's simple experiments reflected the general Puritan respect for logical reasoning as the supreme authority in purely human spheres, like other Puritans he

---

[98] TCD MS 165, fo. 18v, and Harrison, *Description* (1577), fo. 117r; (1587), p. 239; *cf.* Porta, *Natural Magic*, 18. iv. The 1587 *Description* underlined that there were no exceptions to this law.

[99] He gave no details, but presumably his experiments paralleled Porta's in *Natural Magic*, 7. xlviii. The idea derived from a misreading of Pliny's 'alio' for another lodestone, as 'allio' for garlic (*cf.* Pliny, *Historia naturalis*, xxxvi. 25). See W. Gilbert, *De magnete* (London, 1600), p. 2, and ch. 1, *passim*.

[100] Morgan, 'Puritanism and Science', pp. 535–60, quoting Edward Dering on p. 552. See TCD MS 165, fo. 117r, on the futility of human speculations about the cosmos.

knew that rational investigation could never determine matters of faith. A faithful interpretation of natural phenomena could, therefore, only come from consulting with the Scriptures.

Not all natural phenomena could be directly explained from the Scriptures, and in those cases human reason was at liberty to speculate about the cause and meaning of occurrences so long as those speculations did not contradict Scriptural teachings. Thus Harrison felt at liberty to dismiss sinister and superstitious interpretations of the aurora borealis and to expound 'the naturall cause', evidently unknown to those who 'upon the like occasions prognosticate many thinges'. He considered the aurora borealis to be 'a secondary reflexion of the oblique beames of the sonne', and drew a simple diagram to show how 'the sonne casting his oblique beames upon the broode sea, thei do not returne againe toward the center of the planete, but are throwen at large els where, and finding none other obiect betwene them and the clowdy or clere aire, thei there staie and yeld furth these brightnesses, which bring us often to terror', although the movements of the lights, said Harrison, only reflect the movements of the ocean. Harrison felt that he could prove his argument by the 'example' of 'the light that is reflected from a pece of glasse in a mans hand to every corner of the house', so that ignoring the factual errors in his reasoning, we can see that his rational interpretation of natural phenomena preferred experimental to magical explanation.[101]

However, any conclusions about Nature which did not bow to the prior authority of the Scriptures could only reiterate Gentile delusions. Harrison therefore believed that whoever attempted to explain the rainbow without reference to Gen. 9.12–17 was 'not likely to set downe any certeinty'. The schoolmen could analyse its material and efficient causes, and 'experiens' showed that it was created by natural refraction. But regardless of all scholastic opinion Harrison followed 'the sense of the scriptures' in affirming that it was first seen in AM 1656, as a token of God's covenant not to drown the world again. The rainbow was not a natural phenomenon that had occurred regularly since the Creation, but 'the workemanship of God according to nature after the flood'. Thus Harrison shared a heightened awareness of the immanence of God in daily affairs with other Puritans who saw a controlling Providence in every occurrence. However regular the operations of Nature seemed to be, every empirical conclusion had to be cognisant of the Scriptural evidence about Nature. In the same terms that he contrasted theoretical propositions and experimental proof, Harrison contrasted the conclusions of the 'writing philosophers' about the rainbow with his own, which started from the mystical account in Genesis. Thus the Scriptures provided a kind of experimental data for the interpretation of Nature, and while this Puritan commitment to the Scriptural interpretation

[101] TCD MS 165, fo. 269r.

of natural phenomena might vary with individual character, it was the very antithesis of free rational enquiry.[102]

The fact that Harrison's wish to limit the scope and interpretation of human knowledge was shared by other Puritans thus makes it difficult to accept the thesis that Puritanism provided an incentive for the pursuit of the new learning. The proponents of this view have not shown that there was any necessary theological reason for Protestants to support free enquiry, and it is difficult to imagine how Protestantism can be retained as a coherent set of ideas without its Scriptural and theological centre. Those who argue that while Protestant theology restricted scientific enquiry, other elements within Protestant thought promoted it, must acknowledge that those other elements were not unique to Protestantism. To select from Protestantism only those ideas which accord with criteria drawn from an entirely different set of ideas, whether unrestricted scientific enquiry or capitalism, does not prove that Protestantism 'influenced' those sets of ideas, for any number of such 'influences' might be drawn from other intellectual sources, including Catholicism, by the same erroneous method. Once any element in Protestant thought is considered independently of its Scriptural and theological source, it ceases to be Protestant and becomes part of another set of ideas. Thus we need to realise that when it came to the practical application of scientific knowledge, Harrison was acutely aware that unbridled innovation could be not only in direct contravention of God's will but also a more insidious threat to the essentially static godly commonwealth and its limited economy as envisaged by Puritans.[103]

In fact technological innovation could undermine not only the ideal social and economic values demanded by Scriptural revelation but even their imperfect realisation in the contemporary, delicately balanced economy. Certainly Protestants emphasised the need to labour earnestly in the calling, but this did not necessarily condone the capitalist ethos, as the dogged Puritan advocacy of 'commonwealth' legislation makes clear. To concentrate only upon those elements of Protestant thought which contributed to later capitalist values is to give a very selective and distorted picture of the essential nature of Protestantism. In Harrison's case Protestant theology led him

---

[102] Abraham Fleming, editor of *Holinshed's Chronicles* (1587), similarly interpreted the rainbow (*A Treatise of Blazing Sterres in Generall* (Bernard Alsop for Henry Bell: London, 1618), sig. D3v), and Harrison's radical colleague George Withers made it explicit in *An ABC for layemen*, sig. I7v; see the onetime presbyterian William Fulke, *A Most Pleasant Prospect into the Garden of Naturall Contemplation* (London, 1602), sig. E5v, who differed slightly in his view of the rainbow, but affirmed that it must now be seen as a sign of the covenant and the fulfilment of God's promises. Calvin also regarded the natural explanation of the rainbow as less important than its meaning for the covenant (*Commentaire...upon... Genesis*, sigs. P1v–P2r).

[103] TCD MS, fo. 137v, on the economic threat of an alchemical invention such as unbreakable glass, and Harrison's criticisms of enclosures in *Description* (1587), p. 205, and see above, pp. 282–3.

to denigrate technological innovation, entrepreneurial skills and capital formation, because from his viewpoint the driving force of a distorted economy was the pursuit of wealth as an end in itself, by men who were deaf to Scripture's call to the godly life. Capitalist society was the society of natural man, the satanic Gentile parody of godly Israel. Therefore if we want to understand Harrison's Protestant vision properly, we must treat it as an integral whole, and that has been the aim of this study.

Index

Cambridge Studies in the History and Theory of Politics

Editors: Maurice Cowling, G. R. Elton and J. R. Pole

A series in two parts, studies and original texts. The studies are original works on political history and political philosophy while the texts are modern, critical editions of major texts in political thought. The titles include:

TEXTS

Vladimire Akimov on the Dilemmas of Russian Marxism 1895–1903. An English edition of 'A Short History of the Social Democratic Movement in Russia' and 'The Second Congress of the Russian Social Democratic Labour Party', with an introduction and notes by Jonathan Frankel

J. G. Herder on Social and Political Culture, translated and edited with an introduction by F. M. Barnard

Kant's Political Writings, edited with an introduction and notes by Hans Reiss; translated by H. B. Nisbet

Karl Marx's Critique of Hegel's 'Philosophy of Right', edited with an introduction and notes by Joseph O'Malley; translated by Annette Jolin and Joseph O'Malley

The Political Writings of Leibniz, edited and translated by Patrick Riley

Turgot on Progress, Sociology and Economics: A Philosophical Review of the Successive Advances of the Human Mind. On Universal History. Reflections on the Formation and Distribution of Wealth, edited, translated and introduced by Ronald L. Meek

Georg Wilhelm Friedrich Hegel: Lectures on the Philosophy of World History: Reason in History, translated from the German edition of Johannes Hoffmeister by H. B. Nisbet and with an introduction by Duncan Forbes

A Machiavellian Treatise by Stephen Gardiner, edited and translated by Peter S. Donaldson

The Political Works of James Harrington, edited by J. G. A. Pocock

Selected Writings of August Cieszkowski, edited and translated with an introductory essay by André Liebich

De Republica Anglorum by Sir Thomas Smith, edited by Mary Dewar

Sister Peg: A Pamphlet Hitherto Unknown by David Hume, edited with an introduction and notes by David R. Raynor

STUDIES

1867: Disraeli, Gladstone and Revolution: The Passing of the Second Reform Bill, by Maurice Cowling

The Social and Political Thought of Karl Marx, by Shlomo Avineri

Idealism, Politics and History: Sources of Hegelian Thought, by George Armstrong Kelly

Alienation: Marx's Conception of Man in Capitalist Society, by Bertell Ollman

Hegel's Theory of the Modern State, by Shlomo Avineri

The Impact of Hitler: British Politics and British Policy 1933–1940, by Maurice Cowling

The Liberal Mind 1914–1929, by Michael Bentley

Revolution Principles: The Politics of Party 1689–1720, by J. P. Kenyon

John Locke and the Theory of Sovereignty: Mixed Monarchy and the Right of Resistance in the Political Thought of the English Revolution, by Julian H. Franklin